Globalization, Culture and Inequality in Asia

Globalization, Culture and Inequality in Asia

Edited by
Timothy J. Scrase
Todd Joseph Miles Holden
Scott Baum

Trans Pacific Press
Melbourne

This English edition first published in 2003 by
Trans Pacific Press, PO Box 120, Rosanna, Melbourne, Victoria 3084, Australia
Telephone: +61 3 9459 3021   Fax: +61 3 9457 5923
Email: info@transpacificpress.com
Web: http://www.transpacificpress.com

Copyright © Trans Pacific Press 2003

Designed and set by digital environs Melbourne.
enquiries@digitalenvirons.com

Printed by BPA Print Group, Burwood, Victoria, Australia

Distributors

Australia
Bushbooks
PO Box 1958, Gosford, NSW 2250
Telephone: (02) 4323-3274
Fax: (02) 9212-2468
Email: bushbook@ozemail.com.au

USA and Canada
International Specialized Book
Services (ISBS)
920 NE 58th Avenue, Suite 300
Portland, Oregon 97213-3786
USA
Telephone: (800) 944-6190
Fax: (503) 280-8832
Email: orders@isbs.com
Web: http://www.isbs.com

Japan
Kyoto University Press
Kyodai Kaikan
15-9 Yoshida Kawara-cho
Sakyo-ku, Kyoto 606-8305
Telephone: (075) 761-6182
Fax: (075) 761-6190
Email: sales@kyoto-up.gr.jp
Web: http://www.kyoto-up.gr.jp

UK and Europe
Asian Studies Book Services
3554 TT Utrecht
The Netherlands
Telephone: +31 (30) 289 1240
Fax: +31 (30) 289 1249
Email: info@asianstudiesbooks.com
Web: http://www.asianstudiesbooks.com

All rights reserved. No production of any part of this book may take place without the written permission of Trans Pacific Press.

ISBN 1-8768-4394-2 (Hardback)
ISBN 1-8768-4388-8 (Paperback)

National Library of Australia Cataloging in Publication Data

   Globalization, culture and inequality in asia.

     Bibliography.
     ISBN 1 876843 88 8 (pbk.).

     ISBN 1 876843 94 2.
     1. Globalization – Economic aspects – Asia. 2.
     Globalization – Social aspects – Asia. I. Baum, Scott. II.
     Scrase, Timothy J. III. Holden, Todd.

337.5

Contents

Figures	vi
Tables	vii
Notes on Contributors	xi
Acknowledgements	xv

1 Asia's Globalization: A Sociological View   1
  Timothy J. Scrase, T.J.M. Holden and Scott Baum

Part I – Gender, Class and Labour

2 Contesting the New Inequalities: Social Movements in the Asia Pacific   21
  James Goodman

3 Global Norms, Transnational Advocacy Networks and Female Migrant Labor in Asia   48
  Nicola Piper

4 Globalization, Modernity and Gender Equality   68
  Ruchira Ganguly-Scrase

5 Producing on the Margins: Asian Artisans in the Global Economy   95
  Timothy J. Scrase

Part II – Media, Culture and Identity

6 Transnational Identities in the Hmong Diaspora   119
  Roberta Julian

7 Japan's Mediated 'Global' Identities   144
  T.J.M. Holden

8 The Social Meanings of Media for Indonesian Youth   168
  Pam Nilan

9 Talking Sex and Gender from Taiwan's VCD Scandal   191
  Ming-Chu Chen

Part III – Cities and Urbanization

10 Social and Economic Restructuring and the New
   Economy in Singapore   215
   Scott Baum
11 Globalization, Rapid Urbanization and Anomie in
   Dhaka   234
   Zakia Hossain
12 Job Opportunities for Working Children in Jakarta's
   Informal Settlements   249
   Susy Y.R. Sanie and Scott Baum

Part IV – Conclusion

13 Social and Cultural Transformation in Asia:
   A Critical Assessment   269
   Timothy J. Scrase, T.J.M. Holden and Scott Baum

Notes   285
References   299
Name Index   349
Subject Index   358

Figures

2.1	Asian Social Forum 'ASF stage: Another Asia is Possible'	42
2.2	Asian Social Forum 'ASF demonstration: the Communal monster'	42
4.1	Public discourses of gender equality and women's emancipation	76
4.2	Women benefited under liberalization	81
4.3	Household financial conditions improved or deteriorated under economic liberalization	84
4.4	Salary has increased in relation to cost of living	85
5.1	Crafts Museum, New Delhi	110
5.2	Jute artisan in his stall	111
5.3	Terracotta artisan displaying her wares	111
6.1	'Hmong-storycloth'	128
6.2	'Hmong-artists'	138

Tables

8.1	Perceptions of media effect	175
10.1	Occupational distribution, Singapore 1990 and 2000	224
10.2	Educational qualifications, Singapore 1991 to 2001	227
10.3	Resident households by income from work, 1990 and 2000	229
10.4	Individual income, Singapore, 1991 and 2001	230
11.1	Characteristics of survey respondents	237
11.2	Associations between the age of respondent and anomie items	244
11.3	Associations between sex of respondent and anomie items	245
11.4	Associations between employment status and anomie items	246
11.5	Associations between education status and anomie items	247
12.1	Logistic regression results	261

To my mother (Kathleen) and in the memory of my father (Joseph)
T. J. S.

To Takako, Maya Simone and Alexander Seishi:

persuasive evidence of the wonders of
transculturation, hybridization, and indigenization
in everyday life.
T. J. M. H.

To my parents (Arthur & Shirley) and to Briony, Oscar and Salem
S. B.

Notes on Contributors

Scott Baum (PhD, Flinders University, 1995) is an Australian Research Council Senior Research Fellow in the Centre for Research into Sustainable Urban and Regional Futures, University of Queensland, Australia. Trained in economics and sociology his research interests include the socio-economic aspects of urban and regional transformations, including distributional equity, housing preferences and choice, residential mobility and the impact of globalization on cities. He has previously published three books / monographs and 22 articles and book chapters. His books include *Community Opportunity and Vulnerability in Australia's Cities and Towns* and *A Decade of Change: A Social Atlas of Brisbane and the South East Queensland Region*. His current research includes an analysis of home ownership aspirations of young Australians and an analysis of local community performance across Australia's settlement system. His email contact is: S.Baum@uq.edu.au

Ming-Chu Chen is assistant professor of Radio, Television, and Film at Shih Hsin University in Taiwan. She completed her PhD in Communication at the Ohio State University in the United States. Her recent research projects focus on Taiwanese locality and the female phenomenal body in representations of media. Contact her by email at: mbcc89@cc.shu.edu.tw

Ruchira Ganguly-Scrase holds a PhD in Anthropology from the University of Melbourne. She teaches in the Sociology Program at the University of Wollongong, Australia. She is the author of *Global Issues/ Local Contexts: The Rabi Das of West Bengal* (2001, New Delhi: Orient Longman/ London: Sangam Books). Her research interests include comparative sociology, globalization, gender relations in Asia, and ethnographic method. Currently she is completing a book with Tim Scrase on the social consequences of globalization and economic liberalization in India. Her email contact is: rgscrase@uow.edu.au

James Goodman (PhD) is editor of *Protest and Globalization: Prospects for Transnational Solidarity* (2002, Sydney: Pluto), *Moving Mountains: Communities Confront Mining and Globalisation* (2002, London: Zed), *Corporate Power or Peoples Power: Transnational Corporations and Globalisation* (2002, Manila: Asia Pacific Research Network) and *Stopping a Juggernaut: Public Interests Vs. the Multilateral Agreement on Investment* (1998, Sydney: Pluto). He teaches at the University of Technology Sydney where he co-convenes the Research Initiative on International Activism (www.international.activism.uts.edu.au). You can contact him at: james.goodman@uts.edu.au

Todd Joseph Miles Holden (PhD, Syracuse University, 1989) is Professor of Mediated Sociology in the Graduate School of International Cultural Studies at Tohoku University, Sendai, Japan. His research interests encompass social theory, semiology, advertising, gender, political communication and comparative culture. Recent publications include the book *Reading Signs: Language, Culture and Society* (in Japanese), and empirical studies of media in context, including pro-social messages in Malaysian advertising, political commercials in Japan, and Japanese cell phone dating. Up-coming chapters include 'Advertising: a Synthetic Approach' in Sage's *Handbook of Media Studies*; 'Gods in All Things,' a historical treatment of Japanese heroes in literature, painting, film, *manga* and news; and the phenomenon of 'sport exports' as 'information imports' in a forthcoming book on Japan's globalization. His regular column, *ReDotPop,* is published in the e-zine *PopMatters.* All of his writings – including various flights of fiction – can be located on his web site (http://www.langc.tohoku.ac.jp/~holden/index.htm). Direct comments, queries and complaints to: holden@lark.langc.tohoku.ac.jp

Roberta Julian (PhD) is a Senior Lecturer in Sociology at the University of Tasmania, Australia, where she teaches courses on ethnicity, identity, gender, and qualitative research methods. Her publications focus on the Hmong diaspora; citizenship, multiculturalism and refugee resettlement; ethnic identities; health and ethnicity; and the intersection of ethnicity, class and gender. She can be contacted at: Roberta.Julian@utas.edu.au

Pam Nilan (PhD) is a Senior Lecturer in Sociology in the School of Social Sciences at the University of Newcastle, Australia. She has conducted research on education, gender, youth and popular culture in Australia, Vietnam and Indonesia. Articles reporting on this research have been published in a number of international journals. Her major research interest at present is the nexus between youth, politics and media in Australia and also in Indonesia. She can be reached at Pamela.Nilan@newcastle.edu.au

Nicola Piper is Research Fellow at the Australian National University in Canberra. She holds a PhD in Sociology from the University of Sheffield in the UK. Her research has revolved around various aspects of international labor migration in Europe and Asia. She is author of the book *Racism, Nationalism and Citizenship* (1998), the co-editor of the volumes *Women and Work in Globalising Asia* (2002) and *Wife or Worker? Asians Marriage and Migration* (2003) as well as various journal articles. Her current project focuses on the intersection of international law (HR and labor rights) and activism from the perspective of foreign migrant workers. Her email address is: nicola.piper@anu.edu.au

Susy Yunia R Sanie is a senior researcher and research coordinator of Community Welfare Studies, at The Center of Societal Development Studies – Atma Jaya Catholic University, Jakarta, Indonesia. She holds a Master's degree in Regional Development and Planning from Bogor Agricultural University where her research focused on child labor in Jakarta. Her current research focuses on social, economic and health aspects of women and children in poor urban areas, the social impact of the public policies and programs on poverty alleviation, domestic violence and gender issues. Her email address is: syrsanie@lpa.atmajaya.ac.id

Tim Scrase (PhD, La Trobe University, 1990) teaches in the Sociology Program, School of Social Sciences, Media and Communication, University of Wollongong, Australia. His research interests are in the areas of globalization, the sociology of development, and the sociology of media and education. From October 2001 to January 2002 he was an Affiliated Research

Fellow, International Institute for Asian Studies (IIAS), Universities of Leiden and Amsterdam. His publications include two books: *Social Justice and Third World Education* (New York and London: Garland, 1997); and *Image, Ideology and Inequality: Cultural Domination, Hegemony and Schooling in India* (New Delhi, Newbury Park and London: Sage, 1993); and several recent articles on globalisation, development and social and cultural change. His email contact is: tims@uow.edu.au

Zakia Hossain is a Senior Lecturer in the School of Behavioural Sciences, University of Sydney. She holds a PhD in Sociology from The University of Queensland, an MA in Demography from the Australian National University and an MA in Sociology from Dhaka University, Bangladesh. Her research interests include sociology of health and social demography and in is particularly interested in women and children's health, reproductive behaviour and decision making, and cross cultural aspects of health and illnesses. Her email address is: Z.Hossain@fhs.uysd.edu.au

Acknowledgements

This book is an exemplar of the globalization process itself. Its genesis was the idea of a Japanese-born sociology professor who has lived and worked in Melbourne, Australia, for over three decades. While attending an international conference in Brisbane, he approached a Melbourne born sociologist living and working in Wollongong, who then contacted an American born, media sociologist living and working in Japan and an Adelaide born, urban sociologist living and working in Brisbane! The editors and contributors to this book are all members of the Asia Pacific Sociological Association (APSA), a diverse collection of social scientists formed in the mid-1990s to forge greater intellectual and collegial links among sociologists in the region. Among their members are academics from New Zealand to China, South Korea to the Philippines, Viet Nam to Indonesia. While this volume is by no means representative of the various intellectual strands in APSA, it nevertheless is reflective of the cross-fertilization of ideas and issues that sociologists in APSA grapple with at their biennial conferences.

As is true of any publication, this book could not have come to fruition without assists from a number of crucial quarters. Above all, the editors wish to acknowledge the considerable involvement of Professor Yoshio Sugimoto of La Trobe University. It was Yoshio's initial suggestion which spawned this book, and throughout the process he has offered encouragement and support. Second, we wish to thank the individual contributors for their expedited effort: first in transforming rough conference papers into sterling first drafts; and then in quickly re-drafting (and sometimes re-drafting yet again) their chapters. The bulk of this work transpired over the 2002/03 Christmas and New Year holiday period. Throughout, they adhered to the relatively stringent deadlines set by us and did so with unflagging motivation and considerable good cheer. Thirdly, we sincerely appreciate the financial support which has been provided by a number of sources, including: APSA, CAPSTRANS (The Centre for Asia Pacific Social Transformation Studies, University of Wollongong), CR-SURF (Centre for Research into Sustainable Urban and Regional Futures, The University of Queensland), and Tohoku University.

TJS
TJMH
SB

1 Asia's Globalization: A Sociological View

Timothy J. Scrase
T.J.M. Holden
Scott Baum

Globalization, Asia and Social Change

One could fill a good-size bookcase with the volumes penned under the name 'globalization' over the past decade. The topic touches so many of the traditional disciplines that it seems everyone has something to contribute to the conversation. Economists, political scientists, anthropologists, sociologists, historians, geographers, communication researchers – there is no end in sight to the vantage points provided by globalization's multifarious processes. So why one more book? Well, scan that bookcase carefully and one will find the selection of volumes on *Asian* globalization still sparse.

In making this claim, we are not denying that a number of important books on contemporary social change in Asia have not appeared in recent years. For instance, Evans (1993) sought to initiate readers to the anthropology, and Vervoorn (2002) to the sociology, of Asia. By introducing the social scientific study of the region to a broader undergraduate audience, both authors aimed at demystifying the people and practices of Asia. Each author, in his own way, argued that the societies and cultures of the realm are largely misunderstood and this misunderstanding is due to the surface level, superficial understandings and interpretations spouted by Western media, business leaders, politicians and political institutions. Moreover, the common stereotypes of Asia – ranging from the chauvinistic notion of 'Asian' values to the sexist caricature of the 'demure and subservient' Asian woman – are found to be irrelevant when one critically studies the countries and peoples of Asia.

Studies of social change in Asia at a more advanced level have also emerged in recent years. Notable among these are the edited volumes by Robison and Goodman (1996) and Pinches (1999), which focus on the themes of capitalist development and the emergence of the new rich in Asia. In particular, the contributors to both these books explore class and cultural reconfigurations, the nature of consumer behavior, and changing economic and social status brought about by the neo-liberal, capitalist transformation of the region. In a third noteworthy work (Edwards and Roces 2000), the various contributors question the current status of women in Asia, especially in terms of the key social indicators of education, health, population, politics, law, violence and employment.

This recitation of books concerning social change in Asia is obviously truncated, but the significance of the research analyzed in these volumes lies in highlighting the dynamic nature of Asian societies. Rather than being seen as 'traditional', 'conservative' or 'mysterious,' the writers instead emphasize the extent of internal social complexity, social conflict, social and cultural change, exchange, and rapid economic growth – all coursing through and influencing the Asian region.

Now, if one were to search for books specifically attuned to 'globalization' in Asia, the list narrows considerably. Most prominent would likely be Andre Gunder Frank's *ReOrient* (1998), which re-positions Asia as central in the early development of the global economy. A second that springs to mind is Yeung's (2000) exploration of the intricate interplay between globalization, regionalism and localism in the formation of Pacific Asia's urban centers. Wee (2002), in a recent edited collection, considers the manifestation of 'new Asia,' although this discussion transpires largely within a political science framework. The comparative regional analysis is confined more or less to the role of the state in fostering various aspects of economic development. More often, books have attended to global activity within one nation, and then, to date it seems, most often that nation has been Japan (e.g. Clammer 2001; Eades et al., 2000).

Finally, were one to try and locate a book about inequality in Asia arising from global processes, or identity issues, or the activity of the media, the selections would be fewer still. Yamashita and Eades's (2001) anthropological view has touched upon impacts in specific Asian countries pertaining to ethnicity, religion, popular culture, and labor migration; Kinnvall and Jonsson (2002) have discussed the relationship between globalization, identity and democratic developments in the region; and Tehranian (1999) has studied the association between communication technologies and political power. His generalist argument – that global communication can often serve to stimulate cultural and political resistance against 'globalist hegemonies' – extends beyond Asia, and when it does turn its sights to the region, singles out Iran for attention. Virtually none of these laudable additions to the globalization bookshelf address the phenomenon from a sociological perspective.

Asia's Contemporary Global Career

Looking at globalization sociologically, it is almost certain that Asia is a major site for social, political, economic, cultural and moral contestation and change in the new millennium. Over the past decade alone, we have witnessed most, if not all, Asian countries propelled on a roller coaster of economic prosperity, sudden downturn and entrenched recession, with many chugging slowly toward prosperity once more. Political upheaval, as well, has been sudden, dramatic, and its resolution often quite unpredictable. In many cases the political fallout has yet to fully settle and may be years before its effects are fully expressed. Such change has, at times, been prodded by ideas and practices from outside the focal contexts – or else the local reactions to these exogenous elements. The outcomes that have been expressed have not been equally calibrated. Thus, for instance, an uneven pattern of development has resulted across the region; one in which, for instance, a new class of technology rich have come to reside in dazzling, prosperous, 'modern' cities, while other parts of the region are stocked with menial labor, condemned to life in deteriorating industrial, environmental or rural wastelands. Astride these changes are rapid developments in digital media, which offer 'lucky' consumers an array of cultural pursuits and lifestyles 24/7 – from rap music to hip-hop to *Bay Watch* and *The Simpsons*. Such artifacts span national borders, bombarding local cultures and weaving them into a seamless collective tapestry of ideas, words, and practices. And yet not all of these changes are roundly accepted. For, they often exert pressures on local worlds – bringing long held cultural patterns under challenge or outright assault. What is certain is that the changes experienced in the region have been fast-paced and complex and there remains much to be researched, analyzed and theorized.

The chapters in this book seek to do just that. In various ways they describe and assess a number of key aspects of social, economic and cultural change wrought by globalization in the Asian region. The underlying theme in the book is the multi-dimensional way in which globalization – in the form of ideas, practices and technology – have introduced social inequalities in specific contexts. Along the way, themes such as gender, labor, political activism, social movements, diaspora, identity, media, poverty, governmental policy, and development – among others – come to the fore. With so many elements in play, one point that we wish to make is that globalization is not any one thing. There is unevenness in its diffusion, differential expression in the contexts it enters, and widely diverging ways it is experienced and treated by human agents and the structures they have created – either prior to its entry or following human engagement with it. In this way, as one of our authors argues, globalization has a variety of 'careers' – not only between any two spatial contexts, but within any one context or among any given population over time.

The text is divided into four sections. Part I is concerned with delineating and explaining the vagaries of social inequality wrought by globalization in terms of gender, social class and labor. All four chapters in this section demonstrate that the globalization process exerts local impacts, which, in turn, engender complex responses by those who must deal with contemporary social change. Part II centers on the relationship between media and identity in the face of globalization. For the most part the emphasis is on how messages are mediated, experienced and expressed in particular places. The four chapters show that media is often employed as a tool by local users for interpreting, if not remaking, understandings of self, group and society. Part III looks at globalization from the perspective of cities. Among the issues that the three chapters address are: changing urban social structures, quality of life, sustainable urban development, developing civil society, and increasing consumer culture. The emphasis is not only on problems, but solutions; discussing how to: turn local culture to developmental advantage, reverse structural factors that can produce anomie, and attend to situations that necessitate children to go to work. Part IV concludes the book, providing a critical assessment of the social and cultural transformation of contemporary Asia.

Before introducing the contributions in each section, let's consider the core concept underlying this text.

Globalization

The earliest work in globalization theory was macroscopic. From Wallerstein's 'world system analysis' (1976) to Giddens' 'four dimensions of globalization' (1990) the emphasis was on conceptualizing globalization 'from above,' in totalistic form. Beginning with Appadurai (1990), though, a greater attention was laid on context. Focusing on the simultaneous push-pull between cultural homogenization *and* heterogenization, he spoke of 'disjuncture and difference' *in situ*. This dissonance was stimulated by and rendered intelligible via reference to five 'scapes'. Appadurai's approach was attractive because it enabled analysts to say that while 'dimensions of global cultural flow' might be fixed, they are generally expressed differentially as between any two given contexts. The focus on context is present in a number of chapters of this volume, with Bangladesh, Indonesia, India, Japan, Singapore, and Taiwan among the states studied. At the same time, broad population 'flows' across the Asian region are considered – notably Asian artisans, female migrant labor, and the Hmong people – as well as key cohorts located in specific places – including women, child laborers, and young adults.

One factor that nearly all globalization theory has emphasized is economy. It was the entire engine in Wallerstein's conception and, for Giddens, two of his 'four dimensions of globalization' are the world capitalist economy and the international division of labor. In this volume, economy certainly carries an important voice. For instance, in Part I, Timothy Scrase explores Asian artisans in the global economy and Nicola Piper calls attention to female migrant labor in Asia. In Part II, T.J.M. Holden and Pam Nilan both argue that 'lifestyling' predicated on conspicuous consumption of fashion and technology are factors mediating identity formation and expression in Japan and Indonesia, respectively; Ming-Chu Chen, too, implicates capitalist rationality as the motive force leading to the publication of salacious details concerning a female politician in Taiwan. In Part III all authors emphasize the economic fallout of a globalizing Asia, with Scott Baum looking at economic restructuring in Singapore, Zakia Hossain considering social effects of rapid urbanization in Dhaka, and Susy Sanie and Scott Baum studying the working children in the slums of Jakarta.

Without question, it is essential to explore the economic dimensions of social inequality fuelled by globalization processes in Asia, as the gaps between countries, classes and groups is widening. While there has been an explosion in terms of the 'new rich' (Pinches 1999) there remains large numbers of 'old poor' – those who inhabit the shanty towns, urban fringes, or under-resourced rural areas, and work in the informal sector for piecemeal wages in dangerous and demeaning jobs. Moreover, while some celebrate the 'Asian economic miracle,' others point to the fact that it is still largely a 'miracle' for a few, Westernized elites. We are reminded by Vervoorn's (2002: 135) observation – heretofore the classic critique of Western economic development in Asia – that as new economic models are imposed, localized forms of knowledge and institutions are undermined and devalued, and once lost, local knowledge and cultural traditions become lost forever.

Significant as the economic is, Vervoorn's insight reminds us of something Clammer (2002) has also argued: that there is more to globalization than economic processes, changes and outcomes. It is true that as compared to political systems, the economic has been the most adept at facilitating the penetration of goods, values and practices, and the least resistant to the integration of these elements into local contexts. What has been required is a way of conceiving of globalization in less totalizing, less (politically or economically) exclusive terms. For instance, more than seeing a world economy – through the offices of multinational companies – as speeding up the flow of capital (and, consequently, labor) both within and across international boundaries, one must see and attend to the accelerated transmission of values and behaviors, and how they articulate with and are expressed in specific localities. Such views suggest that not only are macro contours important, but micro manifestations, as well. For the editors of this volume, analyzing the cultural, as much as the economic or political is imperative in comprehending the globalization process in Asia. In this respect, a significant concept for analysis in several chapters is 'transculturation' – the 'process in which cultural forms literally move through time and space where they interact with other cultural forms, influence each other, and produce new forms,' (Lull 1995: 153). For instance, Pam Nilan, in her analysis of Indonesian youth's attitudes toward western media, observes just such a process. Invoking Appadurai's now-famous concept 'disjuncture,' Nilan demonstrates that transculturation appears to be a jagged process: equivocal and far from univocal. When Indonesian youth encounter global media and its intellectual products, they are placed in a position of having to negotiate competing discourses of identity: that of modernity and tradition, with responses rarely entirely faithful to one or the other.

One aspect of transculturation is its production of hybrids. These fused cultural forms, T.J.M. Holden shows in his scrutiny of Japanese media, often do little to subvert the integrity of the local. This is a significant departure from much of the earlier thinking about globalization, which presumed a 'hypodermic needle'-like theory of influence: with the exogenous content 'injected' into a local context, thereby exerting a hegemonic effect. In a similar way, the power of locality can be divined in the indigenization of transcultural content. This local coloration of imported forms is what Roberta Julian demonstrates in her chapter on the Hmong diaspora – for instance, in her presentation of a freelance dramatic artist living in America, expressing his Hmong identity via rap music, the language form he perceives as belonging to a fellow-oppressed racial minority in the adopted context.

Indigenization bespeaks local power. Understood thus it is possible to see that local regularities might exist that are relatively impervious (or at least obstructive to) to macro forces. As Santos (2002) observes, it is often the case that indigenous contexts will produce 'resistant local hegemonies' which rise up in response to would-be homogenizing content. This is one of Chen's points in her study of a female politician in Taiwan furtively filmed while having sex with a married man. As the author observes, the local 'rules' of patriarchal order dictated that the single woman was subjected to social opprobrium while the adulterous male passed free of condemnation. Such presumptive hegemonies – and the local response – is also a theme Julian touches upon. For the Hmong, what might at first glance appear to be a globally uniform identity is actually a hegemonic discourse emanating from specific elites – defined by gender, age and profession – who reside in the United States. In the face of such singularity, counter-hegemonic discourses have arisen from voices on the 'periphery' – in particular, Hmong women and youth.

This book's structure

In Part I of this book the first two chapters, by James Goodman and Nicola Piper, are broadly concerned with explaining the inequities of the globalization process in the Asia Pacific region by way of social movement analysis. In Chapter 2, Goodman assesses the changing dimensions of social stratification in the Asia Pacific brought about by factors like an emerging post-colonial political order, the imposition of neo-liberal economic policies, heightened consumption and materialism, and growing social divisions. Taken together, these changes have spawned a range of social movements (some local and others more regional and global in outlook), which challenge, at various levels and in various ways, the established social, political and economic order. As he argues, inequalities in the Asia Pacific region have been dramatically reterritorialized due to the impact of neo-liberal globalism and it is thus imperative to understand the specificity of the localized impacts of such globalism in, and within, particular countries. His chapter ends with the optimistic view that new social movements formed largely in reaction to neo-liberal globalism have strengthened political solidarity and communal bonds between various groups in the region.

The theme of social movements, or more correctly, the movement of peoples across the region, is explored in Chapter 3. Here Nicola Piper considers the case of female migrant labor within and between the various countries of Asia, a phenomenon that has drastically increased in recent years due to the widening economic disparities between rich (mostly north-eastern) and poor (mainly south-eastern) Asian nations. Inequality is essentially at the heart of female labor migration in Asia – they migrate because they face discrimination as women and, by all objective social measures, because they are poor. Significantly, there has been comparatively less sociological research carried out on this topic, partly because many governments wish to deny the extent, levels and forms of exploitation that women and girls face. For the majority of Asian nations, there is simply neither the legislation nor political will to instigate effective labor laws capable of protecting the rights of migrant laborers. This is even more true of female migrant laborers who, in many cases, remain in the host country illegally and are thus vulnerable to a range of criminal activities. Consequently, it is left to various NGOs and advocacy networks to lobby on behalf of these women in order to protect their needs and rights. Yet, as Piper demonstrates, the NGO route toward emancipating female migrant workers is fraught with inconsistencies and difficulties at various levels – individual, local, national, regional and transnational – and, so, her chapter raises important and complex questions regarding the sources of women's inequality in Asia, as well as the practical steps required to eliminate it.

Linking the discussions of neo-liberal globalism (in Chapter 2) and gender inequality in Asia (in Chapter 3), Ruchira Ganguly-Scrase in Chapter 4 explores the consequences of market liberalization for lower middle class women in India. Based on extensive fieldwork and interviews, her findings show that while neo-liberal economic reforms are generally viewed as having been beneficial to society, paradoxically, no direct benefits from economic reforms over the past decade have come to the families of her respondents. Moreover, interviewees state categorically that women's equality has not been secured by the neo-liberal policy agenda. Essentially, one could argue that neo-liberalism is just as much an ideology as it is an economic policy and political agenda. As Gosovic (2000) contends, global intellectual hegemony has become one of the main characteristics of globalization since the early 1990s. The India example described by Ganguly-Scrase is important when considering the changes in Asia over the past 50 years. Once a socialist-oriented, centrally planned economy, India took on board the IMF agenda for economic liberalization and reform in the late 1980s. The past 15 years have been witness to immense changes at the national and local levels, especially with the privatization of many government enterprises and the freeing-up of telecommunications and other key industries in the Indian economy. As a consequence, many middle and lower class employees have lost job security and benefits, inflation is high, consumption and materialism have increased exponentially, and there has been an explosion of the so-called middle classes. While not quite an economic miracle, economists nevertheless point to the Indian economy as a successful case for IMF-derived liberalization policies. Importantly, Ganguly-Scrase goes beyond the rhetoric to expose the localized impacts of an essentially globalized economic agenda – specifically highlighting the fact that any gains for women's emancipation are confined by the inherent patriarchal ideologies of the neo-liberal state.

Tim Scrase, in Chapter 5, considers inequality in Asia particularly in terms of the impact of globalization on work and labor. The emphasis in this chapter is on explaining the situation of a 'traditional', yet marginalized group of producers, namely artisans, and their various survival strategies in the face of increasing global and local market competition. In many ways, the daily life and struggle of Asian artisans has changed little over the past few decades. This is the life of precarious production – a marginalized existence determined by the ever-changing desires of a whimsical global and local consumer market, where the majority of artisans fluctuate between work and unemployment, income and poverty. Scrase describes how the globalization of artisanal crafts has led to the separation of craft from artisan. For instance, many examples exist where specific crafts, weaving designs, or local, indigenous patterns and styles are copied and mass-produced in factories in the industrial centers of Asia for worldwide distribution and consumption. Thus, ironically, the craft itself survives in a hybrid form which may or may not be produced by the original workers. Interviews with artisans and craft consumers also reveal the extent of day-to-day corruption faced by artisans in their quest to market their goods, as well as highlighting the unique ways they attempt to adapt their product to shifting consumer trends and tastes. Like the other three chapters in this section, this chapter reveals the localized impact of the globalization process, and describes and analyzes the complex ways people deal with contemporary social change in Asia.

Part II

It could be argued that the globalization paradigm was born of the assertion by media theorist Marshall McLuhan that 'ours is a brand new *allatonceness*. 'Time' has ceased, 'space' has vanished. We now live in a *global* village…a simultaneous happening.' (1967: 63; emphasis in original). It was this notion that became the fulcrum of Gidden's theorization of globalization, in the form of 'time-space distanciation' – a view that 'society' is no longer a bounded system and, as consequence, social life should be analyzed in terms of how it is ordered across space and time (1991: 64). Robertson's (1992) definition of globalization also accentuated 'the compression of the world and the intensification of consciousness of the world as a whole.'

In point of fact, it is media that largely engineer these 'new spatial dynamics.' According to Morley and Robins (1995: 1) media are 'boundary spanning technologies,' that influence 'patterns of movement and flows of people, culture, goods and information.' In turn, media and the phenomena they touch and influence, are implicated in contemporary identity discourse, the social construction of gender, and the reification of (or challenge to) local beliefs, practices and embedded social inequalities, to name a few significant aspects of social organization. It is precisely these media-related (or what we call here 'mediated') processes that the four chapters in Part II are concerned with.

In Roberta Julian's Chapter 6, it is the boundary-spanning capability of media – with the ability to transcend and compress, unify and facilitate social change – that is on display. Her study of the diaspora of the Hmong people from Laos to Australia, America and France suggests that while they are a people lacking a geographical locus, media such as video, pop songs, journals, the Internet and 'storycloths,' have enabled the collective to maintain threads of commonality, forging what Anderson (1983) has called an 'imagined community.' The 'shared space of dialogue' created by the Hmong exemplifies what Werbner (1998) has labeled the 'diasporic public sphere.' Importantly, Julian shows, this is not necessarily a realm of consensus. Whereas a unitary discourse (emanating from the elder, male, former political elite in Laos) dominated the initial stages of diaspora in the 1970s, now a plurality of voices exists. In place of the traditional Hmong identity – which was originally fused with a myth of the 'American success story' – there has arisen a discourse increasingly female, youth-centered, less ideological, and, importantly, less 'traditional.' Significantly, it is because of media, Julian argues, that contestation appears ascendant. The burgeoning number of outlets for expression has meant a fragmentation of Hmong identity in the face of a diverse chorus of Hmong voices – not necessarily a bad thing, Julian concludes, but a development of 'uncertain-ization' (Slevin 2002) that promises to pose future challenges for this dispersed, territory-less community.

The situation Julian recounts relates to what Giddens (1991) has called the 'narrative of the self' – the story or stories by which self-identity is reflexively understood. In his reckoning media play a prominent role in constructing and communicating such stories. As Gauntlett (2002) explains: 'The media disseminates a huge number of messages about identity and acceptable forms of self-expression, gender, sexuality, and lifestyle.'[1] On such a view, the social construction of identity is an on-going process that is assisted – though not necessarily determined – by media. But what do we mean by media? And is *any* medium a part of this narrative of self or only particular kinds? Answering such questions is one aim of T.J.M. Holden's Chapter 7.

Since McLuhan (1964), there has been a recognition that media not only constitute things that transmit, treat and receive messages, but enable humans to 'extend themselves'.[2] Of course, media is much more complex than that. For one, it comes not only in types (such as TV, cars, flags, jewelry), but in grades of 'formality'. Some, such as radio or videotape or CDs, have been institutionalized – either via their integration into the economy or everyday practice. They most often (though not necessarily) take a technological form. Such media are widespread in their accessibility, 'decodability,' and use, and, because of the relative 'embeddness' in social structure, can be thought of as formal. In every chapter in this second section, the authors contemplate media of this ilk: studying popular music, films, VCD recordings, television, magazines, newspapers and the Internet. There are other media, however, that are less technology-centered, regularized, widely used, or formalized. Our authors point to T-shirts, body adornments and quilts as examples of this. One dimension of Holden's chapter is to explore how identity discourse is communicated through both formal and informal means in Japan – via television food shows, in the case of the former, and female fashion and tattoos, in the latter. Both types of communication vehicle, he shows, are integrative: they help unify subcultures – providing shared codes, experiences, understandings, senses of belonging, and defensive tools. They also serve to demarcate and clarify localized identity and provide ammunition for resisting the influence of exogenous, would-be homogenizing beliefs and practices, often imported through other media. In this regard, Holden argues, Japanese media, regardless of form, are all rather uniform in their content and effect. They not only orient Japanese people to a globalizing world; they serve as conduits for communicating to Japanese their uniqueness – importance, even excellence – in the world beyond sub-group or national borders. They, thus, inoculate media consumers against too much foreign intrusion (cauterizing the local with the global flame), or else inculcate the logic of the local via repetition and valorization. The result is the construction of more impregnable versions of localized identities.

This finding reminds us of something Castells asserts in his *The Rise of the Network Society* (1996): 'we are not living in a global village, but in customized cottages globally produced and locally distributed.'[3] To him communications technologies may have a global reach, but their content is not determined by their structural configuration. This is certainly true of the Internet, where every web author is free to upload and disseminate her own sounds, words and images. However, it is also true of radio and TV networks and cable systems, where programming is subject to local decision, as is the determination of which words or images within those programs will be modified or expurgated. In short, even the certitude of a technology delivering a message is not enough to guarantee what message will be delivered. Beyond this, though, as Pam Nilan makes clear in Chapter 8, there is no certitude whatsoever how whatever message does make it through the administrative gauntlet will be received. Drawing on data derived from eleven focus group interviews conducted with forty-six Indonesian youths (carefully selected to reflect religious affiliation), Nilan persuasively demonstrates that despite the prevalence of western messages in Indonesian society, local filtration is widespread. Significantly, this message 'customization' transpires outside of formal institutional structures (such as media organizations, schools, or the State). Indonesian youth of all religious persuasions actively engage with media, participating in a reflexive process of meaning making. They remember certain messages, and tend to talk about communications that confirm or deny their significant identity discourses. At the same time, although they evaluate media as powerful, they also most often regard it in negative or equivocal terms. This poses a dilemma for this cohort – many of whom will hold significant leadership positions in Indonesia's future. As Nilan reveals, two discordant discourses (of tradition and western modernity) become pitted against one another: on the one hand engagement with media possesses the power to shift Indonesian youth out of traditional frames of self-reference; on the other hand, without continued engagement with media and information technology, Indonesian youth believe that their nation will lag further behind other nations in the future. Given the dual insistence of global media and localized ideas and practices, no easy solution appears in the offing.

The power of media to stimulate or assist social change is a major part of the McLuhan canon. This power lies in part in extension – the alteration of the senses, the stretching of human capability. Extensions can mean the car that transports a human over greater distances than two legs could, or a web page that can instantaneously connect one side of the world with another. Missiles can communicate hatred in minutes; books can encapsulate ideas, enabling humans to extend their existence in perpetuity. Julian's chapter inscribes this aspect of media theory, showing how the Hmong had employed media to nullify (or at least de-emphasize) place as the definitive element in identity formation. This reminds us of Meyerowitz's (1986: 6) contention that 'electronic media affect us, not primarily through their content, but by changing the "situational geography" of social life.'

Another kind of extension, considered by Ming-Chu Chen in Chapter 9, is that of human possibility. Working through the fascinating, multi-act history of a 'sex-VCD scandal' in Taiwan, she shows us how media can be used to change what could be called the *situational structuredness* of social life – the rigid organization of the social world in accord with pre-existing definitions of gender, role, and human possibility. The scandal began when a tabloid freely distributed video recordings depicting a sexual encounter between a former Taiwanese politician and a married businessman. In the months that followed, the incident moved from criminal investigation to scandal to shared voyeuristic extravaganza to public debate about the position of women in a patriarchal society. Copies of the VCD were disseminated worldwide across the Internet, in addition to becoming a local best seller at Taiwan's night markets and bazaars. The politician was not only branded a criminal by the press, she became a victim of peeping by hidden camera delivered to a global public. Forced to endure the humiliation of communal censure, she publicly declared that she had been 'sentenced to death' by a profit-hungry media.

In a stunning reversal, however, the victim employed the very same media that had exploited her private experience, raising her voice against traditional culture, publishing a book, hosting a smash radio and TV show, and debuting as a singer. This reinvention of identity reflects how media can work to extend human possibilities beyond many of the confining ideational and practical shackles of local social structure.

While it may be true, as Tomlinson (1999: 21) has asserted, that globalization is more than media, the four chapters in this section underscore the central role media play in negotiating identity under conditions of contemporary globalization. The contributions here not only reveal the panoply of engagements between mediated communication and everyday lives in Asia, but also validate Appadurai's perspicacity in designating media as one of the 'five dimensions of global cultural flow'.

Part III

As important contemporary sociological issues, the interrelated themes of this book – globalization, culture and inequality – are represented by and deeply ensconced in the urban centers of Asia. Like cities elsewhere in the world, cities in the region are increasingly becoming the sites of varied social processes. The populations of Singapore and Hong Kong are almost 100 per cent urban, while Japan's figure is slightly less (79 per cent). Other countries, Indonesia, India and China (for example) have much smaller urban populations, but these numbers are growing (The World Bank 2000). The World Bank predicts that over the next two decades over half of Asia's population will be urban. Over this same stretch the United Nations predicts that worldwide there will be 358 cities with populations of over one million. Slightly less than half of these will be in Asia (Hall and Pfeiffer 2000). Given this growth, urban places in the region have, over the past few decades, become the focus of increasing sociological research.

A sociology of the cities in the region is driven by a rich history of urban scholarship and is influenced by the pioneering work of two Chicago School sociologists, Park (1967) and Burgess (1967), together with those working later within the new urban sociology, notably Castells (1977), but also a handful of other European social scientists (see Pickvance 1976). More recently the impacts of those interested in a post-modern theory of cities have also influenced thinking (Savage and Warde 1993). Such a rich background means that a diversity of theories, conceptualizations and methodologies naturally drive the sociological treatment of Asian cities, with key interest accorded to the description of how urban social life is being played out. Propelled by this overarching issue, questions of growing inequality associated with increasing levels of urbanization and the impact of a far greater global economic reach have been raised across several research areas (see, for example, Ariffin and Louis 2001; Ho 1997; Hung 1996). So too, questions of increased urban environments, increases in globalization, and an increasing consumer culture have come to the fore in urban-based research, as scholars have attempted to unravel the associated impacts on local populations (see, for example, Clammer 2003; Robison and Goodman 1996). Issues to do with changing urban social structures, quality of life, sustainable urban development and developing civil society are also being discussed. It is these types of questions that the authors of the three chapters dealing with cities have sought to respond to.

In Chapter 10, Scott Baum addresses the impact of Singapore's 'global city status' and the development of significant new knowledge economy sectors on the social structure of the city-state. Placed in the framework established by authors such as Sassen (1991) and Friedmann and Wolff (1982) the analysis in this chapter considers the changes that have taken place in Singapore's occupational structure and income distribution, tying these changes to the increasing presence of Singapore in the network of global urban centers. The patterns identified are different in some ways from those identified elsewhere, a finding which suggests that changes occurring in the world's global cities are influenced by something more than just the impact of global economic sectors. To be sure, local governance and culture also play a role. The author finishes by suggesting that it is the ability to utilize these local factors to mediate the negative social and economic impacts that will be important when dealing with altered or changing situations.

Chapter 11 shifts the focus from Singapore to Bangladesh's capital city Dhaka. Zakia Hossain explores the extent to which rapid social change associated with increasing globalization and urbanization can influence feelings of anomie or anomic structures. Concerns about the impact of rapid social change on social life have been part of sociological inquiry since the birth of the discipline.

The author takes up recent directions in the issue – above all, the reemergence of anomie as a useful sociological concept – and considers how anomic structures might be emerging among a sample of Dhaka residents. Noting that a number of patterns are clearly discernible with regard to anomic structures, Hossain suggests that the rapid social changes that have characterized contemporary society in Dhaka have not been experienced equally. Such a finding – which is in line with several other studies – leads her to contend that governments should consider the ways economic growth and social change can exert differential impacts across different sub-populations.

In Chapter 12, Susy Sanie and Scott Baum turn attention to the position of child workers in informal settlements in Jakarta. Motivated by long-expressed concerns relating to the impact and prevalence of child workers, the authors analyze findings from a small-scale survey. Questions relate to the types of work done, the factors that influenced a child to undertake paid work and the probability of child worker outcomes. Sanie and Baum conclude by arguing that just as the factors that determine child labor are complex, so too are the possible solutions which may be used to address the problems. Here the authors canvass issues that include the need to be aware of unintended impacts resulting from national and international policy on child labor, and the need to address workable solutions.

Reading this book

The team of authors who we have assembled to assess the major challenges to and changes confronting Asian societies in the face of global incursion, we believe, are well suited for the task. They represent a wide range of experience with, location in, and perspectives on globalization in Asia. Moreover, they bring the panoply of viewpoints – social, cultural, political-economic, and philosophical – which they train on global phenomena both within specific countries and across nations. Nearly every contributor seeks to understand globalization conceptually, with an eye for moving beyond the descriptive present into the prescriptive future. Above all, their emphasis is on the scope and complexity of contemporary social and cultural change in the region, in comparative perspective, and in light of two driving forces of change: the intensification of economic globalization and the impact of global cultural flows upon urban spaces, social groups, local cultures and collective identities.

The perspective that our authors adopt – and the spirit in which we hope the book will be read – is sociological in the classical sense. That is, it is at once integrative and synthetic; it recognizes that social phenomena often engage multiple societal 'sectors' at once – the economic, political, social, cultural and moral – often in cross cutting, permeable, polyvalent ways. Moreover, such phenomena express themselves ideationally, practically, spatially and temporally, often simultaneously. For this reason, the kind of intellectual approach that best facilitates appreciation of the full dimensionality or contours of globalization recounted here is the 'sociological imagination' that Mills (1959) argued for: a worldview that is contextual, grounded in empirical observation, aware of and searching for the linkages among the intricately connected institutions and milieux in which we, who are increasingly touched by globalization, ourselves, touch, are touched by, are woven into, and help weave.

Part I
Gender, Class and Labour

2 Contesting the New Inequalities: Social Movements in the Asia Pacific

James Goodman[1]

Introduction

Social movements in the Asia Pacific face a rapidly changing socio-cultural and political context. The movements of today have their roots in state formation and national mobilization. Reflecting the rise of state-centered developmentalism, social movements share a common democratizing impulse and have in many cases successfully transformed national development in favor of popular aspirations. The last decade has dramatically shifted this mobilization framework. National development projects are weakening, in many cases unraveling, shaking the underlying foundations for social movement politics. Where in the past social movements could unify at the national level behind a shared agenda, today there is little common ground. Existing national projects, whether social democratic, anti-colonial, communist or anti-communist, are increasingly stripped of meaning and relevance. Instead, new spheres for social movements are emerging, whether 'below' the state in sub-national territorial and communal conflicts, or 'above' the state, in conflicts around transnational forces, such as corporations, inter-governmental institutions and global norms.

These shifts reflect the impacts of neo-liberal globalism. Sharper sub-national and cross-national inequalities are emerging, and these impose new imperatives for mobilization. The new inequalities, as illustrated elsewhere in this book, have two axes. The first is a social axis: neo-liberal globalism stratifies across peoples, creating a newly transnationalized business class — what Leslie Sklair calls the transnational capitalist class (Sklair 2000). The global corporate diaspora that has emerged from neo-liberalism is articulated into macro-regions such as the Asia Pacific, and also into national contexts, transforming the 'local' political game. Against this diaspora are ranged diverse constituencies of subordinated peoples, who start to recognize common problems, common causes and common enemies. The second axis of stratification is a spatial axis, expressing the geography of subordination. Neo-liberal globalism territorializes at the same time as it globalizes. As it weakens national frameworks for interest articulation and legitimation, it sharpens and opens-up territorial divides, between the regional or local 'haves' and their corresponding 'have-nots'. Inequalities are dramatically reterritorialized, with new divisions between places and the peoples that live in them. The result is the transformation of social movement mobilization. Social movements emerge around a range of sub-national conflicts, and at the same time around new cross-national conflicts.

This chapter explores the changing logic of stratification, debating the redefinition of mobilization. The focus is on the fate of national developmentalism, linking this to shifting forms of mobilization. Section 1 opens with a discussion of hegemonism and 'new-constitutionalism', understood as framing Asia Pacific politics in the current era. Section 2 focuses on the disruption of national 'developmentalism', and the implications for national political elites. Redefinitions of political legitimacy and implications for movements are discussed in Section 3. The final section, Section 4, focuses on mobilization and on responses to neo-liberal globalism, debating the forging of political community around themes of solidarity, decommodification and 'deep democracy'. But before discussing hegemonism, let's briefly consider the role of social movements in the new, economically liberalizing Asia.

Social movements, redefining 'the political'

Debate about the role of social movements necessarily focuses on the boundaries of politics, how they are being policed and where they changing (see Stivens 1991). Two key factors that contain and border 'politics' are the dominant conceptions of political scale and the formal channeling of political power and contestation. Scale is an important means of bounding the political, confining realms of the political to locality, to nation, to region, to the international or to the global. Confinement of political life into levels of institutionalization enables the hierarchic ordering of 'politics', into insiders and outsiders, quite literally into those with speaking rights and those without. Another important confinement device is the process of channeling political contestation into established or formalized structures. The exercise of power outside of these structures may be obscured and naturalized: political struggle then becomes a struggle about contesting the naturalized or 'apolitical' exercise of power, establishing political salience for otherwise invisible political issues.

Under capitalist modes of accumulation there are intermittent waves of stabilization and destabilization, with associated realms of the political. The logic of containment under 'laissez faire' capitalism in the late Nineteenth Century, for instance, dramatically contrasts with the political model under post-War Fordism. In this respect, there is a powerful dialectical relationship between phases of accumulation and political form: the two proceed hand-in-hand through what Karl Polanyi characterized as a 'double movement' (Polanyi 1944). The logic of accumulation creates new avenues for marketization, but at the same time requires and creates new forms socialization and mobilization. The process of creating a new development model out of the ashes of its predecessor is necessarily a process of reframing or re-containering politics. In the current era, as values are increasingly financialized and rendered liquid, positioned as flows rather than situated in places, we are seeing a dramatic reordering of political space. The new hyper-marketized model – a form of neo-liberal globalism – is transforming the framework for social movements. The model though, is a work-in-progress, with multiple in-built instabilities, and appears to be in a state of permanent transition.

The Asia Pacific is a key site for these transformations. The latest wave of neo-liberal globalism has been playing out in the Asia Pacific since the mid-1980s, and the region remains steeped in the marketization process. National development projects, national ideologies and political institutions have undergone dramatic transformations, especially since the financial collapses which beset the region, beginning with Australia and New Zealand in the mid 1980s, through to East Asia in the late 1990s. The ramifications, especially the political ramifications, are arguably still only beginning to be felt. There are dramatic shifts in the frameworks for political culture, for mobilization and contestation. The Asian NGO, ARENA, noted the passing dream: 'Several years ago, world leaders and global capitalists predicted that the Twenty-First Century would be the 'Pacific Century' and that Asia would be the cradle of new global economic power. Today, at the threshold of the so-called 'Pacific Century', Asia stands at the vortex of critical events and processes which spell sweeping and profound changes in its economic, political, social and cultural life' (Asian Regional Exchange for New Alternatives 2000: 3). The vortex may, in this way, become the cradle for future forms of social movement mobilization, and for future re-definitions of 'the political'.

Hegemonism

The Asia Pacific has been a place of imperialist rivalry and domination from the early-modern mercantilist period, through to modern colonial imperialism, and to contemporary modes of hegemonism, played out in today's variously post-colonial, neo-colonial and other late-modern forms of domination. In the era of mercantilism, from at least the Sixteenth Century, with Portuguese, Dutch and British rivalry in the West Pacific, the region became bound into the logic of European expansionism. In the era of colonial imperialism from the Eighteenth Century, the Asia Pacific region was a center for European and briefly Japanese imperialist expansion and domination. Following a wave of decolonizations through the Twentieth Century, colonial imperialism gave way to post-colonial hegemonism, that became increasingly US-centered, especially with the demise of Soviet Communism, and the subsequent effective dismantling of Vietnamese and Chinese communism.

What is understood today as the Asia Pacific – militarily, economically, politically – has its roots in the logic of US Cold War foreign policy. The region began life as a security concept, and fast became an economic concept due to the process of creating economic stability as a bulwark against communism. At the same time, the region was marked by a shared authoritarian political framework – whether communist or anti-communist. Post-Cold War there has been a deliberate effort at creating a pro-market consensus, with the dissemination and institutionalization of the neo-liberal 'Washington Consensus' through various combinations of regionalism and multilateral constitutionalism (Khoo and Smith

2002; Mittelman and Falk 2000; Soederberg 2001). The objective has been to irreversibly transform domestic frameworks of politics in the direction of marketization. Hettne characterizes the subsequent response as an aspect of Polanyi's 'double movement', a 'self-protection of society' (Hettne 1997). As peoples and movements protect themselves, they reflexively construct new fields of politics, and in the process produce new modes of contestation.

A key feature of this contemporary hegemonism, as against colonial imperialism, is its ideological power as a form of self-regulation and self-subjection. Hegemonism, as its name implies, is normalized imperialism, a form of domination that is built into the constitutive foundations that form the normative arenas in which 'politics' is permitted to take place. It is a 'soft' imperialism, one that suffuses political life by living in the interstices or capillaries of politics, defining what it means to be 'political'. Contemporary hegemonism is neoliberal and market-centered. It is enforced not through military coercion or colonial occupation, but through the disciplines of the market, paired with inter-state norms and agreements. Stephen Gill characterizes this as a 'new constitutionalism' – a new framework for the political sphere that differs from the 'old constitutionalism' in being cross-national in scope, interpenetrating and mutually-reinforcing across national borders (Gill 1998). From a very different (and non-critical) perspective, Thomas Friedman describes the phenomenon as a 'straitjacket' on political power – a 'golden straitjacket' that keeps politicians out of the market and in the process delivers prosperity: once wearing it, 'your economy grows and your politics shrinks' (Friedman 1999: 100).

There are deep instabilities written into this model. In the first instance, new constitutionalism is a contradiction in terms: it regulates states to deregulate markets. It seeks to permanently remove the task of economic management from the purview of government – to permanently remove politicians from the marketplace. The model thereby undermines the capacity to reproduce the conditions for accumulation and destabilizes development. Ironically, this leads to intermittent political 'bailouts', via various modes of corporate welfare, where losses are socialized to restore private profit. The mop-up function sees the state reentering by the back door, paying the private costs of crisis, whether financial costs in the form of repayments to the IMF, environmental costs in terms of cleaning-up abandoned projects, social costs in terms of welfare provision, or political costs in terms of political repression. The Polanyian 'double movement' – where socialization of costs proceeds hand-in-hand with marketization – remains very much in evidence. The political context, though, is quite different from Polanyi's, in the early Twentieth Century, as the political room for maneuver is strictly limited. Neo-liberal constitutionalism prevents the creation of frameworks that might provide long-term stability. Members of the elite may call for such frameworks, but they fail to materialize. George Soros and Joseph Stiglitz, and a host of others, have called for a new 'architecture' to contain the volatility of markets, but the ideological model militates against such an outcome (Soros 1998; Stiglitz 2002). Marketization under new constitutionalism thus creates substantial risks and dangers – not least for the US: the 1994 $52 billion bailout of Mexico is a case in point. Neo-liberal constitutionalism offers no way of addressing these risks: it makes them unavoidable. The result is a relatively permanent state of transition and crisis. There are recurrent crises of confidence, expressed in fears of 'contagion' following intermittent financial bubbles and busts. There are also deepening divides between those who benefit from market deregulation (and from intermittent interventions) and those who bear its costs: the lines are often drawn across territory and culture as well as across social category, destabilizing existing polities.

Developmentalism

Until recent years the dominant development ideology in the Asia Pacific defined the state as the vehicle of development. This produced the national development model familiar in the 'developmentalist' states of the region – those 'Newly Industrializing States' (NICs) of East and South East Asia dedicated to relatively high rates of intervention to achieve development goals. These states engaged in industry policy, creating a governed market to promote exports: the state governed via a technocracy of experts operating in a relatively depoliticized environment, insulated from public pressure and from social movements (Johnson 1987). This state was 'catalytic', in the sense that it intervened in the market to create national economic autonomy (Weiss 1998). In doing so, the model edged towards an 'Asian' model of development and version of modernity (Preston 1998: 197).

Through the 1980s the region acquired a remarkable degree of economic autonomy, driving a political agenda of triumphalism amongst the relatively authoritarian governments of the region, expressed in the rhetoric of 'Asian Values' (Uhlin 1999). There are interesting parallels with other non-Asian countries in the region, where a similar national development model predated the NIC emergence, and in some respects was more entrenched. Mexico, Australia, Canada and New Zealand, for instance, all developed their own largely commodity-based economies, protecting and promoting locally-owned industries. National development policies in these countries were unraveling by the 1980s, under pressure from globalizing elites, leaving the Asian develop-mentalist state looking like an exception. Through the 1980s the US Government pressured the NICs to open-up markets to trade and capital flows (Ahn 1997; Khoo and Smith 2002). But the pressures were only successful in the later 1980s as the middle classes of the NICs – much like the middle classes of other countries in the region – became increasingly detached from any commitment to the national development model, and more integrated with transnationalizing elites than with their state elites. Pang makes the point very clear: the developmental state model hinged on the dependence of national business on state finance. From the mid-1980s the internationalization of finance gave business elites new sources of capital, loosening their dependence on the state (Pang 2000). The business diasporas of the region, notably the overseas Chinese diaspora, turned to globalization as 'an alternative growth strategy', seeking 'internal transformations to meet the challenges' (Yeung 2000: 268). Funds flowed into the NICs in the early 1990s, with disastrous consequences when investor confidence was on the wane from 1997: in the process, globalism and financialization forced countries away from statist developmentalism into 'a new development model' (Pang 2000: 584)

The national development model, that had for decades delivered some degree of national political autonomy, was ruptured from within. National business and state elites, that had provided key constituencies for the model, were increasingly defined against it. In Chile in 1974 the transnationalized middle classes – compradors as they were called at the time – could only gain power through the military. From 1984 in New Zealand, 1986 in Australia, 1988 in Canada, 1989 in Mexico, 1994 in the Philippines, 1997 in the NICs, and perhaps from 2002 in China (with its accession to the WTO), the same ideological shift was secured through a combination of elite incorporation, market pressure and inter-state negotiation (Khoo and Smith 2002). As the process of internationalization has unfolded, entire executive classes – public as well as private – have become inter-penetrated, forming a transnational class of technocrats. The personnel have become 'moveable parts of the extensive network of the global public and private financial systems' (Pang 2000: 585). The phenomenon that Leslie Sklair identified in Australia in the mid-1980s, of an emerging transnational capitalist class, was paralleled across the region in New Zealand, Canada and Mexico, and later in the NICs (see Fairbrother *et. al.* 1998, Sklair 1996 and Wiseman 1999, for Australia; Hewison, Robison and Rodan 1993, and Pang 2000, for the NICs; Niblo 1995, for Mexico; Kelsey 1995, for New Zealand; Clarke 1997, for Canada).

The conversion to 'economic rationalism' rendered economies vulnerable to crashes – examples being the 1984 currency crash in New Zealand, the 1991 recession that, according to the Australian Prime Minister, Australia 'had to have', and the 1994 financial crash in Mexico. In the NICs and Japan the liberalization process facilitated a speculative bubble in the early 1990s, which finally burst in 1997–8, forcing several regional governments into reliance on the International Monetary Fund (IMF). IMF Structural Adjustment Programs (SAPs) directly reflected the political agenda of the US, to prise-open the region for US-based corporations, and to force a shift away from interventionist state-led development (Bello 1998; Camilleri 2000). The IMF led the charge, post-crisis, against the region's 'crony capitalist' development model, through the rhetoric of 'good governance' and anti-corruption. The IMF priority was, once and for all, to 'bring an end to East Asian-style statist developmentalism' (Berger 2002: 79).[2] The result was the wholesale dismantling of the developmental state model, and of the legitimacy of developmental authoritarianism. In effect the crisis brought a dramatic 'third worldization' of the region's NICs, demonstrating their lack of autonomy (Chossudovsky 1998; Webber 2001). The arguments for East Asian exceptionalism melted, forcing the 'emerging markets' into conformity with the development model that had been imposed on the post-Communist 'transition' societies of East and Central Europe in the early 1990's. Like the IMF's post-communist 'shock treatment', the new dispensation created new IMF protectorates and zones of dependency (Field and Goodman 1999; Ma 1998).

Crises of national developmentalism had dramatic consequences for regional elites: at one move, the ideological foundation for their political project was washed away. The resulting disarray opened up new political spaces for opposition movements, forcing some limited transitions away from authoritarianism. As Pang notes, 'financial globalization shifts the controlling lever to capital markets, and state power declines. This provokes political and social changes – regimes collapse, the political opposition wins in elections, and new civil society groups emerge' (Pang 2000: 580). Rule by the market does not preclude national politics – including national authoritarianism, but rather reshapes it. Marketization, moreover, seems compatible with state power – most spectacularly in marketized command economies, such as China (currently delivering the 'fastest and longest growth the world has seen'; Flynn 1999: 156). The result is not so much a 'rolling back' of the state, as a shift to a new kind of state. The World Bank in 1997 described a state that was 'steering not rowing', one that facilitated marketization, enabling markets, rather than regulating them (World Bank 1997). The state was changed from a 'bulwark' against global market forces into a 'transmission belt', imposing rather than insulating society from market discipline (Cox 1987). As Camilleri states, 'the task of the state' in the Asia Pacific today is to 'sustain the conditions most conducive to market activities' (Camilleri 2000: 380).

The impact on national political frameworks is widespread. Whether centrally planned, 'socialist' states (Vietnam, China, e.g.), Anglo-American-style capitalist states (Philippines, Mexico, Australia), or developmental-authoritarian states (Singapore, Chile, Malaysia), there is a dramatic shift away from commitments to social and redistributive equity to a preoccupation with economic growth and accumulation. The shift, simply put, is to the 'value of the monetary versus the non-monetary in life' (Malhotra 2002: 35), a shift that reduces state capacity and legitimacy, destabilizing polities across the region. A key component of this is a process of decentralization, and the introduction of 'good governance' provisions, drawn from the 'new public management', centering on the promotion of technical efficiency, achieved for instance through privatization, contracting out and public-private 'partnerships'. The World Bank in 1997 described this as 'bringing the state closer to the people', and the effects are felt in terms of a radical decentering of public power, with the proliferation of private providers, quangos and semi-state agencies, and semi-autonomous governmental units (Turner 1999).

As 'macro-regionalism' squeezes state power from 'above', these 'micro-regional' pressures undermine state legitimacy from 'below', or rather, from 'within' (Morales 1999).[3] Under the new model, a range of new sub-national political spaces open up, with the emergence of global cities or business districts, 'Special Economic Zones', 'Export Processing Zones' and Maquiladoras, as well as various defensible enclaves and gated communities. These disaggregated zones have more in common with their counterparts than with their national hinterlands, contributing to a frag-mentation of national space. The tendencies are recognizable across the region, as cultural and social divides are overlapped and reinforced by marketized stratification – from Los Angeles to Manila (Faust and Franke 2002). Reflecting this, intra-state conflicts between regions, cultures and nationalities within national states are a key focus for political contestation, and, some argue, the key threat to regional political stability (Reilly 2002).

Legitimacy

Political legitimation in the Asia Pacific is highly fluid. Asia Pacific governments are often weakly legitimated, facing multiple regime challenges. In many contexts there is a long history of authoritarianism, with definitions of nation, state, regime and government inter-penetrating, meaning a challenge to one political institution becomes a challenge to all. Pressures for change then precipitate periodical waves of political transformation, sometimes transmitted from country to country. In part this reflects shared social and cultural upheavals, and associated challenges to the political authority of even the most stable regimes. It also reflects the relative lack of traditional foundations for authority, itself a legacy of colonialism, as, 'except for a few cases, colonial rule destroyed or marginalized the traditional bases of domination' (Alagappa 1995: 57).

Post-colonial elites have wrestled with the task of creating a shared normative order as the foundation for authority. Several had well-established principles for rule: in Japan it was the power of the Emperor; in China it was the thought of Mao Zedong; in Vietnam the thought of Ho Chi Minh; in Taiwan the thought of Sun Yat Sen; in Thailand the triad of 'King, nation and religion'; in Burma the 'Way to Socialism'; in Indonesia the five 'Pancasila' principles; in Malaysia the 'Rukeenegara' (National Principles); and in Singapore the five neo-Confucianist 'Shared Values' (Crouch and Morley 1999). These in many respects constituted national norms, offering a cultural foundation for rule. In this way, they are not unlike the American Declaration of Independence, as assertions of the right to rule, and of the principles on which legitimate rule is to be based.

These national principles have proved highly resilient, although substantially reinterpreted and adapted to suit successive regimes. The legitimacy they offer has often been defined against perceived 'threats' – for instance in the form of sub-national separatist and communal challenges, or inter-state security challenges, or ideological challenges from communist movements (Antlov and Tonnesson 1995). In several cases the threats legitimized authoritarianism – and only when they were felt to have subsided were significant concessions made for democracy. In recent years a number of 'hybrid political systems' have emerged, where state elites position themselves between authoritarianism and democratization, mirroring the broader cultural divide between 'westernization and respect for tradition' (Camilleri 2000: 432). The key issue here is an ever-present contestation over the legacies of post-colonialism and post-imperialism, and the search for foundations of national legitimation, for the national polity's cultural place. The struggle is pervasive – for major powers in the region such as Japan, wrestling with the burdens of post-imperialism, as well as for lesser powers such as Australia, juxtapositioned between post-colonialism and post-imperialism, between Euro-centrism and Asia-centrism.

A unifying national ideology is particularly important given the multi-ethnic and multi-national composition of many post-imperial as well as post-colonial societies in the region. In many contexts the state plays a key role in indigenizing and reproducing the 'nation', and state power entails various ethnicization strategies – a 'gargantuan task' for post-colonial elites (Alagappa

1995: 57). The developmentalist state was able to emerge and flourish because business elites failed to play a strong and independent role, and in part this reflected the 'ethnic burden' borne by business classes across the region (Crouch and Morley 1999: 332). In many parts of the region – especially the NICs – business interests were either not national or were ethnic Chinese (interestingly, only in the Philippines was there a large indigenous business elite, which may help explain its relatively early democratization). In these contexts cultural politics was and remains a 'powerful force', with states seeking to construct inclusivity across cultural minorities through shared national aspirations. This is true of Indonesia's striving for 'unity in diversity' through the five Pancasila principles; it also is reflected in Taiwan's ethnic conflict between 'mainlander' and 'indigenous' Han Chinese; another example is Malaysia, where the state carefully manages (and maintains) ethnic divisions between Malays, Indians and Chinese (Crouch and Morley 1999: 334). Ethnic and communal divides can be put to political use in terms of justifying authoritarianism; they may also be an impulse towards pluralism and inclusivity. This is the experience in the Philippines, and also in settler societies, especially in Canada where French Quebecois and indigenous pressures for self-government have encouraged the national government to embark on various multicultural ventures to broaden cultural citizenship (Laxer 1992). Similar tendencies are evident in Mexico, where a hybridized national identity – Mestizo identity – is forced to make concessions to indigenous culture (Hernandez-Diaz 1994).

For much of the last thirty years, then, the national development project mustered significant leverage, delivering meaningful benefits for elites and some subordinates. The authoritarian technocracies could create and exploit the emerging 'New International Division of Labor', shielding themselves from politicization through the rhetoric of development. For a brief period, and with spectacular results, some states in the region were able to hold together market-focused development with state-centered developmentalism. In the late 1990s, with the financial crisis, the contradiction between these strategies was finally resolved in favour of the marketised developmentalism, throwing the state and its 'miracle' economy into disarray, signaling the 'demise of state-guided national development' (Berger 2001b:

211). In this context a shared value-base for political life has been severely shaken, undermining national legitimacy.

Today the new basis for national legitimacy, insofar as it exists, is the drive for markets. Rather than mounting national crusades for or against communism, governments now launch crusades for national competitiveness. As Acharya and Stubbs note, 'the legitimating geopolitical threats associated with the Cold War have been replaced by geo-economic threats associated with survival in an increasingly competitive global economy' (Acharya and Stubbs 1999: 126). One example was the 'Philippine 2000' project launched by President Fidel Ramos in 1994. This was a five year plan that, it was claimed, would elevate the Philippines to 'NIC-hood' by the year 2000 (Pinches 1997). The Plan brought deregulations and marketization of agri-business, minerals production, and the export of labor, but failed to deliver the Philippines into the charmed circle. Instead it created and exacerbated conflicts around regional identity, for instance in Mindanao and the cordillera as it displaced peoples from their means of livelihood, leaving them with little option but to join the ranks of the urban poor (Schmidt 2000; for the mining sector see Tujan and Guzman 1998).

One positive outcome of the recurring crises has been the renewal and strengthening of structures for electoral representation – part of what Huntington has characterized as a new 'wave' of liberal democracy (Huntington 1991). But the process of installing neo-liberal constitutionalism has had deeper political effects. Sharp tensions have opened up between the effects of market-ization, in terms of stratification and fragmentation, and the legitimacy of the national state (Thompson, 1996). There is an intense clash between the 'culture of capitalism' and the 'culture of the nation' (Purushotam, quoted in Malhotra 2002: 3). Developmental authoritarianism is clearly shaken, but what replaces it? If it is the case, as argued by some, that meaningful democratization directly relates to 'a conscious effort on the part of the state to achieve a degree of economic equity', for instance via mass education (Curtis 1998: 220), then the current shift in the role of the state would seem to undermine, not promote, democratic participation. As an alternative, Malhotra (2002) argues for 'socially activist states', and such possibilities are advanced by a series of movements promoting peoples' sovereignty over state sovereignty – asserting a form of democracy that rests with the people rather than with the institutions of the liberal state, and is focused on human and environmental security, and perhaps a 'post-development' future (Berger 2001a; Dokken 2001).

For many, the main source of hope lies in the powerful non-government sector of civil society and social movement organizations, that flourished across the region from the 1990s (see Serrano 1994; Yamamoto 1995). These give rise to political forces that intrude on and extend realms of the political, resisting the containering of democracy within representative structures. As Camilleri argues, 'With few exceptions, civil society had acquired a richer and more variegated organizational texture, especially in the context of family, religion and work, and partly as a consequence, its political space has intruded with increasing frequency and intensity into the political space traditionally occupied by the state' (Camilleri 2000: 403). Indeed, a remark-able feature of Asia Pacific political development is that it has been movements of non-government organizations – not political parties – that have led the multiple political transformations in the region. Western-style political parties are not even especially stable channels for formal political power: of the several hundred political parties across the 41 countries of the Asia Pacific in 1985, only half survived into the mid 1990s (Sachsenroder 1998). The legacy of colonialism, the impact of Cold War and the region's development model have militated against party political development along Western lines. Party political development in the region did not fit the Western institutional matrix – neither did it fit the ideological matrix: reflecting this there is little integration of Asia Pacific political parties into the international confederations. The parties remain idiosyncratic in Western terms.

Taking the long view, the various economic shocks to regime stability – from the 1970's oil crisis, to the 1980s debts crisis and the 1990s financial crisis – have opened up opportunities for civil society organization and social movements. Crises delegitimize the status quo, destabilize elite patronage and politicize social life: they offer a 'democratic moment' (Acharya 1998). Where governments have successfully branded Non-Government Organizations (NGOs) as a threat to political stability, perhaps as communists or separatists, democratization has been blocked (Crouch and Morley 1999: 324). The same factors may come into play in the future, as non-governmental forces seek to forge new constituencies in the context of deepening marketization. The process of transformation, reflecting its historical roots, is not predictable: rather it is centered on the agency of social actors and contingent on modes of cooptation and counter-mobilization. Democratization is necessarily dialectical, offering the possibility that socio-political responses 'from below' will set the agenda for repoliticization of social space.

The potential is especially evident today: as Camilleri argues, the latest 'transition to neo-liberal capitalism had opened a new chapter of social and political ferment at least as turbulent and absorbing as the one that preceded it' (Camilleri 2000: 417). Today, there are multiple dimensions to the politicization process, sharing the theme of asserting values that offer an alternative to the cash nexus promoted under neo-liberalism. NGOs and social move-ments are making manifold assaults on marketised relations, embodied in various demands for meaningful security – understood as human, food, cultural and environmental security (Burke 2001). The affective or moral vacuum of the new constitutionalism, and the materialism it promotes, is both its strength and its weakness. It should come as no surprise that today the key political challenges are soaked in the politics of moral and cultural community, challenging 'the absence of an ethical dimension in neo-liberal globalization, as well as...the cultural consequences of the consumerist ethos' (Mittelman and Falk 2000: 9). Scalapino notes, with concern, 'The declining ability of the secular state to market political values has...resulted in the search by many citizens for viable substitutes to serve their needs' (Scalapino 1998: 230). The political agendas necessarily take the process of contestation beyond the confinements imposed by the minimalist marketised state, demanding political action to achieve goals – for instance, around social justice, gender equity, environmental security and cultural identity.

New constitutionalism is de-centering power, but the political spaces are not innocent of subordination and domination. The overarching political dynamic often sees social set against cultural responses: movements to realize social and democratic rights emerge, but are confronted by movements for cultural self-determination. A key political task has been to bridge these twin dynamics, the first which is often associated with social movements and non-government organizations orientated to cosmopolitan norms, while the second is associated with communalist, regionalist or nationalist movements centered on territory. The task is as urgent for relatively wealthy countries like Canada, Australia and Mexico, as it is for countries such as Indonesia and the Philippines.

Often the counter-pressures emerge simultaneously. One example is the democracy movement that peaked in Indonesia in May 1998 after the Suharto Government finally acceded to the IMF demand that it remove subsidies on rice and fuel; the very same events saw the mobilization of militias intent on diverting discontent into an anti-Chinese pogrom (see Forrester and May 1998). Another example is the emergence of powerful counter-globalist and anti-corporate movements in countries such as Australia, which successfully disrupted the 2000 Asia Pacific World Economic Forum – a meeting of regional corporate elites (Goodman 2001). At the same time Australia had been experiencing a dramatic shift to the right with the emergence of the far-right One Nation party and sustained government attacks on refugees and asylum-seekers (Langton 1997). Another example is Fiji in 1999, which swung from a left-liberal coalition government to a military coup, and away from democratic decision-making (Prasad et. al. 2001). These mobilizations pose the question of political community – a question that still hinges, in many respects, on questions of nationalism and national identity. Most of the national political cultures across the region emerged from colonialism, and their sense of political community is defined by the assertion of national rights to self-determination, viewed through the lens of anti-colonial nationalism. Across the region, 'official' state-sponsored nationalism is ubiquitous, and politics has been primarily a contest for the mantle of anti-colonial or anti-imperialist legitimacy. Social movements still invariably frame their demands within the national framework, making appeals in the name of the nation. In countries such as Indonesia, the Philippines and Mexico for instance, where democracy movements have played a central role in the transformation of political life, there is rarely any attempt to define a politics outside the nation. This has also been true of feminist movements across the region, which in many cases have developed specifically nationalist feminisms (West 1997).

Unlike in Europe – both in the European Economic Community and in the Comecon bloc – nationalism was not 'held back' in the Asia Pacific during the Cold War (Hsiung, 1993). On the contrary, in the aftermath of colonialism, the region may be interpreted in terms of a conflict between anti-communist nationalism and communist nationalism (Antlov and Tonnesson 1995). The territory of three countries was divided by this conflict: Vietnam, Korea and China/Taiwan. In other countries – such as Chile and

Indonesia – the conflict set the terms for political contestation. For others, such as China and Singapore, to take contrast examples, nationalist mobilization, whether communist or anti-communist, was a key element in political development. Similar themes are evident in the post-imperial states of the region, where variants of nationalism retain their power, despite the legacies of imperial nationalism. Nationalism is normalized and banal in the US: assertions of US patriotism remain profoundly un-reflexive. In this, US political culture differs markedly form other post-imperial states in the region – Canada, Australia, New Zealand and Japan – where post-imperial nationalism is foundational but highly contested.

There are powerful sub-national indigenous challenges to hegemonic definitions of the 'nation', but these challenges are rarely directly separatist – rather they assert self-government, cultural autonomy and sovereignty within the existing state. Several sub-national political movements position their aspirations as explicitly state nationalist: Zapatistas in Southern Mexico are Mexican nationalists; the Cordillera people of the Northern Philippines are Filipino nationalists; even the East Timorese movement for self determination defined their aspirations in terms of the Indonesian Pancasila principles, and in terms of the Indonesian 1945 Constitution, claiming the Indonesian occupation of East Timor violated these principles (Goodman 2000a). Even when explicitly separatist, the challenges are rarely non-negotiable, as borne out in Indonesia in relation to Aceh for instance, and in the Philippines in relation to Mindanao.

The strengthening of transnational communities – in the form of social or cultural diasporas – has a parallel impact. Mobility from above, professional migration, is paired with mobility from below in the form of refugees and contract labor flows. Increasingly these flows are gendered, with women especially falling into the latter category, especially as domestic workers (Pettman 1996).[4] There are dual pressures, on the one hand challenging cultural exclusivity, but at the same time creating opportunities for exclusivity, usually national exclusivity. Earlier waves of migration, for instance under colonialism, have placed cultural politics at the center of post-colonial states like Malaysia, Fiji and Indonesia, as well as in the settler states on the region – New Zealand, Canada, the US, and Australia. Contemporary social movements are emerging around migrant advocacy, asserting inclusivity, whether for migrant workers in Japan and from the Philippines or Indonesia (Piper and Ball 2001; see also Piper, this volume). Reflecting a shift away from ideological divides, cultural identity has become increasingly salient and there has been an increased politicization of cultural relations. In many respects this cultural politics is played out across the particularism-versus-universalism divide. State elites use cultural divides to shore up political positions, asserting local values against globalist or Western values. The politics of division serves the powerful, but also sees subordinated groups engaging in communalist clashes, constructing cultural enclaves from which to assert the denial of difference.

Mobilization

The cultural politics of identity, territory and communalism flow through transnationalized contexts, patterning responses to neo-liberal globalism. Feminist, environmental, indigenous, lesbian and gay, human rights, and labor movements have all been dominated by Western perspectives and assumptions. All are now undergoing dramatic reconfiguration, forced by the process of constructing transnational and cross-cultural strategies, and the Asia Pacific is a key site for this process. Feminists have participated in a 'Third Wave' that embeds feminist goals in different cultural contexts, rendering diversity a strength rather that a threat (Heywood and Drake 1997). Environmentalists have moved from the assertion of ecological values against 'development', to embrace social priorities and the politics of 'environmental justice' (Martinez-Alier 2000). Lesbian and gay movements are shifting to what Altman characterizes as 'modern' gay identities, associated with politics of sexual rights as human rights across the Asia Pacific region: here the embodied politics of sexuality meets the cultural politics of diaspora, in a creative process of challenging North American models of activism and identity (Altman, 2000; Gopinath 1996). Human rights advocates have moved from the simple assertion of universal rights to myriad attempts at embedding and balancing rights in local culture and identity, for instance, through collective indigenous rights (Ghai 1996; Maiguashca 1994). Labor movements have shifted dramatically from a universal appeal to the 'workers of the world' to express the interests and aspirations of workers in different cultural contexts, in a new form of 'transnational social movements unionism' that steps out of industrial and national contexts to contest the new sources of corporate power (Munck 2002).

There is much crossing of cultural divides, with attempts at constructing political community around what might be seen as situated universalisms, centered on social justice. These 'reconstituted universals' are sometimes characterized as harboring a 'transversal' mode of politics, geared to superseding polarities between cultural positions (Yuval-Davis 1997). The result is a series of shared political orientations, with various contextual inflexions and specificities, signaling a politics of 'shared humanity' (Stivens 2000: 26). National civil societies, and the politics of social movements and NGOs within those societies, are heavily and increasingly influenced by these various transnational cross-cultural contexts. This point has been argued for the Philippines, in what is perhaps the region's most active civil society, where social movement mobilizations have been a major democratizing force in a largely underdeveloped society (Silliman 1998).

The exercise of power under neo-liberal globalism sets the pace for these social movement reorientations. Three specific targets are evident – global norms, transnational corporations and intergovernmental institutions (Goodman 2000b). All three are under challenge: global norm-formation is assaulted by the assertion of diversity and plurality; corporations are confronted by campaigns for decommodification; intergovernmental organizations are forced to address demands for deep democratization.

Contesting norms

Contesting global norms involves a value orientation, where diverse localized ways of being are counter-posed against the simple idea or ideal of globalized marketization. The politics of solidarity and recognition thus enters by the front door: transnational social movement unionism, 'third wave' feminism, ecological justice, all center on the process of working across cultural contexts to achieve solidarity. These ethics of solidarity offer frameworks for living together centered on mutual recognition and are an expression of the kind of sociability necessary for paradigmatic change. This simple assertion of multiplicity or plurality poses a very powerful challenge to the uniformity required and promoted under neo-liberal globalism.

It is especially powerful when multiple demands for embedded or localized difference are brought together across cultural and national contexts, to challenge the absolutism of corporate globalism.

Such challenges have been occurring in the Asia Pacific with increasing regularity. A good example is the Asian Social Forum (ASF), held in Hyderabad, India, in January 2003. The ASF was modeled on the World Social Forum (WSF), which held its inaugural meeting in 2001 in Porto Alegre, Brazil. The WSF was deliberately timed as a counter to the WEF held in Davos, Switzerland, and its key slogan was 'Another world is possible'. This world is a world of many worlds: the eighth clause of the World Social Forum 'Charter of Principles' states, 'The World Social Forum is a plural, diversified, non-confessional, non-governmental and non-party context that, in a decentralized fashion, interrelates organizations and movements engaged in concrete action at levels from the local to the international to build another world' (World Social Forum 2001: 1).[5] It does so by avoiding political posturing, instead focusing on facilitating dialogue (see Hardt 2002 ; Mertes 2002). The Charter makes the position clear: 'participants in the Forum shall not be called on to take decisions as a body, whether by vote or acclamation, on declarations or proposals for action that would commit all, or the majority…It thus does not constitute a locus of power to be disputed by the participants in its meetings…' (World Social Forum 2001: 1). Reflecting the success of this dialogical model, the WSF grew from 15,000 in 2001, to 70,000 in 2002, and to an expected 100,000 in 2003. More important, the model has disseminated, notably across the Asia Pacific.

The first Asia Pacific meeting of social movements was held in Bangkok in August 2002, to prepare for an ASF. This produced a statement that spoke of a 'second moment in the trajectory of the resistance as many anti-neo-liberal movements become a critical mass impacting on politics at the national level' (Asian Social Movements 2002: 1). This second 'moment' foregrounds the issue of intra- and cross-national coordination and solidarity and this was a major theme at the ensuing Hyderabad Asian Social Forum. The theme of this Forum was 'Connecting across Asia', and the invitation fore-grounded the question of cross-cultural Asia and Pacific solidarity: 'Asia's own diversity and spread invites and demands interaction and connections across the continent. The variety of Asian cultures, faiths and traditions provides to the process a rich resource to explore. The Asia Social Forum 2003 proposes and seeks participation from all the many Asian sub-regions so that the process builds and yields a rich exchange bringing together Central Asia, West Asia/Middle East, South Asia, North Asia, South-East Asia, and reaching out to the Pacific (Asian Social Forum 2002: 1).

At Hyderabad, 15,000 participants participated in a week of events that had the unexpected effect of bringing together formerly-divided movements, offering 'a venue where movements and organizations [could] find ways of working together despite their differences' (Bello 2003). Accordingly, a focus of the Forum was on overcoming communalism and cultural exclusivity, and this was reflected in some of the protests at the Forum (see Figures 2.1 and 2.2).[6] The Forum stressed the 'shrinking of democratic space within the nation-states', and the 'rise of aggressively fundamentalist, intolerant and violent articulations of identities and an increase in the repressive powers of the state and the elites, leading to gross violation of civic and human rights' (Asian Social Forum 2003: 2). The antidote was 'solidarity resisting imperialist domination', entailing 'the need to include many more social movements into this process of resistance and to evolve democratic and transparent processes for coordinating activities and actions' (Asian Social Forum 2003: 3).

Countering commodification

Decommodification, the second theme infusing the region's social movements, involves a radical refusal of marketization. Global hegemonism, under the rhetoric of 'market access', is generating manifold movements for decommodification (Starr 2000). Movements contesting neo-liberal globalism now share a common critique of commodification: the new solidarities, or as Waterman calls them, the 'new internationalisms', weave together a range of agendas defined against the 'market' (Waterman 2002). These movements are often offensive and proactive, seeking not only to defend presently uncommodified zones, but also to decommodify presently privatized aspects of social life. They often generate transformative, or what Castells calls 'project' identities, forcing the emergence of new paradigms for living beyond the market (Castells 1997).

Figure 2.1: Asian Social Forum 'ASF stage: Another Asia is Possible'.

Source: courtesy of *AidWatch*, Sydney.

Figure 2.2: Asian Social Forum 'ASF demonstration: the Communal monster'.

Source: courtesy of *AidWatch*, Sydney.

More specifically, many movements have become infused with the common theme of contesting the exercise of corporate power, and asserting alternative frameworks for existence. Neo-liberal globalism reveals the full force of corporate power, which previously dwelt in the relatively depoliticized harbor of 'domestic' civil society. The myth that business interests are national interests have become increasingly unconvincing, and national corporate 'champions' are revealed as powerful transnational political actors. Corporate power greatly exceeds corporate legitimacy, opening a gap to be exploited by popular movements. Reflecting this, a wave of consumer and producer-led movements have emerged across the Asia Pacific targeting transnational corporations, exploiting their exposure and vulnerability, politicizing their practices, and demanding action (Goodman 2002). Two relatively new pressure points have emerged – mass consumer activism, emerging from the success of cross-national corporate branding, and investor activism, emerging from the volatility and sensitivity of highly inter-connected finance markets (Willetts 1998).

Corporate campaigning has become a genre for social movements, with strategizing across the Asia Pacific (Goodman and Tujan, 2002).[7] New connections are forged between workers and affected peoples on the one hand, and conscientious consumers and investors on the other. Campaigns for industry codes of conduct, often linked to labeling regimes, are proliferating – from the garment trade to GM foods (Diller 1999). These fair trade 'buycotts' emerge as the flip side of consumer boycotts, all manifestations of the mounting revolt against consumerist values. Anti-consumerist alternatives are often community-based collective initiatives, where people disconnect from consumer capitalism. The move towards community gardens, growers markets, organic production, and seed banks are everyday expressions of this phenomena. The Seikatsu Club Consumers' Cooperative, in place since the mid-1960s, and in the 1990s claiming 170,000 member households, calls on the public 'to create a self-managed lifestyle in order to change the present wasteful lifestyle, which is a fall-out of the present capitalist-controlled society' (Yokyo Seikatsusha Network, 1988, quoted in Ekins 1992:132). The Malaysia-based Asia Pacific Pesticides Action Network is only another example, demonstrating how the process of contesting corporate power – in this case the power of oligopolized agro-industry – necessarily entails a process of working for alternative frameworks for living, for instance subsistence organic production and by eating GM-free foods.[8] Another example is the revolt against media conglomerates, expressed in attempts at creating alternative media systems, such as the on-line 'Indymedia' initiative, that has spread across the region.[9] Another campaign sector where significant leverage has emerged is in mining, denigrated by one industry advocate as a 'risk-creation industry that confronts and seeks to deter potential investors in the region', 'contributing to the decline in foreign investment' (Cruz 2002: 26; Evans et. al. 2002).

Counter-corporate movements politicize commodities, expose the social relations embedded in the 'product', injecting political meaning into 'things'. The Nike shoe is not associated with fashion and health, but with exploitation of workers in Indonesia and elsewhere in the region.[10] Chinese-made children's' toys are no longer associated with the joy of growing up but with exploitative and cruel working conditions in export-processing zones.[11] The product comes alive, linking the power of the consumer or investor to the power of the worker, the indigenous person or the environmentalist. Empty materialism is thereby challenged by moral outrage and social solidarity. These movements thus exploit the vacuum at the heart of consumer capitalism – its crisis of meaning. They demand substantive freedoms – the freedom to have a livelihood, to live in healthy environments, to organize in workplaces, to live free from prejudice, to campaign for political change, to be self-governing, to express cultural identity. Such campaigns are multiplying, challenging the costs of 'development' (see Friends of the Earth International 2002).

Deepening democracy

Deep democracy – the third theme – involves the assertion of popular participation in the emerging frameworks for rule. Deep democratization thus denotes the assertion of common realms of collective management and control beyond the increasingly minimalist public sphere. Key drivers are a sense of powerlessness, at various levels of association. There is household resistance to consumerist ethics and the assertion of alternative modes of consumption. There are efforts to democratize the workplace, forcing other actors into the arena of corporate decision-making (Schmidt 2000). There are moves to deglobalize financial and productive relations, creating local embeddedness and accountability. But most noticeable are the many efforts at wresting popular sovereignty from inter-governmental institutions, and from liberalizing states, (re)claiming structures of governance for popular participation, invigorating locality within globality. New constitutionalism exposes the logic of inter-governmentalism, previously defined as foreign or 'external' relations. The resulting regimes are distanced from formal democracy, yet increasingly shape 'domestic' policy (Goodman and Ranald 2000; Goodman, 2002). Movements work together to mirror the scope of these inter-state agreements and institutions, politicizing the new inter-state power sources and arguing for the democratization of transnational relations, whether through national or international mechanisms.

A good example is the reflexive mobilization of regional non-government organizations in opposition to Asia Pacific Economic Cooperation (APEC). As with the logic of IMF-imposed SAPs, deepened marketization through APEC destabilizes the legitimacy structures of states (Ericson and Doyle 2000). A key source of opposition has been the ideological framework for APEC, expressed in its 1996 motto 'APEC means business', and the prominent role accorded to business elites through the APEC Business Council in the formation of APEC policy. Since Kyoto in 1995 and later on a mass scale in Manila in 1996, APEC Heads of Government meetings have been besieged by NGO protestors. Doucet (2001) analyzed this process in 1996, theorizing a dynamic interaction between de-territorialized forms of democratization through inter-NGO solidarities, with and against existing national frameworks for democracy. The protests offered the model for such mobilizations across the region – they were 'dress rehersals' for the dramatic and highly effective anti-World Trade Organization mobilization in Seattle in 1999 (Ravenhill 2001: 172). Since Seattle there has scarcely been a meeting of an inter-state organization without a parallel mobilization of NGOs, whether through a counter-conference, or a blockade prevent the meeting from going ahead (Burgmann 2003). The yearly meetings of the Asian Development Bank, the ASEAN-EU 'ASEM' process, the WTO meetings, and also corporate planning meetings such as the World Economic Forum in Melbourne in 2000, have all been politicized as illegitimate sources of power in the region.

In general terms, then, the recent wave of neo-liberal marketization in the Asia Pacific has been remarkably successful, but the very success of this ideology presages new contradictions and instabilities. In some ways these are more intense than those they replace, and have greater potential of opening up possibilities for social and political transformation. In this double-sided and contradictory way, neo-liberal 'globalism' contains within it the seeds of its own destruction. The seeds have been planted and nourished, extending politics into new realms. We are seeing, as Doucet argues, the politicization of 'that which, prior to the 1990s, tended to fall outside the realm of social contestation' (Doucet 2001: 285). We also see a powerful process of ideological interaction, grounded in cross-cultural solidarity. This creates new frameworks for action overlaying the politics of territoriality and identification: political community finds a new fluidity in the dynamics of contesting globalism (Luke 1997). Increasingly, political action rests on a dynamic interaction across levels of identification. Marchand et. al. (1999: 899) speculate this signals a 'new state of being' that places people in the 'dyad of global local' rather than in the fixed place of the nation-state. The key is the nexus with the territory and place, where the political infrastructures of globalism confront the multifarious instances of local action, that together constitute a reflexive counter-globalism, what some characterize as 'globalisation from below' (Falk 1999).

Conclusion

Since the declaration of the 'Pacific Century' the Asia Pacific has been marked by a dramatic decline in expectations, accompanied by the dissemination of various versions of a broadly liberal model for development and politics. It may be argued that what was once a threat to the global liberal order has been subdued and domesticated. The conversion has been part of a broader trend away from the post-WW2 model of 'embedded liberalism', where international trading and investment flows were 'embedded' in national contexts through state regulation and welfarism (Ruggie 1982). Today's model is a form of *disembedded* liberalism – a domestication of the market mechanism that reflects the neo-liberal revolution in the region from the 1980s (Whitfield 2001).

The implications for state power are central: 'articulation of political space' under 'a hegemonic Western liberal paradigm' where new modes of stratification generate new forms of consciousness and action, has the capacity to reground the public realm through a reconstituted state power (Jarvis and Paolini 1995: 16). This may be thought of as a process of building political space, where reciprocal and reflexive mobilizations lead to the reconstruction of political community in response to internationalizing and regionalizing elites. This search for a 'more durable basis for political authority' is perhaps the region's most 'fundamental political challenge' (Alagappa 1995: 331).

Some observers see the liberal revolution, and believe it is permanent, concluding there is an exhaustion of possibilities, that today we live in a 'world without alternatives' (Kothari 1993; Richardson 1995). The argument made in this paper has been that while there are no ready-made, off-the-shelf alternatives, there are substantial grounds believing that Asia Pacific politics is, perhaps more than ever, a politics of transition and transformation. The new modes of political power are dissolving old political divides, but they are also constituting new constituencies and crystallizing new modes of contestation and mobilization.

In the new context, political cultures may be positioned defensively around forms of reactive mobilization, driving resistance identities. Alternatively they can pose an offensive challenge, mounting forms of proactive mobilization and forming transformative project identities. Those displaced by liberal hegemonism have an immediately-felt shared foundation for reciprocal action and can construct forms of transversal solidarity, driving modes of reflexive action that redefine the meaning of political culture. There are, then, substantial possibilities for disrupting disembedded liberalism via similarly disembedded political projects asserting alternative normative foundations for action, and alternative paradigms for living.

Polanyi's 'double movement' is alive and well in the Asia Pacific (Polanyi 1944). The national and transnational politics of the region is characterized by a fluidity that has not existed since before the Cold War and the advent of authoritarian developmentalism. In multiplying contexts there is a process of politicization that is producing a swarming effect on the region's political institutions. In myriad dimensions and levels there is an enveloping politicization of hegemonism and the agents of new constitutionalism. We find ourselves in a world of alternatives, all defined against the model of one-world liberalism.

3 Global Norms, Transnational Advocacy Networks and Female Migrant Labor in Asia

Nicola Piper

Introduction

Free and rapidly increasing international flows of goods, capital and information are heralded as the hallmarks of the current globalization processes. Movement of people and labor across national, cultural or ethnic borders are often left out of the equation. Yet it is arguably the most complex and controversial of the flows as well as the one with the most far-reaching consequences for both the sending and receiving societies as well as for the individuals concerned. Current experiences of female migration – particularly from Asia, the biggest exporter of female labor – is characterized by the overwhelming presence of women migrants in the category of unskilled labor (which is more often a reflection on the demand side and availability of a limited type of visa rather than a reflection upon these women's actual educational backgrounds). The kinds of jobs open to women are typically in the domestic sphere, the service industry (including entertainment) and to a lesser extent also in factories. In their dual role as women and migrant workers, they are often subject to exploitative or abusive practices in a variety of ways.

Asia has a long history of international labor migration expanding across the globe, but more recently there have been distinctive trends: first, cross-border migration flows within the Asian region have become more significant; and second, in addition to these increasing intra-Asian migratory movements, the feminization of migration has been widely recognized as another new trend (Castles and Miller 1998; Lim and Oishi 1996). Apart from changing patterns of migration, Asia has also witnessed enhanced democratization processes with a revival of civil society and social movements since the 1980s. Labor migration, too, has resulted in increased importance of political organizing aimed at asserting pressure on governments to take action on certain social justice issues by often transgressing national boundaries. The latter typically involves so-called transnational advocacy networks, and on a general level, the importance of theorizing and analyzing such networks has been highlighted to better represent new forms of social practice and political space (Piper and Uhlin 2001; Piper and Uhlin forthcoming). In operational terms, empowerment of migrant labor is an area to be filled by enhanced transnational NGO (Non-Government Organization) activism, particularly in view of the lack of will or ability of various Asian governments to take responsibility for either sending or receiving foreign workers. One aspect of the 'politicization' of labor migration through NGOs is the framing of a migrants rights' agenda.

In terms of existing academic studies, it has been observed that little research has been conducted on NGOs involved in migrant worker advocacy in the specific context of labor migration (Sim 2002). In addition to this lack of research on migrant worker NGOs in East and Southeast Asia[1], not much research has been carried out on the phenomenon of transnational activist networks in this particular part of the world[2] (exceptions are: Aviel 2000; Chen Jie 2001; Gurowitz 1999; Piper and Uhlin 2002; Price 1998). Moreover, also influenced by discourses on globalization, many scholars have neglected the regional – and not global – scope of much transnational activism.

In this chapter, I use the specific example of 'female labor migration' and 'trafficking' of people in Asia to illustrate how issues revolving around this particular type of migration are being dealt with by international law and NGOs which tend to use global norms as tools for their campaigns. I shall thereby pay special attention to exploring the dynamics between the different actors within and across borders. My overall aim is to bring grassroots politics into migration studies by not only highlighting state interventions and their limitations, but more so to discuss transnational NGO activism as an additional, ever increasing force in politics aimed at social change and social justice. This chapter thus offers conceptual ideas underpinned by preliminary empirical illustrations rather than a thorough empirical analysis and suggests a future research agenda.

Changing patterns of gendered migratory movements in Asia

Throughout the 1990s, based on enhanced economic performance and increasing integration of national economies within the ASEAN +3 countries[3], intra-regional flows of migrant labor have begun to exceed inter-regional flows, to the extent that today foreign labor has become a structural part of the national economies in much of Asia (Athukorala and Manning 1999). As a result, since the early 1980s, migration between Asian countries has grown steadily from just over one million Asians to more than 6.5 million by mid-1997 (Human Rights Watch 2000). In addition, there has been a clear trend towards the feminization of labor migration. Not only are increasing numbers of women participating, but they often exceed the numbers of the their male counterparts (*Asian and Pacific Migration Journal* 1996; OECD 1998). For instance, throughout the 1990s, approximately 60% of workers exported from the Philippines were women (POEA 1999), and in 1997, the total number of Indonesian migrant workers was 1.9 million of whom women made up 65% (in the Middle East, Indonesian women constitute more than 90% of all Indonesian migrant workers) (Tirtorsudarmo 1999). The experience of women migrants, however, differs from that of men in many ways, often resulting in higher levels of vulnerability because of a number of factors, such as female migrants' marginal status within the labor market, the nature of the labor they sell, and their labor often not being socially recognized as 'work' (Ito 1996). The latter is related to the traditional division of labor in which women assume care giving and reproductive types of work. Much of the feminization of labor migration in the global economic system is thus a reflection of women's roles as wives and mothers (and also 'dutiful' daughters). In addition, migrants work in domestic or reproductive spheres, even more so when 'illegal', tends to have an isolating effect as it is outside any protective mechanisms and outside the coverage of receiving countries' labor laws (Lawasia 1998; Piper and Ball 2001).

A number of factors have contributed to increasing flows of labor across national borders, with the large differences in economic development and living standards between the countries in Asia being crucial. In the context of the sending and receiving countries being at different stages in their respective demographic and socio-economic developments, lack of employment opportunities 'at home' have led to large scale international migration flows to labor scarce economies such as in East Asia. In addition, improved levels of education in the poorer countries have resulted in better access to information. At the same time, due to avenues for legal migration of unskilled labor being limited, many workers are prompted to migrate in an undocumented manner, often recruited by employers or agencies in the receiving countries and hence related more strongly to the demand than the supply side of labor migration. As undocumented workers, these migrants are typically excluded from labor law protections or other state services. Even when visas or work permits are available, they only allow for short-term periods of stay and renewal may be difficult. Thus, many workers who initially migrated on a contract decide to stay on and subsequently become 'illegal' overstayers (Human Rights Watch 2000). There are no reliable data available for undocumented migrants but it is estimated that they outnumber legal migrant workers by as much as seven to one. Migrant workers from Thailand were estimated to amount to 450,000 in 1995, of which the proportion of undocumented workers was approximately 60% (Phongpaichit 1999: 77). At the same time, Thailand has become destination country for approximately 294,000 registered migrant workers (mostly from Burma) and 733,000 undocumented labor migrants from Laos, Cambodia, and Vietnam (Chantavanich 1999: 161–62). The status of undocumented migrant or overseas contract workers often results in 'repeat' migration after a short return period to the country of origin, with permanent settlement being more and more out of reach for this category of migrants[4].

Although the growing feminization of Asian migration has been acknowledged by mainstream migration scholars, this has mainly been referenced in passing or else in a neutral manner (see, for instance, Castles and Miller 1998). Despite recent signs of a diversification in skill levels and employment opportunities (Kofmann 1999; Piper and Roces forthcoming; Raghuram 2000), the majority of migrant women in Southeast and East Asia still labor as unskilled domestic helpers on short-term work contracts (Chin 1998; Yeoh, Huang and Gonzalez 1999) or in the service sector as 'entertainers' or sex workers, and they typically do so either on short term visas or in the context of trafficking (Piper 1999). In addition, an unknown numbers of undocumented, unskilled women are to be found in labor-short industries such as manufacturing, agriculture and fishing (Yamanaka 1999, 2002). Most of these unskilled women migrate from Southeast Asia, notably the Philippines, Indonesia, Thailand and the Mekong countries.

Underlying the feminization of migration in Asia are long-standing patriarchal traditions and institutions that place young females in the lowest rank within the family, the household and the workforce (Tyner 1999). This social inequality pushes women to migrate in search of better opportunities to improve the household economy or to escape marital problems in the light of non-existence or social unacceptability of divorce. Consequently, female migrants are subject to various kinds and intense levels of prejudice, discrimination, exploitation and violence based not only on their sex, but also on class, nationality and ethnicity (Cox 1997; Shah and Menon 1997). Under prevailing institutional arrangements of migration in Asia, it is difficult to fully protect the rights, physical safety, and psychological health of migrant women. Despite the significant levels of risk and vulnerability they encounter, the precarious situation of migrant women has attracted some scholarly, but still little administrative or public attention in the region (Lim and Oishi 1996). The stereotypical view of women as dependents or secondary earners remains dominant as the gap between scholarly perceptions and the reality of migrant women's lives grows. Most governments have failed to provide protective legislation and services specific to their needs and vulnerabilities. Indifference to feminized migration has led to a lack of relevant policies and public awareness in countries of origin as well as host countries. The few moves towards protective measures which have occurred are typically rooted in a paternalistic approach to women rather than in the notion of empowerment [5] (Piper 2002).

The growth of service sector employment in Asia, as much as elsewhere, contributed to the feminization of labor migration, such that more and more countries are beginning to 'export' increasing numbers of female workers (e.g. Vietnam and Cambodia). Employment in the sex and entertainment industries is interestingly regulated by way of an 'Artist' or 'Entertainers' visa and hence treated as 'skilled'. This is, however, less to offer 'protection' but rather to assert control over these women and also to circumvent the sensitive issue of importing foreign hostesses and sex workers.

A related issue in this context is trafficking. Although trafficking, as such, does not exclusively refer to women, it typically occurs in the context of trafficking for the purpose of prostitution and thus involves large numbers of women and also children (Raymond and Hughes 2001; Ucarer 1999). There is much confusion, however, as to the exact definition of trafficking and its distinction from smuggling (I re-visit this issue in more detail below). East Asia is an important 'receiver' of foreign sex workers, with Japan being the largest in this region, with Korea and Taiwan also offering increasing vacancies for foreign women in this particular sector. In general, both prostitution and labor of unskilled migrants are 'illegal' in East Asia. Thus, foreign women who enter these countries on a tourist visa without any contractual and legal provisions end up being 'illegal' on two counts: firstly, as unskilled laborers and secondly, as prostitutes.

Global mechanisms for protection

In the context of globalized labor markets and the presence of non-national workers, new concepts need to be developed to incorporate changing realities of migrants working outside their country of citizenship. In particular, attention needs to be given to human rights of workers to avoid their being treated as tradable commodities. The institutionalization of rights through the UN Charter of Human Rights, for instance, has been described as a central aspect of the social process surrounding globalization (Turner 1993). International concern with the rights of migrants began with the establishment of the International Labor Organization (ILO) (Ghai 1999), and thanks to its numerous efforts to generate global standards, there are a number of international norms for the protection of migrant workers.[6] There are also UN Conventions such as the 1975 Convention on Basic Human Rights of Migrant Workers and its expanded version of 1990 on the prevention of discrimination against foreign workers. In view of the feminization of international migration, UN conventions specifically targeted at women's welfare, together with the UN Convention of Protection of Rights of All Migrant Workers adopted in 1990, could offer satisfactory protection for migrating women.[7] However, all these initiatives have little support by state governments anywhere in the world. In fact, many migrant host countries in Asia have not even ratified ILO conventions that would guarantee basic rights to their own local workers (Lawasia 1998).

In her specific discussion of protective mechanisms for female migrant workers, Truong (1996) has observed that the UN Convention on the Protection of the Rights of All Migrant Workers has in fact recognized female migrant workers, but not in their role as 'reproductive workers' – a term with which she refers to jobs in 'sex-affective services' and the 'care-taking economy'. The Vienna Human Rights Convention of 1993, on the other hand, recognizes sexual violence and trafficking in women as an aspect of violation of human rights, but does not give prominence to female migrant reproductive workers. To better protect the rights of domestic workers as migrant workers, and so-called 'mail-order-brides' as long-term residents or citizens in the host countries, Truong (1996) argues that their situations must be included in the international frameworks of human rights that specifically concern them. In this sense, addressing particular needs or concerns of female migrants is also an issue for the international women's movement as part of its efforts revolving around the 'women's rights as human rights' campaign (Joachim 1999).

On the whole, when pitting 'rights of states' versus 'rights of migrants' from an international law perspective, it remains a fact that 'states retain the right to set the conditions under which foreigners may enter and reside in their territory' (Weiner 1995: 153). Although those migrants who are holders of work permits tend to be in a better position than undocumented migrants, in many parts of Asia they are obliged to succumb to other state restrictions, including those pertaining to sexual behavior, and they are not granted any citizenship rights (Aguilar 1999).[8] The enforcement of restrictive laws vis-à-vis migrants might not come as a surprise considering that many states enforce similarly restrictive laws vis-à-vis their own citizens (Aguilar 1999; Weekley 1999). This situation is, however, worse for 'undocumented' workers and women. With the dominance of domestic service as an occupation among female migrants, the issue of the private sphere being under little scrutiny by policy makers constitutes a gender specific problem. Domestic service is not covered by national labor laws since the domestic sphere is not defined as a workplace. In so-called 'transition countries' like Vietnam and Cambodia, an additional problem is that the whole concept of 'rights' is fairly new, with legal frameworks and enforcement capacities generally not being in place. Furthermore, high levels of corruption in certain parts of Asia aggravate this situation.

The issue of trafficking is a particularly complex issue and deserves special attention. It is typically neglected by conceptual understandings of what constitutes labor migration – which I have criticized elsewhere by arguing for its inclusion in discussions on labor migration (Piper 1999). I would also argue that the category of 'trafficking' has been over-employed. The situations under which women cross borders and/or 'opt' for work in the sex and entertainment industries have become so diversified – depending on the countries of origin, the type of 'sex work', and the individual women – that it is not helpful to subsume all these incidences under the category of 'trafficking'. In view of much of today's cross-border movements being, or ending up as, 'illegal' largely owing to restrictive immigration policies, one has to distinguish 'trafficking' from 'smuggling'. The latter refers to 'facilitating migration', which is a reflection of the actual process. The aim is to take someone across a border illegally for a fee, as a consequence of the desire of a person who is unable to obtain a visa to travel to another country to work. Smuggling is thus perceived as a crime violating state sovereignty (Human Rights Law Group 2001). Trafficking, on the other hand, always involves the use of deception, coercion or debt bondage at the beginning of a trip or at the end. The aim here is to extract work or services from someone through the use of deception, violence or threat of violence, or debt bondage. This does not always involve the crossing of borders or the illegal crossing of borders. In this sense, trafficking is seen as a crime against the individual (i.e. a violation of human rights) and only secondarily a violation of state sovereignty (Human Rights Law Group 2001). In practice, however, the boundaries between those two distinctions are blurred. A person who hires a 'smuggler' might not know that the 'smuggler' or 'recruiter' is really a trafficker who intends to hold this person in forced labor, servitude or slave-like conditions. At the same time, there is more and more evidence that women migrants usually know what kind of job they are expected to do at the receiving end, but often find the conditions different from what they were promised. I would argue that much of the trafficking or smuggling which occurs should be seen as gender-based violations of women's labor rights – their rights as sex-affective service providers.

When trafficking in women is approached as a human rights issue, the aim is to criminalize the practices of traffickers. As rightly commented upon by Ucarer, though, 'this approach focuses on the *consequences* of trafficking rather than its causes' (1999: 231; original emphasis). The human rights framework emphasizes the sexual exploitation and abuse of women and a distinction between voluntary and involuntary prostitution is often made – an issue on which human rights and women's NGOs are divided. Many feminist NGOs argue that voluntary prostitution does not exist, whereas others portray prostitution as a profession which should be accredited rights, hence leading to the 'sex workers' rights' movement (Kempadoo and Doezema 1999). One major problem in this respect are the different socio-economic contexts in which 'trafficking' occurs, involving different levels of choice. A related problem area is the divergence of national legal approaches and – possibly most crucially – social attitudes in dealing with prostitution which obstruct international efforts in their attempt to develop effective international rules translated into national policies to suppress the trafficking of women (Ucarer 1999) and/or to empower sex workers. It is no surprise, then, to find a lack of consensus on key issues in this debate.

In many respects, the internationally available conventions and standards dealing with migrant workers in general, and migrant women specifically, could offer a lot of protection. However, this is more so in theory than in practice, in that the translation of these conventions into national laws with proper enforcement is an entirely different matter. Rarely do any 'migrant worker receiving countries' sign, let alone implement, such conventions. As rightly commented upon by Gurowitz (1999), states are not paralyzed by international norms as sometimes claimed because these norms are often not binding and not enforceable by any supra-national authority. Hence, international norms can only matter when operationalized domestically. Their impact, thus, varies across time and place. As a result of inadequate responses from governments and state agencies to the vulnerable situation of migrant labor – in general, and female migrants specifically – NGOs and activist groups are needed to fill this gap, and they are in fact increasingly doing so.

Pro-migrant responses from non-state actors

In view of governments' inability or lack of political will to deal with labor migration issues from the perspective of empowerment and rights of foreign workers, it is very much up to non-state actors, such as NGOs, to take up the role as advocates to assert pressure on policymakers. In this context, it has been remarked that one of the impacts of globalization on changing state authority and regulatory capacity has been the opening up of political space for non-state actors (Mills 1998). Conceptually, this links up with the extensive literature on the revival of 'civil society' and social movements, in a national as well as transnational setting. NGOs constitute one such civil society group which have gained great significance as domestic actors using 'international norms to bolster arguments for which they have found few domestic resources and those norms in turn work under particular domestic circumstances' (Gurowitz 1999: 444). Apart from acting on the domestic scene, they are also important as transnational actors (Piper and Uhlin forthcoming).

From the 1980s onward, Asian migratory flows have in fact given rise to many NGOs and other voluntary associations committed to addressing the dire needs and alleviating serious problems of migrants in general and migrant women specifically (for example, Lawasia 1998). At the receiving end, these migrant organizations are often established, staffed and managed by concerned local citizens. They provide migrants with guidance and assistance in such matters as documentation, legal rights and benefits, education and the like. Some such organizations are devoted to sheltering women whose safety is threatened by employers or others (Roberts 2000). Migrants also often organize themselves into mutual help associations based on shared religious or ethnic affiliation. With Filipinos constituting the largest global migratory workforce (Harris 1995), it is not surprising to find supportive NGOs organized by Filipino nationals all over the world.

In Japan, for instance, in response to the harsh immigration policies by the national government, local NGOs have been addressing migrants' work-related and other types of problems for over a decade. Although the percentage of foreigners of the total population (1.2%) is small in comparison to other industrialized countries in the West, by 1997 there were 145 civic groups supporting migrant workers all over the country (Roberts 2000: 276). These groups can be broadly classified into two main types: (1) volunteer-based citizens' organizations, and (2) local labor unions (ibid). The first group can be subdivided into five groups: Christian groups, medical NGOs, lawyers' association

NGOs, concerned citizens groups and women support groups (Shipper 2000). Women-specific NGOs typically include privately run shelters of which there were seven in the Tokyo/ Yokohama area in 1994, addressing domestic violence and divorce issues. There are migrant worker NGOs either set up by Japanese or by mainly Filipinos. Migrant worker NGOs and support groups are increasingly being confronted with problems that have shifted over time from being about 'help to return' to 'livelihood support' in Japan (Roberts 2000: 286). This indicates a shift in approach by these support groups along with prolonged immigration: instead of short-term intervention for people who are considered to be sojourners, there is now a stronger emphasis on settlement and citizenship provisions. There is also another shift as noted by Mackie (1999): today activists emphasize that foreign migrant women are exploited as workers – emphasizing labor rights – with much in common with other groups of 'illegal' immigrants to Japan. This shift was led by local welfare workers but also by the foreign women themselves. Among those located in Japan, women's groups in particular often promote and appeal for strong linkages against human trafficking and the violation of human rights – an aspect which has also been observed in the context of Taiwan (Jie Chen 2001). Most have established local 'networks' within their own country, and some have begun to establish transnational links, particularly with an Asia Pacific focus. This is partly related to already established linkages in that region based on anti-sex tour campaigns in the 1970s and also campaigns for compensation and recognition of the survivors of 'military sexual slavery' committed by Japan during the Second World War (concerning the latter, see Piper 2001). Activists in Korea and Japan have worked tightly together, organizing regional conferences and regional networks, including the Philippines, Taiwan and other Southeast Asian countries. It, therefore, seems that women groups have a particularly strong and broad regional basis for rights activism based on historical and economic links (recognized by feminist groups as having had specific impact upon women) between East and Southeast Asia.

In South Korea, according to a survey by the Christian Institute for the Study of Justice and Development, at least 150 civil, religious, and labor organizations are presently engaged in improving migrant workers' rights and supporting their interests (Lim 2002). Virtually all of these organizations devote the bulk of their efforts to 'labor counseling' (e.g. helping foreign workers collect unpaid wages or severance pay, obtain medical assistance and financial compensation for work-related incidents, receive legal advice, etc.). In the aftermath of the Asian financial crisis, an initiative for a 'Foreign Worker Employment and Human Rights Protection Law' (FWPL) ended up being scrapped. The idea to draft this FWPL was first introduced by a coalition of civic and religious organizations in 1996 and then designed to create a legal basis of equality for foreign migrant workers in Korea. While the passage of the law was always in some doubt, prior to the onset of the Asian crisis, the prospects were fairly good. Indeed, after collecting roughly one million signatures through a nationwide signature campaign,[9] support for the law seemed solid even within the government – both the ruling and opposition parties, as well as key ministries (including the Ministry of Labor), favored passage of a new law along the lines proposed by Korean NGOs. The Asian crisis, however, effectively destroyed official and public support for the law. More than this, the Korean Federation of Small Businesses (KFSB) used the crisis to argue that existing laws and institutions designed to control transnational migrants be adjusted to better meet the needs of the Korean economy (as opposed to the needs of the migrant workers). To make this point, the KFSB even conducted its own 'civil protests' in front of government offices. At this stage, I cannot assess to what extent and effect Korean NGOs have been operating transnationally or whether the setback triggered by the Asian crisis has given new impetus to NGOs to consider transnational networking.

In Hong Kong, Sim (2002) reports of 16 NGOs operating on behalf of Southeast Asian migrant issues. They have been active in educating domestic workers about their rights and have been demanding legislation to eliminate racial discrimination. According to Sim, these NGOs have been able to build coalitions beyond narrow organizational agendas with some success. For instance, they staged a multi-ethnic protest of migrant workers on behalf of Indonesian workers against the imposition of fees by Indonesian authorities for contract renewal. In this sense, she sees the collaborative actions of NGOs as having forged an emerging sense of solidarity and class identity among migrant workers of different ethnicities from different countries (2002: 12). According to Law (forthcoming), NGOs based in Hong Kong which have been formed to support foreign domestic helpers since the 1970s have for the first time created a network of different Asian countries in their fairly recent campaign against wage cuts and hence gone beyond a focus on one specific nationality group. And by targeting not only Hong Kong's policies vis-à-vis migrant labor, but also their country of origin's emigration policies, they are truly operating transnationally on various fronts.

In Taiwan, NGOs concerned with migrant workers' rights and conditions constitute a fairly new phenomenon, as the Taiwanese government's policy of importing unskilled labor has only existed since 1991. Such NGOs, however, are joining an otherwise robust environment of social movement activism and appear to be more 'international' than others in Taiwan because of the nature of the cause they support. Groups like 'Hope Workers' Centre' and 'Migrant Workers' Concerned Desk' have established firm linkages with the Migrant Forum in Asia (based in Manila) and the Asian Migrant Center (based in Hong Kong) which are the two most important umbrella NGO networks on behalf of migrant labor in this region (Jie Chen 2001).

Despite the general observation by scholars that NGOs have been mushrooming in much of Asia, it is still the fact that NGOs meet considerable barriers to their free activism from many governments, particularly in Southeast Asia. The variation between countries is, however, substantial. In Singapore, NGOs are hampered by the state with 'catch all laws' whereby the state can act to hinder development of NGOs and their agendas (Sim 2002). In Malaysia, there are less domestic political opportunities for civil society initiatives than in many other Asian countries. Malaysian groups that are perceived as a threat by the government are systematically harassed. This is especially true for feminists and those focusing on problems of labor migration. The high profile women's group Tenaganita (Women Power) has suffered harassment since it published a well-documented report on the mistreatment of migrants in Malaysian detention camps in 1995 (Uhlin 2001). Concerns about the 'ethnic balance' between ethnic Malays, Chinese and Indians make issues of diversity, including migration, especially sensitive in Malaysia. Unlike in many other countries, NGOs working to protect migrants' human rights have found it hard to use arguments about the multiethnic character of the state when they campaign for fair treatment of immigrants (Gurowitz 2000). Political protest by women and human rights groups are typically dismissed by male leaders as culturally inappropriate and a product of the west (Gurowitz 2000) – a tendency not only to be found in Malaysia but in much of the Asia Pacific region (see Macintyre in Hilsdon et al. 2000). The Philippines, for instance, have a long tradition of a vivid civil society. With the Philippine government having been an active promoter of labor export for a long time, NGOs have been highly involved in this process for a similarly long period of time. Hence, with Filipinos being the most global workforce of whom the majority are women, it is not surprising to find supportive NGOs organized by themselves all over the world. Being largely Catholic, these activist networks also link up with the global presence of the Catholic Church. Indonesia (another major 'exporter' of female workers) under the Suharto regime was highly repressive against all aspects of civil society activism that was perceived as working against the interests of the ruling elite. Although the Indonesian political system has begun to open up significantly since the fall of Suharto in May 1998, civil society initiatives to protect the victims of trafficking and labor migration are still far less extensive and influential than in the Philippines. Furthermore, Indonesian women have been less well organized (since the crushing of radical movements following the coup in 1965) and the number and strength of women's groups is much lower than in the Philippines and Thailand, which have experienced a longer period of more open political systems. Thailand, a country that is both exporting and importing workers, has a relatively strong women's movement and a large number of NGOs focusing on the issue of trafficking. NGO activism in so-called transition countries like Vietnam and Cambodia is particularly hampered by a lack of financial as well as human resources. More or less vibrant activism on behalf of migrants is, however, not only linked to more open or closed political systems, but also to the more or less prolonged history and experience of labor export or import.

The discussion above only offers a glimpse of the type of social and/or political activism on behalf of labor migrants that exists within the Asian region. These responses by NGOs, based in both Asian sending and receiving countries, often operating transnationally, indicate not only a regionalization of labor migration and its feminization, but also a trend toward regionalization of 'migrant politics'. Despite existing local obstacles which obstruct NGO activism more or less severely – in many ways it is actually because of such obstacles – NGOs have made use of global norms of equality in articulating their solidarity with 'local workers' by pointing to UN and ILO conventions on the protection of migrant workers (Law, forthcoming: 216; Piper and Uhlin 2002). International conferences have witnessed calls for the recognition of migrant issues as part of their political agendas (such as the NGO Migrant Caucus at the1995 Fourth World Conference on Women in Beijing; Law forthcoming). Regionally, there is an increase in transnational networks such as the Coalition Against Government Exactions (CAGE) formed in 1998 and the newly formed Asian Migrant Coordinating Body (Chen 2001; Law forthcoming). A campaign organized in 1999 by the 'Migrant Forum in Asia', a network of independent grassroots migrant advocacy and support organization, claiming that 'Migrant's Rights are Human Rights' also shows the increasingly use of a language of 'rights'. This strategy of using a 'rights' frame has created a political opening for discussions about the discriminating tendencies of employment contracts and immigration policy. This does not however work in such a straightforward manner in the context of all types of cross-border migration – as discussed in the following section.

Anti-trafficking activism and NGOs' role

NGOs play an important role in defining the conditions for trafficked women as a problem and they also contribute to policy formulation. Although the anti-trafficking lobby has gained much momentum and impact, it has to be noted that there is much diversity – so much that there is in fact no consensus among NGOs on the definition of 'trafficking' and how to approach this issue. Trafficking is typically linked by NGOs to prostitution, and those NGOs involved in trafficking can roughly be divided into two camps: first, the abolitionists who advocate for the end of all forms of prostitution and trafficking (such as CATW – 'Coalition Against Trafficking in Women'; founder Kathleen Barry); and second, others such as the GAATW ('Global Alliance Against Traffic in Women') which condemn prostitution as a rule but demand a distinction between those women who were 'forced' and those who voluntarily enter prostitution; GAATW are opposed to 'forced' prostitution. NGOs promoting sex worker rights would also fall under this latter category. The abolitionists typically engage in the construction of the passive, poor and unemancipated victim without questioning the wider socioeconomic structures prostitution is embedded within. The efforts by such NGOs to introduce anti-trafficking laws, the indictment of traffickers, and inter-governmental cooperation to stop the trade have been described as expressions of the imposition of middle class morality on the working classes with the promotion of an ideal that is necessarily reactionary (Hemming 2002; Sandy 2002). The focus on sexual exploitation downplays other forms of exploitation and abuses, giving a skewed representation of the situation, leading to a falsely premised solution that fails to solve the problem of abuses.

Although trafficking does not exclusively refer to prostitution – related migratory movements, it numerically occurs mostly, and exactly in this context. Generally, prostitution is illegal in many Asian countries (such as Korea, Cambodia, Vietnam, Japan etc). By defining women engaged in the sex industry as 'fallen women' (as in Korea) or as a 'social vice' (as for instance reflected in the title of the ministry in charge in Vietnam: the Ministry of Social Evil), moral blame is attributed to these women – a practice or attitude which restricts any appeal on these women's behalf to an identification of them as victims to be saved. Attempts to improve working conditions for these women, national or foreign, thus becomes very difficult. In much of NGOs' discourse, moral authority is claimed by constructing women as 'young, innocent, poor, and ignorant'. This victimizing discourse ignores the agency of the women involved, neglecting their capacity to think, decide and desire. Many organizations with a focus on prostitution have hence stopped short of taking part in the sex worker movements predominantly in the West but increasingly in Latin America and slowly also in Asia (Cheng 2002). Discourses of 'sex work' and sex workers' rights have made no entry into many of these activist groups in spite of their awareness of these terms and movements. They seem not yet ready for the idea of prostitution as a legitimate form of work. Moreover, there is evidence of NGOs claiming to work for trafficked women often having little interaction with the actual women on whose behalf they are supposedly active. As a consequence, NGOs have approached the women as 'trafficked women' or 'sexually exploited women' rather than as persons. Cheng (2002) found the lack of concern for research on this topic baffling and the assumption-laden dialogue and efforts problematic. To underpin her findings, she refers to Heather

Montgomery's work as pointing to the aloofness of NGOs concerned with child prostitution in Thailand and how few of them actually work with child prostitutes. Truong Than-Dam's (1996) evaluation that the 1949 UN Convention 'rests mainly at the conceptual level' – i.e. that prostitution is a form of promiscuity which offends public morality – underpins these findings even from the international law perspective.

In Korea, Cheng (2002) has observed that it is the prevalence of abuses and sexual exploitation and the absence of government interventions that NGOs, both local and international, take on the issue of trafficked women. At the same time, failure to exert pressure on the Korean government has allowed the government to remain ignorant of the abuses of foreign women in the sex industry. The Korea-based 'Counseling Center for Migrant Women Workers' (funded by a German Christian organization) makes use of the classic 'victimizing' discourse. So do certain NGOs in Vietnam and Cambodia. Interestingly, efforts by the 'Joint Committee for Migrant Workers in Korea' have made public appeals for recognition of migrant workers in general since the mid-1990s. They have framed their call for justice in the language of human rights and democracy and have in particular pointed to the exploitative industrial trainee system which, as a consequence, is finally about to be scrapped. [10] Their efforts have thus born fruit, especially benefiting a special type of migrant workers namely, foreign trainees (most of whom are male). But Cheng rightly asks (2002: 154) why is there a difference between trainees and entertainers and why have Filipino entertainers not been addressed in these migrant workers' movements? Why do Korean organizations rely only on international support to help these women? Part of the answer to this question is related to the moralistic attitude of middle-class NGO activists who pursue an abolitionist agenda. In addition, there is a lack of cooperation between different women's groups which is partly rooted in a lack of resources inside Korea, but also in the dominance of a moralized and racialized Korean nationalism. At the same time, the issue of international trafficking has become an important platform to gain resources and membership in transnational activism. In this context, Cheng has cynically commented upon the difference between NGOs run by 'local' women on behalf of migrant women (e.g. Koreans on behalf of Filipino entertainers). Here, one can observe the ambition to participate in transnational activist networks. Similar to the Korean case, in Taiwan sex workers have been described as constituting a particularly marginalized group in a highly moralistic society (Jie Chen 2001).

On a more positive line in terms of progressiveness and transnational networking links, a particularly well-known NGO focusing on people trafficking is the previously mentioned Bangkok-based NGO, GAATW. In collaboration with the Dutch 'Foundation Against Trafficking in Women' (STV) this group has proposed a new definition of trafficking which shifts the emphasis to the conditions under which women have to work. In this two-fold definition, it is recognized that women often consent to migrate within their country or abroad for various purposes, including prostitution. They, however, do not agree to work or live under slave-like conditions. In this way, GAATW and STV criticize the terminological distinction between voluntary and involuntary migration for the purpose of sex work, usually understood by law enforcement agencies and policy-makers as the only proper form of trafficking. Coercion is, thus, the central element of a new definition of trafficking produced by an alliance of NGOs. The GAATW, albeit a global network, has also a strong Asia focus. Formed at an international conference in Thailand in 1994, its international coordinating office is based in Bangkok. The GAATW has organized a series of training workshops for activists in Southeast Asia and has started specific projects in the Mekong region and in Burma. The network links organizations and individual activists concerned with protecting the human rights of trafficked persons. The GAATW emphasizes the involvement of grassroots women, aiming at empowering women rather than treating them as victims.

A similar advocacy network operating transnationally is the CATW (previously mentioned), with a sub-network covering the Asia Pacific based in the Philippines. This network consists of feminist groups fighting the sexual exploitation of women, especially related to prostitution and trafficking. Like other transnational advocacy networks in this field, CATW tries to relate to the UN system in its campaigns and the organization has a consultative status under the UN Economic and Social Council since 1989. Women's ability to engage the UN and other multilateral organizations is vital and has been observed as a global phenomenon in connection with the growth of the women's human rights movement (Ho et al. 1996; Pietila and Vickers 1996). UNICEF, for instance, supports transnational advocacy networks focusing on trafficking in children in Asia, such as the 'Child Rights-Asianet' based at the Faculty of Law at Chulalongkorn University in Bangkok. Unlike many other networks, it not only involves non-state organizations, but also state institutions. 'Child Rights-Asianet' is an active partner in the 'United Nations Inter-Agency Project on Trafficking in Women and Children in the Mekong Sub-Region'. This network of UN agencies and NGOs also includes among others the GAATW and Fight Against Child Exploitation (FACE) – a network of Thai NGOs focusing on children's and women's rights.

Another case in which there have been moves away from a victim discourse comes from the Philippines. Filipino activities and discursive practices of networks between local and foreign NGOs carrying out HIV/AIDS education projects have been described as being 'in the process of unsettling the dominant representation of the prostitute as "victim"'(Law 2000: 97). Law found that Filipino NGOs which work with a strong HIV/AIDS agenda, in collaboration with foreign (especially Australian) NGOs, are much more prepared to adopt a rights' approach. In this context, it would be interesting to explore here the question of whether rights awareness was triggered by INGOs' involvement or whether the actual framing as a health, rather than human rights issue, was more crucial in determining a rights-based approach. Also, as opposed to NGOs run by Koreans on behalf of foreign women, Philippine-based NGOs campaigning on behalf of their own nationals might determine the fact that issues are differently framed as they are campaigning on behalf of their compatriots rather than foreigners.

In the context of Japan, much of the activity of Japanese women's groups in relation to illegal women workers focused on an anti-prostitution campaign, with groups such as the 'Temperance Union' and the 'Anti-prostitution Association' particularly active, but nevertheless based on moral issues alone (Buckley 1994: 170). This has caused some uneasiness among the Filipino women themselves who have now begun to take the initiative in organizing their own support groups based on such issues as protection from violence, improved working conditions, legalization of their status, and protection from deportation. This is described by one of the major women shelters, Yokohama's 'Mizura Space for Women', as the development of a new human rights service sector (Mackie 1999: 608) in connection with violence and sex workers' rights campaigns.

Overall, one can distinguish a conceptual from a practical level in terms of NGO involvement in women's rights in Asia.

Conceptually, many NGOs are struggling with integrating sex work into a rights' frame and it is safe to say that campaigns on other types of migrant labor have been more successful in this respect. As far as the practical level is concerned, it has been remarked that there are clear limitations as to what anti-trafficking measures NGOs can achieve. Local NGOs are extremely good at rescuing individual migrants and offering crisis intervention; however their ability to deal with recruiters, traffickers or smugglers, employers and authorities is rather limited (Oxfam GB 2000).

Conclusion

In this chapter, I have discussed how existing international norms in the form of human rights or labor rights have served, or potentially could serve, as a frame for political activism on behalf of migrant labor, and also the way in which migrant worker NGOs in much of Asia have made use of these global norms in their activism and advocacy campaigns. NGOs are often acting on multiple fronts – locally, nationally and transnationally – reflecting contemporary forms of labor migration which are characterized by being either short-term as overseas contract work, or else of an undocumented nature (often involving smuggling or trafficking), whereby settlement is a rare outcome. Instead, migrants spend limited periods abroad, return home and possibly re-migrate. Hence, NGOs cannot purely concentrate on either the sending countries' or the receiving countries' policies, but must adopt a holistic approach to further a migrants' rights' agenda. Gradually more and more NGOs are moving away from a purely service provision and crisis intervention to adopting a rights' agenda (and those which hardly ever engage in advocacy are nevertheless often members of umbrella NGOs which do so) and transnational networking is becoming an important phenomenon. In this sense, there is evidence supporting the argument for an increasing politicization of labor migration within this region. NGOs are, of course, not a monolithic phenomenon, but rather are characterized by considerable diversity which was demonstrated in this chapter in terms of trafficking and sex work where the concerns and needs of the actual women involved are not always served at best. The finer dynamics between local NGOs and across borders, as well as concrete forms of everyday activism, constitutes a subject area to be explored in more depth in future research.

4 Globalization, Modernity and Gender Equality

Ruchira Ganguly-Scrase

Introduction

Global trends towards market economies have signaled the ascendancy of neo-liberal paradigms. Its impact in the Asia Pacific region has brought about significant social and cultural change. Increased commodification of daily life and the mediation of social relationships through the market have taken place. For women the consequences of market liberalization are often complex and contradictory. Developing countries such as India have pursued policies of economic liberalization over the last decade. This chapter examines the experiences of women in the lower middle classes in West Bengal in a globalizing Indian economy.[1] From the mid-1980s India has pursued a policy of economic liberalization, which was a dramatic reversal of earlier policies of protecting domestic industrial capital. Adverse impacts on women have resulted from the privatization of public sector enterprises, reduction in investment in public sector units and lower government expenditure on poverty eradication programs (Panini 1995: 57). Yet, my study reveals that women themselves do not perceive their situation to be detrimental to their lives. Instead they considered themselves to be more empowered compared to an earlier generation of women. This is largely due to their class position. This chapter focuses on the paradox between women's feelings of empowerment and the reality of the overall negative impact of neo-liberal development policies on women. Utilizing an ethnographic approach to analyze my respondents' perceptions, I argue that their contradictory views have been shaped by the ongoing constructions of gender equality.

In their ground breaking cross-cultural study of the impact of global market reforms on women, Einhorn and Yeo (1995) demonstrate that the consequences can be both empowering and constraining. Two major contrasting approaches prevail in India in analyzing the impact of the liberalizing process on women. A number of writers show that there are growing gender inequalities under the New Economic Policy (hereafter NEP) (Arora 1999; Basu 1996; CWDS, 2000; Dewan 1999; Kalpagam 1994; Upadhay 2000). Their major concerns include feminization of poverty, reduced employment opportunities in the formal sector and inadequate protection in the labor force. This contrasts with those works which explore feminine desire and subjectivity precipitated by consumerism in a globalized economy (John 1998; Mankekar1999; Munshi 1998). These latter studies, which link emergent femininities to practices of consumption, have focused on the significance of the images of femininity mediated by the forces of global media corporations. These dichotomous analyses overlook the experiences of people who do not neatly fit into the extreme ends of the social spectrum. Significantly, this chapter takes up the challenge by considering the worldviews and experiences of those within a class fraction of the middle class, namely the lower middle class who have been thus far neglected in academic debate.

My research shows that women do not perceive liberalization as beneficial but deny that they have been disadvantaged by it. Such responses may be understood in the context of changing gender relations, both as a result of women's own changing perceptions as well as the post colonial state's interventions in the spheres of education and employment. However, I concur with Bannerjee's (1999) hypothesis that despite these changes in the globalizing economies of Asia capital has rarely challenged existing patriarchal traditions; rather it has harnessed them for its own benefit. It is here that the intersections of globalization, gender and modernity assume their significance. The ensuing relationship between gender and modernity invariably brings to mind questions regarding women's status. Recent theoretical insights on modernity and female subjectivity in India show that women are assigned a sufficient measure of modernity in order to reinforce rather than challenge hegemonic gender roles (Avasthi and Srivastava 2001; Das 1994; Puri 1999; Sunder Rajan 1993; 1999: 5–8). By exploring the ways in which women have been cast within the narratives of the post colonial state, particularly in terms of those relating to equality and empowerment, my study considers the implication of these narratives in enabling women to expand their opportunities and disrupt hegemonic codes.

Globalization, liberalization and gender equality: the Indian case

Throughout the 1990s the International Monetary Fund (IMF)-derived structural adjustment programs were implemented in India. In July 1991 the New Economic Policy (NEP) was formulated. West Bengal developed its own NEP in 1994. The current economic reforms aim at liberalizing the economy from various bureaucratic regulations and controls that are said to have stifled growth[2]. Making the economy more efficient through increased market orientation is the major goal of the reforms. The central strategy is to secure a greater share of the global market in industry, trade and services through increased productivity. This is in marked contrast to the post independence developmental strategy of self-reliant economic growth and the rhetoric of 'socialism'. Under the earlier five-year plans the government played an interventionist role in industrialization through the public sector, which assumed the 'commanding heights' through licensing and regulatory mechanisms. The new market-oriented state ideology and economic reforms are confusing to many people. This was particularly the case in West Bengal, which has been ruled by a coalition of left political parties since 1977, dominated by the Communist Party of India, Marxist – CPI (M). Initially opposed to market reforms, the Left-Front government has now become vociferous in its attempt to attract foreign transnational corporations into the state. I shall shortly return to the cultural significance of the left parties in West Bengal, when considering the public debates concerning gender equality.

Globalization conceived as an expansion of a neo-liberal market economy is central to my discussions since, as noted above, market and trade liberalization have been the cornerstone of the globalizing process in India. Additionally, Structural Adjustment Programs (SAPs) were integral to economic liberalization. My informants perceived the notion of globalization as an amalgam of social, cultural and economic outcomes resulting from an 'opening-up' of the Indian economy to the global market. For my purposes therefore, the contemporary phase of globalization and economic liberalization are considered as two sides of the same coin. As

Stewart and Berry (1999: 151) assert, '...both conceptually and empirically it is impossible to differentiate globalization and liberalization completely.'

I would argue that globalizing processes work in contradictory ways. Evidently market liberalization and structural adjustment policies may have a contradictory impact on women when we explore the cultural terrain. While new forms of inequality result from economic reforms, there may be other opportunities for greater independence. Such inclusionary and exclusionary processes are increasingly prevalent (Afshar and Barrientos 1999: 1–17). Examining the relationships between market liberalization, women's labor and gender ideology, Moghadam (1999: 128–153) convincingly argues that women's participation in the global economy and national labor force can serve to interrogate and modify gender relations and ideologies. Omvedt's (1997) analysis of women's rights in Indian families in an era of liberalization is also instructive: she contends that in light of democratization of gender relations within the family, the effects of structural adjustment on women has not been as much of a burden as its opponents would claim. Regional patterns of gender relations in India shows the mediating effects of cultural processes as well as the various coping strategies of households with different assets (Agarwal 1992). Therefore, class differentials and cultural specificity are of paramount importance when considering how economic changes have shaped gender relations and people's responses. In the foregoing analysis the specificity of the lower middle class in West Bengal is considered.

Economic liberalization, ethnographic research and the lower middle classes

Adverse impacts of economic liberalization on poor and marginalized groups have been thoroughly detailed elsewhere (Acharya 1995; Dasgupta 1993; Mukherjee 1994). By contrast, I am concerned with studying a class fraction – that is, the lower middle class. For the purposes of my study, I have defined the lower middle class in Bengal in terms of both a particular economic bracket and a cultural milieu. Their mean household income is just under is Rs10,000 per month[3]. In terms of culture, this group forms part of the Bengali *bhadralok*. This term is multivalent but means most of all 'respectable people'. The *bhadralok* were distinguished by their refined behavior and cultivated taste, but not necessarily substantial wealth and power. They emerged as a new social group in the late 18th century in Bengal and were the first to gain entry into urban professional occupations. Although originally linked to upper castes in contemporary Bengali society, they are a distinct status group (in the Weberian sense), which is neither coterminous with caste nor class (Mukherjee 1975). Changed from their original position for two centuries as a reasonably well-off, educated and highly cultured status group, the *bhadralok* are now a heterogeneous group and often indigent. They still seek education above all for their children and attempt to maintain a veneer of their once high social status by engaging in writing, music and the arts, but the economic reality of the present has meant that the penchant for cultural pursuit, the traditional status maintainer, is disappearing. Instead, (often to their disadvantage) conspicuous consumption has increasingly become an important determinant of status (see Scrase 1993). It is important to note that the downward mobility of the *bhadralok* began several decades ago following the partition of Bengal and is not specifically due to globalization.

The self-ascription of informants was often couched in terms of being lower middle class. Indeed, their use of the Bengali term *nimno moddhobitto* (lower middle class) suggested the same classification. Presenting a striking contrast to the real poor, other terms used were 'ordinary folk', or 'common folk', 'people of limited means' or simply 'those dependent on a salary'. The image of a regular salary earner is a powerful one in Bengali culture, which both suggests a distinction from menial wage work as well as earnings from trading. However, it also disguises the real incomes of those civil servants who supplement their total household income by taking bribes. During our fieldwork no one claimed that they were poor, despite their lack of material wealth. On the contrary, there were attempts to distance themselves from the poor in subtle ways.

The group we studied was largely white-collar, salaried persons. Our respondents consisted of clerks, lower level professionals and administrators, as well as sales and service personnel. However, sociological attempts to operationalize class derived from occupational categories and income only partially explain the position my informants. As suggested earlier, these groups are best understood as class fractions. Suffice to say that neo-Weberian and neo-Marxist accounts shed some light on the social location of a marginal middle class consisting of non-manual wage earners and low-grade technicians.[4] Although I utilize these class categories to specify the occupational characteristics of our respondents in terms of their market capacity and thereby show their location within the modern economy, I nevertheless do not claim that any of these definitions are completely adequate in analyzing class relations in Bengal[5].

Significance of analyzing the lower middle classes

I am concerned with studying this class fraction for a number of reasons. Firstly, this group is of particular significance given the elasticity of the category 'middle class' found in many accounts. In India over the past decade much has been said about the growth of the middle class as a consequence of the globalization of the economy (Deshpande 1998; Kulkarni 1993; Lakha 1999). The middle class is said to have expanded greatly and benefited from the structural adjustment reforms to the economy and industry[6]. On the one hand the state's rationale for forging ahead with the economic reforms is an outcome of the policy shift towards neo-liberalism on a global scale[7]. The unswerving faith in liberalization policies as the solution to the overall improvement of the standard of living of the population underpins such a rationale. On the other hand, at the level of social science theory there is a great deal of interest in the life styles of the 'new middle class' on the basis of consumption as the new definer of group identity (see Appadurai and Breckenridge 1995). Yet, as Murdock has argued the theoretical shift to questions centered around identity, consumption and difference 'has coincided almost exactly with the neo-liberal revolution in economic and social policy' and cautions that to ignore the specificities of class is tantamount to colluding with the 'marketers' deceitful celebration of an undifferentiated expansion in choice and opportunity' (Murdock 2000: 8). Elsewhere I have demonstrated that a homogenous Indian middle class as being the undoubted beneficiaries of New Economic Policies is untenable (Ganguly-Scrase 2000; Ganguly-Scrase and Scrase 1999, 2001). The lower middle classes remain both supporters of NEP yet skeptical of whether any benefits will accrue to them. Secondly, it is important to bear in mind the problems of combining the lower and upper levels of the middle classes in Asia. Ideological and policy shifts in development to the open support for structural adjustment have resulted in the differentiation of the middles classes in India (Deshpande 1998). Thirdly, while the lower middle classes in Western Europe and North America are increasingly becoming proletarianized, even lower levels of these strata in contemporary Asia may regard themselves very differently. Therefore these groups should be regarded as class fractions rather than a single unified class (Sen and Stivens 1998: 15).

The study and setting

The narratives of my informants explored in this paper are derived from participant observation and in-depth interviews with low-ranking salaried workers and their families in Calcutta (now Kolkata) and in Siliguri in North Bengal. This research is ethnographic and qualitative in nature. Despite almost a decade of radical economic reform, there remains little in the way of micro-level sociological research documenting the direct, and indirect, effects of this process of economic reforms for communities and local groups. On the whole, most studies highlight a range of macro political-economic transformations taking place in India (see Bhattachraya 1999; Nagaraj 1997; Oshikawa 1999; Pedersen 2000). With few exceptions (Lakha 1999; Van Wessel 1998) there is a paucity of ethnographic research on the social consequences of changing economic relations. Moreover, it is through the ethnographic method that the respondents' paradoxical views towards liberalization and gender equality can be revealed.[8]

Fieldwork was conducted over a four-year period (1998–2002).[9] Utilizing a snowballing method a total 120 people were interviewed (60 in each city). Among the respondents there were 20 key informants, most of whom we had known for over a decade from our earlier research in the late 1980s. Women constituted 48% of our sample, while men were 52%. The overwhelming majority (85%) was employed in the formal or organized sector of the labor force, while 15% were working in the so-called informal sector. While most people worked in the public sector, among the formal sector workforce about a quarter were employed by the private sector. It is important to note however, that none of our respondents had obtained employment in occupations that have specifically sprung-up as a consequence of liberalization. The mean household size was 4.7 persons, with only seven percent of households having more than seven persons residing. The types of families respondents belonged to were roughly divided between joint and nuclear families.

Ideological influences: public debate and popular media

Within lower middle class families decisive factors that have shaped the lives of girls and women is access to education and a lessening of the restricted physical mobility of the past. Women and men of all ages refer to the better opportunities for women in the present generation compared to that of the past. However, improvements in the spheres of education and employment are regarded as being independent of economic reforms. Moreover, while readily admitting that liberalization may not have benefited women in particular, they emphatically deny that women have been disadvantaged. Their views reflect notions of gender equality that are incorporated into the public discourse and popular media. Their assertions as individuals are related to the possibilities debated within the public realm.

Debates on the public visibility of women, their participation in employment and the subsequent emancipation of women have occupied center stage in anti-colonial nationalist discourses as well as in post-colonial developmentalist narratives of nation building. Several distinct narratives may be identified in Figure 4.1 below. These include social reform and nationalist discourses of the 19th and early 20th centuries, narratives of independence and partition during the mid 20th century, ideological pronouncements by the Left Front Government/ Community Party (Marxist) particularly since the 1960s and 1970s and, finally, consumerist and advertising discourses of the last decade. However, my informants did not perceive each of these as unitary system of ideas, but instead as a contradictory set of themes, often incorporating elements from various premises.

Public discourse in the 19th century, particularly the views of social reformers, centered on two opposing categorization: labor force participation of poor women and widows and the employment of upper class women in high status professions. While the former could be tolerated because it was an absolute necessity, the latter was not only desirable, but also a moral obligation, a sense of public duty. For the rest, women's entry into the workforce signaled a loss of respectability. This was not only for the women themselves, but it also meant a loss of familial status. These oppositions are crucial

Figure 4.1: Public discourses of gender equality and women's emancipation: 19th century to end of 20th century

Social Reform and Nationalist Discourses	Independence and Partition	Left Front Government/CPM	Consumerism and Advertising
Poor women's work as a necessity for survival	Massive social dislocation	Women encouraged to participate in wage labor struggles and politics	The 'new' empowered woman
Upper class women's work Moral obligation and duty – desirable	Respectable 'genteel' women forced to enter the workforce		
Work outside the home undesirable for all other women	Powerful imagery in popular fiction – public debate evokes sympathy for women, but does not challenge ideology of domesticity		
Left and Labor Movement	Modernizing ideologies of the Indian State: Education, Development etc		Rhetoric of 'empowerment' in the NEP
Importance of paid work for women's emancipation			
19th to mid-20th C.	1947	Post 1960's 1985	Present

for examining the ethnographic context of my informants because they do not fit either class category.

Exceptions to this dichotomy in the debates on women's public role are to be found in discourses of the left and the labor movement (see Chaudhuri, 1996). Given the importance of left politics in the history of the nationalist struggle in Bengal, these contributions were significant. Nevertheless, public acceptance of these views was not widespread until the 1970s when political parties of the left came into power and thereby began to reshape public discourse about the emancipation of women. Empowerment through employment has been the general developmentalist agenda of the post-colonial state irrespective of the ideologies of various political parties. Nowadays, although developmentalism has been replaced by neo-liberalism, empowerment of women is a critical component of the rhetoric of the latter (Bagchi 1999: 368–370; Mohanty 1995).

Attitudes of women in this study are framed by the confluence of the ideas of the left along with emerging consumer discourses of the woman exercising choice, which have become prominent since the formulation of new economic policies. Although effective empowerment requires to move beyond an individual's own attitudes to the individual's and groups' capacities to initiate social change or influence societal attitudes and behavior, it is not surprising that the language of empowerment is couched in terms of individual choice by respondents. Unless they are actively engaged politically, for most respondents feminist and other emancipatory discourses of collective advancement appear overly abstract. Their perceptions are influenced by the notion of the individual, which has been relentlessly propagated by advertising.

Employment and empowerment

The common theme that typifies the sentiments of most respondents is 'women's advancement'. This is expressed in many ways but primarily in terms of entering the world of work. For men it is recognition of improvement and a sense of pride that 'my' wife goes out to work or 'my' daughter is doing well in her studies and the hope that she will be well-placed in a good job. These are subtly linked to ideologies of consumerism. Women are emphatic in their renewed confidence and convey the sentiment that paid work brings autonomy. One of the crucial markers of emerging class identity among this fraction of the middle class is the desire for the public visibility of women and their relative freedom to pursue careers. A typical response was:

> I don't know whether women have benefited from policies or not. But the women's lot has improved. They have come forward, entered the work force etc. This is a good sign. In every government and non-government organization women have entered in great numbers. This wasn't the case before. They were not visible in great numbers. Women have entered every field. This is very good. Previously women thought that they had to be confined at home. All there was for them was *shongsar, ranna banna* (marriage and cooking). Now they are working for their own advancement and the families have gained too.

Maintaining a contrast between the present and the past, the expression *egie aasha* or 'coming forward' was frequently used to indicate progress. Recalling her own experience, a widowed woman in her late 40s explained the changes in the following way,

Compared to the past the situation of women entering the workforce has improved a lot. Previously those who were just at home are now working, like myself. Young women aren't sitting at home, hoping to be provided for. Women are going out to work. In our youth, it was expected that the wife would stay at home and look after the home and family. Now the circumstances have changed a lot. The opportunities for women working have improved.

Women's absence of opportunities and their rising consciousness as a result of participation in the outside world of work are now commonsense. Young women routinely make statements like,

Women have started to consciously think about themselves; they have begun to obtain more knowledge about the external world, unlike earlier when they hardly used to step out of the threshold. (woman police constable, aged 23)

While the loosening of restrictions on physical mobility are seen as a hallmark of modernity, any attempts to restrict women's access to education constitute proof of 'backwardness'. Certain gender constructs are also utilized to distance themselves from the poor. In the words of a Muslim respondent, 'Who keeps women at home these days? Only the most backward section of our community and poor people!' From the life histories of older women I found that a few decades earlier the same group distinguished itself by confining women within the household as a mark of respectability in opposition to the elite *bhadralok* women who were notably prominent in the public arena. A number of women recollected the tension and the hardship they faced when they first entered the workforce.

My respondents' attitudes are shaped and reshaped by the competing debates on women's work in the public domain. For example, as demonstrated in Figure 4.1, for the most part of the last 100 years there has been a well-defined opposition between poor women as objects of pity – since they have to work – and the idea that respectable women do not work outside their homes. Lodged between these conflicting ideologies women respondents have continually struggled with these dichotomous messages and have attempted to reconcile them in their daily lives. A slight twist to this prevailing dichotomy appeared after partition in 1947. This period marked the end of Colonial rule; the partition of India that ensued created immense social dislocation. Massive numbers of refugees from East Bengal flowed into West Bengal, particularly to the metropolis of Calcutta. It was during this period that economic hardship 'forced' *bhadralok* women from refugee families to enter the paid workforce. This image became particularly compelling in popular fiction (Bandyopadhyay 1958; Kar 1956; Mitra 1957; Mitra 1963). There are numerous stories of genteel women forced to seek work, being ostracized as a consequence, and struggling to reconcile family honor, domestic duty and family survival[10]. While attempts were made to deal with the changes taking place in families in the years following Indian Independence, by and large these accounts evoked sympathy for the women rather than criticizing the dominant ideologies of domesticity and female dependency. Many of the older women talked about the significance of these novels for contemporary times, emphasizing that these issues are finally being discussed within their families, aided by much more open discussion disseminated in the mass media.

Perceptions of gendered liberalization

I had entered the field assuming that the growing gender inequalities stemming from the impact of the new economic policies would be self-evident. However, during fieldwork, my preconceived ideas were challenged. Against the overwhelming evidence of the negative impact of economic liberalization outlined in the earlier part of this chapter, I found that women do not perceive themselves to be the victims of the NEP. Instead they stress their own sense of self-worth and advancement of women's everyday lives, continually emphasizing the difference between the present and the past. For example, a young woman aged 30, who had recently been retrenched from a private airline company, but had found employment elsewhere commented,

> In the past only women in poorer circumstances went to work. Now women from all walks of life are working. Now everyone wants to do something. I think the circumstances for women's work and their career prospects have improved. Previously not many women were in the workforce. Now more women want to work. They want the freedom. They don't want to depend on anyone. There have been tremendous improvements in women's education and employment. Because women

want to work education becomes very important. Everyone wants to stand on her own two feet.

My attempts to identify how the economic reforms had affected women, and explore how this was understood, met with responses that invariably denied a link between female employment and the NEP. If I tried to suggest that there might be fewer opportunities for women, it had the opposite effect, sometimes leading to vehement denials. Their reasons can be understood to a certain extent if we consider the ideologies that underpin the role of the state in relation to women's employment. The idea that women's participation in the public world of work and politics is crucial to their emancipation has been promoted during the twenty-five year rule of the Left Front Government in West Bengal. Although I have noted that the exceptions to the dichotomous debates on women's public role were always present in discourses of the left and the labor movement, public acceptance of these views was not widespread until the latter part of the 20th Century. Since the 1970s political parties of the left, (the CPI (M) as the dominant partner) have been in power, thereby shaping public debates.

In response to issues affecting the status of women under globalization, a notable minority (15%) of all respondents rejected outright the idea that women had made any gains since the economy was liberalized. I found that the respondents in general revealed their skepticism toward the economic benefits of liberalization rather than highlighting the negative outcomes for women.

An overwhelming majority (82%) of respondents argued that women had made considerable gains. However, they held differing views as to whether the gains were independent of economic reforms or not. It is interesting to note that 38% asserted that women had advanced in their everyday lives but simultaneously claimed that this could not be linked to globalization or economic liberalization. Both men and women put forward remarkably similar viewpoints, in vociferously denying the link between NEP and women's employment, but they pursued different explanations. Arguing in favor of women's advancement men tried to identify concrete opportunities that have come about regardless of liberalization whereas women attributed it to their own rising consciousness. The subtle distinctions between men's and women's attitudes become apparent in the following comments. A married man in his mid 30s offered this explanation:

Figure 4.2: Women benefited under liberalization*

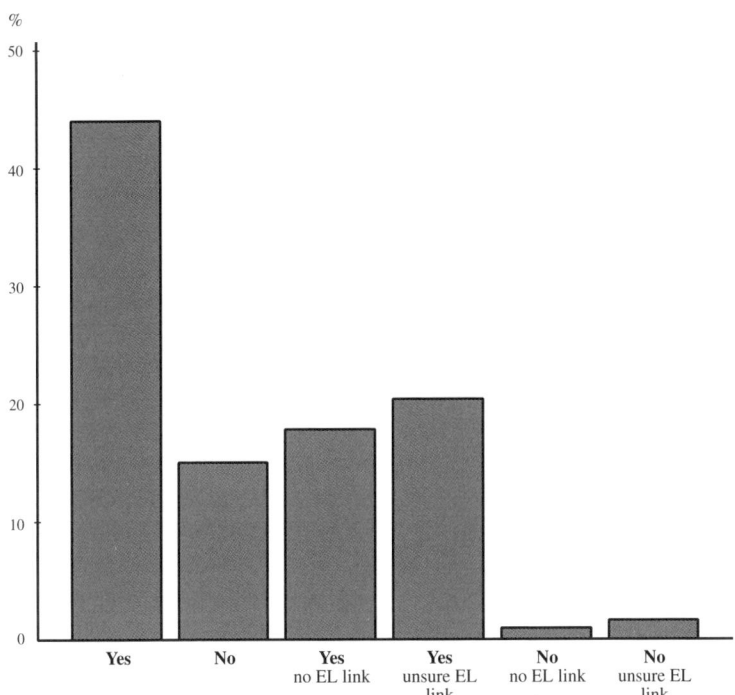

* note: n = 118

Let me put it this way. Opportunities for women have opened up a bit more. You can't link it to liberalization policies. The quota for women for positions, in parliament – all these cannot be linked to liberalization policies, but they have happened during the period of liberalization. More women are recruited in the private sector. Women are more efficient and employers like them.

This may be contrasted with the comments of a married woman aged 38 who worked as a postal clerk:

Some people with high demand skills have definitely benefited from liberalization. However, we have to look at the general benefits for women; it is not enough to only look at its economic aspects. We have to look at the social aspect, the social consciousness that has arisen within ourselves. One advantage on the personal front is the feminist movement. I mean, we women have benefited from the positive aspects of the feminist movement...a number of things never existed in families, but now they do. Some such changes have taken place in case of families, on the social front – I mean within the society. And we do enjoy its consequences.

To support their claims men held the opinion that women are preferred employees because they were more compliant, women interpreted this as 'being keen' and 'making greater effort'. Men frequently turned to indices of 'advancement' whereas women said that this was beside the point; to them the social recognition and status was more important than actual opportunities. Indeed women were often at pains to show that in West Bengal where employment opportunities for all young people were extremely limited, it was meaningless to talk about better opportunities for girls. Nevertheless, they emphasized that young women were more eager to find jobs.

The gains for women were regarded as being the result of an enlightened outlook of, and cultural changes within families together with a range of ongoing political initiatives. Informants often reproduced the state's rhetoric of development and modernization, at times explicitly drawing on the Left Front government's ideological statements concerning the necessity of incorporating women in to wage labor for their emancipation. Although research shows that there is no causal relationship between women's paid employment and status enhancement (Chanana 1996; Desai 1996; Sharma 1986; Standing 1991), the view that women can be empowered through employment holds firm sway with our informants. Women particularly challenged the belief that limited family income compels them to seek employment and they frequently expressed their feeling of increased self-confidence through gainful employment. Even those who held vague ideas about liberalization nevertheless highlighted the strides women had made in the world of work. The idea that employment is a road to independence and rejection of the notion that women only work due to economic hardship exemplify the views of young women. Often the catch-cry is, 'Whatever job she does, small or big, she should be independent and not depend on others'.

However, despite assertions of young women that it is acceptable for girls to take up any occupation no matter how insignificant, clearly in practice this is not the case. *Bhadralok* women are still confined to a restricted range of jobs. Despite the widespread appraisal of women's employment by our informants, in reality there are still only a narrow range of work options that are available to women. The crucial difference between an earlier generation and the contemporary situation for lower middle class women is the firm belief that this class fraction is taking the lead in defying the conventional stereotypical jobs that are open to women and entering these occupations. For example, the explanations are couched in terms of 'women in our kind of families' are taking up previously unacceptable jobs such as medical sales representative, shop keeper and even bus driver or tram conductor. This is qualitatively different from the upper middle class women entering male dominated high status jobs.

These accounts offer some critical challenges to the notions of female dependency, which are characteristic of familial ideologies in West Bengal (see Sen 1997). They are in part shaped by the emerging images of the assertive 'New Woman'. According to Munshi (1998: 573) advertising discourses have constructed this new persona by 'appropriating the discourses of traditional femininity on the one hand and liberating feminist discourses on the other'. This is not to claim the demise of gender hierarchies within families. However, these representations do challenge some aspects of traditional femininity, which women in this study questioned; and they demonstrate the powerful significance of going out to work and the meaning it has for the women. Significantly, my informants do not identify personal disadvantages resulting from the NEP. Instead they wished to emphasize the deteriorating condition of the household and or the absence of any gain for their families.

As Figure 4.3 demonstrates, most respondents noted that there was no marked improvement in their economic conditions since the NEP was implemented. Moreover, Figure 4.4 shows that the overwhelming majority of respondents (86%), regardless of their gender argued that despite actual increases in salaries they still faced financial difficulties due to the rising cost of living.

However, women want to separate the current economic problems their households are facing due to the NEP and their own sense of self and the future, which can only get better. They perceive themselves to be personally better off than their mothers and aunts; they vehemently reject any idea that economic policies are holding

Figure 4.3: Household financial conditions improved or deteriorated under economic liberalization

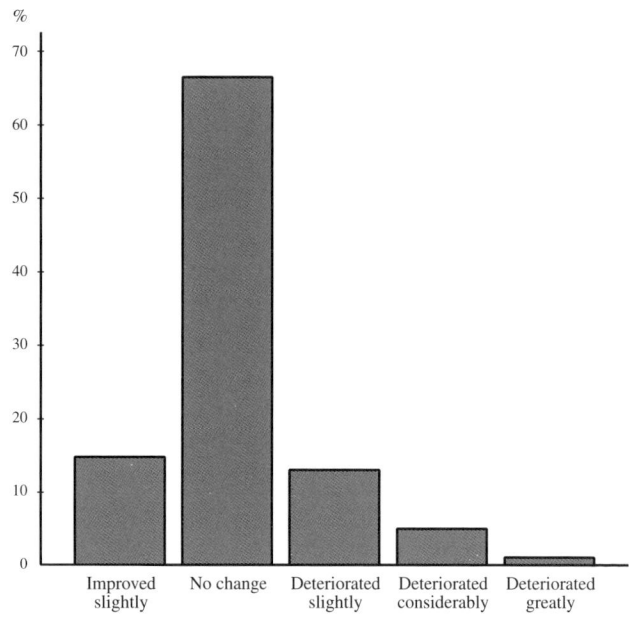

them back. This is in part due to the corporate ideology of the household. It is important to recognize this ideology. As Kabeer (1999: 460) notes, the notion of empowerment must be cognizant of the context. Despite rising wages and employment, in circumstances where the ideology of 'togetherness' prevail, women do not seek to be autonomous beings, separate from their households nor is such a proposition socially acceptable. Yet, if we overlook this contextual possibility, we are likely to miss the significance of transformations taking place.

Interestingly, my informants do not recognize or readily identify any specific gender discrimination or disadvantage that have come about as a result of household budgetary restrictions. For example, no girl has had her education terminated in favor of her brother. A sister has not been forced to obtain employment, while a brother remains unemployed. This however, is entirely consistent with the gender ideology of *bhadralok* families. Unlike poor families, who may have to sacrifice a girl's education in the

Figure 4.4: Salary has increased in relation to cost of living

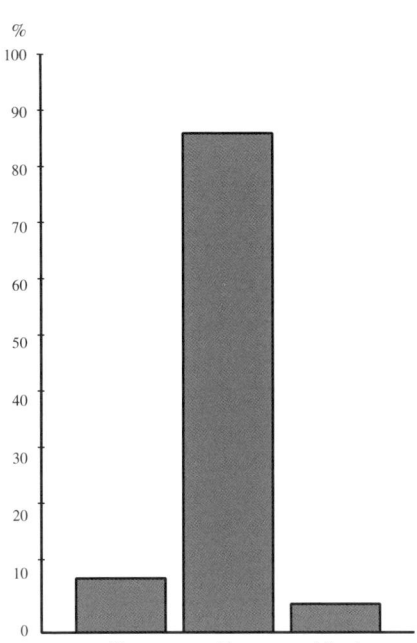

hope that her brother may earn a better living due to few additional years of schooling, *bhadralok* families are prepared to support higher education of daughters, as this is consistent with culturally assigned feminine qualities of greater perseverance and patience. Girls are seen as responsible. Education also acts as a means of keeping control over daughters because of the discipline that is demanded in taking up further education. By comparison, if boys are bored and unsuccessful in their studies they may drop out of college. Parents are more concerned about the idleness of daughters. Yet, this is an unfortunate and unfounded fear since young women themselves are only too keen to obtain additional training in the hope of improving their employment prospects.

While a significant proportion of respondents denied any links between conditions of women's employment and economic reforms, a few pointed out that there was better scope for women in some of the new companies emerging as a result of the opening-up the Indian economy to the global market. It is important to remember that the respondents were not employed in any occupations that have sprung up as a consequence of liberalization. When asked to identify anyone in their families who had gained entry into positions in transnational firms, they were unable to do so and were speaking in abstract terms. Working women generally commented that there were entrepreneurial opportunities for women such as starting a small business. Although many of them were neither self-employed or sub-contracted by private firms, nor did they wished to be, they nevertheless believed that, 'nowadays you find housewives selling saris and cosmetics. There is always something you can do, join a private firm or start a business.' It appears that such opportunities as a result of privatization are often ideological statements emanating from the images promoted in glossy magazines and in television serials and advertisements.

During my fieldwork, the following short story from a women's magazine was narrated by a number of key informants. It is emblematic of an ideology of women's emerging entrepreneurial acumen. The story revolves around a housewife who has been tirelessly carrying out her domestic duties and serving the joint family. One day she confides in one of her unmarried sisters-in-law about her desire to find employment. The college-educated young woman is completely dismissive of her brother's wife's quest for paid work. Undeterred by such ridicule, the woman sets out to find a job. Secretly she attends an interview one afternoon, telling the family she is going to the cinema with her friends. She is successful in her interview. When she breaks the news to the sister-in-law, the latter exclaims, 'you have no qualifications! Who would have given you a job? All you know is how to cook'. The housewife triumphantly declares, 'That's right. It is my cooking experience that has scored me this job. I have been offered the position of catering manager in a hostel. All those of years of looking after you people and managing the family budget are indeed my qual-ifications'. For my informants this story was also used to stress the claims that now it is possible to move beyond the dichotomy of the elite *bhadralok* women's pursuit of high status professional occupations and poor women's financial necessity.

For my informants, the public visibility of women and the freedom to pursue careers are together seen as major achievements for women within their class. They, however, sidestepped any discussion of the negative impact of neo-liberal reforms on women's lives and gender relations. Significantly, they do not see the inequalities stemming from recent economic reforms as a problem of gender inequality for their class. On the one hand the main beneficiaries of liberalization are considered to be the upper middle class described as, 'higher sectors of society, not people like us'. On the other hand, gender disadvantages resulting from liberalization are attributed to 'poorer sections of society'. By comparison, their own concerns are largely couched in terms of consumerism and the commodification of women. These are in relation to the new narratives of consumption through advertising in the electronic and print media, especially glossy women's magazines. Although an overwhelming majority of our respondents subscribe to daily newspapers it is important to note that not many women bought women's magazines regularly because they were simply too expensive. They did however share these magazines around and the story narrated above by my informants is one such example of shared use. More than half the number of households in our sample (54%) also subscribed to cable television. The advertisements found in magazines and cable television for the most part target women as consumers, whose decision-making within the family economy, according to marketing strategists, are considered to exert influence on buying choices. The aim of these advertisements is the continual creation of desires for these products and an accomanying consumer lifestyle.

Consumption, empowerment and modernity

The image that has strongly influenced some of our respondents' desire for consumption is the ideal home, with tastefully decorated interior and furnishings. A number of women identified the pleasure they derived from the imagery of the working wife-mother whose skills in house management and artistic flair create a stylish modern home. Such an ideal of womanhood was to be admired and emulated. However, I do not wish to overstate the extent of the current influence of commercials urging women to embrace a particular ideal of womanhood and domesticity. Being instructed in the art of home making is not a new phenomenon for our women respondents. Through gender socialization women have been already inculcated with the virtues of domestic responsibilities[11] such as cleanliness (including ritual cleanliness) and taught the aesthetic sense of home decoration required to achieve the effect of bright clean homes. Quite a few subscribed to and/or read women's magazines in the pre-liberalization era and some had undertaken domestic science courses as part of their educational training. Therefore they firmly believed in the necessity for a woman to maintain good standards of housekeeping. Many were well aware of the recurrent tips on improving housework and adhered to instructions on self-improvement, such as needlework and embroidery widely covered in women's magazines in earlier times. Indeed many homes proudly displayed a wife or daughter's artistic talents in the form of embroidered wall hangings, tablecloths and doilies. Some chose to adorn their homes with craft items such as brightly printed handloom curtains, bedspreads, cushions and a range of pottery items. The furniture in living room areas consisted of chairs and coffee tables made of pained wickerwork and bamboo. These were obtained from local handicraft fairs, street stalls and markets where they were purchased at wholesale and discounted prices. Aware of their limited budget, these respondents were relatively content with their furnishings and interior decorations.

Another distinct group of respondents emerged who desired a range of household commodities such as the latest electronic, entertainment goods and expensive furnishings that, for them, is symbolic of the 'modern' style which they considered were lacking. While advertisers have continued to capitalize on the dominant ideologies of women's domestic roles, it is the fundamental shifts in the consumption orientation relating to the home that has greatly influenced this segment of our respondents. For this group the imagined home is an arena of leisure, a space of luxury and pleasure rather than merely a space stocked with functional consumption items to alleviate domestic drudgery.

The history of Euro-American housework demonstrates that the mass marketing of domestic appliances promoted the idea of gadgets as labor saving devices (Cowan 1983; Ehrenrich and English 1978; Oakley 1976). Yet, given the large section of working women in our sample, it is interesting to note that the acquisition of domestic appliances were not high on their agenda as the labor of domestic servants renders these commodities as non-essential. For example, 86% of households did not have a washing machine nor did they particularly wish to acquire one. A number of married couples were given a mini grinder/ food processor ('mixie') as wedding gifts but rarely used them.

While the representation of the thrifty housewife in search of cheaper brands of detergents, soaps and toothpastes resonates with the experiences of many of our respondents as they struggle to maintain the household budget, the most important object of fantasy and pleasure for this group is the glamorous woman who goes shopping. Advertising discourses that promote shopping as an enabling force empowering women have captured their imagination. One respondent who was highly critical of market mediated discourses of women's emancipation argued that,

> The main role model for women is the consumer role. This is especially so for married women. Did our mothers and grandmothers find their own independence by shopping? Yes I agree, just because I'm a woman why do I have to be stuck at home all day cooking and cleaning? I can go out and do a bit of shopping. To go shopping is what they show on television: how a woman drives herself to the shops. She drives on her own to school to pick up the children. This has become the dream. Previously it was a man's responsibility to go to the market, to do the shopping. Now you see on foreign programs that it is the women who do the shopping. This is the symbol of the new modern woman!

The positive image of the woman engaged in shopping and its accompanying independence is a strange inverse of everyday life. Traditional middle class sexual division of labor requires men (or servants) to undertake daily food and grocery shopping, as the market constitutes a disagreeable outside environment from which a respectable woman must be protected. Markets are indeed unpleasant dirty spaces, which most women respondents were only too happy to avoid and devolve responsibility to men. The transformation of shopping into a desirable activity for women is alluring when the experience occurs in a department store. For some respondents it is an appealing aspect of a modern life style surrounded by luxury.

Tensions persist however, regarding the ideal 'modern' woman: someone attempting to improve home life through consumption or the woman who is the prudent financial manager? The conflict between these two perspectives was evident in the contrasting attitudes of two sisters-in-law of a joint family that had has recently split up into separate nuclear households. The older sister-in-law had entered the workforce in the early 1980s during a time of financial crisis in the family, although at the time it was unacceptable to do so. She offered a lengthy explanation:

> When I first went to work there was a lot of tension in the family... Eventually I persuaded my mother-in-law to allow me to work. Ever since then I have continued to work. I like it very much. The world of work broadens your horizon. Why should it be that it is only men who have access to this outside world?...Over the years we have struggled and we have managed to get a few of the mod-cons. We now have a fridge, gas stove and there is a good solid TV that my brother gave us, when he got his job as a token of thanks to my husband. We even fitted a geyser for use in the winter months when my mother-in-law's arthritis was unbearable. These were not good enough for her [younger sister-in-law]. She insisted on splitting up and what does she do? Getting fat and watching TV day and night while the husband has to travel 5 hours a day to and from work. *Living in a fantasy world of beauty contests and glamour homes!* (original emphasis). That place is slovenly; you see unwashed utensils in the kitchen; *entho-kanta*[12] (food scraps) everywhere. She is a graduate, I am told. I had suggested she do a Montessori course and get a job. That was the source of her anger. No, staying home is just an excuse to watch serials. (Mrs Gita M.; aged 48)

The real reason underlying the criticism of the younger sister-in-law was the latter's defiance of setting up her own household. The messy kitchen was an easy target of criticism. There was limited space to set aside for dirty dishes, which was possible within the joint household.

The younger sister-in-law, Rinku M. countered the rather dismissive attitude of her older counterpart by arguing that it was an unrealistic expectation to go to work with two small children under the age of five. Further she did not wish to expose her daughters to the poisonous attitudes of affines, which would occur if she went to work and would have to leave the children in the care of joint family members. She retorted by adding,

> She thinks she is high and mighty. The way they live in is a dump. Have you seen the kitchen? Still using the kerosene stove even though there is gas! All that fuss over not using this and that utensil. It is positively barbaric...That dreadful [squat] toilet. I was forever anxious that one of my children was going to fall down into the pan. They could have got a commode...my mother-in-law had terrible arthritis. I am so pleased that

we separated into our own portion of the house. We are finally free to buy things of our choice. (Mrs Rinku M.; aged 31)

Rinku hoped one day she could create a real home of her own that reflected the styles depicted in the advertisements and serials which had the 'right smart fittings in the shower and toilets'.

These contrasting attitudes play-off certain aspects of 'modern' womanhood combined with tradition against each other. They also reflect the tensions in the desire for comfort versus luxury. For Gita to be modern implies the ability to transcend the narrow confines of the home. Entering the public world of work with men signifies her freedom from the backwardness and inferiority of the interior world. Gita's disdain towards consumption beyond one's means is comfortably reconciled with conformity to dominant norms of women's domestic responsibilities. Yet, her disapproval of Rinku for daring to dream a different domestic scenario is indicative of an earlier modern attitude towards the attainment of material comfort and maintenance of a standard of housekeeping through hard work and supervision of servants and younger women. Nevertheless this implicitly female domestic realm considered to be characterized by trivia and gossip must be subordinated to the superior public sphere. Stepping outside is the symbol of the modern progressive woman, who walks side by side with men. This echoes a discourse of nationalist and socialist modernities. By contrast, for Rinku freedom is attainable through consumption while stereotypically adhering to the ideal of staying at home to look after her children. The younger sister-in-law's pursuit of pleasure and association of freedom through the acquisition of commodities is made possible by the availability of moderately priced, mass marketed alternatives; these include mirrors and other fittings, replicas of expensive furniture and so on. It is this group which is most influenced by the glamorous 'new woman' depicted in the advertisements and serials that has attracted most attention in the studies of the media.

Media portrayal and empowerment

The images of women portrayed in these advertisements have attracted considerable criticism concerning the impact of marketization on gender relations (Chakravarti 2000; Chaudhuri, 2001; Scrase, 2002). Utilizing empowerment as a marketing strategy advertisers combine femininity with the rhetoric of feminism and frequently depict women as highly successful independent beings who are astute consumers. Chakravarti (2000) suggests that this 'new woman,' imbued with agency is a new creation marking the arrival of a 'gender-friendly globalized market'. Curiously however, popular representation of women's freedom attainable through consumption[13] found in these advertising narratives of corporate global media interests gloss over the underlying unequal gender relations in Indian society.

In general my respondents were highly concerned about media representations of femininity and its consequences for gender equality. As I have argued above, while many women readily challenge the idea that liberalization policies have not had a detrimental impact on their lives, the focal point of their critique is the visual images of femininity presented particularly in the narratives of advertising. It is here that their paradoxical attitudes towards globalization and liberalization assume their greatest significance. Women I talked to took extreme positions and their responses were age specific. Mainly older women argue that in promoting a consumerist ideology, television portrays derogatory and shameful images of women, which can only have a detrimental impact on women's status. Women are thus reduced to nothing more than sex objects. According to a number of my key informants the commodified femininity threatens women's status subsequently disempowering them vis a vis men.

Women's views differ according to their various locations within the life cycle. There is a generational divide in these responses. While most women are highly critical of the media representation of women a significant proportion do not feel demeaned as a consequence of the commodification of women; they also distinguish between these portrayals and the reality of their lives. Older women view their empowerment in terms of their responsibility within the family and the space they have negotiated to assert themselves. They often felt heartened by seeing strong female characters within popular culture or the leadership of women politicians. By comparison young women regard the glamorous liberated woman as highly desirable.

Using these new images of independent womanhood young women construct oppositional narratives of freedom from traditional patriarchal norms and challenge the gender ideologies in Bengali culture. A significant number argue that television provides a social service in promoting an ideal representation of gender relations and egalitarian conjugal relationships. Their accounts emphasize the viewers' complete freedom in exercising their choice and assert the absence of negative connotations for women in the new media. They evoke the sentiments of constructing choice and empowerment in terms of competitive individualism and consumerism when discussing the significance of the images of women portrayed in the media. While a number of young women aspire to emulate the role model of the modern liberated woman, many feel that the image and reality do not fit within the context of contemporary Bengali society. Women in their 30s are much more ambivalent in their assessment. They point out the unreality of television advertisements in depicting the lives of women. More significantly, given their class position, they emphasized the virtual impossibility of acquiring the life styles conveyed by these images. As noted earlier, these images do not radically subvert gender relations. Nevertheless they provide a scope for a degree of assertiveness and agency, which women identify with. Findings in this study reveal that women are able to negotiate a space for themselves within their families and sometimes feel ultimately vindicated. The market forces, which promote derogatory images of women, are asserted by some and evaded by others.

Conclusion

In this chapter I have highlighted the significance of bringing together the economic and cultural dynamics of the globalizing Indian economy and its consequences for lower middle class women. How these changes are received, interpreted and challenged presents a complex picture. The simultaneous and paradoxical feeling of female empowerment, and the sidestepping of the question of gender discrimination in the NEP evident in the responses, reveals the complex interplay of modernity and female subjectivity. In this instance my findings are consistent with Vina Das' (1994) exegesis on modernity and biography of women's lives in that the opposition between traditional and modern institutions has played an important role in the construction of the feminine self in India. It is apparent that in contemporary urban India, the tensions and ambiguities of this process has resulted in women ensuring that they are neither too traditional nor too modern. The cultural transformation currently taking place continually subverts and appropriates discourses of female emancipation to promote a pro-woman market. These dovetail comfortably with the neo-liberal state's rhetoric of female empowerment in its structural adjustment policies. The Bengali lower middle classes project aspects of gender equality as part of their emerging 'modern' class identity. While some opportunities have risen to challenge pre-existing gender ideologies enabling women to assert their sense of self and personal agency, ultimately their challenges are contained within the confines of patriarchal ideologies of the neo-liberal state.

Finally, this neo-liberal hegemonic project in the making presents a number of dilemmas for the respondents. The minority who were highly critical of liberalization are concerned about the shift from social citizenship to a market citizenship. For others the future is uncertain. The middle classes in India were the main beneficiaries of the state-led development over the decades following Independence. However, since globalization and liberalization have emerged as the new economic dogma, a segment within these middle classes find themselves slowly losing the protection of the state, especially in terms of secure employment and a guaranteed place in a higher education institution. Women in particular emphasize that they feel increasingly insecure in terms of the well being of their families, rather than for themselves. While they welcome some aspects of globalism embodied in the 'new woman,' they don't want to lose the secure safety-net provided by the state. For women, this is a double-edged sword. Many acknowledge the state support in education and employment. While along with other family members they are at times highly critical of the state, at the same time they also want to appeal to the state. The practical gains they have made appear to have been sidelined since gender equality under market liberalization is assumed to have arrived.

5 Producing on the Margins: Asian Artisans in the Global Economy

Timothy J. Scrase

Introduction

This chapter has two key aims[1]. First, it provides an overview and analysis of recent studies of third world artisans, especially those from Asia, in the context of economic globalization. It demonstrates that globalization has intensified the precarious existence of artisan communities due to increasing global competition, the mass-production of craft goods, and shifting trends in fashion, cultural taste and aesthetics. This conclusion is reached after close examination of the extant literature from research carried-out in various countries of not only Asia, but in Central America and Africa. The chapter casts a critical eye over various government and non-government programs aimed at supporting artisan communities primarily because they are limited and, on many occasions, largely ineffectual. An outcome of globalization has been a growing, Western awareness of the struggle of third world peoples and indigenous cultures. This has resulted in recent consumer trends like 'fair-trade' shopping in stores and on the Internet yet, as research has indicated, support through 'fair' trade remains piecemeal and limited in terms of effective and long-term support which can be provided to struggling artisan communities. The second key aim of this chapter, incorporating interviews conducted in New Delhi, India, analyzes the day-to-day problems faced by artisans as workers struggling to survive in an increasingly competitive, globalized market. Survival strategies, ranging from individual skill, innovation and entrepreneurialism to basic bribery and petty corruption, are explored and assessed in light of interview data from both artisans and consumers of craft goods. Underlying the discussion in this chapter is the acknowledgement that there are at least three fundamental dimensions to the ongoing exploitation of artisans: first, their social class; second, their vulnerability in a globalized industrial and trade environment; and third, the very nature of their work and skills which, in many ways, are becoming redundant. When artisans survive, they do so mainly on the periphery of both global and local capitalist economies and this is a situation that has rarely changed over the decades. In various ways, and in specific regional contexts, the globalization of production exacerbates, rather than diminishes, the marginal status of Asian artisan communities.

Artisans in the third world: a review of recent research

The anthropologist, June Nash (1993b), argues that crafts are the medium of communication between people who live profoundly different lives, in different countries, but who can respond to the symbols, textures and forms that express different cultural traditions. She goes on to argue that there is now a reverse flow of goods from the former colonies back to the industrial centers of the world as consumers seek out the exotic and unique objects of handicraft production. Yet despite the intricate designs and high level of skills demonstrated in the production of various crafts, and despite middle class consumer interest in all things 'ethnic', 'traditional' and 'different', the daily life for the majority of third world artisans remains one of struggle, poverty and exploitation. The significance of craft production is that it crosses all sectors of the modern global economy – from pre-industrial, industrial and post-industrial (Dickie and Frank 1996). Moreover, unlike some other forms of labor, artisan production can also enable a degree of labor autonomy for those who have limited access to the cash economy, especially because craft production is generally household-based. Importantly, because it is largely confined to the household, or small village or community, significant questions relating to the organization of craft production in terms of gender or generation are raised.

The precarious and marginalized status of artisans is illustrated by the fact that, according to the United Nations, over the last 30 years the numbers of artisans in India, for instance, have declined by at least 30%. The result is that many artisans now find themselves employed as casual wage laborers, mostly in the informal economy (cited in Seth 1995). Mass produced, cheap factory products have, in many instances, replaced the various goods once produced by the artisans. This is illustrated starkly in Ganguly-Scrase's (2001) ethnography of Indian leather workers who have become displaced as a result of the globalization of the shoe and leather industries, coupled with the introduction of plastics and other synthetic materials for making footwear. As indicative of the sorts of problems artisans face, we see that essential raw materials for their crafts such as various skins and hides, certain types of wood, precious metals and stones, shells and a range of other craft materials have become either too expensive for the artisans to purchase, or else have been diverted for mass production (Knorringa 1999). Many of the artisans that do survive invariably produce for a world market, and so daily confront the vagaries of that market (Anderson 1992; Balkwell and Dickerson 1994; Grimes and Milgram 2000; Nash 1993a). In particular, the fluctuating global demand and the hierarchal, exploitative organization of craft production and sales, is indicative of the findings in these various studies of artisan communities in the developing world.

Despite the fact that artisan production is highly localized and, in many instances, confined to homes or villages, artisan production is nevertheless an extremely contested and antagonistic form of production. The relentless commodification of craft production, inherent gender segregation and discrimination against women and girls, and coupled with a generational divide in many instances, are evident throughout studies of artisan communities. The increasing commodification of craft production is indicative of the increasing globalization of production more generally. Various studies have described the ways artisan communities have attempted to re-organize and adjust to changing global economic circumstances and market demands. One body of literature, for instance, explores this process of internationalized craft commercialization in terms of commodity chains that link artisans, wholesalers and first world department stores (Nash 1993b; Steiner 1994; Tice 1995). The trade in artisanal goods is largely dominated by a handful of importing countries – namely Germany, the USA, the UK and France – illustrating that the industry is subject to the demands and policies of dominant, first world corporations and trading regimes (Kathuria 1988). Other scholars have reported on artisan communities that seek market niches or develop flexible specialization in their manufacturing of crafts in order to survive (Chibnick 2000; Wood 2000). The commercialization and global expansion of certain craft industries concomitantly can lead to severe localized effects. The Indonesian textiles industry, for example, in the late 1970s and early 1980s developed into a large, commercialized manufacturing process which immediately created 80,000 new jobs but subsequently lead to a loss of an estimated 410,000 traditional artisan jobs in weaving and associated crafts like dyeing (Buchanan 1985).

The extent to which global capital transforms artisan communities, however, is neither uniform nor consistent but varies according to local historical developments, experiences and levels of global economic integration. Colloredo-Mansfield (2002) argues in a recent study that increasing competition due to economic neo-liberalism and globalization among artisan communities in Otavalo, Ecuador, has re-vitalized these communities, opening-up new markets and opportunities and re-creating interdependencies between artisans, merchants and shopkeepers. Nevertheless, while there is a sense of community survival there remains a pervasive system of inequality wrought by transnationalism and competition. As he argues: 'I want to analyze the distinctive inequalities that afflict people seeking livelihoods in capitalism's austere margins and explain how internal discourses of "competition" naturalize these inequalities as an acceptable (for the moment) community condition' (Colloredo-Mansfield 2002: 114). Tanya Korovkin (1998) similarly provides detailed evidence concerning recent economic and cultural changes confronting the artisans of Otavalo, which, she argues, led to a transformation in, rather than disappearance of, the local Quichua culture. As she writes: 'Not only did the market expansion in Otavalo fail to destroy the community institutions but is also gave rise to an indigenous intelligentsia whose members redefined Indian identity in accordance with new cultural and economic realities' (Korovkin 1998: 126).

Artisan exploitation: gender and health concerns

It is notable, therefore, that in the mainly ethnographic studies of the localized effects of the commercialization of craft production, complex and subtle social changes are unearthed. For various reasons, craft production is an important industry for the employment of women. Several recent studies of women's home-based, subsistence production in various settings in Asia reveal the unique ways women are exploited by both their class and gender and even, in some specific cases, their religious affiliations (Kaino 1995; MacHenry 2000; Nakatani 1999). Wilkinson-Weber (1997) analyzes the way the embroidery (*chikan*) industry in Lucknow, India, has changed over time – from one which produced highly intricate and expensive embroidery to become a mass-market industry where coarse, cheap product is made for a largely local market. In an important shift in the gender division of labor, this industry was once dominated by highly-skilled male embroiders. However, many of these men are mostly now the agents or middlemen responsible for obtaining the goods from the artisans and shifting them into the markets. The *chikan* industry is now dominated by semi-skilled Muslim women, most of who work from home. This has the effect of keeping these women invisible, in *purdah*, and hence out of the public eye. Moreover, as an 'invisible' form of production, it makes the industry difficult to regulate in terms of wages and other workplace conditions. Comparative, inter-country research reveals conclusively that women lack control over the distribution and marketing of crafts, exacerbating their inequality within the industry. Moreover 'womanly' traits like docility, dexterity and obedience are crucial factors in selecting workers, subsequently denying similar opportunities to those women who do not fit the 'feminine, obedient worker' stereotype. Ideas of domesticity and the 'ideal' role of women intersect at various levels in the craft production process, meaning that many women remain at home, having to mind children, cook and clean as well as produce craft goods when demanded and for low rates of pay (Kaino 1995: 9–11). Moreover, the feminine domestication of craft production intersects with patriarchal perceptions of women's sexuality where, in a case described from the Philippines for example, menstruating women are prohibited from the site of dyeing (Guillermo 1995). Finally, the domestic nature of women's craft production means that it is not only impossible for them to form craft unions, but also difficult for them to develop strategies to overcome entrenched patriarchal structures embedded within artisan industries.

The exploitative nature of craft production is not confined solely to gender discrimination. Much of the industry is piecemeal, repetitive, and based on an intensive and prevailing division of labor determined by both class and gender. Wilkinson-Weber's (1997) study also revealed that, because the artisan is paid per piece, and as the market is demanding more, the artisans themselves are becoming de-skilled, only bothering to learn one or two popular stitches. Even urban artisans in Lucknow were bemoaning the work of rural-based embroiders whose work was the most simplistic. Kathuria et al. (1988), in a comparative study of artisan labor in India, the Philippines and Indonesia, described the persistent and enduring inequalities found in the industry throughout the third world. Craft workers tend to have little formal education, are rarely organized and so are subject to a range of exploitative work conditions like poor safety, low wages and lack of formalization of their craft skills. More recently, Milgram's (1999) study of craft and household production in the northern Philippines indicates that craft production indeed supplemented total household incomes, yet most artisans were required to borrow money from support groups, and households without land were unable to accumulate financial reserves nor were they able to meet everyday needs. Moreover, certain individuals, particularly middle people, continued to exploit artisan households and reap the greater amounts of profit from the localized craft industries. Findings illustrate that not only social, economic, gender, and class inequalities persist in artisan communities, but they also face a range of health and environmental problems. Imhoff (1998) relates an example of a female artisan who, after purchasing cheap dyes from a local market (dyes containing high levels of heavy metals and toxic chemicals), proceeded to empty the used dye water onto her household's garden bed where vegetables are grown for family consumption. In Nepal, there have been serious health and environmental consequences of dumping untreated dye wastewater into rivers and onto agricultural land, and these problems are exacerbated especially when safe drinking water is in short supply (MacHenry 2000).

Craft production, markets and allied industries

There is an intrinsic relationship between various industries and artisan production, especially between tourism and handicraft production. The recent growth in international tourism is matched by an equally high increase in tourist handicraft production of various kinds – ranging from simple trinkets and small mementos to intricate and elaborate art works, carvings and pottery. The tourist handicraft industry is seasonal and fluctuates between various sites depending upon the market, advertising, government support and other factors (Brohman 1996). This is apart from the fact that the handicraft market remains tightly controlled by a few agents, is highly exploitative and can earn relatively little for the individual artisan (Helu-Thaman 1993). The fluidity and precarious nature of third world artisan production is exemplified in the case of the 'rise and fall' of Guatemalan textiles in the early 1990s (Imhoff 1998). In this case, increased demand in the USA and Europe for colorful and exciting designs meant that Guatemalan artisans competed with each other to the point of market-saturation, over-supply and an eventual decline in both prices and market demand. This is despite the attempts of Guatemalan artisans to change strategies by lowering their prices and adapt to market conditions by offering a range of different products. The integration of Latin American artisanal products into USA and global markets faces a number of problems including: dominance of the markets by TNCs and large monopoly retail businesses; changing fashion styles and trends; and general market corruption and unreliability (Nash 1993a). The intricacies of craft work on the Asian periphery is succinctly analyzed in a paper by Kusakabe (2001) where she describes the ways in which women weavers on the Laos-Thailand border experience the highs and lows of producing for a market that is rapidly being subject to liberalizing forces. While opportunities are closed-off for some (the 'old' or 'traditional' weavers), others who are better organized or have more support reap the benefits of a commercialized weaving scene. Other alternatives for survival by artisans competing in the global marketplace, such as small producers binding together and subcontracting their wares, rarely offer long-term gains. In the case of Albay artisan subcontractors in the Philippines, it was found that those that were initially successful preferred to invest their profits in fast-moving, high yielding ventures rather than re-invest in the craft enterprises where the market remains insecure and fickle (Rutten 2002).

Crafts: styles and consumption

The success of artisanal crafts within the wider national and international markets largely depends on the whims of global consumer demand. We can distinguish between artisan crafts for everyday use – 'quotidian crafts' – and those that are fundamentally for status consumption – 'elite crafts'. In terms of a globalized cultural market, following Bourdieu (1984), we can delineate a status distinction in the types of crafts produced and consumed. Artisanal crafts that are seen to be of high quality, rare, with great artistic beauty, or are intricately constructed have a specialized and elite consumer market. These elite consumers are most likely to be able to relate tales concerning the craft involved, where the item is from, specific details about the artisan community, and so forth (Nakatani 2001). On the other hand, there circulates a veritable variety of everyday craft goods like women's cloth bags, backpacks, leather wallets and handbags, wall hangings, floor rugs, and dress jewellery, to name just a few, which are largely for global mass consumption.

At the local level, quotidian crafts are under threat. For instance, cheap plastic sandals are replacing leather ones that, in turn, is displacing the mass of indigenous leather shoemakers in countries such as India (Ganguly-Scrase 2001; Knorringa 1999). Likewise, clay pottery items are being replaced by plastic or aluminum plates, bowls, jugs and cups. Cotton weave is substituted by synthetic cloth, with the advantage that it is lighter, cheaper and rarely needs ironing. There are numerous examples where a traditional craft is subsumed by mass-produced items. Artisans themselves are more than aware of this however and indeed many develop strategies to accommodate fluctuating global markets and interests in their crafts. For example, interviews with several artisans in New Delhi reveal their awareness of the need for change[2]:

> Interviewer: What changes have come in styles of craft?
> Artisan response: During my grandfather's generation there was no style and they worked to pass the time. Coloring was also not popular. They were very poor. But we brothers changed our traditional craft into a new style.
> Interviewer: Where do you get your ideas from?
> Artisan response: Ideas are very natural to the craftsmen. But if anyone gives an order for a new design I can perfectly do it.

Another artisan, when asked about designs and how they get changed, responded by saying that: 'NGOs are supporting us to enrich our designs. Like the new style of *Jou-Lakh* [pottery] crafts that do not get spoilt by water. NGOs are trying to give a little support in ideas and color concepts'. Studies show that artisans, by themselves or with NGO support, can quite readily adapt and change, often producing inferior crafts for a global market that have little resemblance to the meaning-rich, specialized crafts that are reserved for ceremonies or local consumption (Grimes and Milgram 2000; MacHenry 2000; Nash 1993a). Additionally, while artisans recognize the need for modification of craft styles to suit changing market demands, there is a certain inevitable consequence of design copy, with eventual market saturation. As one artisan put it, after attending a workshop on 'Design Development':

> …everything spreads in the market. An instructor from NID (National Institute of Design) gives a series of training workshops in five places and the same design gets popularized in the market in the same period of time, thus becoming too common and of no value. There is no profit in such training. Instead, our traditional designs are much better – the horse, Mother Goddess – these are uncommon to the terracotta craftsmen from other states…Traditional and our own designs are the best for earning profit from the market.

The preservation and continuation of 'traditional' styles may indeed be a more secure route for the survival of, in this case, terracotta artisans. In the opinion of others however, artisan survival must come through change. One consumer noted the fluidity and interchange between traditional and modern styles that can give a certain aesthetic appeal to everyday office wear[3].

> Interviewer: You also talked about changing market conditions – do you think the artisans should also do something to change their styles?
> Respondent: Absolutely. They are doing it. They are extremely savvy. If you go and see artisans at Dilli Haat – there is nature bazaar! You will see mirror work. Originally this was done on *lehengas* [traditional mirrored skirts] by the women of Kutch. They used to wear 80 *kalis lehenga* [i.e. extremely heavy] that nobody could wear in an urban center. But the very fact that it is now being done on *kurtas* [long shirts] that women can wear to their office means that these artisans have developed.

For this consumer, traditional styles interwoven with modern ones certainly have a place in the contemporary world of the fashionable, Indian middle and upper class professional – it invokes a sense of being at once modern, stylish and traditional, giving one a visible, Indian identity. As another consumer remarked: 'I think heritage is not something that is static. For it to even remain as heritage, it has to constantly evolve. Tradition is not static and conservative'.

Craft consumption

In contrast with the numerous studies of craft production, research focusing on craft consumption – the meaning, motivations and reasons for consuming artisanal crafts and analyses of the interrelationships that develop between third world artisans and Western, or local consumers for that matter – is comparatively rare. In the context of marketing theory and research, for instance, Basu (1995) makes the point that relatively little is actually understood concerning the relationship between consumers and craft producers. For upper and middle class consumers in Delhi, handicrafts consumption is certainly fashionable. A self-employed professional woman in her early 30s made the following remarks:

> Interviewer: Do you like Indian handicrafts? Do you find them unique?
> Respondent: Definitely I find them unique. In fact as far as decoration is…that is my taste. It is very ethnic. Handicrafts are more what I prefer in terms of things to use and to wear.
> Interviewer: Is it fashionable also?
> Respondent: Definitely fashionable. There is a certain kind of fashion. It is a fashion statement that I like to make (laughs).
> Interviewer: So your group of people would also like to make such fashion statements?
> Respondent: Definitely. I think a lot of my friends have similar tastes and they would like to buy a lot of handicrafts and a lot of hand crafted decoration things.

With the emergence of 'ethnic *chic*', the hybridization of fashion, and a return to 'earthy' and 'natural' forms and colors in interior design, then third world craft goods and patterns have become popular, both in the West and in the local country.

> Interviewer: Why do you think that crafts are fashionable?
> Respondent: Well, I don't know why – the trends of fashion that are created are definitely in two directions – one is the ultra modern and the other is ultra traditional. That has been the

fashion for those creations. I don't know why that has happened but is has happened. 'Ethnic' is also fashionable. It is definitely because of its uniqueness and also because of its boldness. There is certain bold quality to most ethnic crafts. The colors are mostly primary. They are bold. The materials used are bigger, larger. Somehow there is boldness attached to it. That inherent quality makes it an interesting fashion.

Yet, even in terms of the appeals and suitability of 'ethnic *chic*' there remains a significant cultural distinction between the more liberal, professional upper middle classes (employed in the new, high-tech industries and educational institutions), and those from the 'traditional' business and corporate world. When asked if she thought it fashionable for the Indian upper classes to like things that are 'ethnic', one woman responded:

I do not think so. It depends in the circles you move in. Till a year ago, I just had cane furniture and sitting on the ground with lots of ethnic stuff. But it became unsuitable for my husband, who is a corporate person. It depends in the world you move in. In JNU [Jawaharlal Nehru University], it is very chic and ethnic to have those kinds of things. His world is different. It is the corporate world. Finally we had to find a midway.

Research from other countries has also, to some extent, revealed the intersection of the traditional and modern mediated in craft production and consumption. A study of the culture market of Niger, for example, Davis (1999) describes the ways economically successful Tuareg artisans re-define their 'traditional' craft and their place within the conventional socio-classificatory system. As Davis (1999: 498–9) explains in her conclusion:

'Modern' artisanal objects thus represent a striking transformation between Westerners and non-Westerners. For Westerners, Tuareg artisans appeal to a contemporary political consciousness that drives expatriates to develop egalitarian relationships with local people…For Tuareg artisans, Western expatriates comprise a new and reliable clientele who grant to artisans a novel cultural status, along with wealth and esteem refused by their traditional noble patrons. 'Modern' artisanal objects mirror these changes: their Western utility, indelible Tuareg style, and novelty represent the adjustment of Tuaregs and Westerners to each other and to an as-yet obscure ideal of postcolonial modernity.

In certain circumstances, therefore, there is a sense of political and social unity felt by the Western consumer in 'helping-out' the struggling or marginal artisan peoples.

Apart from overseas travel, it is largely by way of catalogues and visits to 'fair-trade' stores that enables Western consumers to purchase 'authentic' artisanal products. Apart from mail-order catalogues, Internet websites have also become important promoters of third world artisanal goods.[4] In this context, Hendrickson (1996) analyses the portrayal of Mayan and Guatemalan clothing and handicraft items in a range of mail-order catalogues circulating in the USA. She reveals the various ways these catalogues construct the 'natural', 'traditional' and even, in some cases, 'primitive' images of Guatemalan life that are used to appeal to consumers. Western consumers sometimes '...*are* made more aware of the situation in that country and Maya *do* earn money from these businesses' (Hendrickson 1996: 118; orig. emphasis). But, in each case, products have to be tailored to suit the foreign audience, the 'horror' stories of certain communities are toned-down, and the fact that the crafts marketed overseas are produced according to strict quality control measures is never revealed. 'Fair trade' shopping, which involves the marketing of third world artisanal crafts and produce, with the intended aim of linking first world consumers to third world producers, has been critiqued in terms of counter-hegemonic consumerism. In this context, Johnson (2002) critically explores how fair-trade discourse constructs various understandings of development, consumerism, and social justice and what these discourses reveal about issues like over-consumption in the industrialized cores and globalized structural inequality. She finds that fair trade discourse tends to '...rely on individualistic notions of choice and consumer sovereignty, obscures the structural linkages between core and periphery in a globalized economy, and belies the collective environmental implications of individual free choice in the marketplace' (Johnson 2002: 55). Significantly, she also points-out that fair trade discourse, rather than provide or stimulate any serious discussion of structural inequality, instead supports a more liberal, de-politicized vision of cultural difference. In this context, 'ethnic branding', 'traditional', and 'authenticity' thereby become important features in the marketing of crafts. To illustrate this trend, Lynn Stephen (1993) reports on the integration and 'ethnicization' of Mexican rugs in the North American consumer markets, showing how the 'branding' of ethnic identity is an important marketing tool despite the revelation that the majority of 'Mexican' rugs are now made in India.

When interviewed, Indian consumers were well aware of the role and place of artisans and their crafts in the wider religious history and culture of India; they had a fair understanding of traditional styles and designs and what made an item unique. Take the following exchange:

> Interviewer: Why Indian crafts? Do you find the Indian handicrafts to be good?
> Respondent: Yes, they are. I think they are the best.
> Interviewer: In what way? Is the quality good?
> Respondent: The quality and the style, you know, that the craft has and the design the artefact has. Take the example of *Ganesha* [elephant god] – that I bought from Lajpat Nagar [market] – I bought a beautiful *Ganesha* from there – with a lotus flower that closes. It is a very unique piece. That is because it is also made of metal [rather than terracotta].

In addition, crafts should not only be unique, but equally be of some use. As one 34 year old consumer, who works as a consultant in an export firm, put it when asked, 'Why do you like Indian crafts?':

> I like them for two reasons. Because they are aesthetically very nice and because they appeal to me. It is totally my choice. Secondly, they are very user friendly. They have been made very contemporary. The crafts still remain very traditional but the shapes and the forms, the cuts [designs] have been contemporized for someone like me who lives in an urban center.

Here the respondent is clearly identifying herself as part of the upwardly mobile, urban middle class and significantly, her consumption of contemporary crafts is an important signifier of her status and cultural taste – a modern woman but still with passion for the values and heritage of 'traditional' India.

The resurrection and increasing popularity of 'native', 'traditional' or 'authentic' Indian arts and crafts can be seen in the context of the Indian urban elite and diasporic community of professional migrants seeking to interrogate and reconstruct their identities, through literature, film and art, in a fragmented and globalizing world (Appadurai 1996). Jain (1995) argues that a great divide now exists in India between the mainstream elite artists who work in studios and sell through organized galleries and the 'everyday' artisans and craftspeople. This latter group:

> ...mainly thrive on the new urban patronage which has arisen as a result of protection and patronizing developmental endeavours on the part of the government. The government encourages these with a view to keeping the artisans self-employed and to earning precious foreign exchange by exporting manufactured craft products. Once it is established that the 'crafts' are primarily 'commercial' rather than 'cultural' in nature, their treatment involves different strategies, one of which must be that the criteria for design and aesthetics are oriented to commerce-related development (Jain 1995: 29).

Jain goes on to write that a schism evolves wherein tribal and village artistic products are rarely considered part of contemporary 'art'. Rather, the 'art' of rural artisans, or more correctly 'artists', is predominantly mass-produced, commercially-driven 'handicrafts'.

Government and NGO support for artisans

Specialized government agencies and various NGOs have aimed to preserve the range of crafts unique to their nations. Notwithstanding the good intent of state or national policies to preserve 'traditional' crafts, there is nevertheless an underlying paternalism in such policies when the very same state is pursuing a broader global industrial and manufacturing agenda that competes with, and will ultimately lead to the marginalization, or even complete demise, of local artisan industries. Government policies and bureaucracies, set-up to promote artisan industries in various third world countries, have been criticized for their failure to properly recognize and promote the needs of craft workers (Suratman 1991). The failure to recognize 'on-the-ground', local knowledge and incorporate this into employment policies and planning shows a disdain for marginal workers and so reproduces the failures of top-down policy making so indicative of ill-conceived, developmentalist policies. Moreover, who decides what activities are worth supporting and what specific crafts are considered unique to a nation and its peoples and why is a significant question to pose. In this sense, the state involves itself in a process of what I term 'selective traditionalizing', a process which can assist some communities to survive but may condemn the fate of many others.

At the more mundane level, Indian artisans themselves were often highly critical of government support for several reasons. Petty corruption was at the forefront of their complaints, however, as the following account reveals:

>Interviewer: What other support is there from the government?
>Artisan response: To get to a fair we have to give money then only do we get an approval letter. Again we have to pay money to the officers at the fair.
>Interviewer: How much?
>Artisan response: For a letter it is 1500–5000 rupees.
>Interviewer: Receiving the letter confirms your participation in the fair?
>Artisan response: No. To get information about the fair we have to pay more money. We are ready [willing] to pay to get to a fair. Government organizes fairs free of cost yet we still have to pay the officers. We are also entitled for TA/DA [travel and dearness allowances] but that money goes to officers' pockets in addition to the other money we pay. If someone else gives more money than us then the [approval] letter will be issued for him and not for us. So even if we pay bribes, our participation in a fair is not confirmed.

Corruption is not just confined to participation in fairs but is virtually in all stages and levels of the display and marketing of crafts.

>Interviewer: Do the wholesalers send crafts to *Manjusha* or *Tantuja* [various state government emporiums]?
>Artisan response: If you know any officer in the cottage emporium then you can enter your crafts by bribing them. They are all corrupted. You also have to bribe the 4th class staff to display your crafts so that a sale can possibly take place, especially as the manager is not going to help you. Payment is on the sale basis and you earn a

Interviewer: check every month. If no craft item is sold then they will return it to you after 3–4 years.
Interviewer: Are societies [NGOs] more helpful in getting information and reciprocation for fairs?
Artisan response: Artisan societies are there. But now all the channels are corrupted. To make a society 10–15 members are needed and are fulfilled by own family members and friends. Whatever money is sanctioned by the NGO or other public/private organizations is then put into personal pockets.

Unlike state-supported systems, the situation at the non-governmental level is somewhat different. While the support of various NGOs, the establishment of artisan cooperatives, and the emergence of various fair trade schemes are welcome, there remains a sense of hopelessness as artisans employed by these various NGOs have to compete in a global market. For example, a 1997 report by the United Nations Development Fund for Women (UNIFEM) on women artisans in India describes the rise of artisan sweatshops where NGO staff on good salaries, with leave and other job benefits, supervise the work of women who are barley

Figure 5.1: Crafts Museum, New Delhi

Source: Ms Sayani Das

Figure 5.2: Jute artisan in his stall.

Source: Ms Sayani Das

struggling to survive on a subsistence income. In one case, orders for Belgian lace were rejected on the grounds of poor quality. The income from sales, more than ten times the cost of its manufacture, is largely shared by the charity and the NGO that buys it, with only a subsistence level of wages trickling down to the artisans. The various fair trade bodies, with their focus on a fair price, are also criticized for failing to ensure that the artisans are accorded just and reasonable wages and suitable employment conditions and rights (UNIFEM 1997). Moreover, the fickle nature of the global marketplace means that various crafts come in and out of fashion leading to problems of dwindling markets and oversupply.

Another way in which artisan labor has the potential to survive, with both government and NGO assistance, is through the imposition of intellectual property rights. The globalization of production has given rise to several well-known cases of copyright and patent violations in relation to medicines, music and literature. However, one of the key problems that emerges is that artisanal crafts and skills are shared, owned and practiced by a community and so stand in stark contrast to the Western view of knowledge as a commodity owned by an individual or an incorporated company. Furthermore, what happens when another marginalized group uses similar patterns or crafts to enter the marketplace? Moreover, can a society hold onto its intellectual property when businesses from another country decide to use the same patterns and designs? (Riley and Moran 2001). As most artisans remarked during their interviews, the problem of copying designs and then mass-producing them cheaply is rife in India.

Skills training of artisan laborers

> ...But these people are unskilled and are not professionals. They work when they want to. That is why a lot of export orders are rejected and are delayed. Education should be improved to a certain extent. If they get too educated, they will not do hard work. (24 year old male export dealer).

The quote above is all too indicative of the patronizing and stereotypical attitudes of the Indian upper middle classes concerning the lower classes (and castes). Yet, it does lead to two important questions: Is there the need, and advantage, for specific skills training and education for artisans? And, should the skills of the artisans be formalized and would any benefit be derived if this were to happen? In the area of skills training and the social and economic improvement of artisan communities, the majority of

Figure 5.3: Terracotta artisan displaying her wares.

Source: Ms Sayani Das

research undertaken points to the advantages of forming artisan cooperatives which are managed by, or in linkage with, fair trade organizations (see Grimes and Milgram 2000; MacHenry 2000). Various international groups have recently been formed to assist and train artisan communities from around the globe. One such group is the 'Artisan Enterprise Network' (AEN). As they point-out in their publicity, they have a goal of '...empowering owners of micro and small businesses to be entrepreneurs in the global marketplace'. The AEN was established after being one of 44 winners of a World Bank competition for innovative ideas to reduce world poverty and spur development. Essentially, the AEN sets out to establish and ferment an entrepreneurial spirit and organization among artisan communities. Included in the AEN is an artisan/entrepreneur curriculum that teaches small business planning and entrepreneurial skills.[5]

Many other organizations provide assistance and training for artisans. At the international governmental level, SEED (Boosting Employment Through Small EnterprisE Development) is a program of the International Labor Organization (ILO) to capitalize on the ILO's work in supporting micro and small-scale enterprises. For example, in Mali the ILO assisted in establishing the National Federation of Artisans that has over 20,000 members and assists these workers in having a representative voice in government affairs. Moreover, the ILO is developing a range of guidelines, manuals and training programs for capacity building among marginal working communities like artisans and handicraft workers. At the non-profit level, 'The Crafts Center' is an organization that connects artisans to potential buyers and assistance organizations like micro-credit agencies and various NGOs. It also educates and trains artisans and their development partners about product quality, sound business practices and market trends, 'best practice' in production and marketing, and raises general consumer interest and appreciation for handicrafts.[6]

All artisans interviewed in New Delhi expressed the desire for more training and financial assistance to enable them to compete and survive in the marketplace. However, numerous obstacles stood in their way: corruption and bribery; lack of market knowledge; poor or uneven quality of their goods. Even with a 'fashionable' or high demand product, there remains in the world of private production the inherent problems of fluctuating market demand, intense local and global competition, lack of social power and hence a lack of effective bargaining and negotiating skills, and a general reduction in secure and meaningful employment once the skills of the artisan become commercialized.

Concluding comments

> These particular crafts are made by people. They are not particularly artists. They are whole communities. So there are a lot of people who probably moved out of doing that because there is no livelihood to be made from it. So if there was a viable livelihood to be made from it, a lot of people would move back to it. There would be no shortage of people to do it. There would be whole villages. If you travel in the North East you will find that there are whole villages who make baskets or do bamboo work and things like that. There is a whole team. The old woman does a particular part of the job, the young man does a particular part of the job, the little child does a particular...The whole family is involved. So there will be no dearth of that [skilled artisans] (self-employed professional woman, aged 31).

As this interviewee points-out, if more people came to respect and support Indian artisans their craft, along with their communities, would survive. Craft consumption is significant because, in the act of buying an artisanal commodity, the consumer is buying the experience of authenticity and traditionalism, establishing a connection that symbolically links the commodity back to the artisan and their community. This is reinforced by a direct experience of buying from the producer, as in a tourist encounter, at a crafts market, fair or festival, or from a fair trade shop or through a catalogue, where the details of the craft and the producers themselves are provided (Hendrickson, 1996). Crafts retain many of the qualities that imbue them with a sense of tradition and uniqueness. Ayami Nakatani (2001) recounts the tales of Japanese middle class consumers, and the various women's' magazines aimed at this market, which personalize the consumption of craft goods. She explains:

> The Japanese consumers, predominantly women, crave for the stories and 'biographical' details about these goods. Responding to those needs, the magazine articles and import dealers provide some ideas about the context of production; their discourse tends to create a highly romanticized, and static view of local producers. On the part of the purchasers, they turn the

goods into personalized possessions and display them in an effort to express their individuality (Nakatani 2001: 13).

Thus, in a hyperreal world of mass, packaged consumption, global telecommunication and virtual relationships, the purchase of an artisan craft may act to temporarily anchor the consumer in a real world of labor production (Featherstone 1991; Fine and Leopold 1993; Miller 1995).

Despite shifts to the 'smart' economy, fostered and fed by the globalization of culture and the economy, in many ways, the daily life and struggle of Asian artisans have changed little over the past few decades. This is the life of precarious production – a marginalized existence determined by the ever-changing desires of a whimsical global consumer market. Tourists can come and go, wars and civil disruption can occur, and various raw materials can become too expensive or disappear forever. To be an artisan is thus a contingent and relative experience, whereby the majority of artisans fluctuate between work and unemployment, income and poverty. Just as the life of the artisan is precarious, so too is the craft itself. The globalization of artisanal crafts has led to the separation of the craft from the actual artisan. For example, China mass-produces and markets 'sari' cloth, based on Indian designs, which finds it way into Western supermarkets and discount fabric stores, as tablecloths, placemats and bedding linen. Thus, it may be now possible to speak of the 'virtual artisan', meaning that the craft itself survives in a hybrid form that may or may not be produced by the original workers. Coupled with this is the concomitant emergence of artisanal or craft bricolage, whereby the artisanal product becomes an assemblage of popular patterns and designs, often used out of context, and with the finished good a mere resemblance of its former self.

Finally, in many respects the contemporary artisan, like the urban professional middle classes and savvy cosmopolitans, has developed a hybrid identity: some retain traditionalism in their craft while simultaneously producing for a global or local consumer market. Moreover, the vestiges of the craft itself survive despite its material transference from design to artifact to mass-produced commodity. Either way, the identity of the artisan is imbued in the craft piece itself – whether it is on the design of the embroidery, the shape of the pot, the style of weaving, or the colors and patterns of the cloth. In other words, unlike the displaced or marginalized wage worker, artisan crafts carry with them a piece of the identity of the makers themselves and so circulate in the global consumer markets of department stores, fair trade shops or local bazaars and markets. Thus, despite the precarious nature of artisan production, their crafts and skills survive.

Part II
Media, Culture and Identity

6 Transnational Identities in the Hmong Diaspora

Roberta Julian

Introduction

In 1973 the first Hmong person arrived in Tasmania, the small island state at the southeastern tip of Australia. He was a Colombo Plan[1] student named Vue Thaow. After the fall of Vientiane in 1975, Vue Thaow sponsored his wife and two children to Australia, followed by his parents, his siblings, other clan members, and then relatives of those who had married into his clan. Thus began two decades of chain migration of Hmong refugees from Laos to Tasmania, via refugee camps in Thailand. By the mid-1990s, the emerging Hmong community in Tasmania numbered about 500, comprised of five clans. In the early 1990s I was commissioned to undertake research in Tasmania on the settlement experiences of recently arrived refugees. Not only did I meet Vue Thaow and the Hmong in Tasmania, I also embarked on a decade-long journey of discovery of Hmong people worldwide. Observing this Asian diaspora first hand has stimulated in me an almost obsessive fascination with Hmong culture(s) and identity/ies.

This chapter on the Hmong diaspora is based on my association with Hmong people living mainly in Tasmania and the United States, but also in Thailand. It draws on an array of ethnographic data: observation and participant observation, in-depth semi-structured interviews, a survey, structured interviews, document analysis (including books, newsletters, articles on the Internet, keynote addresses), analysis of scholarly publications (by both Hmong and non-Hmong), autobiographies and biographies, cultural artefacts and non-traditional media (such as storycloths), plays, museum displays, comedy skits and videos, and poetry and short stories. Much of this media serves to create what can be called a 'diasporic public sphere,' a venue where Hmong identity is negotiated and constructed.

The research has been guided by two general questions: 'who are the Hmong?' and 'what does it mean to be Hmong?' These questions are of interest to sociologists and anthropologists (e.g. Schein 1999) in that they provide an opportunity to examine processes of identity construction under conditions of postmodernity and in the context of globalization. Most importantly, however, these questions are of immediate significance to members of the Hmong diaspora themselves. Illustrative of this concern with identity is the fact that the Hmong National Development (HND) conference, held annually in the United States, selected 'The Complexity of Hmong Identity' as its 2002 theme.

My analysis of identity construction and change in the Hmong diaspora draws in particular on ideas developed by Stuart Hall (1990, 1992), Pnina Werbner (1998), Denis-Constant Martin (1995), Robin Cohen (1997) and Avtah Brah (1998). It examines a number of inter-related themes including:

- the processes of identity construction among the people of a diaspora with a focus on the tensions between local and global dimensions;
- the tensions between identity as discourse or narrative on the one hand, and the performative aspects of identity on the other hand; that is, identity as both narrated and enacted through cultural practices;
- the crucial significance of the media in the construction and transformation of diasporic identities in the 'age of globalization';
- the problematic relationship between diasporas and nation-states as potentially competing forms of social organization.

Let's consider these themes in greater detail.

Globalization, diaspora and identity

Stuart Hall defines globalization as 'those processes, operating on a global scale, which cut across national boundaries, integrating and connecting communities and organizations in new space-time combinations, making the world in reality and in experience more interconnected' (1992: 299). Rex (1995) emphasizes globalization's role in stimulating emergent forms of social organization, saying:

(globalization refers to a process in which) the bounding of social life by such political units as nation-states has been superseded by a state of affairs in which the social relations and networks in which individuals are involved, as well as the cultural influences to which they are subject, tend to have global, rather than purely national character (1995: 21–22).

These views considered, it can be argued that globalization processes are conducive to the development of diasporas. As Cohen states:

> Globalization and diasporization are separate phenomena with no necessary causal connection, but they "go together" extraordinarily well…Globalization has enhanced the practical, economic and affective roles of diasporas, showing them to be particularly adaptive forms of social organization (1997: 175–6).

Similarly, Sinclair and Cunningham theorise that 'to the extent that globalisation presents more and more people with the experience of difference and displacement, the diasporic experience becomes not so much a metaphor as the archetype for the kind of cultural adaptiveness which our era demands.' (2000: 14).

What are the implications of transnational networks and diasporas for the cultural identities of those involved? Hall argues that globalization has 'the effect of contesting and dislocating the centred and "closed" identities of a national culture' (1992: 309). For Cohen, the so-called 'age of globalization' has produced 'an increasing proliferation of diasporic, subnational and ethnic identities that cannot easily be contained in the nation-state system' (1997: 520). As I demonstrate here, the Hmong diaspora provides a fascinating case study of the identification processes that Hall, Rex and Cohen have recognized as central to globalization.

Following Werbner, I conceive of diasporas as 'communities of co-responsibility.' In such a way I 'recognis(e)…not simply their loyalty but their existential connections to "co-diasporans" elsewhere' (1998: 12). Whereas much contemporary literature limits its focus to the aesthetic and experiential dimensions of diaspora (for example, Bhabha, 1994; Brah, 1996), Werbner 'seeks to retain a prior emphasis on the compelling nature of the *obligations* "diasporans" feel across space and national boundary' (1998: 12).

In this way, diasporas are what Anderson (1983) calls 'imagined communities.' Communities, he suggests, are imagined in a variety of ways. First, there is the belief of belonging to a shared community – even though it is often the case that fellow members will never know or meet one another. Second, the community is imagined as having finite boundaries beyond which lie 'other' communities. Third, it is imagined as sovereign, with members dreaming of freedom from external interference. Finally, it is imagined as based on 'a deep, horizontal comradeship' that denies (or at least 'glosses') the existence of inequalities among its members.

Taking up the ideas of differentiation and inequality, Brah (1996) has noted that diasporas are no more unified and homogenous than cultures or communities are. They are 'lived and re-lived through multiple modalities' as 'differentiated, heterogeneous and contested spaces, even as they are implicated in the construction of a common "we"' (Brah 1996: 184).

As with all communities, identity processes are integral to the construction of a 'diasporic community.' It is useful to adopt Hall's (1990: 53) perspective here, viewing identities as 'points of identification, the unstable points of identification or suture, which are made, within the discourses of history and culture. Not an essence but a *positioning*. Hence, there is always a politics of identity, a politics of position, which has no absolute guarantee in an unproblematic, transcendental "law of origin".'

For diasporas the arena in which such *positioning* takes place is described by Werbner as the 'diasporic public sphere'. This is: 'conceived of as a space in which different transnational imaginaries are interpreted and argued over, where aesthetic and moral fables of diaspora are formulated, and political mobilisation generated in response to global social dramas.' (1998: 11).

Importantly, however, such debate and contestation 'presumes a *shared space of dialogue;* a space that has to be *created* through voluntary efforts and investments...' (Werbner 1998: 25). This chapter not only argues, but demonstrates, that in the case of the Hmong, media comprise a powerful avenue for the creation of a diasporic public sphere. Furthermore, they play a significant role in *how* the diasporic identity is constructed and represented.

To show this I begin by exploring the social construction of a transnational/diasporic Hmong identity. I then analyse the evolution of a 'diasporic public sphere' and the *positioning* of a diasporic Hmong identity through a variety of media. Given the nature of the transnational community that has emerged among

Hmong refugees, it is important to recognise that processes of identity construction at the local level are necessarily implicated in processes of identity construction at the global level, and vice versa. As Luke and Luke have noted, 'identities emerge within specific localised contexts of domination and resistance' (2000: 48). At the same time, however, 'locales are thoroughly permeated and shaped by distant social influences' (Luke and Luke 2000: 63). It is important to ask, then, what relations of domination and resistance are (re)produced through processes of identity construction in the Hmong diaspora? This is a question I attend to here.

This chapter also demonstrates that debate in the diasporic public sphere is gendered. Importantly, however, this gendered debate is cross-cut by divisions based on age and generation. On the one hand, men (especially, but not only, older men) typically support an essentialist notion of Hmong identity. The strategies they adopt at both the local and the global level reify 'culture' and treat 'tradition' as relatively fixed, uncontested, and uncontestable. On the other hand, Hmong women and some young men, see Hmong identity as open to change – even transformation – in the context of resettlement, modernity and globalization.

This tension between these alternative identity types under conditions of globalization has been addressed by Hall:

> Some identities gravitate to what Robins calls 'Tradition', attempting to restore their former purity and recover the unities and certainties which are felt as being lost. Others accept that identity is subject to the play of history, politics, representation and difference, so that they are unlikely ever again to be 'pure'; and these consequently gravitate towards what Robins (following Homi Bhabha) calls 'Translation' (1992: 309).

The paradox of the Hmong is that they are engaged in both processes. It is through a reassertion of 'tradition' at the local level, together with the resistance and negotiation undertaken by the next generation (and especially women), that new global Hmong identities are emerging within the context of diaspora. Perhaps this is true of all diasporas and contributes to their success as a form of organization in the 'age of globalization'. Bearing this larger possibility in mind, let us now consider the Hmong diaspora in greater detail.

The Hmong diaspora

The history of the Hmong can be traced back over four thousand years. Legend has it that they originated in Mesopotamia, then migrated to southern China. As a result of persecution by the Chinese an element of the Hmong crossed China's southern frontiers in the mid-nineteenth century, settling in the uninhabited mountainous areas of northern Vietnam, Laos and Thailand (Cooper et al. 1995: 5–6; Quincey 1995). The majority of the Hmong in the 'west' are from Laos where, as one of the two main ethnic groups living in the highest mountain regions, they were allocated a minority status vis-a-vis the dominant group, the lowland Lao (Chan 1994; Yang Dao 1993). In short, the Hmong have no nation and no homeland and, consequently, birthplace is not a major component of Hmong identity (see Donnelly 1994: 84–86).

Between 1949 and 1975 the Hmong found themselves caught up in the Indo-Chinese wars in South East Asia and the civil war in Laos. While in the early years some Hmong fought with the communist forces (the Pathet Lao), in later years the majority joined the anti-communist General Vang Pao. During this period they supported the Americans and many assisted the CIA as secret anti-communist guerrillas. After 1975, in response to persecution by the communist Lao government, many were forced to retreat into the jungle, becoming refugees in their 'own' country before escaping to refugee camps in Thailand (Dean 1993). By 1990 more than 120,000 Hmong had fled Laos; over 80,000 have since resettled overseas where they have been accepted in countries such as the United States, France, Canada, Australia and French Guiana, on humanitarian grounds (Cooper et al. 1995: 8).

Significant class and status differences are apparent in the Hmong diaspora. The first Hmong émigrés consisted of the political and military elite who were able to exploit pre-war connections with politicians and educators in France or else manage a CIA-sponsored airlift from the military base at Long Tieng. For those who escaped to a refugee camp in Thailand, initial candidates for resettlement went to the United States. These refugees were the most educated, who had held higher positions within General Vang Pao's army. By 2002, 186,000 Hmong refugees and their descendants were residing in the United States (Hmong Resource Center 2002). Within the context of U.S. race relations, their identity has gradually shifted from that of 'migrants' to 'racial minority' (Hein 1994). Inequality is a feature of the Hmong-American community. There is an identifiable elite which has achieved educational and material success, as well as a larger percentage which is welfare-dependant and struggling economically. By contrast, the Hmong community in Australia is more homogenous. The majority were 'foot soldiers' in General Vang Pao's army, and most arrived after spending a number of years in Thai refugee camps. Australia is now home to approximately 2,000 Hmong.

A global Hmong identity

When I originally began exploring the question 'Who are the Hmong?' I discovered a highly visible, well-articulated and almost *unitary* narrative. In books and videos, as well as in interviews with Hmong in Australia and in the United States, the same story was told about Hmong identity. After a decade of researching this question I can now argue with confidence that a dominant part of this identity narrative appears to be a hegemonic discourse emanating from Hmong-America and adopted by Hmong throughout their diaspora. This global identity construction is made possible by the existence of clan ties across nation-states together with technological advances in communication (such as the Internet) that enable the maintenance of social ties and the transmission of information on a global scale (Gorman and McLean 2003). However, rather than seeing this unitary narrative as representing internal homogeneity based on 'authenticity,' I wish to follow Werbner's (1998) lead in asserting that this is the outcome of mono-aural media and limited debate in the diasporic public sphere. In point of fact, other strands of identity can be discerned.

To see that, let's ask: what precisely are the characteristics of the global identity narrative being constructed by Hmong in the diasporic public sphere? Who is involved in its construction? And what media serve as conduits for this narrative?

The refugee discourse

The dominant identity narrative could be described as the quintessential 'refugee story' – a version of the well known

'immigrant success story'. It is a 'heroic' narrative that incorporates a number of themes:
- the war and the military (the starting point for the diasporic narrative);
- the refugee experience (including flight across the Mekong River and languishing in Thai refugee camps for many years);
- continuity with the past through recognition of the value of clan ties and 'traditional' Hmong culture (e.g. shamanism);
- symbols of movement into the future (the modern or the postmodern) by emphasizing educational achievement.

There are two heroes of this narrative, in particular, who represent the link with the past and the move into the future. The first is General Vang Pao, acknowledged leader of the Hmong diaspora, who symbolises the military basis of the Hmong identity. Vang Pao lives in Santa Ana, California, and it is often said that 'he has no power any more.' The other hero is Dr Yang Dao, the first Hmong to receive a PhD (in Political Science from a French university). Yang Dao, who lives in St. Paul, Minnesota, is considered the patron of Hmong education and symbolises the way ahead. He personally knows all Hmong who have received a PhD and has sponsored or mentored many of them in their quest for higher education.

Numerous videos and books 'tell' the history of the Hmong exodus from Laos to resettlement in the west. Scholarly publications – the majority written by non-Hmong – recount Hmong involvement in the Vietnam War and the difficulties associated with resettlement. Emphasis is placed on the effort to manage a 'traditional' culture in the context of modern western society. The Hmong have made numerous videos for the extensive US market (both Hmong and non-Hmong) as well as the global Hmong market. These videos, like the books, recount the same story: first, of a 'brotherhood' with US citizens as a consequence of fighting side-by-side in the Vietnam War, and second, of 'successful' adaptation to American society (evidenced by educational success) alongside the maintenance of 'traditional' cultural practices (such as shamanism).

Typical of books in this genre is the following opening paragraph, based on the translation of an interview with a Hmong man, Chia Koua Xiong, who resettled in the United States:

> Who are the Hmong?...
>   In Laos, we helped you fight the war. The Americans came to live with our leaders in our country…We provided food…If the Americans came

to our house, whatever we ate we treated the Americans equally...If we found an injured soldier...we...carried the American to the base...In some dangerous situations we were willing to let ten Hmong soldiers die so that one of your leaders could live...

We considered Americans as our own brothers...Now we have lost our own country...Those who made it here, they have the opportunity for education and jobs...We started a new life so that our children would have a better life (Pfaff 1995: 7).

While this narrative is predominantly articulated by male elites, it is also enacted and perpetuated by ordinary men and women. For example, women reproduce this narrative in the 'storycloth' (*paj ndau*), a new form of media that originated in the refugee camps in Thailand. The first storycloths were made around 1976 in Ban Vinai refugee camp (Anderson 1996: 30), combining traditional needlework techniques with innovative imagery. In Anderson's description:

> the designs are stitched on flat pieces of fabric varying in size from small twelve-inch squares to rectangular panels four feet by three feet or larger. The textile is called a 'story' cloth because the picture, like a narrative text, follows a chronological sequence of events or activities that portray the experiences and traditional folkways of the Hmong people (Anderson 1996:28).

Commonly, the storycloths chronicle village life in the mountains of Laos, depict religious ceremonies, or illustrate Hmong folktales. The majority created in the 'west' or for the western market, however, recount the escape from Laos after the Vietnam War. In Anderson's (1996: 28) estimate 'these pictures stand as graphic statements of the horrors of war and show people carrying their babies and all their worldly possessions across the Mekong River into Thailand, dodging the gunfire and helicopters overhead.'

Such themes – of war, exodus and refugee status – have emerged as central to the representation of a diasporic identity among the Hmong. Anderson explains why:

> The storycloths are a link with the past. They are shared memories captured in visual images, with the embroiderer's needle rather than the camera or the written word. As episodes of social history, they record and pass on information about Hmong customs to the younger

Figure 6.1 A Hmong paj ndau *'storycloth' depicting the forced exodus from village life in Laos to refugee camps in Thailand and finally to the planes that would take them to 'freedom' in the 'west'.*

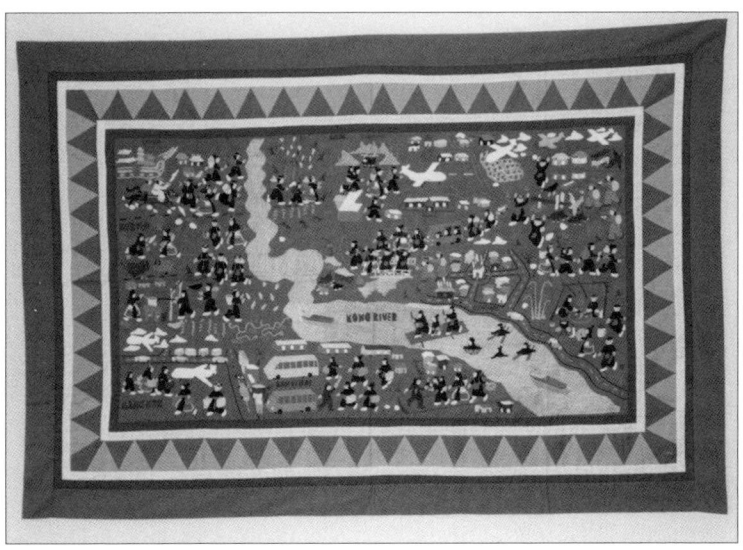

generation, especially those born in the United States with no first-hand knowledge of Laos...They are a form of non-verbal communication that transcend [sic] language barriers (1996: 28).

It is not only the storycloths that carry this narrative, though. Public events involving Hmong almost always contain accounts of refugees enduring forced migration. Typical is the following keynote speech, from the Fourth Annual National Hmong Conference held in Denver, Colorado in April, 1998. Dr. Mymee Her, a young Hmong psychologist from California, declared:

> The Hmong are classified as REFUGEES...Hmong refugees come to the United States wounded. Most have been beaten up physically and emotionally. They seek out shelter from whatever country will offer them safety. They have no anticipation of what life holds for them in the country of refuge. They are in a state of shock, not realizing what had just happened (Her 1998).

The main focus of such narratives is on maintaining continuity with the past while taking advantage of opportunities for educational and material success in the west. Thus, Her began her speech by intoning:

> When I was asked to deliver a keynote address...I was told that the conference theme was living the American dream. I was ecstatic, relieved that for once I did not have to talk about the struggles and suffering of the Hmong people...But as I sat down to think about what I was going to say...(I realized that it is) impossible to talk about our people living the American dream without talking about the history that has brought us to America, including the struggles and sufferings everyone must endure as part of our American Dream...

In such narratives, Hmong identity is forged on a past relationship with the United States in Laos. The Hmong are provided with a unique identity vis-a-vis America, establishing and reinforcing a relationship of patronage. In general, this has been a successful strategy for Hmong-Americans, 'voiced' loudest and most articulately by Hmong male elites. As we see above, however, a supporting 'cast' of ordinary Hmong men and women also exists. As Denis-Constant Martin has pointed out: 'It takes political brokers *and* ordinary people...to tangle strategies and feelings into a narrative which will raise an echo' (Martin 1995: 11).

The traditional discourse

In terms of identity politics, this strategy supports and reinforces an essentialist notion of Hmongness and encourages the maintenance of ideas of 'tradition' and 'authenticity'. In turn, this gives vent to other strands of identity discourse: unitary, but not necessarily refugee-based or American-tinged.

When 'traditional' Hmongness is emphasized, those in the west attempting to reconstruct it look to Thailand and Laos for 'authenticity'. For many young Hmong, visits to northern Thailand and Laos are viewed with enthusiasm and are encouraged by parents as a way of reclaiming traditional Hmongness. For some Hmong men in the west, marrying Thai Hmong women is a way of maintaining traditional Hmongness. It can be argued that the maintenance of such connections with the past involves a *reinvention* of tradition which takes the form of a 'strategic essentialism' (Ang 1993; Spivak 1990).

Alternate unities

Paradoxically, this strategy serves to both inhibit and encourage change in cultural practices. For example, 'traditional' views of Hmong femininity are sustained, as Hmong women are expected to be the bearers of cultural tradition (see Ganguly-Scrase and Julian 1999; Julian 1998). So, too, gender inequalities that existed in Laos remain unchallenged. On the other hand, emphasis on links with the past has led to the (re)discovery of Hmong 'roots' in China (Schein, 2000) and a consequent process of sinicization of contemporary Hmong identity (Tapp 2000). One of the dominant signifiers of this sinicized Hmong identity is the Chinese Hmong costume, which has been increasingly adopted by young Hmong women at New Year celebrations throughout the diaspora. Significantly, the Chinese Hmong skirt is now mass-produced in China and exported to Hmong women worldwide who wear it in favour of the hand-made skirts that their mothers laboured over (Friend 2002). There is, in this global flow, a universalization of a different kind of Hmong identity.

While it has greatest strategic value in the local contexts of various states in the United States, this diasporic identity is also evident among Hmong on the diaspora's periphery, particularly in Canada, France and Australia. The boundaries of this imagined community, though, are not spatial; they are grounded in the social networks that constitute the diaspora. This is evidenced by the fact that financial remittances are sent between the United States and refugees in Wat Thamkrabok, while Hmong in Bangkok communicate regularly on the Internet with Hmong in the United States, Australia and Canada.[2]

The role of media

Representations of a unitary Hmong identity are transmitted throughout the diaspora via videos, books, Internet web sites, tourism, and 'travelling' museum displays. Gary Yia Lee, the only Hmong in Australia to yet gain a PhD, articulates this goal very clearly in one of his articles on the Internet:

> The ability to travel freely to other countries where Hmong live and the informal Hmong mass media have allowed the Hmong people to rediscover each other, to see each other on videos...

> The Hmong, no matter where they are, need to know that the total sum is always bigger than its parts: the overall global Hmong identity is greater than its many local differences and groups...The biggest challenge for all Hmong is...to turn our diverse language and customs into one unified and one Hmong/Miao[3] identity...(Lee 1996).

The media used in accomplishing this project – such as Internet web sites and videos – create a market for a unitary global identity out of dislocated Hmong people. This is a capability Slevin sees when he writes: 'communication media facilitate the representation of...constructed "reality" by making possible the transmission of shared histories of common "hows" and shared landscapes of common "essences".' (2002: 149–50).

The data presented here demonstrate this. Media are not only avenues for transmitting shared histories, but sites for constructing them. They both reflect the Hmong diaspora and re/produce the identity/ies necessary to sustain it.

Counter-hegemonic discourses

The previous section began by identifying a unitary 'global' Hmong identity emanating from Hmong-America, one that is in evidence throughout the Hmong diaspora. On closer examination, however, the existence of alternative subaltern voices is also discernable in the diasporic public sphere. These may constitute resistances and/or challenges to the hegemonic discourse. It is possible that they are counter-hegemonic discourses articulated by voices on the diasporic periphery.

Such resistances arise where the narrative of the 'refugee success story' does not resonate with lived experience. The voices that arise in local contexts – both inside and outside the United States – reflect differences within the Hmong diaspora based on gender, age, class, religion, 'migrantness' and place. They are what Werbner (1998: 12) refers to as voices of 'argument and imaginative creativity.' Hard to hear, since they do not dominate the major media in the diasporic public sphere (videos, books and 'ethnic' cultural displays); still, they are present and can be gleaned in 'new,' less traditional media.

The voices of resistance are predominantly those of educated Hmong women. However, they have been joined more recently by the voices of young Hmong people, both male and female. The main topics of contestation and debate include clan structure; youthful marriage; cross-cultural marriage; polygamy and levirate; 'kidnap' marriages; women's education; and the significance of Hmong language for Hmong identity.

Surely, the first generation of successful young Hmong men in the United States are living symbols of the 'truth' behind the 'refugee success story.' Many are doctors, lawyers and teachers who have strived to maintain a traditional Hmongness during the process of adaptation. Yet, the 'new' generation of young Hmong men and women feel less obliged to follow these 'safe' paths toward educational success and material wealth – the 'American Dream.' They have risked the adulation of their parents and their community by negotiating new pathways through less traditional American careers. In doing so, they have created new forums for the articulation and expression of Hmong identity – some hybrid, others oppositional – that stand in contrast to the domination of the hegemonic discourse. In these new contexts, such 'new identity producers' are free to creatively 'translate' the meaning of Hmongness in the diaspora.

New media and global Hmong community

There are two main arenas emerging as significant sites for this translation of Hmongness: 'new' media (especially the Internet) and the arts (with a particular emphasis on popular culture and popular music). The Internet is an important site of contestation and debate in the diasporic public sphere, with an on-line Hmong Journal and at least one Hmong home page in both America and Australia. Young Hmong people in the United States, Australia, Canada, Thailand and Laos discuss issues surrounding Hmong identity in various chat rooms. New electronic media thus make an important contribution not only to the translation of Hmong identity, but to the construction of community itself. Associations are established and solidarities created via discourse on the web. Not only does it serve as a means of communication among members of a pre-existing transnational community, the Internet is a mechanism for the creative construction of a new global reality: the Hmong diaspora. This diaspora comprises Hmong refugees but also includes their descendants, many of whom have never set foot in Laos and whose own subjectivities are constructed in various geographical and social locations throughout the world.

It should come as little surprise that this social formation – transgenerational, transnational, electronically mediated – constitutes a public sphere rife with contestation and debate.

Popular culture as expression of resistance

Popular culture is emerging as a potentially more powerful site of translation, for the act of adopting pop symbolizes a shift away from identification with refugee or migrant status. Consider Tou Ger Xiong, a freelance dramatic artist and stand-up comedian. His use of rap to narrate and 'translate' Hmongness not only creates an identification with African-Americans, but posits Hmong as racial minority, rather than refugee. Tou Ger Xiong's message of Hmongness sounds like this:

> As you can see I'm Asian; yeah, I'm not black.
> What I'm about to say might sound like slack,
> But just lend me your ears, and hear me out,
> I've come to tell you what I'm all about.
> Yes my name is Tou, and I've come to say
> that I'm special, talented in many ways.
> Yes I know kung fu, and martial arts,
> You try to go get me, man I'll tear you apart.
> Yeah I'm bad, mean, and tough is my game.
> They call me the master; yes, it's my name.
> Well you might think it's weird, to see that I'm Asian,
>
> Bussing some rhymes on such an occasion.
> Well let me tell you, how I came to be,
> I was born in Laos in seventy-three.
> In my culture, we sing and dance,
> But I'm a style rapper, yeah I take my chance.
> Yo, even though this, is my first rap,
> You don't have to like it, and you don't have to clap.
> To those who listen, it might be nice,
> To see this Hmong boy, kickin' like Vanilla Ice (Xiong 1998).

This perception of racial minority resonates strongly with many young Hmong in the United States. No longer defining themselves as refugees, their performances at the 2002 Hmong National Development Conference Youth Forum in Milwaukee placed a wide range of popular cultural acts on display – from break dancing to poetry.

New 'alternative' journals also serve to deliver discordant voice. One of these, *Paj Ntaub Voice*, is subtitled *'A Journal Giving Expression to Hmoob[4] Voices'*. In the Winter 2001 edition entitled 'Silence' the Editor, Mai Neng Moua (a writer herself), states:

> When I think of silence, I hear my mother telling me not to ask so many questions, to not speak with so much passion with my hands and face or in the presence of older Hmoob men. I usually associate silence with powerlessness, punishment, and control...silence is also peace and quiet...
>
> The focus of this issue is silence. The point was to give voice to those who had not been heard before, to shed light on and talk about issues that have been pushed aside or hidden. This task...was in line with *Paj Ntaub Voice's* goals of encouraging Hmoob writers to write their own stories and create their own images of themselves...
>
> Writing and publishing for Hmoob writers are courageous acts... Moving from saying nothing to expression, to shouting and loudness takes courage. It is, to borrow bell hook's expression, an 'act of resistance' – of refusing to remain silent, or rejecting the stories and images others have created of us, of refusing to lie down and die quietly, of 'talking back' (2001: 4).

In a word, *Paj Ntaub Voice* creates a space for oppositional subjectivities to become visible; it serves as a tool for offering resistance.

Hmong resistance interpreted: through the filter of media theory

In his now-classic analysis of television discourse, Hall (1976/2002) identified three positions from which to decode media texts. The first is the *dominant-hegemonic* position, where the reader operates inside the dominant code, thereby interpreting the message as it is encoded. The second is the *negotiated position*, characterised by a mixture of adaptive and oppositional elements. Here the reader acknowledges the legitimacy of the hegemonic definitions but takes into account local conditions. The negotiated version of understanding reflects 'particular or situated logics ...their differential position...in the spectrum...(and) their differential and unequal relation to power.' (Hall 2002: 307). Negotiated versions of the dominant ideology are rife with contradictions although these are rarely fully visible. Finally, Hall's third position is *oppositional.* Here the reader recognizes the hegemonic encoding but is determined 'to decode the message in a globally contrary way'; that is, to recode the message within an alternative frame of reference. This is the most radical of the three positions and is extremely consequential for the politics of identity.

If we apply Hall's model to the meanings of Hmongness produced via the media in the diasporic public sphere, we can immediately see the political significance of the current moment in Hmong history. Since their dislocation from Laos and subsequent dispersal to various countries of resettlement, Hmong refugee women have been employing strategies of resistance to the dominant discourse of Hmong identity. Their new social locations required them to behave in ways that challenged 'traditional' versions of Hmong femininity – despite the global (re)articulation of such traditions, described above.

The result has been the emergence of alternative constructions of Hmong femininity (Julian, 1998) that challenge ideas of 'tradition' and 'authenticity.' Initially, these resistances reflected *negotiated positions.* The major sites of such response were the education system, the workplace, and public spaces such as roads and public conferences. In the case of these last two, negotiated resistance has taken the form of obtaining licenses to drive, which, in turn, has afforded women freedom from surveillance by Hmong men. So, too, have The Hmong National Development Conferences, initiated in 1995, also served as important sites for resistance. Hmong refugee women, educated in the United States, have dominated the planning and organization of these conferences and, in such a way, have located a strategy for presenting alternative versions of Hmong femininity. Importantly, however, these articulations have transpired within a frame that acknowledges the overall legitimacy of the hegemonic discourse.

Since the late 1990s new strategies of resistance have been emerging among second-generation Hmong-Americans. These strategies are much more radical, and reflect the adoption of *oppositional* positions. Such a stance is made explicit in the following excerpt from *Pan Ntaub Voice*:

It is disturbingly ironic that although Hmong means "free", the majority of us feel just the opposite, "trapped". How then, can we be Hmong? The truth is, how we lived in China, Laos, and Thailand cannot explain what we feel or justify who we are today in America. This discrepancy clearly confirms that we must redefine Hmong in the context of our contemporary issues (Cha 2001: 8).

The following poem published in the same journal expresses another young Hmong woman's oppositional positioning in relation to her Hmong identity.

> Everyday.
> Between personal and professional:
> The world does not consist
> Of Hmong issues alone.
> Even though they hit closer to home.
> There is no global, 'bigger' picture
> In the Hmong community.
> We're all struggling.
>
> It hurts to read the paper these days.
> Between individual, family and community
> Because I am a lone Hmong woman
> I'm appreciated more outside of the home.
> My individuality is validated.
> I'm expected to compete.
> Not for affection.
>
> While my sister waits to have
> A late night conversation with me,
> And the dishes lie dirty in the sink.
> Letters unanswered.
> One more meal with the relatives, missed.
>
> One less argument I get to hear.
>
> Between sinner and saint:
> The amorphous, ever-present double standard
> That slips unacknowledged to the back of our minds.
> The 'good Hmong girl' façade
> I will never be able to live up to

Believe me, I've tried.
For 18 years, I've tried.
And the label I now carry
In private, in jest...

Just another day. (Yang 2001:46).

Here, the hegemonic discourse of Hmongness 'naturalises' community as an essential component of Hmong identity. So, too, the family embodies aspects of that community, causing tension and conflict, which the author must oppose. Much of her subjectivity lies outside the Hmong 'community,' in a more global, professional, individually validating world.

The oppositional voices of Hmong women and the young are also being heard in other arenas such as theaters and art galleries. In Minneapolis, Minnesota, the new 'Theater Mu' has become an avenue for Hmong actors and Hmong plays, and in April 2002, an alternative art gallery held an exhibition of works by Hmong-American artists. Theater Mu's 2001–2002 program asserts

> (our outreach programs) combine the power and beauty of Asian music and dance with the immediacy of contemporary drama and culture. We have brought our unique perspective to schools, colleges, community organizations and corporations throughout the upper Midwest and as far afield as Alaska.

Oppositional voices in media have given vent to alternative interpretations of Hmongness, which, in turn, has exerted a powerful impact on cultural practices. This is exemplified by 'The Sounders,' a musical group whose first album, *Leej Twg Lub Paj Rose*, was released in 1994. In the first edition of the *Hmong American Journal*, journalist Pa Houa Lee explained:

> They are considered by many as one of the pioneers of modern Hmong music due to the music they have created. Before Sounders, most Hmong parties were conducted in a structured and orderly manner. Eligible young women would sit in chairs at the front of the audience. When each song begins (sic), the men would go up and find an available partner to dance with...
>
> Then came Sounders. With their non-traditional music, they have forever changed the way Hmong parties are conducted. Their music

demands new moves. Their music demands new ways of getting into and out of the dance floors quickly. For the first year or so, people were confused and wondered if they should adapt to this new music or if they should just ignore parties totally.

But then, Sounder's music became more and more enticing and before they knew it, all the front chairs disappeared and the ladies were no longer 'just available' for the convenience of men...

As time went on and people started catching up to Sounder's innovative music, new rules were made. Now everyone is just there (at the concert) to dance and party the night away...(2002: 36).

Figure 6.2 Two young Hmong-American artists, Ka Vang and Bryan Thao Worra, at an exhibition of 'new' Hmong-American art in St.Paul, Minnesota, April 2002.

In Sum

This brief analysis of the mediated public sphere has provided evidence of dissonant, resistant Hmong 'voices' that run counter to the hegemonic discourse identified earlier. In practice the multiplicity of voices, streaming through a variety of media, produce numerous *positionings* regarding 'Hmongness.' Unlike the hegemonic discourse that attempts to impose a unitary Hmong identity throughout the diaspora, counter-hegemonic discourses are marked by fragmentation and multiplicity. In this sense, the characteristics of the Hmong diaspora are not unlike those of *all* communities in late modernity, described as:

> hard work and uphill struggle...The foremost paradox of the frantic search for communal grounds of consensus is that it results in more dissipation and fragmentation, more heterogeneity...The only consensus likely to stand a chance of success is the acceptance of heterogeneity of dissensions (Bauman, as quoted in Slevin 2002: 151)

The media, the diasporic public sphere and Hmong identity

Since Hall's pioneering work, briefed above, a wealth of studies has examined the polysemic nature of communications and assayed the potential for multiple readings of media messages by audiences. While that strain has emphasized media *consumption,* this chapter has predominantly focussed on media *production.* In so doing, it acknowledges that the representation of a unitary global Hmong identity privileges the encoding practices of the elite and also recognizes the limits of resistance: that is, bounds on message consumers' capacity to counter dominant messages. At the same time, this chapter has not ceded the possibility of resistant readings. It has worked to identify in actual media productions an alternative strategy of resistance: the active, reflexive construction of new spaces for the expression of alternative (in this case hybrid and oppositional) meanings of Hmongness.

A review of the field of media studies reveals that 'treatments of diasporic identity have concentrated on issues of representation *by* mainstream media *of* ethnic and racial identities' (Sinclair and Cunningham 2000: 5). Such studies typically focus on the 'othering' of minority cultures and identities perpetrated in mainstream media. This chapter has offered a different view, focusing on how media has been used to actively construct a 'third space' (Bhaba 1994) within the diasporic public sphere. There, through the aegis of media, hybrid and oppositional identities can be articulated. In such a way, this chapter has revealed how specific cultural strategies have 'become active forms of resistance to domination and marginalisation' (Sinclair and Cunningham 2000: 9) – opposed to hegemonic definitions both within the diasporic public sphere and the wider public sphere.

Admittedly, at this point in time, there appears to be a relatively high degree of consensus as to the meaning of Hmong identity in the diaspora. This is predominantly a consequence of the limited range of those hitherto active in constructing this identity in the disaporic public sphere: namely the political elites. The major point of cleavage is based on gender, with women's voices less visible than those of men. However, as we have seen, the annual HND conferences, the Internet, arts, and popular culture have initiated a broadening in the scope and complexion of the diasporic public sphere. This is a reconfiguration that decentralizes control, enabling more people to speak *as Hmong*. As more and more young people become participants in this debate, the boundaries of the diasporic public sphere will continue to widen, due to their mobilization of new media. Such widening will inevitably lead to even further definitions of Hmongness, as well as deepening cleavages in the debate over what it means to be Hmong under conditions of contemporary globalization.

Ultimately, what I believe this means is that, for the Hmong, the diasporic public sphere will become Werbner's prototypical 'arena of argument and imaginative creativity' (1998: 12). As she explains:

> Diasporic unity is…to be understood in transcendental terms: as the product of shared foci of passionate debate rather then internal homogeneity and agreement; of intermittently agreed upon procedural strategies for joint mobilisation rather than centralised control, or, for that matter, external definitions of identity imposed upon diasporas by the state (1998: 12–13).

Viewing the messages flowing through Hmong media today, it is hard not to believe that such a day will soon be at hand.

Conclusion

This analysis of the Hmong diasporic public sphere suggests some key themes. First, the geographical 'center' of the Hmong diaspora is located in the United States, with its social center comprised of the political and military elite who escaped from Laos to the United States. This has resulted in the representation of a unitary global or diasporic Hmong identity emanating from Hmong-America that denies the existence of contestation and dissent. In turn, this hegemonic construct has produced inequalities in the Hmong diaspora and in the global politics of identity. Hmong on the periphery (including those outside the United States, as well as women, youth and poorer Hmong in the U.S.) have had a limited capacity to articulate Hmongness in the public sphere.

Second, this analysis has shown that, far from the hegemonic construct representing 'authentic' Hmongness, the meaning of Hmongness is subject to ongoing discursive struggle and negotiation among members of the diaspora. As argued initially by Gramsci (1971), hegemony involves a struggle between forms of domination and resistance. In the diasporic 'public sphere,' numerous 'topics' of contestation can be heard, including: the significance of clan structure, youthful marriages, cross-cultural marriages, polygamy and levirate, 'kidnap' marriages, women's education, and Hmong language for Hmong identity. All of these topics relate in some way to Hmong identity and the ways in which they are negotiated have significant implications for the meaning and performance of 'Hmongness' at both local and global levels. Importantly, the very fact of negotiation is likely to lead to variations in the practice of Hmongness in different local contexts.

Third, there is a gendered dimension to this debate. Since resistance often arises out of contradictions between lived experiences and hegemonic discourse, it is unsurprising to find that the spirit of dissonance emerged initially among Hmong women educated in the United States. These women began constructing sites (such as women's groups and the HND conferences) in which alternative versions of Hmong femininity could be *negotiated*. Doing so, they modelled strategies of resistance that were later adopted by Hmong youth (although still more prominently by women than men). Such voices have more recently adopted an explicitly *oppositional* stance, as they more assertively strive to redress visible inequalities within the Hmong diaspora. Following

Hall, this points to the political significance of the current moment in Hmong history and politics. It is likely that these contestations will increase in both number and complexity as they are cross-cut by differences of age, generation, class, religion, 'migrantness' and place.

Finally, it is important to recognise the heavy reliance on media in the construction of a diasporic public sphere. Initially the global characteristic of the diaspora was made possible not only by the existence of clan ties, but also the development of transnational communication technologies that linked distant spaces. Of late, however, new media such as the Internet have been introduced into the diasporic public sphere, 'opening up opportunities for new forms of human association' (Slevin 2002: 152) among the Hmong. Such technologies have provided a space for contestation and debate over identity. There have been greater opportunities for resistance and opposition to the narrative of Hmong as refugees and a stronger representation of alternative, counter-hegemonic representations of Hmong which might 'translate' the meaning of Hmongness. The importance of such sites is evident in the opening paragraph of a contribution to *Hnub Tshiab*, a Hmong women's publication:

> As I thought of this article, many of the issues I have faced as a single Hmong woman in her mid-twenties came to mind. Should I discuss the functional reasons why marriage is so important in the Hmong culture, especially for women? Or do I talk about the lack of eligible, older Hmong men? Better yet, should I complain about the attempts by my relatives to find me a good husband as if it were an unfortunate circumstance that I was single instead of a conscious choice? Thinking it over, though, I decided that all those questions boiled down to one fundamental truth – the Hmong community is still trying to learn how to treat the increasing number of Hmong women who, like me, are making the choice to stay single in their mid-twenties (Yang 2002: 1).

The steadily accreting articulation of such oppositional positionings is producing an increasingly 'noisy' diasporic public sphere; one in which contestation over the meaning of Hmongness is likely to increase. Slevin sees this tendency in communities generally, commenting that 'this process of "uncertainization" is one which is bound to continue and intensify in later modernity' (2002: 151). Whether voices from the social periphery – such as Hmong in America – or along the spatial periphery – such as Australia – will become increasingly audible may depend very much on the extent to which Hmong on the periphery can skilfully manipulate the 'new media' of the 21st century.

7 Japan's Mediated 'Global' Identities

Todd Joseph Miles Holden[1]

Three Japanese salarymen sit in a smoky bar after a long day of work. One man, in white collar, dark suit and loosened tie, wipes his hands and face with a moist towelette. He rants: 'All this talk about globalization, etcetera...but Japan is made a fool of by the world...Once and for all we have to speak out *gatsun.*'[2] *The man pushes his glasses atop his head.* 'If it were me, I would say it!' *He works the cloth vigorously over his face.* 'I'd say it, *gatsun.*' *The frame fades to black and white, then freezes. Superimposed over the man's image is personal data:* Itoh Masayuki, 37 years, corporate man. *Action resumes with Itoh throwing his towel down in disgust and declaring*: 'Because I'm that type!'

Cut to an extreme close-up of the yellow towelette – now lying on someone's knee. Panning back the camera reveals that the knee belongs to Bill Clinton – or, someone of surprising likeness. The American president is seated opposite salaryman Itoh in a room that looks very much like the Oval Office. Ringing the two men are translators, advisors and security guards. Flicking the towel off his leg, the president utters in his distinctive southern drawl: 'So! I'd like to hear your honest opinions...' *To the swell of spaghetti western showdown music Itoh gulps hard, stares vacantly at his interlocutor and tries to muster that suddenly elusive 'gatsun'.*

Whether it is true, as so many argue (cf. Barber 1995; Clammer 2002; Eriksen 1999; Irvine 1998; Kinnvall and Jonsson 2002), that identity is increasingly mediated by globalization, it is certainly correct that in Japan, discourse about globalization and identity are implicated in processes of mediation. These two elements may not always appear together – as they do in the television advertisement recounted above. Sometimes one arises as a consequence of the other; other times they appear independently. In advertising, sustained commentary on self, group and nation can be found (Holden 2000). To be sure, such '*adentity*' messages are not always engendered by globalization; at the same time, under current conditions, it is difficult *not* to encounter dimensions of 'globality' in *any* mediation of identity.

It is precisely this angle I wish to pursue here. Looking at an assortment of media – television, magazines and body adornments – we discover not only the panoply of forms through which identity discourse courses in contemporary Japan, but also specific ways in which the media carrying this discourse engage globalization. What emerges is recognition that despite (or often, because of) the presence of exogenous elements, identity discourse is largely a local affair. And this is likely true not only in Japan, but by extrapolation, elsewhere. After all, in a uniformly globalized world, would a loud-mouthed Indonesian or Malaysian salaryman who finally received the opportunity to speak his mind to the most powerful politician in the world, comport himself as worker Itoh did? Is it likely that Bill Clinton would have gotten the final say in South Korea? In Viet Nam? Or Australia? Would a salaryman even signify the never-catch-a-break, workaday stiff in India? Thailand? China?

What is uniform is this: in Japan, as elsewhere, identity is constructed via connection to exogenous referents – things outside national community, sub-groups, and individual actors – which help conjugate and crystallize it. The smoky pub defines the salaryman; his assertion of '*gatsun*' talk situates the people he represents historically; the American President modifies Japanese character. Also uniform is the fact that media is complicit in this process. It locates audiences, delivers content, and helps determine how that content will be received. It isn't only the kinds of media available, but the manner in which they communicate, that bear on the types of identity discourse and specific identifications streaming toward message recipients. In the case of the mediations considered here, while they often appear 'global' the identifications that result are heavily Japan-centered. Perhaps no different than media anywhere else in the world, they enable message recipients to engage in discourse with themselves, about themselves.

Globalization, media and identity

A basic framework

Twelve assumptions inform this analysis:
1 Globalization is a process involving 'time-space distanciation' (Giddens 1990; McLuhan 1964; McLuhan and Fiore 1967;

Robertson 1992). While earliest conceptions viewed it in economic (e.g. Wallerstein 1976) or political economic (e.g. Giddens 1990) terms, here globalization is seen as social and cultural.

2. It is also contextual (e.g. Appadurai 1990), with local regularities often resistant to macro forces (e.g. Santos 2002). Such localized phenomena – particularly in the cultural realm – bespeak global diversity as much as uniformity (e.g. Eades et al. 2000).

3. This contextuality owes to the various *careers* countries manifest vis-à-vis globalization. Rarely does a *career stage* mimic its precursors; nor do *career paths* resemble those of other nations.

4. Part and parcel of any global career is media: a core, though not exclusive, organizing element.

5. Global and local are implicated in identity discourse. Sometimes events or forces external to a context affect localized identity discourse; at other times, indigenous elements may operate outside the context and/or bear on (exo)local identity discourse.

6. Identity is understood interactively and institutionally. The former endorses Woodward's (1997: 1–2) view that identity is 'the interface between subjective positions and social and cultural situations (that) gives us an idea of who we are and of how we relate to others and to the world in which we live.' The latter champions Hall's (1996: 4) recognition that identity is 'produced within specific historical and institutional sites within specific discursive formations and practices, by specific enunciative strategies.'

7. 'Mediated identity' is different still. Both interactive and institutional, it involves:
   - significations,
   - conveyed through representations of sameness and difference,
   - by media, and
   - brought into relief by:
     (a) references to (socially constructed) group-based traits, and
     (b) the depiction of relationship(s) between individuals and/or groups.

8. Identity discourse can be understood as transpiring at 'levels' or zones by which people arrange themselves in 'social space'; these include the nation, group and individual.

9. Relatively independent of these zones of social configuration are the specific media through which identity discourse passes.

'Media' encompasses any means of communication – from *formal*, organized, institutional structures and devices (such as advertising, television, music, or cell phones), to *informal* systems of symbolization (such as slang, tattoos, body piercing, make-up and apparel).

10 Aside from the variegated *forms* through which identity discourse streams, is the *content*: the wide array of themes and ideas communicating identification.

11 Relatedly, within each medium (though, generally, the more formal, institutionalized and, hence, well developed ones), content often is packaged as genres, which are multiple, relatively hermetic, and often elaborate. Genres here include TV food shows, fashion magazines, body decoration and sports news.

12 *Effects* of this mediated discourse are multiple and diffuse and, therefore, often difficult to trace. Nonetheless, effects *do* exist.

Media and identity

In the opening chapter the intimate relationship between media and identity was briefed. We saw that various forms of communication serve as filter and vehicle for the 'narrative of the self' (Giddens 1991). Media's ability to alter situational geographies (Meyerowitz 1986) also affects the definition, expression and experience of self. Thus, for instance, a Japanese who has been constrained by environmental conditions – limited physical space, scarce resources, rigid hierarchy, rules of social deference – can, because of exposure to media, suddenly spy alternative, possible worlds: spaces where salarymen complain to American presidents and home-grown soccer players display individual flair and assertiveness on the European pitch. Such images can prompt the average media consumer to rethink what it means to be Japanese in contemporary society.

On the other hand, the representative 'tribe' member of the opening example – workaholic, salaryman Itoh – manifests stereotypical features of Japanese identity rooted in an earlier era: reluctance to utter innermost sentiments and an inability to take a firm public stand. This becomes obvious once Itoh is *de-placed*, suddenly face to face with *the* signifier of free-speaking opinion. In this way, 'true' local identity is communicated via contact with globality. The ad consumer is invited to rue, ridicule or reject that identification; yet such freedom doesn't alter the fact that the older version of identity has been highlighted as a feature of everyday existence.

This binary character of contemporary identity discourse – of old versus new, local versus global – not only pervades the social construction of *adentity*; due to the transcultural nature of contemporary mediation (Lull 1995), equally complex, globally-conjugated, local identifications crop up in countless media products. Before demonstrating this (and to better appreciate it), let's briefly consider some background features of Japan: its globalization 'career,' media milieu, and identity profile.

Japan and globalization

There is a tendency to see Japan's encounters with globalization from an 'outside-in' perspective – perceiving an isolated nation that either: has remained relatively intact despite encounters with exogenous values and practices (i.e. Gibney 1975:12; Reischauer 1972:8), or else is 'becoming a synthesis that is equal parts Japanese and Western, or even more Western than Japanese.' (Halloran 1985: xix). Another approach is to view Japan's globalization 'inside-out.' Focusing on diaspora, Befu (2000) identifies three distinct eras: from the 15th to 17th century; the mid-19th century through 1945; and the period following the Pacific War. The first was populated by pirates and traders; the second given over to colonizers; the last, most active, period has featured eight types of outward population flow, notably 'war brides,' international marriages, multinational business expatriates, infrastructure service providers, and the excluded, neglected or social drop-outs.[3]

The 'careers' of globalization

Viewing this history one can appreciate that every nation's globalization 'signature' will differ. Matched up with the global career of another country – say, the Philippines or South Korea or Australia – Japan possesses its own unique profile. This is attributable to its ethnic composition, cultural history, religious practices, technological development, political structure, economic system, and resource mix. Important, too, has been its history of global inflow and outflow, and the 'sectors' (i.e. economic, political, social, cultural and moral) engaged by such transcultural flow. In short, there are distinct local 'careers' to globalization – the result of encounters between local and global for any given analytic unit (whether region, nation state, context, or human group). More, such careers are comprised of various 'stages,' meaning that the local globalization footprint for each of those units may differ from the imprimatur of previous eras.

Applied to Japan, globalization may have originally been predominantly political, then economic and cultural, but by the latter 20th century, the stage of its global career was almost entirely economic. The current stage, heavily oriented toward '*sport export/media reimport*' (Holden forthcoming), is both cultural and moral. This transcultural process is unrelated to national aggression or political-economic policy, as was true of sports such as cricket or squash that passed between nations as a result of colonialism. Rather, Japan's current stage is tied to exogenous economic activity at the supra and sub-national levels; the result has been a diaspora of the domestic workforce (and, parasitically, an inflow of ideas and practices from outside). Other stages will certainly follow.

Far from simplistic reduction to mere trade, military aggression, or societal occupation and reconstruction, Japan's global career is more dynamic, robust, and complex than past theorization would have it.

Japan's media milieu

Castells (1996) has claimed that in urban societies media consumption is the second largest category of activity (behind work). This is certainly true in Japan, where televisions often play soundlessly in offices, commuters listen to walkmans while reading or accessing the Internet, and pedestrians talk on their cell phones or thumb email. The two major forms of mass media – television and newspapers – are consumed by nearly the entire population. 95% watch TV daily: on average, three hours twenty-eight minutes (Kamimura, Ikoma and Nakano 2000); 86% read a daily newspaper.[4] Other media also generate impressive figures. For instance, in 2000 the total number of books printed was 1.42 billion, or about 11.2 books per Japanese citizen;[5] the totals for magazines are even more astonishing: 4.88 billion magazines were printed, or 38.4 magazines per person. Of this figure 22.2 were monthlies and 16.2 weeklies. The number of titles was 4,533, comprised of 2,856 monthlies and 1,677 weeklies.[6]

In terms of time invested, a 1997 study revealed that, combined, radio, comics, books, magazines, newspapers, videotapes and CDs yield a daily average of one hour and 21 minutes. A recent NHK survey (Kamimura and Ida 2002) has determined that the general population devotes 10 minutes to mobile phone use and 5 minutes to Internet each day – figures about on a par with videos and CDs, respectively. To the casual observer, though, this figure seems grossly underreported: as every street, coffee shop, train, passing car, even health club treadmill teem with people operating mobile phones.

In fact, with a 75% ownership rate of Internet-enabled cell phones, Japan is among the world's most 'wired' nations. These devices serve as the platform of preference for email and rudimentary web tasks, such as downloading news, recipes, or weather reports.[7] Most importantly, for particular gender, generational, occupational and behavioral cohorts,[8] they are a fertile medium for identity discourse.[9]

Japanese identity

Following the Pacific War the commonly held perception of Japanese identity was a population that was unified, relatively uniform, and distinct from other peoples of the world (Befu 2001).

It wasn't just foreign analysts who spoke of '*ware ware Nihonjin*' (we Japanese); Japanese scholars contributed mightily to this so-called '*nihonjinron*' (theory of Japanese uniqueness).[10] In recent decades consensus has crumbled (Lebra and Lebra 1986). Moeur and Sugimoto (1986), who helped lead this challenge, counter that 'the Japanese have rather developed, though different, concepts of privacy and the self...a close look at Japanese society will reveal healthy expressions of self-interest, non-conformity and the differentiation of one individual from another.' (1986: 210). It is now fashionable to assert that the once-prevalent identity discourse was merely a 'myth of Japanese uniqueness' (Dale 1986).

The truth, though, probably lies somewhere in between. Signs of collective identification are pervasive in contemporary Japan – the most prominent markers being uniforms (during school years), suits (for salaried workers), smocks (for housewives), and hair coloring and body piercing (for those outside traditional institutional and organizational structures). Still; identity is rarely rigidly fixed and statements of individual difference can easily be located. Even within traditional contexts – where constituents are compelled to don uniforms – differentiation transpires via accessories such as buttons, pins, shoelaces and bows. In Holden's (1994: 218) words, tokens serve as 'discreet statements of difference for those wishing to be considered as discrete statements.'[11] McVeigh (2003), discerning copious evidence of such expression among the college-aged, labels it 'personalized individualization.'

Mediated Japanese identity: three levels, three cases

Having briefed Japan's global career, its media milieu and constituent identity, let's explore three contemporary cases of mediated discourse. The first is food on Japanese television; the second, '*gyaru*' fashion as depicted in mass-circulation magazines; the third, 'street lifestyle' communicated through body adornment. By design, these cases point up connections between identity discourse and nation, interest group, and individual, respectively.

Let's also refer back to Hall (1996: 4), recognizing that each of these mediations:
- is historically situated (born of activities past, sustained by practices present);
- fits within an institutional site (communications generally tied to the economy);
- operates within specific discursive formations (for instance, nation, sub-group, and self);
- serves as a statement of affiliation, marked by clear practices, involving specific strategies (that are unique to each medium but also to each identity-context or identification-group).

What this analysis will reveal is the contextually contingent nature of identity in contemporary Japan.

Television food shows

Food is not a trifling matter on Japanese television. Aired year-round and positioned on every channel in every time period throughout the broadcast day, food discourse works (both in isolation and as a unity) to reproduce traditional Japanese cuisine and cultural mores, educating viewers about regional customs and history. Food talk is insular, exclusionary, reproductive, and, therefore, serves as a powerful pull toward 'the local,' reinforcing cultural nationalism.[12] This differs from a country like America, which has no 'national food' – rather a collection of ethnic and regional cuisines helping to balkanize identity. By contrast, Japan's culinary culture – though diverse – emerges through the unending stream of television segments as a seamless cloth. The ingredients, utensils, vernacular, and approaches are similar enough to form a unity. At the same time, food shows are 'internationalizers': they document the 'peculiar' practices of far-away countries, exposing viewers to ideas, words, people and ways of life beyond Japan's borders. In such a way, these shows assist in integrating outside influences and lifestyles into Japan, as well as differentiating indigenous from exogenous. The effect is construction of a singular national identity.

Although TV shows devoted primarily on food comprise only 5% of the programming between 6 a.m. and 6 p.m.,[13] by other measures food discourse is much more extensive. A 2001 sampling of one month's television commercials determined that food accounted for 20% of all ads broadcast (681 of 3,656) – second-most among ad categories.[14] Further, when categorized, *cooking with guests* and *food as entertainment* average 2 hours each per day, while non-cooking shows (*talk, variety*; and *travel*) constantly feature food.

Inadvertent discourse

In short, delimiting food-talk to food-only categories does not reflect the extensive presence of food on TV. A bounty of what can be called 'inadvertent food discourse' – food that appears in quiz shows, dramas, news, or sporting events – exists. For instance, *Mezamashi Telebi* ('Alarm Clock Television' – akin to America's *Today Show*) – features daily segments on rural activities and urban trends. And though neither exclusively emphasizes food, such discourse invariably appears. A locality's specialty is introduced – along with the people and methods involved in growing, catching, preparing, selling or eating it; culinary currents are reported – the desserts, health foods, breads, pastas and vitamin drinks that city residents are consuming. The effect is a bipolar 'global' discourse – local paired with national; rural with urban; domestic with foreign.

In fact, scores of examples can be marshalled, collectively demonstrating the extent to which food serves as a standard

communication trope on Japanese TV, irrespective of genre. Consider:
- May 9, 2001, during the late night period. *Binbaba*, an entertainment show with singing and light talk, ran a segment in which guests and staff sampled exotic foods, such as toasted scorpions. Following that, *Tonight 2*, an adult infotainment show sent two reporters to Nagoya to sample parfaits, fried rice and Italian food. They introduced a local dessert shop, a bistro, and brought ice cream back to the (Tokyo) studio for on-air sampling.
- May 25, 2002, *NHK's 7:00 p.m. News*. A visit by the Slovenian soccer team to an elementary school in the small Japanese city hosting them during the World Cup was reported. The story emphasized that Slovenian food was on the lunch menu for the week and showed players dining with students. That same evening, all four networks sent their sports reporters to introduce (and sample) the eleven-course meal that would be offered to VIP ticket holders at the up-coming World Cup event.
- February 20, 2003, *Foreign Food Ingredients*. This late night talk show hosted by a famous comedian, featured a 28 year-old former 'office lady' who went to Germany for a three-year apprenticeship as pastry-maker in a small town. Her dream, she confessed, was 'to open a shop back home in Japan with her mother.' Viewers observed her grueling routine: pre-dawn rise, interactions with the German chef and his staff ('because of the language I'm always one step slow'), baking miscues, and life in her one-room apartment. Presented with gifts from home – instant noodles and fermented soybeans – she broke down in tears; 'I love this stuff, but I can't eat it: it would be a waste if I did.'

As this anecdotal evidence makes clear, it is not only food on display. Behind the denotation lies secondary connotation: discourse about individual, local and national identity. This is true, too, of long-running shows such as '*Zumu-in Asa*' (Zoom-in Morning) or '*Letsu! Okusama Hiken*' (Allow us! Wife Must See). In the former, regional reporters stationed throughout Japan introduce the cuisine in their particular local 'beat.' In the latter, a reporter strolls through a neighborhood, knocking on doors, inviting himself in, showing the TV audience what is on tonight's dinner menu. Like the *Mezamashi Telebi* morning reports, these 'peeks inside' enable Japanese from around the country to observe how others live; it also binds the nation into one local community. Food serves the mediative function; effectually, it is socializer, educator, comparative, unifier.

In the same way, reports about Japanese food in the world, or the reverse – world food, itself – serve as peeks outside, thereby clarifying local identity, while at the same time rendering the 'global' less foreign. Consider a weekly Saturday evening show about Japanese lives around the world. In successive weeks in February 2003, a sushi chef operating a restaurant in Los Angeles and an actor working in England were featured. The audience observed the former training his American staff, shopping in the wholesale market, interacting with his American customers, and going through daily paces with his wife and Americanized children. As for the latter, it wasn't only rehearsals and performances, but also the pub fare – such as baked beans on toast – that was introduced to viewers. Additionally, this foreign 'delicacy' was sampled by in-studio guests. Similarly, a December 2002 evening sportscast featured an extended segment on the 'World's Toughest Firefighter Competition' in New Zealand. In addition to footage of firefighters dragging a 90 kilogram dummy 100 meters and ascending seven stories in full gear, the cooking competition between fire department chefs was covered. The report detailed how chefs from around the world prepared food, what it tasted like, and who was adjudged the victor.

Regular programming
The above examples underscore the prominence of inadvertent food discourse in Japanese TV. And because of television's ubiquity and reproductive power, such continuous recurrence unquestionably mediates the global identity of Japanese viewers. However, when it comes to regular programming, the quintessential show inscribing identity discourse has to be *Douchi!? no ryori syou* (Which One!? Cooking Show).[15] In this Thursday evening 'golden hour' show, two dishes are placed in competition for the favor of seven celebrity guests. Co-hosts serve as hawkers for the opposing foods, trying to sway guests to their side. Rival chefs prepare the foods in the studio and infotainment segments introduce the audience to various ingredients. During these segments, the localities furnishing these ingredients are detailed – including ways of life, histories and residents' values.

One of *Dochi*'s tendencies is to pit a foreign food – such as spaghetti with meatballs – against a comparable indigenized one – say, *tarako* (spicy fish roe) spaghetti. The local food almost always prevails. One week it is *won ton* soup (Asian fare) besting minestrone (the Italian import); the next week it is California roll (a sushi hybrid) prevailing over a clubhouse sandwich. A constant message is that Japanese or Japan*ized*) food is distinct, special, irreplaceable, and generally unbeatable. So, too, does *Dochi* reinforce the pull of national identity in its selection and use of panelists. In the cases where foreign guests appear (a French Canadian raised in Japan or a Hong Kong singer now based in Japan), they invariably choose the local item – their reasons varying from 'my own nation's food seems so plain' or 'when I thought about it, the Japanese food was just too enticing.' When ice cream was recently pitted against rice cake topped with sweet bean paste the American who has lived in Japan for over two decades led the 5 to 2 charge toward the indigenous dessert. His explanation ('it reminded me of the sweets I had when I first came to Hokkaido!') is but a variation on the claim often uttered by Japanese panelists: 'you can't beat home-cooking.'

Commercials
Advertising is no less fertile a source for national identity (Holden 1999b). Most apparent are the corporate logos that mimic the national flag. Beyond this, though, ad text often employs food to symbolize nation, as for example the ad in which a man cracks open an egg in his kitchen, only to find himself transported onto a tennis court, facing a powerful foreign player. After this rival delivers an ace – and glares tauntingly – the bewildered Japanese pulls off his glasses, sets his jaw, then smashes an exceptional return with the only tool at his disposal: his frying pan. The next frame shows an egg sizzling in the pan – icon for the Japanese flag – a signification (in this particular context) for a Japan that can improvise and overcome foreign rivals.

In Sum
What food mediations provide the nation is a discourse about itself. The controlled exposure to 'cultures beyond' Japan's borders can have the effect of inoculating viewers against too much foreign intrusion. It can cauterize the local with the global flame, providing a more impregnable version of indigenous identity. It is not the case

that this smorgasbord of food discourse works exclusively to nurture *nihonjinron*. Surely, the widespread reproduction of traditional Japanese cuisine and cultural mores, the education about regional customs and history, *can* contribute a certain measure of belief about the uniqueness of Japanese culture. At the same time, though, food talk assists the integration of outside influences and lifestyles into Japanese society – limited though that may be. As such, a society member's 'cultural stock of knowledge' (Berger and Luckmann 1966) is bolstered and identity is more than simply reproduced. It is quite possibly reformulated – though this may be in less visible, incremental, indigenized ways.

Lifestyle magazines

Compared to many fellow Asians, Japanese are awash in media options – with upwards of 2,800 weekly magazine titles, alone, to choose from. Many of these sources directly address themes of identity – lending weight to Hall's (1996) assertion that under conditions of advanced modernity identity representations are proliferating. Certainly in the area of fashion an array of magazine types abound, tailored to specific gender and age groups, and lifestyles. According to publisher's websites and research center publications,[16] female fashion magazines separate into the following age and occupational groups: high school, junior and technical college, university, later-twenties/OL,[17] and housewives. Here I focus on the first two groups – a 'class' comprised of 16 to 20 year-olds – for whom 18 magazines exist, with aggregate circulation figures of 43,470,000 per issue.[18] The class possesses its own sub-groups – characterized by particular styles of dress, owing to specific social circumstances – each of which constitutes a distinct discursive formation.

The collective considered here are those adopting the '*gyaru*' (gal) look. One reason they are noteworthy is because their look is widely distributed: *Cawaii!* (Cute!) boasts the fourth largest circulation in this teen cohort, at 350,000.[19] A second reason is that such widespread communication of what amounts to a minority lifestyle underscores how far-ranging (and, thereby, developed) identity discourse has become in contemporary Japanese media. In this way, we apprehend the extent to which group identity has been built into the economy and operates as a central feature of the (popular) cultural system.

Background

The etiology of the *gyaru* lifestyle is fuzzy, though it appears to have derived in roughly equal measure from the *kogal* trend of the early 1990s (where young women aspired to 'cute') and the *ganguro* trend of the late '90s (where women sought a coarser image). In *Cawaii!* These twin strands are reflected in *kirekawa* (a fused word meaning 'pretty/cute') and *dabokawa* (a neologism denoting 'big/cute'). In the case of the former, the derivation is the overly youthful high school look; in the latter, the loose, rougher style of '*B-kei*' (or 'black type').

In both of these threads, one finds elements of globalization. For instance, the *kogal* took the indigenous high school uniform and modified it with elements alien to the hermetic school culture: waist bands rolled so high that sweaters fell below hemlines, socks worn 'loose', locks tinting and permed in violation of school codes, bodies accessorized with piercings, and ungainly platform boots. *Ganguro*, by contrast, bore fingerprints of import. Its origins are often traced to Amuro Namie – a dark-skinned pop diva hailing from Okinawa – and Naomi Campbell – the popular black supermodel from the west. One sub-type of *ganguro* hitting closer to home was *yamamba* – the name for a hideous mythological mountain witch. Contemporary urban *yamamba* tanned or painted their faces brown, colored their lips white, caked rings of white shadow around their eyes, and dyed their hair white. Fittingly, *ganguro*'s etiology is said to derive from the vulgar onomatopoetic word '*gan-gan*' (meaning 'fucking') and '*kuro*' ('black').[20]

While *ganguro* has receded as a widespread look, it persists. One reason is that it wasn't only a fashion trend; but a *space of identity* for an entire class. While a Japan MTV director derisively avers '(*ganguro gyarus*) are another culture completely,'[21] a social analyst positively asserts '*ganguro*...has become a cultural identity and personal commitment,' (Talarowska-Kacprzak 2001). A powerful aid to persistence has been commercial media, which enabled *ganguro* to locate one another, express themselves, and become redirected once the trend subsided. *Cawaii!*, for instance, features spreads with models whose current look is contrasted with their *ganguro* candids from a couple years ago. Comments accompany the snapshots, such as: 'I was once a *ganguro*, but now that's old'; or 'when I view that panda style now, it's scary'; or 'I can't imagine walking down the street like that. Thinking about it now is embarrassing!' Self-identity is implicated in this comparison of past and present, with one model writing: 'as I look back at when I used the *ganguro* make-up (style), I feel like I was a child,' and another commenting: 'when I think of my past (look), I can see that my current self is "adult".'

In some ways, though, *Cawaii!* is akin to its fashion precursor. Like the *ganguro* movement, the magazine provides a means of identification, a space of belonging. Nearly every page teems with the word *'uchira'* (literally 'our gang'),[22] reinforcing the idea of a distinct tribe. One headline declares: 'Our gang's decision: Mijean's (a brand name) knits are Number 1!' Another proclaims: *'Mini-bottom* (hot pants/miniskirts) are our gang's uniform,' A third boasts: 'gathering attention is our gang's rule!'

Ganguro arose, in part, because of this cohort's marginality. Individually, demarcated by difference, *ganguro* were treated as outcasts; subjected to ridicule and scorn. *Ganguro*, themselves, admitted to feeling uncomfortable anywhere except with those of similar appearance and behavior. As one informant reported: 'I can fit in, in a normal way, when (I'm) with other girls with the same style. I don't feel out of place. I'm even approached by and able to talk normally with girls I've never met before.' (Nomura 2000). Reflecting on her *ganguro* past, one of the models in *Cawaii!* commented: 'maybe being *ganguro* was strange, but there was power there.' Other informants have suggested that *ganguro* offered a safe harbor; a port of last resort for lives that had run out of options (Waltrous 2000).

Creating a consumption community

The aphorism most often invoked to explain Japan's famous pressure to conform is 'the nail that sticks up gets pounded down.' Thus, most marginal or deviant groups in society – from the ethnic *ainu* to those of Korean ancestry to western-styled individualists – often face ridicule or censure. Fortuitously, the inequalities confronting *ganguro gyarus* were mitigated by the availability of commercial outlets whose aim was to unify the group into a consumption community. Fashion magazines such as *Egg*, *Ego*system*, and *Cawaii!* were created which communicated a coherent, meaningful, integrative discourse, first to *ganguro* and now to reformed *ganguro gyarus*. The discourse operates at two levels. First, it treats readers as a specialized community possessing their own set of values and practices – thereby socializing them into or else reinforcing the *gyaru* identity. At the same time, it seeks to educate the cohort into the ways of consumption – thereby linking them to the larger society beyond.

Examples of the former course through *Cawaii!* with 'leaders' (featured models approaching the 'graduation age' of twenty) speaking directly to readers. One cautions: 'be careful not to adopt too much of a male look!' Another admonishes: 'too much hip-hop is not good.' A third advises: 'If you wear boots, place the pants inside'; a fourth asserts: 'if you dress like this, you'll find it fashionable.' In such a way, the so-called 'Rules of Fashion' are explained to *gyaru* aspirants. 'Let's become pure in our look,' one leader exhorts. 'If you wear big bracelets, then others can see that you understand the trend,' another declares. Compared to originality, a departing leader reminds readers, 'following the trend is more important.' One caption intones: '(Girls), this is the "appeal" (request) you are sending out to the world.' Aggregated, such text inculcates *gyaru* identity; it enfolds readers into the *gyaru* clique.

In other media, identity is often communicated via juxtaposition and association.[23] For example, in one TV ad a Japanese woman bumps into an Indian man wearing a Pugree, thinks: 'curry!', then dashes home to consume it. For *Cawaii!* difference is also employed to reinforce *gyaru* identity. One page concerning make-up, contrasts the various approaches adopted by distinct groups – OLs, college students, and *gyarus* preferring the '*Harajiku* look.'[24] For the older OLs, a combination of money and knowledge determines their make-up approach; for college students it is a brown and gold look, combined with a hint of adulthood; and for young *Harajiku* women, it is a natural look that is both 'pop and cute.' By comparison, *Cawaii!* declares 'for our group – who like make-up and style – large expenditures are inevitable!' Here, then, is another hint of the magazine's role as nexus between sub-group and larger society, via consumption.

Theorizing *gyarus*

In reading *Cawaii!* outsiders cannot help but be struck by the verity that 'media continually visit social locations. (They) disclose…the private aspect of each identity group to us (which) was previously open only to its own members' (Uður 1996). Certainly, media like *Cawaii!* provide a glimpse into a prototypical 'secret society' (Simmel 1950: 362–375). Outsiders become privy to an enclave offering freedom to its members, while also affording dislocation from society. Of course, such identity spaces have received heavy criticism. Japanese analysts see them as encouraging pursuit of egoistic goals, which begets social disengagement, thereby producing collective dysfunction.[25]

Nevertheless, one might also say that for the *ganguro* girls, specialty magazines such as *Cawaii!* provide a secure social niche; a place in the social order where before there was none. Through mediation, subgroup identity has become a preserve, attracting people who normally occupy the margins of Japanese society, providing a protective space demarcated by common values and collective practices.[26] At the same time, the domestication of *ganguro* style into a hipper, stylish '*gyaru*' persona via magazines like *Cawaii!* has worked to develop greater acceptance for this identity group in the larger society.

Body adornment

Another fashion subculture worth discussing are aficionados of tattoo. Unlike the *ganguro* lifestyle, tattoo has an enduring presence – extending as far back in Japanese history as 500 B.C. Like *ganguro*, however, tattoo is viewed with disapproval, if not opprobrium. The major reason, according to Burton (2002), is that 'Chinese and Japanese...disapproved of...any puncturing of the skin as it disrespected their Confucian ideals of filial piety. One should not pierce the body given to you by your parents and so to tattoo somebody was necessarily to set them apart from the community.' For this reason, tattoos became the province of criminals and lower classes. Negative connotations persist even today, with a particular – Japanese – style (called '*irezumi*') associated with organized crime. Tellingly, the tattoos now fashionable with Japanese youth tend to be western in design – possibly signifying a rejection of the local and preference for the exogenous or 'global'.

Medium and audience

The current tattoo fashion is called *sutorēto kei tatū raifusutairu* (Street type tattoo lifestyle). While informants confess to furtiveness, embarrassment and stigma regarding their body designs (Burton 2002), tattoo has grown in popularity among a certain segment of the population. As of this writing, nearly 17,000 tattoo-related web sites are listed by Yahoo Japan. And at least two mass-circulation magazines cater to this community. *Tattoo Burst* (created in 1998) and *Tattoo Tribal* (born in 2002) are both published six times a year. According to *Burst*'s editors their target audience is 'hard core' tattoo lovers – neither beginners nor simple hobbyists – ranging in age from 18 to 60. The magazine's circulation is a modest 30,000 per issue and includes *irezumi*. *Tribal*, by contrast, refrains from depicting *irezumi* or the lifestyle associated with traditional Japanese tattoos. Its readership falls between age 20 and 30, with a 60:40 or 70:30 male/female split. Surprisingly, *Tribal*'s circulation approaches 100,000.

Cognizant of sales, both magazines try to feature famous people or events where tattoos figure in. Thus, for instance, *Burst* ran a special issue featuring Dragon Ash, a popular rock band whose members sport tattoos. Similarly, it covers *matsuri* – traditional festivals in which bearers of portable shrines strip to loin cloths – because many participants bear body paintings. In this way, the local, rather than the global, is reproduced. *Tribal*'s approach differs. While it features tattoos on real models and profiles designers, it also interviews people who have chosen adornment as a lifestyle. In this respect – and no different than the *gyaru* magazines – *Tribal* emphasizes sub-group identification. Additionally, its selection of designs and interviewees has the effect of placing the global over local. For instance, in a Winter 2002 edition, two snow-boarders were featured who acquired their tattoos during a competition in Canada.

Identity discourse: collective or individual?
Not unlike the *gyaru* magazines, tattoo publications are chock-full of palpable identity messages. For instance, a hot-rodder asserts: 'tattoos, are the same as cars: an expression of identity.' *Tribal* reinforces this idea with a section labeled 'ID Girls' – a soft-porn spread with a woman lounging in a China dress, displaying her shoulder, back and thigh tattoos. What *kind* of identity is this, though? When queried about his section title, *Tribal*'s editor stated 'I.D.' means that 'tattoos are akin to an identity card, rather than a statement of personal definition.' So, too, with the hot-rodder: tattoos, like the car and the club in which he belongs, serve as collective, rather than purely individualistic, identifications; they prove membership in a select group.

This is at odds with statements from other tattoo bearers – for instance, the graffiti artist who informs: 'the tattoo on my chest is of cherry blossoms falling. The message it communicates is for me to find my true inner self.' Another interviewee intones: 'my tattoo is a symbol of my (conscious) decision...when people say: "how can you do that to the body your parents gave you?" I reply: "it is *because* I received this body that I freely want to use it!" The tattoo exemplifies my free lifestyle.' In short, these bearers view tattoos as unique expressions of self.

One indicator that liberation and individuation are on the agenda is the language used in tattooing. Thumbing through *Tribal* or scanning samples on web pages, one is struck by the large number of designs carrying English inscriptions – signifiers in Japan for a freedom that can't easily be had in the indigenous realm. Among the many scripts observable: 'Memory of Father,' 'Love,' 'Delta,' 'Rancid,' 'My Families,' 'De Light,' 'Jesus Do,' 'Fantastic Days' and 'A BLIGHTLY SHINNING STAR FROM MY HEART' (sic).

But in determining why younger people tattoo or how they became initiated into the lifestyle, a less individualist portrait re-emerges. According to the assistant editor of *Burst*, 'such designs are for people interested in rockabilly – or else their friends or *sempai* (seniors) have tattoos.' Besides, she continued, 'it is not the general people (who have them). It is people who have no norms or exist outside barriers policing them.' In her cynical view '(tattooees) aren't free thinking or (they) lack resistance.' Some evidence of this can be found in one magazine interview where the bearer opined: 'I saw a kung fu movie, so I selected a dragon.' Another confessed: 'I first saw tattoo in a movie and thought: "that's cool!" After I got mine, a friend got his because of me.' Identifications, then, may have less to do with personal belief than social influence.

Tribal's editor (who sports a tattoo, himself) admits that collectivism may be at play, but argues that body adornment is a motivated activity and any number of influential factors exists. For instance, some seek to emulate their favorite singer who has a tattoo, often acquiring the identical design. Others select tattoos because they believe it is fashionable. This appears the case of one bearer who gushed, 'I saw an American pro wrestler with a tattoo when I was a junior high student and thought: "that is the image of a true man!".' Another confessed that because his uncle had *irezumi*, he'd always wanted a tattoo. *Tribal*'s editor suggested that some people tattoo because they love rap and tattoos are part of that lifestyle. Finally – and supportive of some of the evidence reviewed above – the editor asserted that many tattoos are selected as markers of selfhood. Tattoos commemorate birthdays, a job switch, or some major event in one's life. 'Rather than putting information like a girlfriend's name on their skin,' the editor asserted, 'users tend to select something more personal (about their lives).' To cite a couple of examples, one tatooee selected a gun for his lower back. To him it was a way of signifying that he would always defend himself. A fellow twenty-two year old selected the nickname his family and friends call him, 'in order to force myself to be honest – (true to myself) – at all times.'

Theorizing tattoo
At first blush the evidence suggests that this new, youth-oriented tattoo universe differs from its indigenous forebear. Unlike the *yakuza* world, which employs tattoo as a statement of collective identity, newer wearers appear to regard tattoos as statements of individual identity. However, while interviews suggest that tattoo-based identity representations are more authentic expressions of individuation than, for instance, *gyaru* fashion, tattoo magazines imply something not dissimilar. For, statements inscribed (often in English) on the page read like pleas to the congregation to keep the faith:
- 'I think everybody can understand about it'
- 'All sort of things will make your body rock,'
- 'We just need a good friends,it's call fire our friends,'
- 'It's no one else like me'

Further, picture after picture is posed not only to display adornment, but to invite readers to share in a highly stylized – even eroticized – presentation of self. Like the *gyaru* magazines, these identity expressions are neither rootless nor random; they fit within a clearly demarcated sub-culture with its own rules, meanings and social supports. Moreover, these representations operate to lock presenter and viewer in a relationship of significatory congress. Or, as Frith explains: 'one can never really express oneself "autonomously." Self-identity *is* cultural identity; claims to individual difference depend on audience appreciation, on shared performing, and narrative rules.' (1996: 125). This is true of the *gyaru* tribe seeking to interpret, realize, and express their identity via their media of choice (clothing and make-up). It is also true of all other forms of fashion – even individualist-seeming tattoo.

Globalizing society or hermetic nation?

While we must be cognizant of the insights of cultural studies – that 'meaning is not fixed but is produced through the interaction between text and the socially situated discourses of audiences' (Curran and Gurevitch 1991: 10) – as sociologists we must still inquire 'from above.' Globally, what does the flood of identity discourse flowing through Japan's contemporary media amount to? In a word, it bespeaks the preeminence of national identity.

Nation

One bias of the literature on globalization, Curran correctly observes, is a nearly uniform tendency to 'understate the extent of continuity with the past.' (2002: 182–3). The data reviewed in this chapter challenges this bias, suggesting profound continuity. Like many TV food shows, *Dochi* emphasizes nation via repeated attention to domestic and indigenized cuisine, regional practices and history. Aggregated, such shows serve as evidence that globality may be less transformative than generally suspected. TV discourse underscores Curran's (2002: 183) view that, in media, 'the nation is still a very important marker of difference.' Mediations as diverse as fashion magazines and skin art (with its cherry blossoms and gibberish English) confirm that – demonstrating that despite continuities with other contexts, 'nations have different languages, political systems, power structures, cultural traditions, economies, international links and histories (which) find continual expression in the media of different nation states.' (Curran ibid.).

Transculturation

Of course, it is not *all* nationally organized or oriented. *Gyaru* magazines may be part of a system of national production, distribution and consumption, but they are not tied exclusively to national values. The fact that *Cawaii!* publishes a Taiwanese edition is a good example of this. *Tattoo Tribal*'s intentional neglect of indigenous *irezumi* is another indicator. Moreover, tattoos, as currently understood and consumed, carry distinct marks of the other. Their scent is of an exogenous, global world.

These data are consistent with accounts of globalization that perceive culture as having 'overflowed its boundaries'. Such framings generally emphasize centuries of forced population transfers, diaspora, exile, technological proliferation, linguistic and religious diffusion, trade and war, among others. What has been less common is emphasis on mélange – as in the case of 'street-linked lifestyle' being appropriated and integrated into a local cultural rhythm. The case of tattoos – more so even than food shows – poses questions of hybridization. It also lends credence to Nedvereen Pieterse's (2002: 231) claim that 'a distinctive feature of contemporary times is that they are times of *accelerated mixing*. It is not mixing that is new, but the scope and speed of mixing' – a view consonant with the social theory (recounted in Chapter One) which has postulated media as a major expeditor of acceleration.

Resistance

Less common in globalization theory has been the voice of empowered localism – what Santos (2002) has dubbed 'counter hegemonic globalizations'. Such localized discourses of 'territorial cultures' (Hannerz 1992), may be the voices of 'the losers' or those under assault, but as Clammer (2002: 99) observes, globalization is paradoxical in that while it integrates at certain levels (such as the economic), it also affords room for difference at others. On this account, globalization provides not only the conditions for polysemy (e.g. Fiske 1989) or oppositional code reading (Hall 1980), it possibly even prefers the local, due to the harsh, stench-like odor of the global invader.

Clearly, this kind of dynamic is at work in food shows. Aggregated, the genre strongly communicates localized discourse. 'We Japanese' eat this sort of food – not simply because of the taste; rather due to the tradition, practices, and ways of life that under gird these food choices. This differs from foreign understandings, practices, and tastes – as becomes abundantly clear when the America-born, Japanese-naturalized, *sumo* grand master appears in his *yukata* (summer kimono) and selects spaghetti with meatballs, because 'it's what my momma always cooked for me.' At this level, little of the aberrant subaltern exists in identity discourse. It is a dominant cultural practice – front and center – writ nationwide: shared by all and resistant to external pressure to change.

The local nation

Historically Japan has been perceived as a 'quick borrowing and adaptation' country (Ozaki 1978: 29). From language to Confucianism to political and educational systems to pop culture, this propensity has been a central response to globality. Robertson (1997) reflects this view in his assertion that 'because of the indigenous nature of the concept of glocalization the Japanese are in a particularly strong position to identify themselves as genuinely global people, in a way which the Americans are not.' Nevertheless, as we have seen here, mediated identifications in contemporary Japan generally emphasize the local over the global, and even are preferred over the hybridized or indigenized. Exogenous food more often plays foil to Japanese cuisine; it is the '*kawaii*' school girl – not the western supermodel – look that is favored and reproduced; Japanese tattoo preferences, according to an American designer, differ from people of other countries. 'Japanese people want tattoos that are subdued: black and navy blue and quiet colors…And first timers want big tattoos – which is surprising. Whereas first-timers (from other countries) want small adornments on the shoulder and arms, Japanese first-timers want big designs on their backs.'[27] In all these cases local is quite distinct from global.

The future of mediated identity

These local differences – and the trends they intersect, influence and are expressed through – extend well beyond the realms we have explored here; into – for instance – popular music, Internet home pages, and news and sports reportage. This constitutes an empirical claim worthy of future attention. To offer one example, though, consider the daily attention accorded to 'sport exports' in newspapers, television morning and 'wide shows', evening news programs and advertising. The exports, themselves, constitute a discursive formation: highly visible and extensive – due to the involvement of the commercial media which seek to buy viewers by 'reimporting' information about them. This discourse serves to re/produce Japanese identity. As is common to much identity discourse, the exogenous (or global) is used to refract, modify and/ or solidify definitions of local (again, to attract or 'buy' viewers). Thus, daily attention is accorded to local lads (the discourse centers almost exclusively on men) performing 'overseas.' Each penalty kick, strikeout, assist and base hit carries the tone of national validation. Deliverance hangs in every newspaper headline, pride in every video highlight, replayed morning, noon, and night.

This emphasis on how Japanese are successfully competing in the larger world of sport carries a metaphoric power: it suggests Japan's place and efficacy in the world of nations. Beyond this (and in an ironic twist) these reports tend to cast the foreign as exotic – based on different customs, rules and practices, which can, nonetheless, be mastered. In such a way the global world is presented as no longer impenetrable or daunting for Japanese. Such sports reports merge with the torrent of other contemporary communications concerning identity – from newscasts to personal websites, billboards to neon displays, pop songs to loudspeakers mounted on nationalist-trucks cruising city streets. As viewed in the opening commercial, those statements of identity can poke fun; on the other hand, as the daily reports of sports exports suggest, they can buttress the foundation of national pride and achievement.

In this way, contemporary media not only orient Japanese to a globalizing world; they serve as conduit for communicating to Japanese their competence – even excellence – in the world beyond domestic borders. They assist Japanese in interpreting themselves. In the hands of today's media, in the age of globalization, for the Japanese, local is fine enough indeed.

8 The Social Meanings of Media for Indonesian Youth

Pam Nilan

Introduction

This chapter discusses media and identity in the current generation of Indonesian youth. It draws on data derived from eleven focus group interviews conducted with eighteen Hindus in Singaraja, North Bali, in October 1999, and nineteen Muslims and nine Christians in Makassar, South Sulawesi, in January 2002.[1] Interviewee ages ranged from 19 to 28. All were purposefully selected for tertiary education, community group membership, public speaking skills and strength of religious convictions – qualities deemed indicative of future leadership. During the course of the interviews they considered the impact of mass media on young Indonesians.[2] Although the two interview trials were conducted nearly two years apart, in different regions of Indonesia, and involved young people of different religious persuasions, the answers given were remarkably similar.

On these pages, interviewee comments on mass media effect are analysed in a broad discussion of the role of media in the formation of identities among contemporary Indonesian youth. It was found that Indonesian youth evaluate media as powerful, though most often in negative or equivocal terms. More importantly, though, what lies beneath their responses might be called 'competing identity discourses': tradition against modernity. Media pose a double bind for many Indonesian youth. On the one hand engagement with media possesses the power to shift Indonesian youth out of traditional frames of self-reference; on the other hand, without continued engagement with media and information technology, Indonesian youth perceive that the progress of their beloved nation may become ever more impeded. How Indonesia's youth manage their engagement with these competing identity discourses in the years to come may very well determine the future of the nation.

Indonesian youth and mediated modernity

In the following analysis participants' comments on media influence are not used as straightforward evidence of a direct link between media and identity, for a number of reasons. Firstly, the questions posed to the focus groups were not specifically couched in terms of identity or formulated with identity primarily in mind. Nonetheless, considerable identity discourse could be gleaned from informant responses – a factor impelling pursuit of this topic. Secondly, answers tended to be formulaic and negative. For the most part informants vigorously asserted the 'bad' effects of mass media, invoking pre-packaged discourses about media influence on young Asians. The media were said to:
- 'westernize' youth, turning them into mindless consumers of fashion and trends;
- persuade young people to abandon tradition and religion;
- encourage youth to become promiscuous, drink alcohol and take drugs;
- develop a taste for pornography and nudity;
- stimulate delinquency and criminality.

To those familiar with Indonesia, such comments are striking: they read as verbatim restatements of New Order propaganda.[3] Until 1998 messages about the pernicious effects of Western-influenced mass media were routinely broadcast and printed, reflecting the philosophy that public media should serve as a pedagogic tool for the development of nationalism, unity and passive citizenship (Sen and Hill 2000). Parker (2000) describes the New Order national education system as the paradigmatic instrument for the creation of Indonesian citizens. New Order propaganda was heavily promoted while these young people were growing up and, thus, some of the points listed above would have literally been learned by heart at school or university during Civics Education, Moral Education, Pancasila Studies or Religious Studies.[4]

However, as this chapter reveals, this is not the only way to read their responses. While clearly negative, a different impression about the informants' views on 'the West' and media influence is obtained by assessing other data from these interviews. In particular, what the respondents were wearing, how they behaved and some of the media products they were consuming. Before proceeding to that analysis, let's further consider the Indonesian context.

The milieu

Modernity and religion, development and tradition sit somewhat uneasily together in Indonesia, configured differently from region to region. The interviews recorded here reflect this complexity and unease. Indonesia has undergone a period of rapid social and political transformation which has seen the ascendency of a high-consuming middle-class, as well as a devastating societal-wide economic collapse in 1997/98, from which there has yet to be real recovery. Ethnic and religious tensions threaten stability, stoked by strong pressure from the IMF to fast-track reform. International radical Islamic terrorism is now a publicly-acknowledged part of the climate of unrest. However, even in 1999 the kind of tension that prompted strong calls for the imposition of Sha'ria (Islamic) Law in South Sulawesi (Pradadimara and Junedding 2002), and led to the eventual bombing of tourist nightclubs in Kuta, Bali on October 12, 2002, already existed. Under mounting pressure from all sides, the current government of Megawati Sukarnoputri cannot seem to satisfy anyone's interests and, as the world anxiously awaits resolution to the intractable problems in the Middle East, tensions in Indonesia have not eased. A major focus is anti-Westernism, rather than theological Islamic fundamentalism as such. The 'free' Indonesian press provides a unified anti-Western discourse, and religious leaders of all three major denominations reinforce this line. In the interviews moral concerns about the prospect of Western cultural hegemony eclipsing Indonesian culture and social values was expressed not only by Muslim respondents, but by Hindu and Christian youth. 'Mass media' are widely blamed, just as they have been since the 1960s (Romano 1999).

Media and identity

Though complex, the relationship between media and identity can best be understood as a two-way constitution of subjectivity. On the one hand, individuals bring both actual and potential identity

discourses to their moments of media engagement. For Indonesians, these discourses derive mostly from the following sources:
- ethno-locality
- tradition/religion
- modernity
- nationalism

Mass media, on the other hand, offer a hugely diverse range of discourses – some of which may bear on the identity discourses above, others which may not. Part of this determination lies in media form and content, both of which have the ability to confer salience to, and symbolic power upon, certain discourses, while suppressing others. At the same time, it is only through actual engagement by the individual, as an embodied subject, with the identity discourses transmitted by the media, that an effect constitutive of identity can possibly occur.

Along these lines, let's note: firstly, constitutive effect will generally not be confined to the level of the individual. Secondly, this is especially true in Indonesia where media reception is a group phenomenon. Thirdly, connection between locally existing identity discourses and technologically-mediated identity discourses can be either affirmative or oppositional. Finally, the media recipient reacts by deeming the media content: meaningful (informative or provocative), or else immaterial to local identity. Importantly, if there is little or no affinity between these identity discourses – no provocation between the two sets of discursive 'prompts' – then media content may be ignored. To offer an example, most Indonesian men completely ignore women's daytime television programs, even when the show plays in their presence.

Media and Indonesian identity

How do the media affect the identity of young people in Indonesia? Like Morley and Robins (1995: 44), we should reject any simplistic model where technology is seen as exerting impacts 'on a set of pre-given objects, national (or cultural) identities.' Indonesian people have engaged with forms of global media (broadly speaking) for a very long time. Furthermore, while young Indonesians comprise an age cohort, they are not homogenous. At the very least, the four identity discourses listed above mediate both individual and group experiences of media. Liechty has captured this verity well when he argues: 'identity refers to a person's sense of inclusion in (or exclusion from) a range of social roles and ways of being, both 'real' (those derived from lived experience) and 'imagined' (those encountered in realms beyond the everyday: tales, religious epics, *mass media* etc.)' (1995: 167; emphasis added).

Despite the propagandistic approach embodied in New Order communications and the 'free' Indonesian press, mass media do not usually preach at, or even speak directly to people in the evocation of discourse. More often they address consumers indirectly, by representation. Yet media representations encode particularly powerful identity messages, operating as they do through embodiment, voice (including written media), and acts which directly appeal to emotions and moral values. It has been argued that media consumers 'cruise' texts such as media products, constantly seeking representations through which they might reconstitute fragile subjectivity as stable and strong (Barthes 1977). Through the appropriation of offered discourses, media 'play a pivotal role in organizing the images and discourses through which people make sense of the world' (Golding and Murdock 1996: 11), and make sense of their own identity.

This is precisely what the data reported here reveal. Above all: Indonesian youth actively engage with media. They participate in a reflexive process of meaning-making in interaction with media. Specifically, certain media messages *are* remembered; and youth tend to talk about communications that confirm or deny their significant identity discourses. Thus we can say that mass media are active in the re-constitution and re-invigoration of identity discourses in society, and may contribute to the production of new identity discourses – a major cause of concern to upholders of tradition.

Indonesian identity and globalization

In a globalized media world, diverse populations engage with a constant flow of images and messages which may be remote from their personal experience. As Leichty (1995: 167) puts it 'identity formation occurs within communities, but in the late twentieth century the factors that shape identities increasingly transcend the boundaries of locale.' Often these global media products challenge the moral foundations of strong local identities, and provoke a reaction. For example, *Friends*, a Hollywood sitcom, flopped in Indonesia, but *Xena*, a US-produced television series about a mythical warrior princess, remains popular. To understand why, we may need to look at cultural 'fit' between media discourses and local identity frames. *Xena* is not unlike the Hong Kong martial arts movies so popular throughout Asia. The widespread consumption of such media productions almost certainly stems from their overlap with Asian traditional/supernatural epic narrative genres. They are simple moral tales in which good battles evil, with fighting aplenty, heroism, special effects, magic, and transformation. By contrast, *Friends* depicts the casual urban cohabitation of mixed sex age peers, a scenario that can only fail to strike chords of affinity in a country where Islam is the majority religion, premarital sex is rarely openly discussed, and family and *adat* (tradition) are the pre-emptive defining discourses of people's non-working lives.

Beyond television, the relentless flow of globally distributed media products that come to roost in Indonesia unquestionably impacts on the choice of youth leisure activities. Thus fashion trends, listening to popular music, engaging in and watching sport, playing electronic games, and reading romance novels and magazines[5] are among the exogenous cultural activities commonly undertaken. Transnational media advertising drives the purchase of brand-name icons of global youth culture: music, clothes, shoes, jargon, food and drink (Ainger 2001: 10; Klein 2000). At the same time, global media provide a pedagogic service: young people in Indonesia are able to engage with events, and learn about worlds – real and imaginary – that extend beyond the sphere of their everyday lives (Thompson 1995), as well as their 'possible lives' (Appadurai 1990:9).

The cultural contradictions of modernity

Are such trends disruptive of normative identity frames? Not necessarily. The young Indonesians in my sample were highly critical of 'mass media' influence, speaking often as defenders of culture and tradition. Mimicking the state propaganda which continues to depict the ideal citizen as both modern and traditional at once, my informants identified Western visual media – television and films – as their primary target. Nevertheless, while articulating this discourse, they also wore clothing and carried items which indicated they actively followed global popular cultural youth trends. All interviewees adopted the demeanor of urban dwellers, dressing in fashionable (often brand name) clothing and shoes; their speech peppered with English expressions and trendy Jakarta youth slang *(bahasa prokem)*. This was true even for the six veiled Muslim women who agreed to be interviewed.[6] By their own account, all the young people interviewed went shopping in the mall and sometimes ate Western-style fast food. Some carried mobile phones and portable CD players. Unsurprisingly, it appeared that they wanted the best of both worlds. Rather than hypocritical, this appeared a good example of Appadurai's (1990) 'disjuncture'. Local identities are not fixed and linear, but constructed by habitus as largely self-defining constitutions of self (Robinson 2002: 159). In the non-western context, the cultural constitution of self – the defining of identity – largely occurs through the iteration of difference, through distinctions with and oppositions to Western culture. 'Difference is constitutive of identity,' Morley and Robins (1995: 45) write. But for the majority of Indonesian youth this does not mean a lack of familiarity with Western things. Indeed, quite the opposite.

Local youth identities are embedded in economic and political relations that in themselves embody contradiction. Perhaps the gap between what the focus group interviewees say (discourse) and what they do (enactment) is an instance of what Bhabha (1990) has theorized: the contrast between the *pedagogical* and the *performative*. By the former he intends the homogenous, horizontal version of modernity expressed as an articulation which joins people together in a single nationalist discourse; by the latter he means those taken-for-granted acts of everyday life through which the 'nation' is actually represented (Bhabha 1990: 297). It is in the performative that we see the greatest evidence of disjuncture and contradiction. It is also possible though that, in this apparent disjuncture, we are catching glimpses of something altogether different: the emergence of the late modern entrepreneurial individual described by Beck (2000); a person who deals with risk by adjusting public identity signifiers in a manner capable of signalling prosperity and promise (Nilan 2001: 5).

Views of media effect

Up to this point I have spoken generally about the local context, identity discourse, and youth attitudes toward mass media under conditions of globalization. In this section I wish to explore attitudes about media effect in greater detail. Table 8.1 summarizes the data concerning perceptions of effect for all 46 respondents.

Table 8.1: Perceptions of media effect

[Responses to the Questions: 'What is the influence of the mass media and electronic media on Indonesia?'; 'What is the effect (of mass and electronic media) on young people?']

Focus Group		Positive Effect	Negative Effect	Undecided/Both
BaliFG1	(Hindu)	2 [1fH][1mH]	1 [1fH]	1 [1mH]
BaliFG2	(Hindu)	0	2 [1fH][1mH]	2 [1fH][1mH]
BaliFG3	(Hindu)	0	2 [2fH]	3 [1fH][2mH]
BaliFG4	(Hindu)	0	3 [1fH][2mH]	2 [1fH][1mH]
SulawesiFG1	(Muslim)	1 [1fM]	3 [1fM][2mM]	0
SulawesiFG2	(Muslim)	1 [1mM]	2 [2fM]	1 [1mM]
SulawesiFG3	(Muslim & Christian)	1 [1fC]	3 [1mC][2mM]	0
SulawesiFG4	(Christian)	2 [2fC]	1 [1mC]	1 [1mC]
SulawesiFG5	(Christian)	0	2 [2mC]	1 [1mC]
SulawesiFG6	(Muslim)	0	0	5 [3fM][2mM]
SulawesiFG7	(Muslim)	0	3 [1fM][2mM]	1 [1fM]
Total		7	22	17

m = male f = female H = Hindu M = Muslim C = Christian

General overview

In both Bali and Sulawesi informants emphasizing negative effects of media and technology (N = 22) far outnumbered those who spoke primarily of positive effects (N = 7). In between, seventeen speakers evaluated the positive and negative equally. Typical of these latter cases was the following:

> Mass media can sway public opinion. It depends on the audience and which media are used as the source. Different media represent different interests. If it is in the interests of the media to encourage young people to learn then the effect will be positive. But if a media interest sets out to corrupt young people then the effect will be bad (Sili-Suli, Sulawesi, FG4, [m] [C]).[7]

Television

In the focus groups, speakers appeared to instantly assume that the question about media influence concerned television. For example Rudi said:

> When teenagers see a new hair style on TV, they immediately imitate the style, no matter if it suits them or not. They feel that it must be good because it's just like what they saw on TV (Rudi, Sulawesi, FG5, [m] [C]).

Such a statement reminds us of Barker's (1999: 3) assertion that television is the major source of global cultural capital. So, too, has Lent (1995: 3) claimed that in Asia 'the most significant carrier of Western popular culture is television.' In his study of Indian television, Johnson (2001:152) found that the medium's influence on youth was most noticeable in 'their approach to clothes, their concepts of beauty and their commitment to modern lifestyles' – elements present in the focus group data reported here.

In Indonesia since the time of Suharto saturation advertising of Western-style products has been allowed under local licence. The same has been true in neighboring Malaysia, with the aim of facilitating rapid domestic economic growth through consumerism (Holden 2001: 281). In both these predominantly Muslim countries this consumer-stimulus tactic has stood alongside strident media propaganda about the superiority of 'Asian values' – self-sacrifice and collectivism – over 'Western values' – personal satisfaction and individualism (Holden 2001: 283). What is most striking in the focus group data is that it is this same Asia-centric, nationalistic discourse that so flavoured the negative responses.

The positive view

Most talk about media effects, then, was gloomy, tending to characterize the young person as the passive subject of modernity. Indicative was the comment by Firman, a male Muslim from Sulawesi: 'since youth imitate the behaviour of westerners, they become just like them.' Still, not all comments were negative. Media was occasionally viewed in a positive light, for example: 'All parts of the world can be easily accessed. This will improve and broaden the knowledge and perceptions of Balinese teenagers.' (Daranya, Bali, FG1, [m] [H]).

Generally, those offering positive evaluations ascribed youth greater agency. This 'active consumer' position is exemplified by the following comments:

> We can learn something from a TV series. TV series nowadays mostly feature a glamorous life style and this can motivate us. As teenagers, we might have a fantasy of becoming like them, so if we look at the positive

effect of the series we will be motivated to study hard in order to be successful people (Hazairin, Sulawesi, FG2, [m] [M]).

The positive position on media must be viewed against the general backdrop of contemporary Indonesia. Above all, it is a society at 'risk' (Beck 1992, 1999, 2000), under conditions Castells (1997) has called the 'global/informational economy.' For each of these theorists, a new world order is characterized by greater corporatization, as well as rapidly fragmenting nation states. Beck maintains (1999: 83) the state, through its administrative and political institutions, has distributed and delegated responsibility for the social management of 'risk' (be it health, financial, social, criminal, or otherwise) down to the level of citizens and small groups. A telling example of this strategy was Indonesia's recent regional autonomy act. Such provisions prod youth who have grown up in an unstable economy, to see themselves as beyond simply being 'at risk' from poverty, political unrest and unemployment; it counsels them on the need to take primary responsibility as individuals for managing the local risks in their personal lives. To do so, they have to operate in a context of 'detraditionalization.' This is what Cieslik and Pollock (2002: 3) intend in observing 'norms and values which act as collective cultural guides in our lives are waning in influence and this is reflected in a much more fluid understanding of families, employment and community life.'

Putting these elements together we see that within a climate of risk, commercial media discourses come to constitute significant advisory forces in the lives of young people. To negotiate and survive 'risk society' the young are compelled to take up a typically modern entrepreneurial version of the self. One strategy is reflected in Hazairin's comment, above: to make use of the motivational potential of glamorous lifestyles and affluence depicted on TV. Such a strategy links media and identity insofar as it reveals how young people in the global/informational society have become more 'self-conscious' as they attempt to 'successfully manage their biographies in contemporary societies' (Cieslik and Pollock 2002: 3).

In this data, then, positive comments about media and the management of identity stressed the educative and informational aspects of mass media, as well as its potential for motivating young people to become materially successful. This echoes the popular view that the mass media in Indonesia needs to be pro-development giving 'positive news' to citizens (Romano 1999:47). Such remarks also point strongly toward the 'detraditionalisation' trend described by Beck and others. However, these comments cannot be read independent of critical statements about media from these same young informants – in particular, their assertion of the need for cultural filtering. Viewed thus, it must be observed that all comments generally reflect a dialectical engagement with globally inflected media; one in which identity claims activate traditional, religious and moral discourses in the process of striving for what Giddens (1991a: 84; 1991b: 131) has called 'ontological security.'

The negative view
A central aspect of ontological security appears to be preserving Indonesia's moral and cultural heritage. Not coincidentally, these twin elements appear to fuel the negative view toward media. For instance, respondents said that Western-derived television, satellite broadcasting, VCD and DVD would definitively change the 'Asian' worldview of young Indonesians. To wit:

> Contemporary mass media do not match the identity and characteristics of our culture of the east where no behaviours that contradict norms are allowed. Thus something provocative, like *'Bandung Lautan Asmara'*[8] is really at odds with the norms of Indonesia, where communal values are stressed in society (Ervan, Sulawesi, FG3, [m] [C]).

Were it to be pointed out to Ervan that the DVD he mentioned is an Indonesian product, he would very likely rebut that Indonesian pornography derives from Western influences. Such order of comment was typical among focus group members, many of whom condemned Western lifestyles, 'free' sex, a 'freer lifestyle' and the role that media and technology play in their proliferation. Consider a few of this ilk:

> The parabolic aerial is widely used to catch international TV channels, which sometimes broadcast pornographic scenes and coarse language (Eka, Bali, FG1, [m] [H]).

> In Bali, open discussion or depiction of sexual relations is still regarded as taboo. However, through the development of modern technology

products, such as TV, people everywhere can easily watch scenes of Western sexual intercourse (Meri, Bali, FG1, [f] [H]).

Obviously many of the young generation nowadays are involved in free sex behaviour. On TV, there are cosmetic products and girls want to try them because they want to be beautiful. So the effects are very strong (Naila, Sulawesi, FG1, [f] [M]).

Above all, for those who perceived media to be strongly detrimental, there was a concomitant tendency to see the information consumer as pliable and weak. As Sutedja, a Hindu male from Bali, put it: 'teenagers are in the habit of liking to watch Western films, and so their ways of thinking will automatically change. For example free sex and violence' (Sutedja, Bali, FG4, [m] [H]). As we shall see, this perception of weakness in the face of culturally challenging identity discourses may be kindling the reinvigoration of 'traditional' identity discourse among contemporary youth.

The Internet

Internet cafes are now found in all but the smallest and most remote villages of Indonesia. Young people queue outside cafes and telecommunication outlets to access the web, and home connections are increasing exponentially. Interviewees seemed to view the Internet with greater optimism than TV and DVDs. Daranya asserted, 'through the Internet, all parts of the world can be easily accessed,' 'This will improve and broaden the knowledge and perceptions of Balinese teenagers,' (Daranya, Bali, FG1, [m] [H]). Some stressed the positive link between the Internet and 'development.' Rudi, a Christian male replied, 'The advancement of mass media and information technology means development. But youth must be educated either by family or society. There must be effective ways to make them aware of modern developments in technology, mass media, TV, or the Internet.' (Rudi, Sulawesi, FG5, [m] [C]).

At the same time, negative views were expressed about the effects of the Internet on youth; for example 'the Internet sometimes presents pornographic pictures, such as a naked actress, which not only impact on the religious faith of teenagers, but also have a negative effect on Balinese traditional customs.' (Ayu Putri, Bali, FG2, [f] [H]). A different order of criticism came in the lament that 'in the past children went everywhere around to play, but now they stay at their own house and play on the Internet, individually, or in small groups (Fenijati, Sulawesi, FG4, [f] [C]). This comment is worthy of attention. For, while this is a widespread complaint in the West (e.g. Livingstone 2002), my long-term observations do not confirm this as a commonplace concern in Indonesia. Only affluent homes have a computer, and children are not usually allowed to 'play' on it. Thus, Fenijati's worry appears more likely evidence of youth re-iterating public discourse about deleterious media 'effects.' I will address this tendency to parrot public discourse at greater length, below.

As in the West, despite a boom in Internet use, there is little reliable data about exactly what most young people in Indonesia are actually doing online. Viewing the use of parallel technologies – such as SMS text messaging on mobile phones (which is ubiquitous) – it is probable that these young people mainly use technological devices for entertainment and communication (Facer & Furlong 2001: 457) – above all, games, popstar biopics, and fan sites. Information search and retrieval can also be inferred from the interview data, in the following way. Most of these informants were involved in religious activism. Their responses to other questions revealed that, while their idealism reached back into an imagined golden past, information about current religious causes and issues came from the latest technology, especially the Internet. As well as formal sites for global Islam, Hinduism and Christianity, the Internet carries many radical fundamentalist sites devoted to insurgency and armed struggle. However, it was difficult to ascertain how much, if at all, informants had accessed such sites.

Assessing views toward media

In concluding this section, I will sketch a number of themes that the informants' views of media influence open into. Six in particular bear on issues of media, globalization and identity.

1 Technology and control
The prevalence of technology enabling access to western-style content, is precisely a condition that some Asian governments have sought to exploit. Citing Western cultural threat, they have sought

to justify tightening media controls. In truth, this is usually done for reasons of political dominion, as well as for the purposes of forging national identity out of cultural and/or ethnic diversity (see Van den Bulck 2001: 55).[9] Some nations in the Middle East and Asia have installed firewalls blocking political and pornographic content on the Internet (Mitchell 2001: 43). Such intervention renders Gan's (2001:139) observation that cyberspace is perhaps the only global 'democratic space,' a bit quixotic. As for Internet users, themselves, Vatikiotis (2001) maintains that a recent survey in Singapore revealed the majority were 'in favour of censorship of Web content' (148), especially of sites which threatened 'Asian values' and political stability. In the Indonesian focus groups, as well, such sentiments were vividly articulated. In short, culturally and politically challenging media discourses are filtered locally, both during transmission and reception.

2 Stereotypes

Conversely, when media can operate freely, it would do well to bear in mind Said's (1978: 26) suggestion about innovation in communications technology. Where he saw media expansion and sophistication as working to further Oriental stereotypes, one could argue that global expansion of media has had the simultaneous, reverse effect of reinforcing Occidental stereotypes in Asia. Consequently, one sees in young Indonesian's comments about the effects of mass media, a tendency to reiterate incendiary messages about western hegemony which still sell newspapers and boost ratings in the current climate of unrest and, in turn, work to incite cultural and moral panic in the active consuming public.

3 Socialization

Viewing this process at work, consider the example Sen & Hill (2000: 127) locate in a 1996 government publication: 'the impact of international culture sometimes brings negative consequences which lead to the flourishing of teenage delinquency. This is being monitored.' This statement communicates the notion that Indonesian youth are weak and vulnerable. Implicitly, it argues that there is a need for government surveillance. This is but one example from a communication context rife with 'parental' messages of oversight. Is it any surprise, then, that when asked about 'media effects,' young people tend to offer 'answers' identical to those rampant in the communication milieu?

This prospect of parroting behaviour (*membebek* in Indonesian) is not without precedent in the culture. Leigh (2002) attributes it to the dominant pedagogic practice of the Indonesian schooling system: rote learning and repetition. She maintains that young people will repeat competing viewpoints word for word without reflection. In terms of the focus group data, it is difficult to establish the extent to which parroting might be at play. However, it is conceivable that the 'stock' nature of responses in the focus groups reflects a semantic encoding of distance on the part of the speaker (and by implication the co-speakers in the same group) from the described negative effects. The responses read as if this has not happened to them, but describes the experiences of other, more vulnerable young people – imagined or perhaps filtered through media reports.

4 Media anxiety

Similar to what Scrase (2002: 333) found in contemporary West Bengal, negative responses among these Indonesian informants confirm that much anxiety about media revolves around the depiction of women and, especially, sexual relations. For example, one of the Balinese Hindu female interviewees said 'maybe Westerners think that watching such TV programs is really OK. Free sex relationships in Western countries may be OK. But this, of course, can easily influence the ideas of Balinese teenagers,' (Meri, Bali, fFG1, [f] [H]). It seems significant that over two years later much the same claim was made by a male Muslim in Sulawesi: 'a very obvious example of media influence would be the life of teenagers: free life, free sex and all that. Drugs and stuff. Those habits are from outside Indonesia and we imitate them. Since young people imitate Westerners' behaviors, that strongly affects their own behavior.' (Firman, Sulawesi, FG1, [m] [M]).

However, while the threat of Western media/cultural hegemony was palpable among informants, there was also a sense of not wanting to be left behind the rest of the rapidly modernising, developing world. It is this dilemma which drove Vietnam and Singapore to implement Internet access restrictions as a means of protecting national culture and unity (by keeping out the 'bad'), while facilitating rapid economic progress. Some of these young informants argued for such measures when talking about television, and one assumes that this also goes for Internet content. As upwardly mobile young Indonesians it is easy to understand their bind: avoid falling behind in the race to modernize, yet refrain from courting the risk of losing their current strong sense of ethno-local identity.

5 Global information flow

Anthony Giddens has argued that 'one of the fundamental consequences of modernity...is globalisation,' (1991b: 137), which he describes as a 'juggernaut – a runaway engine of enormous power...' which we can drive to some extent (but which can also) crush those who resist it.' (Giddens 1991b: 139). Barker (1999) refutes this claim, maintaining that the global flows of cultural discourse are no 'longer constituted as one-way-traffic from the "west-to-the-rest"' (1999: 38) and, further, that 'in so far as the predominant flow of cultural discourse is from west to east and north to south, this is not necessarily to be understood as a form of domination' (1999: 38). On both these claims the focus group data appears to offer dispute. Firstly, participants *do* see the global flow of cultural discourse as one way: westward-out. As one Sulawesi respondent stated, 'maybe it's because of the impact of modernization. Too much information. Images shown in America today can be seen in Indonesia just the next day because of modernization and globalization.' (Rosdiana, Sulawesi, FG2, [f] [M]).

Secondly, the respondents clearly *do* perceive this flow as a form of domination which results in cultural loss. For example, Sutedja, in Bali, asserted, 'through their fondness for watching Western films, their ways of thinking will automatically change' (Sutedja, Bali, FG4, [m] [H]). And while less critical of Internet than TV, respondents seemed to see not only a tool with positive power, but also a potential Pandora's box. The collapsing of temporal and spatial boundaries was one concern. So, too, the ability to know what is real. In Anwar's words: 'what's happening in the other parts of the world can be instantly accessed from here. But the problem is the validity of the information cannot be guaranteed.' (Anwar, Sulawesi, FG7, [m] [M]).

6 Local resistance

How, then, can we reconcile the fact that cultural theorists (both Western and non-Western[10]) confidently refute Gidden's 'juggernaut' idea, while local people in developing countries appear to concur with the view of cultural domination? How can cultural theory counter the claims of situated media consumers who believe that 'media have a great impact on customs and traditions, especially for youth who leave it all behind and move towards modernization, imitating what they have seen through the media' (Saipul, Sulawesi, FG3, [m] [M])?

Part of the answer lies in the fact that in Indonesia mass media are viewed as a key component of *globalisasi* (globalisation). The Indonesian term 'refers to forces that people perceive to be largely out of their control' (Connor and Rubinstein 1999: 5) – not unlike Gidden's description of the juggernaut. Another part of the answer lies in local reaction to the dramatic increase in sexually explicit content found in so-called global 'family viewing' over the past ten years (CNN 2001). This increase has provoked a certain amount of outcry from religious groups of most persuasions in most non-Western countries (see Scrase 2002). Thus, in countries such as Saudi Arabia and Iran, satellite dishes, foreign DVDs and free Internet access are banned as a way of curbing the cultural assault of foreign (read Western) cultures against the Islamic state (Tomlinson 1997: 127). Much of the content – from sexually explicit images, to depictions of drug and alcohol consumption, to foul language, to the pursuit of hedonistic, individualistic lifestyles – runs counter to tradition in many non-Western nations, provoking outrage.

Some of the focus group comments reflected this moral impulse, as when Yuliana maintained: 'Youth make use of the mass media for entertainment, but it contains things which are not in accordance with our traditional norms. For example, like what has been mentioned before, pornographic videos. They make them have a desire to do it but it's not in accordance with our ways.' (Yuliana, Sulawesi, FG7, [f] [M]).

Identity, cultural filtration and risk

Having looked at youth's views about media – and, in particular, television and the Internet – we might question what kind of identity 'work' lies within this discourse. Rather than treating their statements as *prima facie* truth claims, we could profitably analyse them as constituting a mediated discourse of identity. At the outset, I distinguished between locally existing and representational (or mediated) identity discourses. Both reflect mediation, though judging from the statements by focus group members, the pull (and power) of the mediators is clearly not equal.

Hall (1991: 21) has claimed that 'identity is always...a structural representation which only achieves its positive through the narrow eye of the negative. It has to go through the eye of the needle of the other before it can construct itself.' Those claiming negative effects may be partly describing strategies for dealing with the challenging identity discourses that globally-inflected media present. Consider the words of Dewa Ayu Eka, a female Hindu from Bali: 'Teenagers need to filter out all the foreign culture influences coming to Bali.' Or as Agung, a Balinese Hindu male asserted, 'I think the teenagers here will only be a little bit influenced by the current media messages, because they still put tradition and religion as their first priority.'

While these views suggest filtration at the individual level, some respondents offered 'macro' filtering strategies. For example, 'I was educated in a Muslim religious school myself, but parents must give strong guidance otherwise the young generation will be torn apart by being too much exposed to immoral scenes,' (Rosdiana, Sulawesi, FG2, [f] [M]). At an even greater level of filtration, one respondent offered: 'We know that high rating programs on TV nowadays have some scenes which are really not supposed to be on air. So a wise government would select serials on TV, deciding which one is suitable for broadcast and which one is not.' (Hazairin, Sulawesi, FG2, [m] [M]).

Clearly, such comments imply a cultural filtering process whereby media discourses incompatible with major local identity frames are subjected to manipulation and control, and even elimination from channels of consumption. In this way a whole set of undesirable 'possible lives' (Appadurai 1990:9) are cancelled out. The major cultural mechanism at play here seems to be religious faith, which guarantees a kind of moral armour against the incursion of exogenous, culturally challenging identity discourse. This is consistent with Vickers's (2002: 82) view that in the 1990s 'religious difference for Balinese Hindus became a defining point of identity: the unity of religion, 'tradition' and ethnicity was elevated as a major feature of being Balinese.' Indeed, this notion of resistance repeatedly appeared in the Bali focus groups, for example:

> Balinese youth have to firmly hold on to their religious teaching. They have to have a very strong religious knowledge or understanding. In theory, if they are strong enough or have adequate religious knowledge,

they will not be influenced by the negative impact of the mass media (Ayu Putri, Bali, FG2, [f] [H]).

Following on the earlier discussion, risk management in Indonesia may involve filtering and modifying media content in order to retain 'ontological security.' Beck (1992) has argued that in the new global modernity, predictabilities and certainties are threatened, and a new set of risks and opportunities are brought into existence (see also Furlong and Cartmel 1997: 3). In an atmosphere of heightened risk, the surety of tradition is called into question. Under such conditions 'the looming threat of personal meaninglessness' (Giddens 1991a: 201) arises. So religious fundamentalism comes to provide a significant measure of security. Certainly it would seem that one could read the wealth of comments by Muslim youth in the focus groups in such a way. Concern about the corrupting influence of Western media attests to the strength of local Islamic religious discourse in providing moral ammunition against perceived Western media hegemony.

This contemporary response may be understood as part of a search for ontological security. It is certainly not without precedent. As Hourani (1946) demonstrated, the original encounter between modern Arab and Islamic culture and the West produced in the former a sense of 'secondariness' or marginality. This has, over time, come to feed the Islamic revival movement, not unlike what we are now witnessing in Indonesia today. Put another way, identity discourses emanating from Western media have been dismantled or, at the very least, are being devalued as a result of powerful counter discourses flowing from sources such as ethno-locality, tradition, religion and nationalism.

Identity, tradition and modernity

Indonesia entered the electronic information age some time ago. Radio first, then television, then computers became commonplace. At present, mobile phones with text capabilities, electronic games and personal organisers are all mainstays of affluent urban 'lifestyling.' The young Indonesians presented in this chapter can all be described as the offspring of the upwardly mobile citizens who prospered under the New Order regime, not least of all because they received tertiary education (Bayhaqi 2000: 241). Yet for young people beyond Jakarta, life in a post-*reformasi*, decentralising nation is constituted within significant discourses of fracture, coalition, and disjuncture in the expression and performance of identity. Life for rural youth differs considerably from that of their peers in major urban centers, where concrete evidence of the material and cultural processes of globalisation has amassed: shopping malls, fast-food outlets, cinemas, Internet cafes, dance venues, and outlets for prestige electrical goods, designer clothing and footwear.

Contemporary Indonesia, then, represents a semantic space of cultural production and identity representation; one simultaneously becoming *more globalised*, yet emphatically *more localized* (see Wilson & Dissanayake 1996). While international capital shapes its economy and exerts pressure toward conspicuous consumption, strident claims to ethno-local identity are seen and heard. Ethnic, religious and regional movements have rapidly gained in popularity (Robinson 2002, Vickers 2002).

Gerke (2000) argues that in contemporary Indonesia, membership of the middle-class is defined more by social behaviour and lifestyling than income. Display of Western-style commodities signals the upward mobility of social elites (Cribb 2001: 232). Informants perceived this impulse to keep up appearances, especially in light of the country's economic decline, and regarded media as playing a central role in this process. As Akzar indicates: 'When they see something in the media that they consider modern they imitate that thing. They tear holes in their pants, or grow their hair long. And because Westerners have blonde hair they dye their hair blonde, despite their dark complexion.' (Akzar, Sulawesi, FG2, [m] [M]).

However, keeping up appearances for respectable young people not only means reflecting modernity, but tradition, as well. Media is crucial because it disseminates information which is particularly useful for the modern entrepreneurial Indonesian individual (Nilan 2001: 2) who wants to keep one reassuring foot in the past and the other in the promise of the present.

A good example of reassurance lies in the considerable religious material carried on television and in newspapers. All three major religious faiths are growing in strength, particularly among the young. Recent world events have certainly played a part, but both Muslim (Hassan 2002) and Hindu (Vickers 2002) fundamentalism was evident even during the New Order. Religious fundamentalism conflates anti-Westernism and pro-Asian discourses. This is reflected in the ratings decline for American programs and films while other exogenous content – South American soap operas, Bollywood films,[11] and Hong Kong martial arts epics – remain hugely popular (see Abu-Lughod 1991: 132). Japanese cartoons such as Dragonball, Hello Kitty and Pokemon (in both paper and electronic form, and with associated games, toys and figures) are also popular. At the same time, the amount of strongly Islamic content in commercial media has vastly increased, in keeping with the middle-class *santri*fication of Indonesian Muslims (Barton 2001: 245; Hassan 2002). So, too, in Hindu Bali and Christian areas of the archipelago, do specialised media convey powerful religious messages bearing global footprints. It is safe to assume that the religious faiths of the young people interviewed are actively invigorated by the media.

It is this split trajectory – perhaps ill-described as 'disjuncture' – which characterizes the identity framing of young middle-class people in Indonesia. Although they are actively engaged with the global/informational economy, young people are still 'situated' (or 'locatable') in their local communities with specific cultural histories. It is from this position that they engage with media materials, and from which multiple readings of, and/or resistances to, media texts may arise. Examples abound, but consider the matter of global terrorism. Despite the relatively low key, non-inflammatory way that mainstream Indonesian media dealt with the September 11th attacks (quietly condemning global terrorism), this did little to affect the cult-like hero worship of Osama Bin Laden among some sectors of radical Muslim youth (see Brayne 2002: 23).[12] In Makassar in January 2002 the three great 'enemies of the west' – Osama Bin Laden, Sadam Hussein and Yasser Arafat – could be found arranged in a grinning pantheon on market-stall t-shirts and posters, beneath the slogan 'ANTI-USA.' Similar reactions were articulated followed the Bali bombing on October 12th 2002 with wide spread public assertions that the attacks were a CIA conspiracy. Considering these outcomes, it could be argued that increased access has enabled Indonesian youth to engage globally distributed media in multiple ways: that which encourages Western-style hedonism and consumption and that which purports to oppose those values.

As mentioned earlier, contemporary identity is produced partly through an engagement with the 'possible lives' (Appadurai 1990) offered by the media. Thus is it that young middle-class people in

Indonesia (as elsewhere in the world) are targets for transnational television marketing campaigns, lifestyling information, media innovations, and religious fundamentalist propaganda – local *and* global. This status as subjects to be seduced into possible lives reminds us of Liechty's (1995: 194) observation that 'to experience modernity is to engage in some way – even if only in reaction or as a sense of longing – the cultural economy of the transnational sphere.' Interestingly, these middle class youth may not always see their subject status. Although they will readily assert the strength of Western media hegemony, they fail to acknowledge that other media sources preaching (local and/or moral) messages are just as powerful, equally hegemonic; their content no less propagandistic.

Some Asian nations, such as Burma and Iran, have banned all mediated representations of global youth culture. Others, such as Indonesia, have deliberately represented globalization as 'yet another and more pernicious phase of media imperialism, marked by more Western messages beaming down from the sky' (Sen and Hill 2000: 15). This was one of the dominant messages of the New Order regime, a message the members of all the focus groups grew up processing. Should it come as a surprise, then, that they reproduce it so faithfully?

Conclusion: mediating the discourses of engagement

This chapter proposes that media are central to changes in social identity frames associated with modernity. At the same time, the data underscore what other theorists (e.g. Giddens 1991a; Thompson 1995: 192) have suggested about globalization: that persistence of traditional ways and the adoption of modern lifestyles are not mutually exclusive. One interviewee even verbalized this fact wistfully: 'we should be aiming for a balance while following guidelines which we can derive from the cultural traditions of Indonesia' (Muhammed Iram Khai, Sualwesi, FG6, [m] [M]).

This snapshot of the engagement between Indonesian youth and media illustrates the coterminous location of traditional ways and modern lifestyling in everyday lives. This coexistence was nowhere more evident than in the large number of informants bearing trendy clothing and footwear, mobile phones, Discmans and Gameboys, on the one hand, and their spirited defense of traditional values, on the other. This is why it is hard to accept Lent's assessment that the 'infatuation' with Western popular culture forms in Asia – and especially media – is 'traceable to colonialism or to commercial and military relationships with the United States or Europe (1995: 2). The data here certainly do not support the simple thesis of 'infatuation' with Western popular cultural forms.

Instead, in their responses these young Indonesians position themselves between two major *discourses of engagement* with media. The first discourse asserts that Western cultural influences from mass media and information technology possess the power to shift Indonesian youth out of traditional frames of self-reference; and significantly that this potential constitutes a risk to ethno/local or religious cultural identity.

The second discourse of engagement holds that mass media and information technology have to be mastered, understood and embraced, if the Indonesian state is to advance economically, and if young citizens want to avoid the risk of future decline in economic and social status.

To be sure, the cohorts given voice here are middle-class, tertiary-educated, confident, politically active, and strongly devout. They cannot be taken as representative of Indonesian youth who are poor, barely-educated, with limited access to technology. Nevertheless, it is precisely because of the above-listed characteristics that young people like these will assume positions of legal and theological influence in the future. Given that one of the consistent forces for change in Indonesia has been the appropriation of new institutions that operate as catalysts for the upward mobility of social elites, this youthful cohort will be instrumental in deliberating the future of mass media and information technology in Indonesia. Judging from the focus group interviews, it is likely that a complex mediation between traditional and modern identity discourses will be adopted.

9 Talking Sex and Gender from Taiwan's VCD Scandal

Ming-Chu Chen

Taiwan's sex-VCD scandal

On December 17, 2001, the tabloid *Scoop Weekly* freely distributed VCDs[1] depicting an alleged sexual encounter between a former Taiwanese politician and a married businessman. The surreptitiously-recorded VCD at the center of the furor purported to show Chu Mei-feng, the 36-year-old former director of the Hsinchu Bureau of Cultural Affairs, engaging in intercourse in her bedroom. Chu was a former member of the New Party in Taiwan who rose to prominence in 1997 after becoming the first to denounce a cult leader who claimed to have supernatural powers. At the time of her election nine years before, Chu had been the youngest Taipei City councilor. Her most recent bid for a legislative seat, however, had been unsuccessful.

When word of Chu's possible presence on the VCD became known, the Government Information Office (GIO) in Taiwan quickly moved to seize the film, arguing that the Broadcasting and Television Law stipulates that any VCD, DVD or videotape must be viewed by the GIO before it can be released. This for the purpose of 'management and consultation over broadcasting.' In rebuttal, *Scoop Weekly*'s publisher and owner claimed that the public's right to know justified the release of the VCD. The publisher emphasized that because Chu was a public figure her behavior must be scrutinized by the public. In addition, adultery is a criminal offense in Taiwan, punishable by up to one year in prison for both the adulterer and his or her unmarried partner. Certainly this fact warranted public exposure.

In the months that followed, the sex-VCD incident moved from criminal investigation to scandal to public debate about the position of women in a patriarchal society to shared voyeuristic extravaganza. Through mass reproduction, copies of the VCD were disseminated worldwide across the Internet, in addition to becoming a local best seller at Taiwan's night markets and bazaars. It might be said that the image of the female body depicted on the VCD or Internet was transformed into an object for public voyeurism as well as the controversial subject of popular discussion. Chu was not only branded a criminal by the press, she became a victim of peeping by hidden camera delivered to a global public. Chu was forced to move from denial to public apology to shame and censure to claiming that she had been 'sentenced to death' by the actions of the media. Yet, employing the very same media that had exploited her private experience, Chu raised her voice against traditional culture, publishing a book, hosting a radio and TV show, and debuting as a singer. In this way she managed a miraculous reincarnation.

This chapter studies the many dimensions of this fascinating story. Throughout, the focus is on gender issues emanating from media. My aim is to rethink the cultural and social implications of the female image represented by media, especially in the epoch of new communications technology such as the Internet. Mechanisms capable of distributing images (and ideas) globally in real time, I will show, are not without their local manifestations. We see, for instance, that gender identity is ideologically reflected in local media discourses, as well as public discussion; we also see how the female image creates a polysemic textual field. Because of this plurality, media texts and audience's reading practices can actually challenge the dominant gender identity rooted in Taiwanese society.

Core issues

Chu's case highlights a number of elements of concern in this book; among them: media technologies, representation, gender, identity, inequality, global and local, public and private, traditional versus contemporary morality, audience and voyeurism. Concretely, let's look at a few ways in which these aspects fit together in the sex VCD story.

Gender and local values

About the size of the American states Massachusetts and Connecticut combined, Taiwan is located in the western Pacific Ocean, 100 miles off the coast of mainland China, 200 miles north of the Philippines and about 700 miles south of Japan. From a historical perspective,[2] Taiwanese culture is a hybrid, influenced by eastern and western cultures, owing to governance by China, the Netherlands, and Japan. However, Taiwan has deeply inherited Chinese traditional culture due to the control of Chiang Kai-Shek's government. Thus, the traditional Confucian concept of females being inferior to males has also influenced Taiwanese familial relationships and even education. When the sex-VCD scandal broke in late 2001, the first reaction from the general public indicated that the fault lay entirely with Chu. The reading of the media audience was expressed in traditional gender identity terms. However, following the dramatic development of the story, different voices present in the local context were expressed. A major one was for women's rights.

Globalization and the Internet

Internet played a major role in this affair, spreading the video across the Asian region, and even throughout the world.[3] As an advanced representation system, Internet communication accelerates the mechanism of distribution and reproduction. However, it does something more: it can lead to the multiplicity of meanings surrounding any given media product, as it is transmitted to more and more media consumers. These consumers, the reader/user of the Internet, become something more than passive receivers; they also become active *re-producers* of the text. Conceivably, the reader-producer can produce different visions about a text and construct various implications from the referents. In effect, textual polysemy ripples through the process of media consumption. In terms of matters of identity, plural decodings are surely possible.

The Internet, self and other in society

A second dimension of the Internet involves the violation of private space (belonging to the self) by others (in the social world). In some ways secret video-taping of intimate acts and their rapid public dissemination via Internet technology can be viewed as a violent behavior that, though not necessarily directed at women, may serve as one of the biggest future threats to the female private sphere. Certainly in Chu's case, the surreptitious recording and public distribution without her knowledge and consent served as a tool of violence that harmed her reputation, and her personal and emotional well-being. The Internet was employed as a mechanism for the satisfaction of voyeuristic desire. Posting and reproducing the recording illustrates the pleasure of patriarchal cultural practices. In this way, one can see, new communication technology may not protect people from psychological, moral, economic and political violence, but conversely enables and even encourages users to conspire in crime globally.

Audience, gendered discourse and polysemy

The sex-VCD scandal stimulated an enormous range of discourse, as well as feverish debate. These communications were not only in the physical spaces of Taiwanese society, but on the Internet, as well. On pornographic websites, web users publicly inquired where they could obtain a copy of the VCD. Reflecting the gendering of much the discourse, there was considerable discussion of the behavior and physical attributes of the woman in the video. On some discussion sites, enormous chauvinistic scorn was directed toward Chu, who was seen as a home wrecker and, from the view of traditional Chinese culture, as someone who was getting what she deserved. At the same time, the VCD episode spurred serious debate about human rights, privacy, and the public interest implications of the furtive video recording. Some indicated that the great attention to the video reflected a serious voyeuristic tendency on the part of the public, a loss of humanity and sympathy for others. Women's rights activists have asserted that secret video recording is a violation of human rights and a rape of individual privacy. They have complained that the rapid increase of secret filming has served to erode media ethics in Taiwan. They have also called for decriminalization of adultery. Through this full public chorus – no matter what position was adopted – it seemed that nearly every one had openly consumed the pornographic images via traditional media such as newspaper, magazine or television, or else through the Internet.

Representation and meaning

Clearly, Chu's case stands for more than simply the story of a female politician whose private life was made public. At a greater level of extrapolation, the private image of 'the female' was re/produced by a representation system (here, the Internet and more traditional media). Further, due to its complexity, as well as its large number of audiences, the sex-VCD case could be viewed as a poli-centric dialogical field interweaving media ethics, political economic interests, morality, law, human rights, humanity, cultural identity, social values, and likely more.

As we can gather from the foregoing, specific interpretations of what Chu's case was about differ. This reflects the basic problem of all representation: in a word, how to read what media communicates. This problem is well captured by Haraway (1988: 587) in the following set of questions:

> How to see? Where to see from? What limits to vision? What to see for? Whom to see with? Who gets to have more than one point of view? Who gets blinded? Who wears blinders? Who interprets the visual field? What other sensory powers do we wish to cultivate besides vision?

Haraway's questions bear on issues of power, ideology, public and private, polysemy, technological capabilities and moral and legal restraints. Let's explore some of these aspects in greater detail.

Media and representation

The December 17, 2001, issue of the tabloid *Scoop Weekly* not only reported Chu Mei-feng's promiscuity, but freely distributed the VCD allegedly depicting that sexual behavior. *Scoop Weekly* strongly asserted its belief that the VCD would serve as a visual aid, either evidence to bolster the claim of the politician's identity, or else as a reference for the reader to know more about the story. It cannot be denied, however, that strong economic motives may have underpinned that choice. The news media's decision to visually publicize the sexual life of a female politician certainly served to attract a maximum number of readers. With the capitalist goal of maximizing profit on full display, the newspaper treated the female image as a commercial product to be consumed by the masses.

Gaze

One problem here is that the images of the female body contained in the VCD were represented from the viewpoint of a 'secret filming' (i.e. without the awareness of the participants); further, it was examined by the public from a specific position of (dominant) gender identity. These twin components of 'the gaze' when applied to the reading of the female image might influence how a reader would come to interpret the story. To help understand this point, consider what Mulvey (1989: 19) says about the determining gaze of different gender roles:

> In a world ordered by sexual imbalance, pleasure in looking has been split between active/male and passive/female. The determining male gaze projects its fantasy onto the female figure, which is styled accordingly. In their traditional exhibitionist role women are simultaneously looked at and displayed, with their appearance coded for strong visual and erotic impact so that they can be said to connote to-be-looked-at-ness.

As Chu's sex-VCD came to be reported in the media and distributed over the Internet, the female bodily experience was transformed from an intimate private act into an exhibitionist image. The act of secret filming renders the female body naked, not simply nude, in front of a determining male gaze. The female private sphere is truly intruded upon and her bodily experience is taken from her and exploited for the pleasure (and economic benefit) of others. The female image visually connotes 'to-be-looked-at-ness' through a representative practice linking the hidden camera, VCD, and the Internet.

Gendered identity

It is important to note that although the VCD presents a woman and a man having a sexual encounter, the process described above served to bypass the man, almost entirely. Directly put, the gendered nature of male and female sexualities in Taiwanese society meant that each 'actor' in the VCD possessed different destinies. The public discussion focused on Chu, more than on the married man, who, once forgiven by his wife, faded from public consciousness. It could be argued that more attention was accorded to the woman not because of her gender, rather because the woman in the video resembled a public figure well known to the public. The manner and treatment of the video by the news media and over the Internet, however, makes it quite clear that this woman was being observed and examined not only in her capacity as actor in a VCD but also within a patriarchal ideology. In short, the media not only visualized and commercialized female bodily experiences to make a profit; in so doing – whether intentional or not – they asserted and maintained dominant cultural views of gender identity through representational and reading practices.

Berger indicates that the relationship between images and readers depends on how a man makes, reads and consumes the image. 'All images are man-made' he writes (Berger 1972: 9). But, the big problem here is: who is this 'man.' If 'man' represents only one sex, there would be only one gaze served, only one gaze provided, which worked to maintain only one, dominant, culture. The one disseminating the image could control the process of representation and empower his idea of strengthening the dominant social identity.

Ideology: reality versus truth

Under the circumstances described in the VCD scandal, the female body has been framed, delivered and examined 'ideologically': under a *male-made* culture. This is how Althusser talks about media representation: in terms of constructing ideology rather than discerning or presenting the real condition of the incident. Ideology lies behind the imaginary representation – even distortion – of the real world. 'It is not their real conditions of human existence, their real world, that "man" "represent to themselves" in ideology,' Althusser says, 'but above all it is their relation to those conditions of existence which is represented to them there.' (Althusser 1971: 164).

Importantly, once in the realm of representation, the ideological aspect of this process creates 'truth' no matter whether the media has actually captured the truth or not. What the magazine sold was not only the news story, but also the female bodily experience captured in her 'natural' private world. Whether the identity of the woman on film was truly Chu or not is unimportant. The point is that the image of private female experience is more 'real' than the truth and, thus, could be commercialized as a product. This is what Baudrillard (1988) means by 'simulacrum': 'the generation by models of a real without origin or reality'; or better, 'the truth which conceals that there is none.' (1988: 166).

The truth behind the image is no longer significant under the mechanism of simulation. The video as a simulacrum presents a 'reality' signified by the phenomenal objects that can be transformed into commercial products. 'Real' reality is not important in the process of media representation. The most important thing is what those objects represent and how they represent it. Thus, even if it is a false reality that is being produced and disseminated, it is a powerful one; one with the capacity for organizing human thought and action. The signification of the image might serve as a mechanism of identification. Thus, for instance, when *Weekly Scoop* broke the story, it was the male gaze brought by its readers that imposed the dominant gendered identity. What circulated was the image of improper female sexuality, an image that prompted widespread public condemnation.

Textual polysemy

In part this definitional outcome was assisted by the action of government officials in the GIO who defined the VCD as a 'pornographic film.' This they had done to enable the confiscation of the VCD and assist in cracking down on the tabloid's market. It is unlikely that they would have confiscated the VCD simply for reasons associated with the intrusion into someone's private life by hidden camera. More, the determination that the VCD was pornographic – as a pretext for intervention – ended up labeling Chu, typing female behavior in general, and, ultimately, defining female identity.

It turns out, though, that sexuality and gender were not the only discourses generated by the VCD scandal. Some studiously ignored the gender dimension, focusing instead on issues of law, privacy, and media practice. In this way one can argue that the sex-VCD was a polysemic text, one capable of being read by different groups in different ways, for different purposes. Let's consider each reading, in turn.

The VCD case as a legal text

Attorneys for the magazine claimed that the government's actions violated the right to a free press. The chairwoman of the magazine also emphasized that the video was newsworthy and the public had the right to know its contents. Rather than pornography, the VCD provided evidence to back up the press report. A politician's life bears on the public and should be examined. Did others deem the

VCD pornographic? Michael Logan, a Taipei-based journalist, wrote that 'this was a simple act of lovemaking – common to any bedroom in Taiwan – albeit one caught on camera.' (*Taipei Times*, December 21, 2001).

By contrast, the GIO stated that the Broadcasting and Television Law empowers the government to ban the broadcasting of materials 'inimical to the well-being of children and to good conduct.' Further, the magazine was under legal obligation to submit the VCD to the GIO for examination prior to publication. The magazine's free give-away was considered a distribution in violation of the law. The GIO officials also claimed that this magazine was simply trying to sell pornographic material for the purpose of making a profit, and that those obscene pictures would challenge traditional Taiwanese moral standards. The magazine's conduct might very well be punishable by law, as Article 235 of the Criminal Code makes the distribution, sale and public display of indecent materials a criminal offense. Article 315, as well, bans the circulation and sale of illegally taped films of another person's private conduct.

Some disagreed with the GIO's interpretation of purview. 'The government doesn't have the power to ban the VCD under the Broadcasting and Television Law,' one writer articulated in the *Taipei Times*, 'since that law applies only to VCDs, DVDs, and CDs that are publicly broadcast.' (December 21, 2001).

The VCD case as a privacy text

It was ironic that the major administrative concern was for the so-called 'immoral content' of the video rather than the human right to privacy. For some, this was worthy of comment. Chen Mei-hua, the secretary-general of the Awakening Foundation,[4] noted that people are naturally curious about the behavior of others, but 'rather than creating more laws, people need to learn the value of human rights and privacy and they should also learn to respect them.' (*Taipei Times*, December 23, 2001). For Huang Cheng-yi, the matter was one of unclear demarcation between public and private spheres, which has traditional roots and, possibly, ramifications for contemporary Taiwanese identity. As she put it:

> Within the Confucianized code of the Ching dynasty, some ethical issues in the private domain can also be expanded and judged in the public sphere. Sometimes, the public and private domains are seen as two sides

of the same coin and there is no clear boundary between them. We still carry residues of such a cultural character, confusing our understanding of what is private and what is public. What clearly belongs to the private domain, such as sex, can be pulled into the public domain, freedom of speech, through the argument that the morality of politicians can be publicly judged. (*Taipei Times*, December 27, 2001)

The unclear boundary between the public and private spheres results in ambiguity in interpreting the sex-VCD case. Is the private life of a public figure a public affair or a private matter? Should privately expressed behaviors be made public, and conversely, publicly-aired documents be suppressed? By exposing private desire in the public sphere, were the publishers of *Weekly Scoop* seeking to confuse the private and public spheres as a means of securing profit? It is true that Chu's love affair might have offended traditional Chinese morality, however, it cannot be denied that she was also a victim of predatory peeping. It wasn't only the tabloid magazine, but also those who posted footage on the Internet who abused Chu's right to privacy in her own home.

Connected with privacy is the preservation of human dignity. Huang Cheng-yi elaborated on this in posing the hypothetical situation in which Chu could be forced to serve as defense witness in any court action.

> (Chu) could even become the subject of forensic tests in which the unique characteristics of her body would be examined. For the person involved in these procedures, formal protections, such as a closed court hearing or a reading of evidence in camera, are no guarantee that dignity will be preserved or that one's past personal experiences won't be unscrupulously exposed to the public. (*Taipei Times*, December 27, 2001).

On this scenario, female privacy – measured in terms of moral, psychological and physical integrity – could be exploited by lawyers, the media and consuming public, all viewing gender behaviour and identity through the lenses of traditional Chinese morality, law, and man-made definition.

The VCD case as a media practices text

Since the Chu case, media watchdog organizations have been extremely critical of the behavior of Taiwan's broadcast and print media. They charge that newspapers' collective aggressiveness not only amplified the gravity of the incident, but elevated it to the level of national or even regional attention. True, *Scoop Weekly* was the only magazine circulating the VCD publicly, yet coverage by other media organizations – in part spurred by their own economic self-interest – helped to inflate the size and intensity of the story. This sensationalist impulse has not diminished since the original case died down. For this reason, the political economy of media representation, as well as the propriety of media practice, have became other topics debated within the public sphere.

Media technologies and public voyeurism

Chu's case was heavily influenced by media. In large part this was because of the prominent position of media in Taiwanese society, engaging publics and circulating values. Not all of this led to particularly positive results, certainly for Chu, but also women in general. Let's consider some manifestations and outcomes.

Hidden cameras

The sex-VCD scandal began because Chu and her lover were captured engaging in sex via a hidden pinhole camera. Surreptitious filming has become a disturbingly popular phenomenon in Taiwan. Pinhole cameras can be found not only in public toilets and hotel rooms, but also prying into private bedrooms. The scandal has sparked a heated debate about morality and fears that Taiwan will become an Orwellian society, especially for celebrities. Cameras become tools for invasion and possible blackmail, intimidation, harassment, and exploitation. In his 1937 discussion of photographs Walter Benjamin (1968: 226) acutely observed that photos are made 'for the purpose of establishing evidence...photographs become standard evidence (of) historical occurrences, and acquire a hidden political significance.' It would seem that nowadays, a video camera has acquired that same hidden political status. In Chu's case, at least, the video became evidence with political significance measured in terms of sexuality, political economy, gender equality, morality, law, and culture.

The Internet

It was Internet communication that transformed Chu's into a household name – not only in Taiwan, but abroad as well. According to *The Taipei Times Online*, the sex-VCD riveted Singapore Internet users, who became the largest national block to seek updates on the story. Lycos.com reported on February 5, 2002, that twenty-three percent of web searches originated from Singapore; with twelve percent from Thailand, four percent from Malaysia, one percent from China, and, interestingly, only one percent from Taiwan. Searches also were undertaken from the US (fourteen percent), Australia and Canada.

Prior to *Scoop Weekly*'s story, there were rumors of the secretly taped VCD circulating on the Internet. After the story broke, web users divided into two diametrically opposed camps. On one media watchgroup's web site a user wrote that *Scoop Weekly*'s behavior was shameless and deplorable and the publisher was damaging Taiwan's moral fiber. By contrast, another user applauded the weekly's action, arguing that nothing less than the truth itself was at stake. Ten days after the sex-VCD incident was reported, Taipei prosecutors questioned and arrested more than twenty people – mostly college and university students – for reproducing and distributing the VCD. According to a prosecutor, many college students were selling the pirated VCD to their schoolmates or posting it on their web sites. Prosecutors emphasized that even those who sent the video footage to their friends via e-mail on the Internet were violating an article of the Criminal Code, which makes it illegal to violate a person's privacy.

Benjamin (1968) claimed that 'the desire of contemporary masses to bring things "closer" spatially and humanly,' is what motivates their media use (for him mechanical reproduction). Certainly, the Internet helps users realize that desire. However, it also does more; for instance, advanced communication technologies provide editing functions by which individuals can easily reproduce the image and create different versions on their own. Distribution is also rendered more efficient – reducing time and spanning greater distance. In this way, the Internet enables the contemporary mass to be something more than simple media readers; they are also message producers and reproducers. These same attributes mean that the Internet can also serve as the best tool for encroaching on someone's private life. Stolen images are quickly disseminated to viewers who possess the desire to render another person's private world closer to them. The Internet has become a mechanism that makes public voyeurism possible, irrespective of concern for whether the reproductive action invades individual privacy. The real problem lies not only in the capabilities of the technology, but in the ethics of the distributor, as well as the existence of a market driven by voyeuristic impulses.

The voyeuristic public

Because of the Internet numerous versions of the VCD were distributed locally, regionally and globally, with downloads available for free on personal websites as well as for money on porn mega sites. However, the video was not distributed exclusively via the Internet; copies were also sold at night markets and bazaars in Taiwan prior to government confiscation.

What accounts for this voracious public appetite for Chu's VCD? Many have pointed to the voyeuristic tendency of the Taiwanese people. As one letter to the editor asserted 'without our insatiable appetite for scandal, perhaps this ordeal could have been avoided.' (*Taipei Times*, December 30, 2001). Another writer offered:

> (the public are) voyeur(s), eas(ily) titillated and the media pander to them...*Scoop Weekly*, which distributed the VCD free with its latest edition, was sold out shortly...Before then, the video was burning up the hard drives of Web surfers around the nation as it made the rounds on the Internet – that medium which is synonymous with sex. (*Taipei Times*, December 21, 2001)

Technologies reproducing gender inequality

According to the Modern Women's Foundation in Taiwan, the fear of being caught on film by a hidden camera was a top concern for women polled in both 1998 and 2000. Several photographs and videos of women at subway stations were distributed over the Internet, prompting police to pay attention to the issue. Photos of women using public restrooms – many apparently filmed with hidden cameras – have become rampant on the Internet, as well. It is almost exclusively women who are the targets of secret filming and, via Internet distribution, the private incursion – and their victimization – is amplified.

The fact is that women are consistently treated as objects to be looked at in most cultures. This perception – backed up by technological intrusions such as pinhole surveillance distributed over the Internet – means that a dominant cultural ideology prevails; it continually imposes a dominant gendered identity on women. At the same time, these technologies work to satisfy the public's voyeuristic pleasure. As Hsu Chia-ching, the secretary-general of the Taiwan Women's League, argues:

> ...the media's performance falls short of what a civilized society can tolerate in a number of ways: secret filming, the distribution of the video and media coverage of the case. Not only were a citizen's basic rights violated, but the meaning of free speech and free press was trampled in the process. (*Taipei Times*, December 29, 2001).

Summary

In short, media technologies conspired to reinforce the patriarchal ideology of a traditional Chinese culture. Although in theory Internet communication enables the airing of different voices and multiple, pluralistic readings, in this case it facilitated the further subjugation of women, especially by abetting satisfaction of the human voyeuristic impulse. New communication technologies, such as pinhole cameras, Internet communication and Web sites – though potentially liberating – acted in this case to play to and even activate voyeuristic and fetishistic mechanisms. Such impulses reinforced cultural practices of representation to support the invasion of privacy and exploitation of a woman's personal bodily experience.

Mediated gender inequalities

In a letter to the public Chu Mei-feng wrote of herself:

> Chu Mei-feng is dead. No matter what the truth is, Chu Mei-feng has suffered physically and psychologically. Within the imaginary report from the media, I am sentenced to death...No matter how strong I am, I could not arm myself. It has been said that Mei-feng was a good-looking and sincere woman, but now I would say that I'm just an ordinary woman...How could our society so cruelly allow *Scoop Weekly* to tear me down? It might present our unbalanced social perspective on female performance. (*China Times*, December 20, 2001)

It was three days after the story ran that Chu Mei-feng broke her silence, asserting that *Scoop Weekly*'s unsubstantiated report and distribution of a video featuring a woman who resembled her was tantamount to a death sentence. Nonetheless, appearing on television, Chu apologized for having erred and bowed for causing a societal uproar. Responding to her public disclaimers, some readers of the *Taipei Times* stated that it might be wrong that Chu had sex with a married man, however, Chu herself was single. It was the man who broke his marriage vows, they pointed out, a criminal offense in Taiwan. The married man was subject to one year in prison, yet Chu was the one being publicly condemned. In both media treatment of the affair and also general public reaction considerable gender inequality can be discerned.

Gender in traditional Taiwanese culture

Historically, when men betrayed their marriage vows in traditional Chinese culture, women have been far from advantaged. They have suffered the double victimization of a cheating husband who they must, nonetheless, excuse and accept back. This is the result of 'rules' imposed by a patriarchal society which keep women financially dependent on men. In Chu's case, while she was not married, the public treated her as an adulterer and, therefore, a criminal. The wife of Chu's adulterous partner was no less a victim, of course, as her husband broke his marriage vows, but was almost immediately forgiven. He quickly disappeared from the public eye. In that sense, while both women were victims, the man escaped societal censure because of traditional cultural definitions of sexuality and immorality.

In ancient Chinese culture, men who had several female lovers were often described as possessing a 'casual and elegant bearing' as well as being 'charming,' or 'dashing.' By contrast, a woman having more than one male lover was often described as 'fickle and lascivious.' Men could enjoy many concubines; but women were property who belonged to the man following marriage. Any woman engaging in an affair after marriage, not only was guilty of adultery, but would be expelled from the family and shunned by neighbors. Obviously, then, significant double standards concerning sexual roles, practices and possibilities existed in the past, but have continued into the present. A double standard is also reflected in the etymology of certain Chinese characters. For instance, the word 'marry' used for females consists of a woman and a home, meaning 'a woman finds a home.' However, the male version consists of a woman and the word 'gain,' meaning 'gaining a woman in his home.' This thought-pattern is reflected in actual household behavior, where, in traditional Chinese culture, a daughter fulfills her duties by obeying her father at home, her husband once married off, and her son after her husband is dead. Female as subject never ceases on this account of gender identity; female subjectivity never exists under such a double standard – one which is deeply ingrained in Taiwanese society.

Adultery by gender in contemporary Taiwan

As public debate swelled in the aftermath of the sex-VCD scandal, gender inequality was hotly debated in terms of enduring double standards, obstacles to life chances, and necessary revisions in the law. Reflecting on the first two points, Hsu Chia-ching, the secretary-general of the Taiwan Women's League, wrote:

> The affair exposed our society's deeply entrenched hypocrisy and chauvinistic culture. Why can a man involved in an extra-marital affair escape moral condemnation and legal responsibility…while the woman must bear a cross for their sins?…Please first look clearly at whether you are also guilty of collusion with traditional patriarchal society and the media before examining the moral standards of others…The women of Taiwan wish to sing their own songs without being maliciously hurt or hounded by the shameless media. (*Taipei Times*, December 29, 2001).

On this view, female development is limited by cultural and sexual biases that place extremely high expectations of sexual morality on women that don't seem to apply to men. In turn, a possible result might be a serious reduction in the desire of women to work and establish their power in the public sphere.

As for the legal debate, women's groups argued that Taiwan is burdened by an outdated system. Those subject to prosecution for adultery required protection and an effort should be made to decriminalize adultery. The reason, some groups asserted, is that in a traditional society such as Taiwan, women are always victimized by sex scandals. As Wang Ping put it:

> The adultery law is unfair to women. It takes two people to engage in sex – both a man and a woman. If it is not a rape case, then it will mean that both parties agreed to have sex. As a result, adultery is an act in which both parties are responsible. However, in a patriarchal country when adultery accusations are made, people usually blame women. Men are forgiven…Patriarchal thought will only restrict the freedom of women…[Adultery] is not a crime. It is improper behavior. (*Taipei Times*, December 31, 2001).

Rather than affixing legal culpability, some critics emphasized that adultery ought not to be within the purview of the criminal justice system. Instead, the Civil Code should be amended to protect women's property rights. Such alterations, they stressed, ought not be effected *before* adultery is removed from the Criminal Code, however, in order to avoid the misperception that a woman's rights to both justice and property are being eroded. Fear of a tightening of patriarchal control remained high.

The concern about over-legislation prompted the *Taipei Times* to assert that although adultery was possibly immoral, certain matters are better left between the adulterer and his or her own conscience, free of intrusion by the law. Relative economic power is an important consideration here, as is a highly regimented gender system:

> Some argue that criminal sanctions for adultery protect women, because they are often the weaker partner in marriage. But when this is the case, it is because they are financially and emotionally dependent on their husbands. So why not address such problems at their roots? Empower women financially and emotionally by giving them social, cultural and work environments that do not discriminate and handicap them because of their sex. (*Taipei Times*, December 23, 2001).

Women's place in Taiwanese society

'If society will accept me again, I want to do more good deeds,' Chu Mei-feng declared on February 7, 2002. However, the question 'what kind of deed would be deemed good in Taiwanese society' is worthy of consideration. What deeds, one might ask, can satisfy a voyeuristic society? What deeds would satisfy a patriarchal society? Should a woman act in ways that adhere to the social rules of a patriarchal society, thereby limiting her development? Such societies (and their cultural support structures) can only restrain women from career development. Women will always end up subject to and victimized within a culture of gender inequality. As Lingis (1984) explains, the female body is a savage body; it is culturally inscribed to be submissive and obedient. The body of a savage is not, as ours is for us, an expression belonging to oneself. Its identity belongs to, and is defined by, others.

This view finds support in Gatens (1996). The modern body politic, she writes,

> ...is based on an image of a masculine body which reflects fantasies about the value and capacities of that body. The effects of this image show its contemporary influence (on) our social and political behavior which continues to implicitly accord privilege to particular bodies and their concerns as they are reflected in our ways of speaking and in what we speak about. (Gatens 1996: 25).

The image of the female – for instance, of Chu on the VCD, or Chu apologizing in public, or of women in cases of adultery – signifies cultural structure and practices and beliefs. As we consider in the following section, the female body is defined within a system of power relations. Gender identity is constructed and maintained to legitimate a social order in which males are superior (and rule) while females are inferior (and submit). What is most noteworthy about the Chu case, is that for once this traditional view of gender identity was turned on its head.

Reinventing identity

In the sex-VCD scandal, the female was both criminal and victim, surveilled by hidden camera, public, and an unequal, gendered culture. Female experience – intended to be privately performed – was placed in public space through the form of images universally disbursed over the Internet. Whoever received the VCD – by whatever electronic means – came to possess the criminal/victim's experience and body. Once appropriated and distributed these elements were transformed into public belongings. This reminds us of Nelson (1989: 225), who states: 'women's bodies have been controlled by and described by men, for purposes prescribed by and perpetuated by men, just as the bodies/selves of prisoners and delinquents are inscribed and constrained by institutional structures of power.'

It is true that women in traditional Chinese culture have been tightly bound by a set of ethics designed by and for the benefit of men. However, in the contemporary era we have come to believe that identity is subjective and constructed; it is neither fixed nor stable. In Woodward's (1997: 2) words 'identities are produced, consumed and regulated within culture-creating meanings through symbolic systems of representation about the identity positions which we *might* adopt' (emphasis added).

Media consumers are provided texts that emanate from particular institutional and power relations. Those texts contain identifications, the implication of which operates on the mechanism of subject identification. It is up to the readers to interpret these texts by recourse to their own identities. Thus, although gender identity is a determinate type that is constructed within and as a result of certain power relations (e.g. Grosz 1994: 149), subjective identity is not necessarily fixed; it is not necessarily determined by the cultural identification predominant in the given milieu. The female could be an active subject that might re-invent and change the original identity.

This is precisely what occurred in the case of Chu Mei-feng. Despite being bounded by a traditional patriarchal culture, Chu decided to be something more than a docile body. Employing the same media that had exploited her private experience, Chu raised her voice against traditional culture and spoke to anyone who could accept her and listen to her. This did not sit well with public opinion. The public thought that Chu should keep silent and disappear. A female adulterer, the conservative line went, should live in seclusion to repent for her shameless behavior, just as an immoral woman would be expelled by her people in traditional Chinese culture.

Quite the contrary, Chu took positive action, fighting to reclaim her dignity and identity. After she apologized to the public for causing such a public disturbance, Chu published a book, *Love Confession*, in February 2002, which revealed relationships with more than a dozen men. The public, generally appalled, criticized Chu of trying to cash in on the VCD scandal. Rather than respond to these criticisms, Chu forged ahead, taking a job a month later as host of a radio show named 'Power Secret Garden.' Facing severe public condemnation Chu argued, 'I haven't had a job for half a year. Working to make a bit of money is not a sin.' Although public scorn might normally restrict a woman's career development, a week later, on March 11, Chu showed up on television as host of a regular talk show, 'Female Secret Garden.' The purpose of this program was to discuss topics related to female independence.

Not much later, in mid-March 2002, Chu made her public singing debut in Singapore – the site of greatest interest in the original scandal. Chu Mei-feng, the politician-turned-writer-turned-media personality-turned singer, was paid roughly eighty-six thousand U.S. dollars for three days of performances. However, she was barred from performing in Malaysia, when she was described as a bad role model for young people. Again refusing to lie quiet, Chu brought a civil action against the eleven criminal defendants in the sex-VCD case on April 11th, 2002. She demanded NT $133 million. In open court Chu admitted for the first time that she was the woman on the sex-VCD.

Chu's revival through a variety of media was certainly astonishing. Her appearance in books, on radio, television, on stage, in the courts and tabloids, violated the rule of traditional gendered identity in which the female wrongdoer should keep her mouth shut and shy away from public. Her reinvented image challenged traditional Chinese cultural identity and contradicted the Taiwanese public's expectations. Such actions clearly demonstrate that this particular female identity, at least, was, to quote Battersby (1998: 7) 'not a fixed, permanent or pre-given "thing" or "substance" that undergoes metamorphosis, but that nevertheless remains always unaltered through change.' Chu actively performed as a host and a singer in the media and for the public that once harmed her physically and psychologically through a process of violent, non-consensual signification. Her performative bodily actions attempted to (and did) subvert the traditional female identity.

Foucault was perhaps the first to observe that the body is directly constituted in a political field. 'Power relations have an immediate hold upon it,' he wrote; 'they invest it, mark it, train it, torture it, force it to carry out tasks, to perform ceremonies, to emit signs. This political investment of the body is bound up, in accordance with complex reciprocal relations…'(Foucault 1979: 25). While Foucault saw the body as caught up in a 'system of subjugation' (ibid.: 26), observing Chu's post-VCD acts, one could argue that the female body was less subject; that her expression of self-identity reflected subjective awareness and personal power. Viewed in terms of reciprocal relations, Chu refused to remain subject; she ignored the conservative public expectations that she hide herself like a prisoner into the private sphere or silence herself in the public sphere. Instead, she reinvented her self through media and in public, creating possibilities for cultural emancipation. Chu did not allow her identity to be subordinated by a traditional patriarchal society in which inequalities in gender are constructed, regulated and maintained. Her female body became independent to the degree that it re-created its own performative stage, even as the public was trapped within a gendered culture. It is as Judith Butler asserts in her book *Gender Trouble*: plural possibilities can exist for the culturally constructed body. There are subversive bodily acts by which the gendered culture can be overcome, by which the self can be liberated.

> If subversion is possible, it will be a subversion from within the terms of the law, through the possibilities that emerge when the law turns against itself and spawns unexpected permutations of itself. The culturally constructed body will then be liberated, neither to its 'natural' past, nor to its original pleasures, but to an open future of cultural possibilities. (Butler 1990: 93).

It is almost as if Butler were writing with Chu's case in mind.

Conclusion

In the sex-VCD case the process of representation, in the first instance, commercialized the female bodily experience as a product capable of titillating the voyeuristic public via media reports and Internet downloads. However, in the second instance, the reading practices of all participants relied on the identifications of the actors being represented in the text, as well as the reader's identity. Because identities are constructed within discourse, as Hall (1996: 17) indicates, 'we need to understand them as produced in specific historical and institutional sites within specific discursive formations and practices, by specific enunciative strategies.' Gender identity as a political field is based on relations between multiple and unstable forces coming from politics, economy, morality, ethics, law, society, and culture.

The furor caused by this sex-VCD scandal was not only public astonishment about the improper behavior of a young female politician, but also the challenge Chu waged against traditional gender identity. As a politician, a criminal, a voyeuristic object, a victim, a dead person, a writer, a radio and TV hostess, and a singer, Chu embodied mobile and unstable identities. Singing on her stage and dancing across the cultural boundary, Chu reinventing the female identity imposed on her by Taiwanese society, media, and consuming public, alike. Her act of reinventing self provided possibilities of resistance and created her own subjectivity beyond traditional cultural limits.

Part III
Cities and Urbanization

10 Social and Economic Restructuring and the New Economy in Singapore

Scott Baum

Introduction

In the sociological literature dealing with cities, a common theme has continued to be the association between economic restructuring and unequal social outcomes. While these concerns have a long history, dating back to the earliest sociological treatment of cities, the contemporary manifestations of this research interest have focused on the impacts that globalization and the increasing importance of new economy sectors have on the social structures of cities, especially cities that play important global roles. Like earlier work into the social impact of economic change within cities, that focusing on the contemporary rounds of restructuring have attempted to identify the winners and losers in terms of economic resources, the role of the state and civil society and the possible consequences of long term sustained changes. While the concerns and outcomes are in some ways similar to earlier work, it is the causal nature of the changes that is said to be different.

Heavily influenced by the work by Sassen (1991) and that of Friedmann and Wolff (1982) contemporary work on economic restructuring-mainly seen as the outcome of increased economic globalization – and its social outcomes within a growing band of world or global cities has largely come to the conclusion that

> major cities are increasingly being divided into a growing highly skilled and highly paid upper stratum and a growing low-skilled, low-income stratum...The middle stratum is declining, both absolutely and relatively (Hamnett 1996: 1407).

This change in the social structure (measured narrowly in terms of occupation and income) became through the 1990s the dominant interpretation of change occurring in global cities. It is reflected most eloquently in the work by Marcuse (1989: 699) who states that

> The best image...is perhaps that of the egg and the hour glass: the population of the city is normally distributed like an egg, widest in the middle and tapering off at both ends; when it becomes polarized the middle is squeezed and the ends expand till it looks like an hour glass. The middle of the egg may be defined as intermediate social strata...Or if the polarization is between rich and poor, the middle of the egg refers to the middle income group...The metaphor is not structural dividing lines, but a continuum, whose distribution is becoming increasingly bi-modal.

The evidence and argument relating to the uneven nature of social outcomes associated with globalization has been focused largely on North American cities and those in Europe and the United Kingdom (see for example Hamnett and Cross 1996; Harrison and Bluestone 1988; Kuttner 1983; Lawrence 1984; Levy 1987; Smith and Timberlake 1995; Stark 1992), with a growing collection of material focusing on the Asia Pacific region (See for example, Baum 1997; Cho 1997; Hung 1996; Lepani 1994).

While there is little disagreement that the economic restructuring is manifesting itself within large cities in terms of an increasing group of winners and losers, there still remains a strong debate regarding the actual shape of these outcomes. With reference to this issue, Hamnett (1996) has been an ardent antagonist. Hamnett (1996) argues that much of the global city-social polarization research, especially that emanating from North America has tended to adopt a mono-causal approach when describing social polarization rather than a multi-causal approach. In analyzing social polarization in global cites there has been an implication that global forces are the most important factors in explaining levels of social polarization. However, such a direct and mono-causal approach needs to be questioned as it is insufficient to look at social polarization without considering the social, historical and economic development of particular nation states. That is, both global and local forces must be seen as interacting to produce given social outcomes. Here Hamnett (1996: 1411) argues that 'what is happening in certain cities in the US in not necessarily happening in similar cities in other countries because of differences in the economic, social and institutional context'. Local processes, including different welfare and labor force policy, different migration patterns and different occupation and labor force structure, must be seen as being influential.

This chapter is placed in the context of the discussion above and focuses on the city-state of Singapore. Importantly it discusses Singapore's role as a key urban node in a number of 'new economy' activities both regionally and on the wider global stage and provides a commentary on the changing nature of occupations and incomes that are a result of these changes. In this sense the chapter provides further analysis of the urban impacts of the current bout of global economic restructuring, adding to what has become a growing body of literature on the subject. In what follows, the changing position of Singapore as a global city and the rise of new economy sectors will be discussed, before turning to consider the outcomes in terms of occupational restructuring and growing socio-economic disparities.

Singapore in the global economy

Any casual observer of cities would easily identify several places across the globe that fit the model of world or global cities. Hymer (1972) produced one of the first lists of global cities based on a hierarchy of Trans-national Corporations and since that time various places have been identified as global cities based on their economic functions (Fujita 1991; King 1990; Markusen and Gwiasda 1994; Pryke 1991; Sassen 1991, 1994; Taylor and Walker 2001; Thrift 1994; Zukin 1992).

Within the Asia region, Tokyo has always played a key role in the global urban network. However, following in the wake of Japan's post-war economic ascendancy several cities in the region including the city states of Singapore and Hong Kong, together with Seoul and Taipei have come to play increasingly important global roles. Moreover, in recent times cities including Osaka, Manila, Bangkok, Kuala Lumpur, Jakarta and more recently Shanghai have risen to global city status. Outside the immediate Asia Region are cities including Sydney and Melbourne in Australia which play a role in the new global economy.

With specific reference to Singapore, the city-state has during much of the past decade been increasingly labeled as an important global urban node. Since its separation from Malaysia in 1965 till the present time the Singapore government has strived to mould the city-state as an important global player. In this sense Singapore's leadership, through economic and social policy and infrastructure planning, have 'labored to transform the city-state into a linchpin of the new global capitalism '(Beng 1993: 105). Both in terms of physical infrastructure and leading economic sectors, Singapore's global position is evident.

Urban infrastructure in the global city

As cities become even more focused as hubs for information flows, finance and business and high-end ancillary services, the terms of trade will shift to favor those who can successfully manage and coordinate resources. As part of this management, urban governments must provide efficient and timely infrastructure that both maintains economic momentum and re-engineers past successes and attracts new economic activity.

With reference to Singapore's successful transition to a global city, it is recognized that the city-state has met many of the infrastructure challenges thrown up by greater global integration. Here Yuan and Choo (1995: 91) assert that 'Singapore's potential as an international business centre was increasingly recognized, and major governmental decisions were taken to support this by creating the basic infrastructure needed'. On a number of measures the city-state shows significant improvement in urban infrastructure provision.

In telecommunications, the number of dial up Internet subscribers has increased from 2000 in 1994 to 1 318 000 in 2001, while mobile phone usage increased by 96.1% from 110 000 in 1992 to 2 859 000 in 2001. Moreover, with reference to Singapore's global linkages the level of international telecommunications traffic has increased significantly. International phone calls increased from 284 million minutes in 1991 to 2561 million minutes in 2001 (Singapore Department of Statistics 2002a).

Moreover, a strategy to link Singaporeans into the information economy through the integration of 800 000 households centrally into two service providers – Singapore Telecommunications and Singapore Cable Vision – has been developed. The main objective of this strategy has to make Singapore a highly networked 'e-society' and develop a seamless integrated system of cyber space in which just about every activity can be performed from the workplace, school and home: online shopping, studying, watching movies and other entertainment programs, video conferencing, paying bills and receiving all sorts of information (Savage and Pow 2001:111).

In 1990, the World Competitiveness Report already ranked Singapore number one in IT usage and management amongst nine other developing nations. A report in 2000 by the Infocomm Development Authority of Singapore shows that about three in five (59 per cent) houses in Singapore had a computer – higher than in the USA (54 per cent), Australia (47 per cent), and Japan (42 per cent) (The Straits Times 21 January 2000:74).

Transport infrastructure has also been upgraded with a land transport policy which 'strives to provide a world-class land transport system – one that is integrated, efficient, affordable, with smooth-flowing traffic and that will meet the people's needs and support economic and environmental goals' (Ministry of Transport 2001: n.p.). A key has been the introduction of the Mass Rapid Transit system that provides approximately 1.1 million passengers per day an efficient public transport system, covering 49 stations and stretching a total of 91 kilometers (Ministry of Information, Communication and the Arts 2002a; Singapore Department of Statistics 2002a). Over and above this, policies that aim to reduce the impact of private vehicles on roads such as a vehicle quota system and electronic road pricing, also contribute to quality transport infrastructure.

The city-state's position as an international transport hub is well known and is an important component of the government's globalization/ internationalization goals. Over the decade 1991 to 2001 civil aircraft landings increased from just over 54 000 annually to over 89 000 annually. The number of arriving passenger including those in transit increased from 8.8 million to 14.8 million and Singapore's Changi International airport has consistently won awards for the best airport worldwide. The role of Singapore as an important seaport has long been crucial for the city-state's economic growth. Reflecting the continuing importance the total sea cargo, vessel arrivals increased from 70 345 in 1991 to 146 265 in 2001 with a total cargo of over 313 million tones (Singapore Department of Statistics 2002a).

Singapore's reputation as a clean, green and efficient city and as an attractive place for business has been predicated in part by its urban planning, and the provision of social infrastructure such as housing and health care. As noted by Savage and Pow (2001: 118)

> It is clear that grand economic strategies would ultimately be unsustainable in the long run without adequate provision for the local population and work force. This is particularly true in the case of Singapore where human resources are critical to the development of the city-state. In a new "people driven" Knowledge Based Economy, long-term investments in housing, education and healthcare must continue to be a priority on the agenda of city governments

On several measures Singapore scores highly. Over 85 per cent of the population is housed in Housing Development Board flats, with many estates providing fully integrated community facilities, retail outlets and public transport hubs. This compares with the 1950s and 1960s when approximately 45% of Singapore households lived in slums and squatter settlements. Moreover, the success of the housing system in Singapore is evidenced by the superior rate of home ownership with 9 per cent of residents owning their homes compared with only 9 per cent when the Housing Development Board was first established (Savage and Pow 2001).

On health care statistics, Singapore rates amongst more developed countries. The World Health Organization ranked the city-state 6th on health care provision behind countries such as Japan and the United States (The Straits Times 21 June, 2000: 3). Health care is provided through 17 outpatient polyclinics, 1200 private medical practitioners clinics and another 27 health care institutions including a total of 11 897 hospital beds (Ministry of information, Communications and the Arts 2002a). The government annually expends approximately $4194 million or 2.7 per cent of DDP (Ministry of information and the Arts 1999).

External linkages and the growth of key economic sectors

The level of external linkages both in terms of transnational flows into Singapore and those from Singapore to elsewhere is an important indicator of the level of global connectedness of the city-state. Enhancing external linkages is a key policy focus in Singapore and is an important part of globalization strategy. The ability to attract foreign investment has been a key to these linkages. For Singapore attracting foreign capital is

> Essential in view of the weak domestic technological base and the long lead-time needed to transform domestic entrepot traders and small scale entrepreneurs into a dynamic industrial entrepreneurial class able to compete in the global market (Chia 1997: 32).

Reflecting this strategy foreign investment in the city-state's economy increased significantly from 7900 foreign owned firms in 1989 contributing 47 billion Singapore dollars in equity to over 19 000 firms in 1999 contributing 178 billion Singapore dollars in equity. The cluster of finance and business firms attracted the highest proportion (38.6 per cent 1999) while manufacturing accounted for a further 53 billion Singapore dollars or 30.3 per cent. (Singapore Department of Statistics 2002a).

While the push to attract foreign investment into Singapore has been important, increasingly there has been a two-way flow with Singapore now contributing equity to overseas ventures. As an important strategy to strengthen Singapore's global competitiveness, the push for a greater regional and global presence through international investment has given rise to a number of projects with Singaporean backing. The establishment of the Singapore-Johore-Riau Growth Triangle in the late 1980s signaled an important step in the level of Singapore investment abroad and was viewed by many as a good base with which to take Singaporean capital onto the international stage (Macleod and McGee 1996). More recently, initiatives such as the establishment of overseas business networks – the Majulah connection – are seen as a key to continuing the internationalization drive (Lim 2002). Figures from the Department of Statistics illustrate the recent extent of Singapore's overseas investment commitments. Between 1994 and 1999 the level of Singapore's equity investment abroad increased from 33% of Gross Domestic Product to 52% of Gross Domestic Product a large proportion being targeted in Asia, especially in China, Malaysia and Indonesia (Singapore Department of Statistics 2002a).

As a result of Singapore's push for greater global interconnectedness and polices aimed at strengthening economic development, the city state has witnessed significant changes in the make up of key economic sectors. As some observers suggest

The achievements already attained by the city-state can be observed in the changes in its economic structure. Over the past three decades, manufacturing and financial and business services have become the two most important categories in economic activity...These changes enabled the city-state to create a more developed, diversified and globally integrated economy. In both its exports and imports, Singapore's trade is moving towards technology intensive and human capital-intensive commodities (Yamazaawa et al., 1991 quoted in Beng, 1993: 104–105)

This position has not evolved by accident, but rather the government of Singapore is constantly re-engineering its industrialization strategies to take advantage of its comparative advantage. The drive towards promoting greater inroads into new economic sectors has been guided by specific strategies. To promote and develop knowledge driven industries, currently six initiatives have been set out:
1 the 'Industry 21' program to attract investments in high growth, high value-added industries focusing on electronics, chemicals, life sciences and engineering clients;
2 'Trade 21' which seeks to make Singapore a global city of international trade and services;
3 'Tourism 21' which provides a blueprint for the development of a world-class tourism industry;
4 'ICT 21', an information and telecommunications technology plan to harness ICT for national competitiveness;
5 building a world class financial centre; and
6 a 'Technopreneurship 21' initiative involving public officials and private business leaders to development entrepreneurial high-tech businesses in Singapore.

The aim of these strategies is to 'build and sustain vibrant industries through greater diversification within and among key industry clusters, and promote knowledge driven activities across the value chain' (Ministry of information, Communications and the Arts 2002a: 131).

Reflecting the success of strategies such as these, the level of output across new economy sectors has increased. At a general level the contribution of service producing industries to GDP has increased over the past decade, especially business and financial services which now collectively account for 28 per cent of the city-state's GDP. In contrast, the manufacturing industry saw a decline in share of GDP to 23 per cent, from around 30 per cent a decade earlier (Singapore Department of Statistics 2002a).

Clearly then, Singapore's role in the network of global cities is illustrated by its global and regional functions and its increased international reach. The extent to which the emergence of Singapore as an important node in the collection of global cities is associated with outcomes including transformations in occupation and income distribution is discussed in the remainder of this chapter.

The new economy and global city occupational structures

The changes that occur in the economic functions of cities inevitably result in transitions occurring in the occupational structure.

> The disproportionate concentration of major growth industries in global cities...result in a distinct restructuring of the job supply in such cities...Thus, a changing incidence of a few major industries in the economic base of localities can bring about major shifts in the socio-economic characteristics of the labor force (Sassen-Koob 1994: 52).

This 'fact' of economic restructuring has been an important part of the understanding of the social impacts of global city networks. Sassen (1994: 102) refers to what she sees as a polarizing trend in occupations as the growth in service based occupations results in 'an increasing polarization of employment opportunities with new types of social divisions'. Following Sassen's work the growth of new class divisions along occupational lines within the network of global cities have been tested and although there has been some debate as to the eventual shape of the new class divisions (Hamnett 1994) change in the overall composition of the labor force within global cities has become a certainty.

The change in the occupational characteristics of the Singapore labor force reflects wider industrialization policies focusing on service based jobs and upper-end manufacturing positions. Over the decade 1990–2000 there was an increase in the proportion of the labor force characterized as administrators and managers, professionals, technical and related personnel and clerical workers. The category 'cleaners and laborers' showed only a small increase, while the category sales and services and production and related workers accounted for a reduced share of the total labor force. Specifically, clerical workers recorded the largest increase in share, accounting for a further 11.4 per cent of the employed labor force (13.0 per cent to 24.4 per cent), with the other increasing categories accounting for between 3 and 4 percent extra over the decade. The decline in employment in the category of 'production and related jobs' stood at 6.4 percentage points, from 30.8 per cent in 1990 to 24.4 per cent in 2000. The occupational class 'sales and services' declined in importance by 2.6 percentage points (table 10.1).

These figures suggest that like global cities elsewhere, Singapore has undergone changes in the make up of its occupational structure. Whether these depict an increasingly polarized structure in Sassen's terms or a move towards a more professionalized structure (as Hamnett 1994 would argue), they are clearly an outcome of the strategies employed by the government to position the city-state as an important economic node in the global network. Over and above these aggregate level indicators, two other characteristics have come to influence the labor force in global cities; these are the increasing presence of expatriate experts and the rise in low skilled immigrant labor.

Global city occupational structure – the emerging cosmopolitan elite

A feature of the changing nature of the occupational structure in global cities, and one that has become increasingly important in Singapore has been the involvement of "large clusters of high-

Table 10.1: Occupational distribution, Singapore 1990 & 2000

	1990 (%)	2000 (%)	Change
Administrative & Managerial	8.6	11.9	+3.3
Professional	4.9	8.9	+4.0
Technical & Related	10.8	14.9	+4.1
Clerical	13.0	24.4	+11.4
Sales & Services	12.7	10.1	−2.6
Production and Related	30.8	24.4	−6.4
Cleaners & Laborers	15.0	16.0	+1.0
Others	4.3	2.6	−1.7

Source: Ministry of Manpower, 2002

waged professional and managerial expatriate workers (Beaverstock 1996: 424). Kanter (1997: 22–23) refers to these expatriate workers as 'cosmopolitans'.

> Cosmopolitans are card carrying members of the world class-often literally card carrying, with passports or air tickets serving to admit them. They lead companies that are linked to global chains. Comfortable in many places and able to understand and bridge the differences among them, cosmopolitans possess portable skills and a broad outlook. Cosmopolitans are rich in three intangible assets...concepts,... competence...and connections.

Cosmopolitans have become an important segment of the new economy occupational structure often attracting large salaries.

In Singapore's case, the ability to attract 'foreign talent' has been an important part of industrialization strategy. Recognizing this fact the government has followed a policy of 'gathering global talent' and 'making Singapore a cosmopolitan city' (Prime Minister Goh, quoted in Yeoh and Chang 2001). Workers entering Singapore are granted either an employment pass or a work permit. Employment passes are reserved for professionals and skilled workers with recognized qualifications, while work permits are reserved for unskilled and semi-skilled workers. It is the former category that constitutes Kanter's (1997) cosmopolitans.

Between 1990 and 2000 the annual average growth of nonresident workers in Singapore was 9.4 per cent representing an increase over ten years of 364 000 persons, with approximately one-fifth being classified as administrative/ managerial, professionals or technical and related workers. This compares to the resident worker category which had an annual average rate of growth of only 1.4 per cent – an increase of 557 800 persons. (Singapore Department of Statistics 2000).

Global city occupation structure – low skilled immigrant workers

The trans-national flows of labor into global cities is not only restricted to Kanter's cosmopolitan elite. Increasingly, an important segment of the local economy in these cities has been the presence of low waged, low skilled workers, who in many cases are foreign workers or immigrants. Sassen (1991) in her exploration of the labor force characteristics of New York, London and Tokyo recognized the important role that low skilled workers, often immigrants, would have in the restructured labor markets as a means of providing ancillary services for the growing number of professionals.

Foreign workers meet a significant proportion of Singapore's low skilled labor requirements. These workers are generally employed on work permits and are located in the construction industry or as domestic labor. In 2000 foreign workers in occupations classified as production and related workers or cleaners and laborers account for three-quarters of all foreign workers. In contrast, only one-quarter of Singaporean residents were employed in these two categories. Quoting figures from 1999 Savage and Pow (2001) provide an indication of the size of this component of the non-resident work force. The authors suggest that 'there are more than 200 000 foreign construction workers (mainly from Thailand, Myanmar, Bangladesh, India and China) and more than 100 000 foreign domestic workers from the Philippines, Sri Lanka and Indonesia' (Savage and Pow 2001: 108).

Occupational upgrading associated with educational upgrading

Hand in hand with the changing occupational structure have been the changes that have taken place in the educational structure, with a clear shift towards educational upgrading. The link between occupation and education is important given that the higher level of skills required in occupations associated the new economy also require a commensurate level of education. According to the International Monetary Fund (1997: 59), "education and training are essential, since these are important means by which workers... can upgrade their skills to match the demands of the changing global economy". Within the Singapore context, the link between education and occupation is especially important given that the government, through educational reforms, has managed to link the curriculum and structure of the education system to the needs of the global economic strategy (Dicken 1987). Indeed, government expenditure on education and vocational training has increased faster than many other categories of social expenditure (Deyo 1991).

In general terms, the level of educational attainment in Singapore is high and has risen steadily. In 2001 the city-state recorded a literacy rate for the population aged 15 years and over of 93.2 per

Table 10.2: Educational qualifications, Singapore 1991 to 2001

	1991	2001
Holds no formal qualifications or only lower primary school level education	16.7	14.2
Holds primary school level education	13.5	5.6
Holds lower secondary school level education	15.9	14.1
Holds secondary school level education	30.7	28.1
Holds post secondary school level education	11.4	10.5
Holds a diploma	4.7	10.6
Holds a degree	7.1	17.0
Total	1 524 315	2 046 744

Source: Ministry of manpower, 2002

cent, and over the decade 1991 to 2001 the mean years of schooling for residents aged 25 years and over increased from 6.8 years (1991) to 8.4 years in 2001. Over this same period, the proportion attaining higher educational qualifications has also increased reaching 17 per cent in 2001 up from 7.1 per cent in 1991 (Table 10.2).

Additionally, the extent to which the work force has been willing to undertake educational upgrading is seen to be important. 'To help business and people thrive at home in the global economy, cities must become centers of globally relevant skills, offering ways their occupants can link to the world' (Kanter 1997: 355) – upgrading of skills and qualifications is one avenue to achieve this. In Singapore skills upgrading is seen as an important obligation of all workers. According to Dr Lee Boon Yang, Minister for Manpower,

> …building our human capital is critical for Singapore's continued success. Our efforts to retrain and upgrade workers with New Economy skills will ensure investors that we are serious about realigning the economy to meet the needs of changing technology and an increasingly borderless world market…Increasingly, we must invest in training and upgrading workers with marketable skills to help them remain employable. However, the challenge of skills upgrading cannot be completely tackled by Government alone. It requires tripartite effort. Employers must support upgrading of their workers…In the New Economy, the most successful companies are likely to be those which have invested heavily in their people…Last but certainly not least, every worker must also feel the urgency and need to go

for retraining and skills upgrading. Not to do so would result in being left behind as technology changes and old skills become irrelevant (Ministry of Manpower 2000: 2).

Among residents who did not hold a university or other tertiary qualification in 2000, 13 per cent had received technical, commercial or vocational qualifications after leaving school. This is higher than the figures five years earlier (1995) when only 9.2 per cent had undertaken some form of qualifications upgrading (Singapore Department of Statistics 2002b).

Has restructuring resulted in growing disparities in income?

In an essay focusing on the global economy and urban society in Asia, Ho (1997) comments on the work of Louis Wirth (1969: 155) and in particular his observation that cities resemble a 'mosaic of social worlds where the transition from one to the other is abrupt'. Reflecting on Wirth's observations Ho recounts how

> globalization in the form of the internationalization of production and the integration of cities into the global and Pacific Asia economy contributes to this shifting mosaic through its impact on metropolitan economies and associated changes in the stratification system (1997: 285).

This concern, that global integration has resulted in increasing disparities within society, has become one of the much-researched topics in the literature on globalization. In the work of Sassen and others the focus has been on the argument that 'major growth industries show a greater incidence of jobs at the high- and low-paying ends of the scale than do the older industries now in decline' (Sassen 1991: 9). In Marcuse's terms a shift from an egg shaped distribution towards one shaped like an hour glass.

Within the context of the forgoing discussion, it is interesting to consider the experience of Singapore and the extent to which the emerging income structure has become polarized. Certainly there has been a change in the characteristics of the occupational structure, but has this resulted in a changing distribution of remuneration? Table three presents data for resident household income for 1990 and 2000, while table four presents similar data (1991–2001) for individuals, both of which are used to determine the extent of any income polarization. Both the data for household income and that for individuals illustrate a trend towards an expanding middle income stratum.

For resident households, the two bottom income categories (below $1000 and $1000 to $2999) both declined in share – minus 3.4 percentage points and minus 18.5 percentage points respectively – while the remaining categories all recorded increasing shares. The largest increase was recorded by the highest income category, which increased from a 2.8 per cent share to a 10.3 per cent share, an increase of 7.5 percentage points. Over the time frame considered, the distribution of households by income categories shifted from a negatively skewed distribution towards a distribution characterized by high proportions of middle-income earners (Table 10.3).

Similarly, for individual incomes the lowest two categories (less than $599 and $600 to $999) recorded declining shares of recipients, while the other categories recorded increasing shares. The largest increase was recorded by the second highest category ($3000 to $4999), which recorded an increase of 11.4 percentage points (5.1 percent to 16.5 percent). The distribution of individual income has, like household incomes, become characterized by a larger middle stratum (Table 10.4).

The fact that there is no polarization of incomes does not imply that increasing global integration has not resulted in adverse changes to the income structure. In fact since the changes wrought on the Asian economies by the economic crisis in 1997 and the economic slowdown beginning in 2000–2001, debate in Singapore has turned to discuss disparities in incomes that according so some

Table 10.3: Resident households by income from work, 1990 and 2000

	1990 (%)	2000 (%)	Change
Below $1000	16.0	12.6	–3.4
$1000 to $2999	47.2	28.7	–18.5
$3000 to $4999	21.2	26.4	+5.2
$5000 to $6999	8.4	14.8	+6.4
$7000 to $9999	4.5	10.6	+6.1
$10000 and over	2.8	10.3	+7.5
	100	100	

Source: Singapore Department of Statistics 2002

Table 10.4: Individual income, Singapore, 1991 and 2001

	1990 (%)	2000 (%)	Change
Less than $599	24.2	12.9	−11.3
$600 to $999	31.4	8.8	−22.6
$1000 to $1999	27.7	29.9	+2.2
$2000 to $2999	8.3	19.2	+10.9
$3000 to $4999	5.1	16.5	+11.4
$5000 and over	3.3	12.7	+9.4
	100	100	

Source: Ministry of Manpower 2002

reports appear to be growing. The flavor of such discussion is reflected in comments by Deputy Prime Minister Lee Hsien Loong who spoke about the disparity between highly skilled workers receiving 'first world wages' and lower skilled workers receiving 'third world wages' (Savage and Pow 2001 112–113), and those of George Yeo, Minister for Trade and Industry, who in discussing the unavoidable challenges of globalization commented that

> Globalization is an unavoidable challenge. Countries, companies, NGOs and individuals which respond quickly and effectively to it will succeed while those which are unable to will be left behind. There will be new winners and losers...Unfortunately, many countries are unable to do this. Globalization of the labor market increases income inequality in every country (Ministry of information, Communications and the Arts 2002b: 4).

This increasing disparity between first world wages and third world wages is reflected in Department of Statistics data which illustrates that over time the percentage of income earned by the bottom 20 per cent of households has declined, while the percentage of income going to the top 20 per cent of households has increased. In 1990 the bottom 20 per cent of households earned 4.3% of the income while the top 20 per cent earned 48.1 per cent of the income. By 2000 the bottom 20 per cent earned only 2.4 per cent of the income, while the proportion earned by the top 20 per cent had increased to 51 per cent. Considering this in terms of a ratio of incomes, the top 20% of households in 1990 earned 11.4 times the incomes of the lowest 20 per cent of households, while by 2000 this had increased to 20.9 times (Singapore Department of Statistics 2002).

This disparity between high-income groups and low-income groups has increasingly concerned public policy makers and academics and some possible implications arising from these changes are addressed in the concluding section.

New economy transitions and transforming social structures: Some implications

Questions surrounding economic restructuring and the social outcomes in terms of incomes have become an important topic in the social sciences literature dealing with cities. While the debates around these changes have been part of the literature for some time, the contemporary manifestations of these debates focus on the impact of economic restructuring in the so-called global cities and the shift in economic structure towards new knowledge sectors. This chapter has discussed these issues with reference to Singapore. As Singapore has matured towards a more globally integrated economy and society, and as new economic sectors have come to dominate, transitions in occupations and incomes have resulted in increasing socio-economic disparities becoming evident.

While these changes can be attributed in some part to changes accompanying wider global factors such as Singapore's position as a key urban centre within the global economy, they are also influenced by conditions at the local level. In particular the nation state has had an important mediating influence on economic and social outcomes taking place. Considering this in the wider Asia context Martin and Schumann (1997: 143) argue

> The Asian boom has little to do with the laissez-faire capitalism of most OECD countries. Without exception, the rising economies of the Far East adopted a strategy which is effectively scorned in the west: namely massive state intervention at every level of economic activity. Instead of letting themselves be led like lambs to the slaughter of international competition...the dragons...from Jakarta to Beijing have developed a wide range of institutions with which to keep control over development.

In terms of the current chapter, it becomes clear that 'Singapore's transition as part of world city formation intersects with local development ambition and political management' (Perry et al. 1997: 20) and that the combination of these factors results in differing patterns of social and economic change being registered in different places throughout the global network of cities. Consequently, to accept well used concepts such as Sassen's arguments surrounding social polarization as the norm is being uncritical. As Hamnett (1996: 1408) argues 'we should not fall into the trap of uncritically accepting the existence of polarisation as a demonstratable fact of contemporary urban life'.

While the patterns in Singapore do not mirror those found in other global cities, the growing inequality in incomes and the increase in middle classness raises several issues, including the divisions that occur between global and local interests. A dilemma confronting globalizing economies is the conflict between global and local interests and the impact of globalizing tendencies on local communities and residents. Within Singapore this has translated into concerns regarding the possibility that highly skilled professionals, increasingly tied to the global economy, may lose sight of their local connections and in some cases 'may not feel obliged to stay and contribute to Singapore's success' (Savage and Pow 2001: 113). This concern has impacted across the policy arena within Singapore. In the 2001 National Day Speech, Prime Minister Goh Chok Tong referred to the divisions between Singaporeans who are stayers and those who are quitters and earlier had made reference to the problems of growing inequality and a divisive tendency creeping into Singaporean society. In an earlier speech the Prime Minister considered that

> ...our society is showing signs of becoming more stratified by education and income groups. Many Singaporeans aspire to drive bigger cars, live in private properties, send their children to top schools. This desire to succeed and upgrade is natural and to be encouraged. But for some, it goes beyond that. They have become snobbish and status conscious. They want to 'move along', to show their peers that they have arrived...I understand why people want to upgrade to private property when they can afford it. But a desire to distance oneself from the majority will weaken our social fabric. A class-conscious Singapore will be a weaker society, unable to stay cohesive and give of its best. Unless we correct this trend among the more successful, it will divide and weaken our society (The Straits Time Interactive, 1997: 2).

In short this is a concern about being global but remaining local and also about the impacts of growing inequalities. Recognizing these problems, the government has begun to pursue a more active form of civil society and in particular is devolving 'power to the lowest level in order to optimize domestic consensus' (The Straits Times, 27 January 2000). The encouragement of local community groups and the establishment of grassroots councils (Community Development Councils) are a key to nurturing civil society. Accordingly, the success of these programs will be seen as a complement to the State and will provide citizens a sense of stakeholdership in the nation-state. A successful civil society will be as Ooi and Koh (1998: 103) argue 'the social glue among citizens and strengthen citizens' sense of belonging [and]...will help to address the problem of rootlessness often attributed to the younger generation of Singaporeans'. Whether a strong civil society is achievable within the Singaporean context or will result in desired outcomes has been debated (see Savage and Pow 2001). Whatever the outcome, it is recognized that 'a vibrant civil society will provide the arena in which Singaporeans can have a stake in shaping their destiny as individuals, local communities and as a nation in an otherwise disorienting and disempowering Information Age' (Ooi and Koh 1998: 108).

Clearly, governments whether they are at the local city level or at higher levels must be aware of the changes to society's social fabric including shifts in incomes and occupational structures. To ignore these may result in wider social divisions and potential social upheaval. In addressing issues governments and the general public, while accepting change must look for new ways of adapting. Referring to these dilemmas in Singapore, Prime Minister Goh Chok Tong has warned

> we can not be locked into old thinking and continue frozen in the model of yesteryear. However, successful this old model was, in the changed world it will not bring us to greater heights (Ministry of information, Communications and the Arts 2002c: 2).

11 Globalization, Rapid Urbanization and Anomie in Dhaka

Zakia Hossian

Introduction

Factors including globalization and increased urbanization have come to characterize cities in the Asia region. Many cities have become important global hubs for trade, finance, transport and communications (see for example Baum this volume; also Fujita 1991; Lo and Yeung 1996). Additionally, the beginning of the so-called 'urban century' has seen the number of very large cities increase with these mega-cities becoming part of the Asian urban settlement hierarchy. The changes in the structures of cities initiated in part by the forces of globalization and urbanization, but also being affected by levels of mass migration and by social and economic policies of governments bring with them a range of social changes both desirable and undesirable.

Social change and the outcomes of change have been part of sociological scholarship since the beginnings of the discipline with several concepts being developed to deal with and explain the outcomes of change. The study of anomie, which Talcott Parsons once referred to as one of the only few truly sociological concepts (Deflem 1999), fits into this area of sociological study. As an important sociological concept anomie is associated with Emile Durkheim (1893) and his treatment of social change at the beginning of the last century and the work by Robert Merton (1968).

As a classical term anomie 'means normlessness, lawlessness and no sense of social identity, being "socially lost"' (Atteslander 1995: 13). Durkheim used the term anomie to describe a condition of deregulation that was occurring in society. This meant that rules on how people ought to behave with each other were breaking down and thus people did not know what to expect from one another.

Merton (1968) in a similar vein to Durkheim's writings was interested in the connection between culture, social structure and anomie. For Merton, culture is 'that organized set of normative values governing behavior which is common to members of a designated society or group', while social structure is 'that organized set of social relationships in which members of the society or group are variously implicated'. Anomie occurs 'when there is an acute disjunction between the cultural norms and goals and the socially structured capacities of members of the group to act in accord with them' (Merton 1968:216).

Research into and theorizing of anomie was popular at the time of Merton's writings during the 1950s and 1960s, but declined thereafter as functionalism began to lose ground to other theoretical schools of thought. As a concept however, the notion of anomie and anomic structures has begun a renaissance and has been increasingly used to explain outcomes in rapidly changing societies in the contemporary world (see Arts et al. 2000; Atteslander, Grasnow and Western 1999; Passas and Agnew 1997). Applying Merton's ideas to rapidly changing contemporary societies Atteslander (1999: 13) suggests that anomie can be described as

> A condition of social-economic structures which are characterized by rapid structural change whereby the social systematic processes which reinforce social integration decline in salience and force. At the same time the disintegration of social and cultural structures are simultaneously heightened.

Contemporary research into anomie and anomic structures view changes in terms of the impact of a range of post-modernizing forces that may include globalization, urbanization and mass migration. Post-modernizing forces impact on pre-existing structures and result in rapid change, with the outcomes being that new changed structures and patterns come into being that are inherently unstable in nature. The flow on from this for the individual is reflected in terms of

> great difficulties in individual adaptation, resulting in a loss of general social orientations, the development of feelings of insecurity and marginalization, uncontrolled rising expectations and the questioning of the legitimacy of core values (Atteslander 1999:12).

It is within the context of rapid social change and the rise of anomic structures that the current chapter is set. Dhaka, Bangladesh has grown to become one of the Asia's new mega cities. Both increasing globalizing forces as well as increasing rates of urbanization characterize the city's development and it is these changes that have flowed through to the anomic structures briefly outlined above. In order to understand the possible outcomes in terms of anomie and anomic structures the chapter investigates the findings from a social survey conducted in Dhaka.

A methodological note

The primary data discussed in this chapter is taken from the Dhaka Anomie Project. The Dhaka Anomie Project is part of a large collaborative research project being coordinated through the Swiss Academy for Development and uses a survey instrument heavily influenced by similar conceptual and theoretical frameworks developed for use in the Australian Anomie Project and the Chinese Anomie Project (Li, Atteslander, Tanur and Wang, 1999; Western and Lanyon 1999).

A total of 504 adults were interviewed for the Dhaka Anomie Project using a structured questionnaire and a face-to-face interview technique. For the purpose of the research a two stage sampling design was used. Initially four residential zones – Mirpur, Lalbag, Mohammadpur, and Motijheel – were randomly selected. From within these zones, a sample of 480 households was randomly selected from electoral rolls. The characteristics of the respondents are presented in table 11.1. The study populations are grouped into young, middle and old in terms of their age. Young are those aged between 25–29, middle are those between aged 30–49 and old are those aged 50+. A little over 60 per cent of the study population is in the middle age group. More than half of the study populations are males (51 per cent) and overwhelmingly Muslim (95.6 per cent). Eleven per cent of the study population had not received formal education while 42 per cent had completed primary to high school education and 46 per cent had more than secondary education. The majority, 52.8 per cent were employed.

The information of most interest is that relating to the Margin of Society Scale (MOS) first developed by Travis (1993). This scale is designed specifically to address concerns relating to anomie and alienation and contains seven individual items. The original items

Table 11.1: Characteristics of survey respondents

Background	Frequency	Per cent
Sex		
Male	258	51.2
Female	246	48.8
Age		
Less than 30 years old	96	19.1
30 to 39 years old	204	40.6
40 to 49 years old	120	23.9
50 years old and older	83	16.5
Marital Status		
Not married	2	0.4
Married	494	98.0
Divorced	8	1.6
Religion		
Muslim	482	95.6
Hindu	18	3.6
Other	4	0.8
Education		
No education	58	11.5
Primary	52	10.3
SSC	109	21.6
HSC	53	10.5
Higher education	232	46.0
Employment status		
Employed	266	52.8
Unemployed	233	46.2
Missing	5	1.0

used by Travis were adjusted to account for differences in language and culture. In this chapter I report on six of the seven items, these being:
- I feel all alone these days;
- No matter how hard people try in life, it does not make any difference;
- I feel discriminated against;
- My whole world feels like it's falling apart;
- I wish I were someone important;
- It's hard for me to tell just what is right and wrong these days.

These questions, according to Travis (1993) provide a useful set of indicators with which to understand anomie and anomic structures. Respondents were asked to indicate the extent of their agreement with each of the items using a five point scale varying from strongly agree to strongly disagree. To simplify the data presented in this chapter these five categories were collapsed into agree and disagree, with a third category (neutral) not reported here.

Background to Bangladesh and Dhaka

As one of the Asia's developing economies and societies Bangladesh is characterized by many of the features that have come to typify countries going through rapid modernization. Increasing globalization – Bangladesh is among the World Bank's most 'globalizing countries in the developing world (World Bank 2002) – rapid rates of urbanization and rapid social change, including increases in collective social problems have become the defining features of modern Bangladesh society.

Across a number of measures, Bangladesh's economic performance over the past decade has been significant. Real Gross Domestic Product increased substantially (60 per cent) returning an average annual rate of growth of approximately 5 per cent, while over the same period the ratio of trade to Gross Domestic Product more than doubled indicating greater linkages to the global economy (Asian Development Bank 2002c). The country has developed several niche industries including ready-made garment manufacturing and has seen industry grow by 7 per cent (1990–98) and the service sector grow by 5.2 per cent (World Bank 2000). Moreover, both of these sectors now contribute much higher proportions to the county's Gross Domestic Product than in the past (Asian Development Bank 2002c). Levels of unemployment have been low by historical world standards and commensurately the country has witnessed significant growth in employment. In 1984 Bangladesh's unemployment rate stood at 11.5 per cent. Following significant economic reform, unemployment fell to around 2 per cent at the end of the 1990s. Over the same period of time, the number of people employed has grown from around 25 million to nearly 60 million (Asian Development Bank 2002c).

Greater economic performance, conditioned in part by greater ties to the global economic market place has filtered down to the population by way of reductions in poverty. World Bank data suggests that the total population under the poverty line fell from 42.2 per cent in 1991–92 to 35.6 per cent in 1995–96. Poverty was worse in rural areas – 39.8 per cent of the rural population was living below the poverty line in 1995–96, although the proportion in this position had declined from 46.0 per cent in 1991–92. The proportion of the urban population living below the poverty line in 1995–96 was 14.3 per cent, a decline from 23.2 per cent in the previous survey period (World Bank 2000; 1997; see also Asian Development Bank 2002a). Recent Asian Development Bank data shows that during the late 1990s, approximately 29 per cent of Bangladesh's population was surviving on US$1 per day (Asian Development Bank 2002c).

As a rapidly developing county, Bangladesh has increasingly taken on a distinctly urban character. In 1974 only 8.8 per cent of the population lived in urban areas. In 1981 this had increased to 15.2 per cent and by 1998 was 20 per cent (World Bank 1997; 2000). Approximately 9 per cent of the population lives in very large cities – those with populations of 1 million or more (Gunewardena 1999). This increase in the rate of urbanization has meant that Bangladesh, like other countries in the region, has seen uncontrolled growth in its major cities, especially Dhaka, the capital and by far the largest metropolis in the country.

Dhaka's population places it firmly within the list of the world's mega-cities. From a relatively small population base, the city's population sat at 7.8 million in 1995 and reached 10 million by the end of the 1990. Population projections place Dhaka's population at 18.9 million by 2015 (Bhuiyanm 1999; Hall and Pfeiffer 2000). Factors contributing to this growth have been the rate of natural population growth, migration of people from rural areas into the city and the annexation over time of new urban areas.

Rapid growth, combined with uneven economic outcomes and the consequences of government policy have resulted in a range of social problems in the city including changing income inequality, high rates of poverty and crime, inadequate housing, poor social and infrastructure services and environmental problems such as increased traffic congestion.

The extremes in social outcomes in Dhaka are nowhere more apparent than the contrast between the rich and poor. Bhuiyanm (1999:1) states that Dhaka is 'perhaps the poorest mega-city in the world' with a per capita annual income of only US$500 in 1997. According to GOV-ADB (1996) about 55 per cent of the city's population can be classified as being absolute poor, while 32 per cent are classified as hard-core poor.

Housing the city's growing population, especially the urban poor has been a constant challenge, one that has not been met by a significant level of success with overcrowded slums and poorly constructed informal settlements being widespread. Approximately 56 per cent of the city's population live in slums and squatter settlements, the great many of which can be found on poor quality land including the edges of lakes, rivers, sewers and railways tracks. A significant proportion (approximately 40 per cent) of houses do not have piped water supply and only 20 per cent have access to satisfactory sanitation. Such adverse surroundings when coupled with high rates of population density result in significant social, health and environmental issues (Hall and Pfeiffer 2000; Siddiqui 2000; Temple 2002). Siddiqui (2000) shows that the housing problem has been made particularly acute by the alarming rise in the value of land, high cost and shortage of modern building materials as well as indigenous construction materials, such as bamboo and timber, complicated land acquisition procedures and disorganized and inadequate housing finance.

Among the urban social problems that have come to plague Dhaka, crime and violence has become one of the most pressing. In part as a result of the inability of law enforcement agencies to address the problems of social unrest, violence, theft, robbery, looting, murder, hijacking, arson and the illegal use of fire arms have become much more widespread in the city (Siddiqui 2000). Ahmed & Baqee (1996) show that almost 61 per cent of crimes recorded in Bangladesh only occurred in Dhaka and the number of registered criminal cases rose from 12 095 in 1993 to 17 895 in 1997 (Shahjahan, 1998). Moreover, trade in illegal narcotics including hashish and heroin has increased with many women and children easily trapped into trafficking these drugs as a result of their poverty and vulnerability (Siddiqui 2000). Such widespread crime has significant impacts on the level of livability in the city.

An important part of urban livability has to do with the quality and extent of publicly provided services and infrastructure. Citizens of Dhaka city are faced with serious problems in relation to infrastructure provision. Facilities such as electricity are inadequately supplied with those living in squatter settlements receiving limited supply or in many cases supply through illegal connections. While these illegal connections do provide electricity that aids in improving life in these settlements, they do raise other issues including the potential danger from fire and electrocution

(Hardoy, Cairncross and Satterthwaite 1990). As noted earlier, only a small number of households have access to piped water with the majority relying on water from private wells and surface water. According to Hardoy, Mitlin and Satterthwaite (1992) where residents have got access to piped water, the quantity of the water that can be accessed depends very much on the logistics of transporting and accessing the water. According to these authors, a survey in Dhaka found that averages of one tap per 1513 persons were not uncommon. The sanitary system of the city is also highly unsatisfactory. Research by Louis Berger International (1991) shows that between 15 per cent to 20 per cent of the city population is serviced by a sewer and sewage treatment system, 25 per cent are serviced by on site septic tanks, 15 per cent by sanitary pit latrines and about 5 per cent by bucket latrines. In addition only a small proportion of the garbage generated by households is collected by the city, resulting in increasing risk of wide spread environmental problems and increased health risks (Enayetullah and Sinha 2001; Hardoy, Mitlin and Satterthwaite 1992).

Associated with infrastructure provision are the problems caused by Dhaka's worsening traffic congestion. Rapid population and economic growth has resulted in increasing demands for transport for both humans and for the goods and services they consume. Much of the city's road network is poorly maintained and the large variety of vehicles using public roads result in lengthy traffic jams. Moreover, poorly enforced traffics rules further add to congestion problems. Hossain (1987) notes that parking on the street, ignoring traffic signals and avoiding the city flyovers also cause traffic congestion and accidents in the city.

It is clear that as Dhaka has continued to develop so to have the range of urban problems confronting residents. Surveys of Dhaka's residents illustrate that the urban problems noted above impinge on daily livability in the city. Public opinion surveys by the World Bank in conjunction with local entities suggest that Dhaka's citizens are distrustful of public officials and show a high level of dissatisfaction with public services (Asian Development Bank 2002b). Within Dhaka tolerance of the judiciary was much lower than other places with 8 per cent of respondents being dissatisfied with the actions of judicial officers. Distrust of the police force was also higher in Dhaka, although in this case only 2 per cent of respondents were dissatisfied with police and this was not significantly higher than other cities. Considering the provision of services, the survey results show that more than other cities in Bangladesh, residents in Dhaka show a high level of dissatisfaction with garbage disposal, sewage and sanitation services and the supply of drinking water. With respect to the provision of drinking water and garbage disposal, the level of dissatisfaction was significantly higher in Dhaka than in any of the other cities considered.

An understanding of the way quality of life is perceived by residents of Dhaka can also be gauged by selected responses to questions contained in the Dhaka Anomie Project. Two sets of questions – one dealing with the local neighborhood and the other dealing more widely with the quality of life are taken from the survey. The questions dealing with local neighborhood satisfaction included statements such as 'I feel satisfied living in this neighborhood' or 'People in this neighborhood are willing to help each other out' and respondents were asked to state the level at which they agreed or disagreed. Large numbers of respondents (over 60 per cent in both cases) agreed, suggesting that at the local level strong neighborhood attachment or feelings of community were present. Additionally, respondents also considered that the provision of services such as transport was adequate at the level of the local neighborhood and that there was little problem with crime or vandalism. At the wider city level, responses to questions such as 'there are too many people in Dhaka', 'Dhaka is becoming more polluted' or 'Urban sprawl is a problem' reflect that on a wider city scale satisfaction with quality of life was low. Respondents are mostly dissatisfied with the pollution, rubbish and sewerage system, clean water, the provision of public toilets and the level of urban sprawl. High numbers of respondents also considered that traffic congestion was a problem.

Anomic structures

This chapter began by considering social changes such as those being experienced in Dhaka in terms of increasing levels of anomie and anomic structures. In line with the brief discussion in the introduction and given the background to Dhaka outlined above, it is interesting to consider the outcomes of the anomie project conducted across the four selected residential zones. The six individual MOS items are all considered in terms of their association with respondent's age, sex, employment status and educational level.

There appears to be little association with age and emerging anomie (table 11.2). Only two of the questions included are significantly related to age. One question, 'No matter how hard people try in life it does not make any difference' did show some differentiation with older persons being less likely to agree with this statement than younger respondents. Of the respondents aged 50 years and above only 11 per cent agreed with this statement, while approximately one-quarter of respondents in the younger age groups (less than 40 years old) agreed. For the question 'I wish I was someone important', younger respondents were more likely to agree (63 per cent of respondents aged less than 30 years agreed), while older respondents were less likely to agree (51 per cent of respondents aged 40–49 years agreed and 53 per cent of respondents aged 50 years and over agreed).

The association between the sex of the respondents and each of the items selected from the anomie questionnaire is shown in Table 11.3. The data presented in this table shows a clear difference when comparing responses given by males and females to items included in the MOS scale. Females are more likely to feel all alone (25.7 per cent) and discriminated against (14.0 per cent) than their male counterparts and they were also more likely to wish that they were someone important (61.3 per cent). Moreover, the responses to the statement 'No matter how hard people try in life it does not make any difference' also differ significantly according to sex of the respondent. Males were less likely to agree with the statement (19.8 per cent) in comparison to females (26.1 per cent). Women are more likely to be confused – 'my whole world feels like it is falling apart' (14.1 per cent) – and are unable to distinguished between 'what is right and what is wrong these days' (61.0 per cent) in comparison to men.

The association between respondent's employment status and the items from the questionnaire is shown in Table 11.4. The association between respondent's employment status and the items included in the MOS scale indicate that those who were unemployed at the time of survey were more likely to be lonely, depressed and feel discriminated against and less enthusiastic about life compared to respondents who were employed. For example for the question 'I feel all alone these days' 27.7 per cent of respondents who were unemployed agreed, while only 10.8 per

Table 11.2: Associations between the age of respondent and anomie items

Anomie Items	Age	Disagree	Agree
I feel all alone these days			
	<30	68.0	24.0
	30–39	70.0	17.0
	40–49	74.0	16.0
	50+	89.0	20.0
No matter how hard people try in life, it doesn't make any difference**			
	<30	64.0	25.0
	30–39	62.0	26.0
	40–49	61.0	24.0
	50+	83.0	11.0
I feel discriminated against			
	<30	850	9.0
	30–39	82.0	13.0
	40–49	86.0	10.0
	50+	84.0	12.0
My whole world feels like it is falling apart			
	<30	86.0	8.0
	30–39	82.0	13.0
	40–49	83.0	12.0
	50+	84.0	13.0
I wish I were someone important**			
	<30	20.0	63.0
	30–39	35.0	55.0
	40–49	34.0	51.0
	50+	41.0	53.0
It's hard for me to tell just what is right and wrong these days			
	<30	33.0	59.0
	30–39	33.0	58.0
	40–49	35.0	59.0
	50+	49.0	45.0

** = significant at the 0.05 level

cent of employed respondents agreed. The difference between these two groups is statistically significant at .05 level. Unemployed respondents are also more likely to agree with the statement 'No matter how hard people try in life, it doesn't make any difference'. A quarter of respondents who were unemployed at the time of the survey agreed with this statement compared to approximately one-fifth of employed respondents.

Table 11.3: Associations between sex of respondent and anomie items

Anomie Items	Sex	Disagree	Agree
I feel all alone these days**			
	Male	80.4	11.8
	Female	60.2	25.7
No matter how hard people try in life, it doesn't make any difference**			
	Male	75.4	19.8
	Female	55.2	26.1
I feel discriminated against**			
	Male	87.8	8.7
	Female	79.8	14.0
My whole world feels like it is falling apart**			
	Male	87.5	10.2
	Female	79.2	14.1
I wish I were someone important**			
	Male	40.4	49.2
	Female	25.1	61.3
It's hard for me to tell just what is right and wrong these days**			
	Male	44.8	51.1
	Female	26.9	61.0

** = significant at the 0.05 level

Finally, when we consider the association between educational status and the anomie items from the questionnaire, it appears that level of education is a significant discriminator between responses (table 11.5). Respondents with no formal education at the time of survey were more likely to be lonely, depressed and feel discriminated against and less enthusiastic about life compared to respondents who had some to higher education. For example 45 per cent of respondents with no education agreed with the statement 'I feel all alone these days', compared to only 8 per cent of respondents with higher education. The difference between the groups is statistically significant at .05 level. This group is also more likely to agree with the statement that says 'No matter how hard people try in life, it doesn't make any difference'. Over 50 per cent of respondents with no education agreed with this statement.

In terms of anomie research these findings are interesting. They suggest that higher levels of anomie are likely to be present in

Table 11.4: Associations between employment status and anomie items

Anomie Items	Employment status	Disagree	Agree
I feel all alone these days**			
	Employed	80.2	10.8
	Unemployed	59.3	27.7
No matter how hard people try in life, it doesn't make any difference**			
	Employed	70.1	20.3
	Unemployed	60.7	25.4
I feel discriminated against**			
	Employed	87.3	9.7
	Unemployed	79.5	13.4
My whole world feels like it is falling apart**			
	Employed	87.5	9.6
	Unemployed	78.4	15.3
I wish I were someone important**			
	Employed	37.5	51.1
	Unemployed	27.1	60.4
It's hard for me to tell just what is right and wrong these days**			
	Employed	42.3	49.8
	Unemployed	28.4	63.1

** = significant at the 0.05 level

particular social relations which may include the role of women in Bangladesh society and the position of the lower educated and unemployed vis-à-vis other social groups. The association between age and some of the anomie items may be a result of the lack of stable social relationships early in life (Western and Lanyon 1995).

Concluding comments

This chapter has considered the rapid social change occurring in Dhaka, Bangladesh and commented on the outcomes of these changes in terms of anomie and anomic structures. Bangladesh is among the region's fast developing countries and has been branded by the World Bank as part of the developing world's 'rapid globalizers' and as such, social change in the country in general but more particularly in Dhaka, has been rapid and characterized by increased globalization and rapid rates of urbanization. What have

Table 11.5: Associations between education status and anomie items

Anomie Items	Education status	Disagree	Agree
I feel all alone these days**			
	No education	44.0	45.0
	Some primary	55.0	29.0
	Some secondary	73.0	15.0
	Higher education	84.0	8.0
No matter how hard people try in life, it doesn't make any difference**			
	No education	33.0	56.0
	Some primary	62.0	31.0
	Some secondary	64.0	20.0
	Higher education	76.0	12.0
I feel discriminated against**			
	No education	55.0	41.0
	Some primary	80.0	15.0
	Some secondary	85.0	7.0
	Higher education	92.0	4.0
My whole world feels like it is falling apart**			
	No education	57.0	38.0
	Some primary	83.0	11.0
	Some secondary	85.0	10.0
	Higher education	89.0	7.0
I wish I were someone important**			
	No education	27.0	64.0
	Some primary	28.0	55.0
	Some secondary	25.0	61.0
	Higher education	40.0	50.0
It's hard for me to tell just what is right and wrong these days**			
	No education	19.0	77.0
	Some primary	31.0	63.0
	Some secondary	34.0	56.0
	Higher education	43.0	47.0

** = significant at the 0.05 level

been referred to as a set of post-modernizing forces has transformed the city bringing both positive changes together with a range of negative externalities.

The analysis of the anomie items in terms of their associations with age, sex, employment status and educational status suggested that for some sub-groups of the sample the changes taking place in Dhaka have resulted in increasing anomic outcomes. Females, young, unemployed and respondents with lower levels of education appeared to display higher levels of anomie than other respondents. Some of the patterns identified support other earlier work like for instance the results of the Australian Anomie Project where rapid social change in the South East Queensland region was seen to be associated with increased anomie for sub-groups such as the young and the unemployed (Western and Lanyon 1999). Like that study, the patterns identified in the current study would benefit from further multivariate statistical analysis in order to more completely develop the associations between anomie and a range socioeconomic factors including those discussed here.

The findings from the chapter raise issues with reference to understanding the outcomes of social change in the contemporary era, especially as it takes place in developing societies. Greater economic development that may bring with it improvements in technology, greater prosperity and other positive outcomes is not received by everyone in the same way. Growth does not translate into equality and for those who are marginalized by the changes accompanying growth progress in economic and social terms does not seem like a reality. For some of these people, rapid social change may result in increased levels of anomie. The pressing issue for governments is to capitalize on the benefits of development while at the same time minimizing the risks to particular groups (Eichengreen 2002). This means introducing appropriate safety nets and providing the mechanisms to catch those who fall through the cracks. Whether this is achieved through a more top down approach or through greater use of grassroots movements and a reliance of civil society mechanisms the difficulty comes in ensuring that policies and programs are appropriate, meet the needs of diverse groups and are delivered in a timely and responsive manner.

12 Job Opportunities for Working Children in Jakarta's Informal Settlements

Susy Sanie
Scott Baum

Introduction

Increasingly, aspects of globalization have come to impact on all areas of society. In large cities, especially in the developing world, the recent period of increased global interconnectedness has been associated with periods of increasing urbanization, both of which have been associated with increasing affluence, together with increasing disadvantage. Within the literature dealing with cities there has grown, as a result of these changes, concerns relating to the ways in which these outcomes translate into social divisions. Concerns include the problems of growing inequality and other social malaise in large cities (see Baum this volume and also Ariffin and Louis 2001; Atteslander et al. 1999; Marcuse 1997), the problems of environmental degradation as an outcome of increasing population pressure and urbanization (see Brookfield and Byron 1993; Forbes 1996) and questions of local governance and civil society in an increasingly globalizing world (see Gilbert et al. 1996; Mahizhnan and Yuan 1998; Williams and Stimson 2001) and the questions of sustainable urban development (Hall and Pfeiffer 2000).

The existence of informal settlements in many of the rapidly urbanizing cities of Asia is a reflection in the built form of the divisions that exist. The quality of life of their inhabitants and the social and economic outcomes characteristic of these places reflect in many cases the worst of urban outcomes. Informal settlements are as the name implies often illegal and are more often than not poorly constructed and maintained. They have been identified as communities of disadvantage and have a range of inherent social problems including issues of health and safety, the ability to find regular sustainable employment, security of tenure and the ability to raise a family in a stable environment (Angel et al. 1983; Hardoy, Cairncross and Satterthwaite 1990; Hardoy and Satterthwaite 1989). The people living in these informal settlement while they live in the city, are not really of the city for they have little or no status, they command no economic power and in many cases are seen as simply an urban nuisance (Hall and Pfeiffer 2000).

Of all the populations living in informal settlements, it is perhaps working children that are the least empowered. Their status as workers is not recognized and they are open to abuse, poor working conditions and a lack of legal protection. They are however for many families an important part of their economic and social survival. The circumstances and characteristics of child labor are however not merely associated with survival, but rather exhibit a range of causes and outcomes. This chapter considers some of these with relation to child workers in Jakarta. A sample of working children living in informal settlements is analyzed to understand the nature of their child work and the circumstances surrounding children's decisions to enter into paid employment.

The importance of child labor as a development issue has received wide coverage, both from academics working in the area, as well as international agencies including the World Health Organization, UNICEF and the International Labor Organization (ILO). While attention has been paid to child labor in rural areas (see for example Levy 1985), there has also developed a body of literature investigating the significance and process of child labor within major urban centers (see for example Ahmed 1991; Delap 2001; Gunn and Ostos 1992; Nangia 1994).

Among governments and international agencies alike, interest in child labor has resulted largely because of the negative impacts that are often associated with child labor. A general review of the literature suggests that child labor is often exploitative and acts to reduce opportunities for children to participate in the formal education process and to lead a normal childhood (ILO 1992; Kaur 1997; UNICEF 1986). According to Kaur (1997: 129) child labor may be

> considered exploitive when children work too young (e.g. starting at 5 years) impeding access to education, and detrimental to their social and psychological development; work too many hours; work under excessive physical, social and psycho-social stress; work for too little wages or

remuneration; work with too much responsibility placed on them, with no time for play and recreation; work in situations that inhibit their self-confidence and self esteem, (for example bonded laborers); and work as substitutes for adult labor.

Child labor is also widely condemned due to its potential health outcomes. As has been noted elsewhere '[t]he effects of exertion, fatigue and over work on the developing body are bound to hinder, counteract, retard or even halt growth'(Bouhdiba 1982: 11). In this respect, UNICEF (1991) estimates that approximately 80% of all child workers are employed in conditions which are so onerous or involve such long hours that it compromises their physical development. Furthermore, health problems are exacerbated due to exposure to industrial chemicals and waste and the possibility of industrial accidents. Referring to the hazards faced by children working at the garbage dumps in Manila, Gunn and Ostos (1992: 632) suggest that,

> perhaps most serious, however, are the invisible hazards. Manila's garbage includes hospital wastes (used dressings, needles, radioactive substances), chemical and pharmaceutical rejects (drugs and caustic substances), occasionally corpses, and a wide variety of explosive, combustible, and decayed materials. Children do not know the risks, nor are the effects always immediately apparent.

It is not only the immediate impacts of child labor that are of concern. One paradoxical outcome of work during childhood is that as a result of low educational levels and retarded physical development, many child workers face the likelihood of reduced earning capacity once they reach adulthood (Nangia 1994). To this extent it is well argued that 'childhood is a period of life that should be devoted to education and training, not work. Child labor, by its very nature, often compromises children's potential to become productive and useful adults in society' (Hasnat 1995:421–422). To this end, Psacharopoulos (1997) shows in an empirical analysis that in situations where a child is working, the likelihood of failing subjects at school is high and reduces the level of educational attainment by one or two years.

Against these concerns are the views expressed in some areas that the hypothesized negative impacts do not automatically accrue to child workers and that some forms of work can be important to socialization and may provide important 'non-formal' means of training. In support of these views Rodgers and Standing (1981: 33) argue that 'we have to be careful not to make an automatic assumption that work by children impairs education and intellectual development...work itself may be an important component of "education" especially in household-based production systems ...Similarly, in a study published in the mid 1990s Grootaert and Kanbur (1995: 193) note that 'In an economic environment where survival depends on work in the informal sector, many parents conclude that taking children out of school and putting them to work is the most sensible solution for survival and the education method which offers the best prospects for the future'.

Clearly the extent to which child labor is associated with positive or negative outcomes depends to a large degree on how it is defined and measured. Some measures include only the most exploitive types of labor such as bonded labor or child prostitution or hazardous work such as scavenging, types of labor which are clearly working to the detriment of children involved. Other measures combine all types of child labor regardless of the work conditions or time spent in work. These types of measures are likely to result in some confusion over child labor that is detrimental and that which may, at the margins, provide some benefit.

Although the extent of child labor is difficult to measure accurately, an estimate by the International Labor Office suggests that in 1996, approximately 250 million children were working in developing countries – 61 per cent being in Asia (UN Chronicle 1996). The largest proportions of child workers are found in agricultural activity in rural areas. While the engagement of children in agricultural activity can not be condoned, it has attracted far less attention and concern than that occurring in urban areas. In other sectors of the economy, such as manufacturing, trade, services and illegal activities (i.e. bonded labor, prostitution) the percentage of child labor is much lower, however, it is these areas of economic activity that do however attract the most attention (Falkus et al. 1997). Country specific figures suggest that there may well be significant variation in the extent of child labor and that these figures may be between the 20 and 60 per cent range (Grootaert and Kanbur 1995). Within Indonesia, the exact numbers of working children are not known. According to official statistics, there are about two million children aged between 10 and 14 who are economically active in urban and rural areas (1994). Of these, the majority is found in rural areas (87 per cent), while the remaining 13 per cent are found in urban areas (Blackburn 1997).

Determinants of child labor

The determinants of child labor are many and varied. Studies associated with determining the extent and background to child labor have in most cases argued that the causes and correlations associated with child labor are not simple, but are complex and multi-faceted (Delap 2001; Grootaert and Kanbur 1995; Nangia 1994; White 1994). While various economic motives and incentives are often considered the most likely causes of child labor, other cultural factors have also been considered.

The existence of families living in poverty has been the most popular reason put forward to explain child labor. As Ahmed (1991: 262) explains 'poverty of the masses is considered the principal cause of child labor...[Where] income disparities are extreme, and a majority of the population lives on the verge of starvation' it is impossible for many parents to provide for the basic needs of their families. Consequently, children may be seen as important economic commodities, whose labor parents can utilize to enhance household earnings. Indeed, as Ahmed (1991) suggests with reference to Pakistan, many children are raised to accept their position as a supplementary income source within the family. The author goes on to report that besides simply stating 'personal choice' as a reason for undertaking work, children in his sample said that poverty and survival were reasons for them seeking paid employment. Similarly, Sharma and Mitter (1990) report that within their sample, a negative correlation existed between child labor and the number of adult earners in the household, and that further, there is a negative correlation between the number of adult earners and households in poverty, suggesting that 'as in most countries, an obvious cause of child labor is poverty' (Blackburn 1997: 96).

Associated with the 'child labor as poverty reduction' argument is the view that considers child labor in terms of the household's exposure to risk. That is, 'child labor can be part of a strategy to minimize the risk of interruption of a household's income stream, and hence to reduce the potential impact of job loss by a family member, of a failed harvest, etc.'(Grootaert and Kanbur 1995:194). In this case, rather than children simply acting as a supplementary source of income, their paid employment forms part of an insurance policy in what is generally a precarious economic position. Such risk minimization is expected to be more prevalent among poor households. Reflecting this assessment, research in rural India illustrates that as household income fluctuates with changes in season, so does children's school attendance. The authors suggest that this was especially the case whenever there was an external shock that may influence earnings (Jacoby and Skoufias 1994 referred to in Grootaert and Kanbur 1995).

Other economic factors implicated in the child labor decisions are the operation of the labor market and flexible wages that act to make children a substitute for adults in the market place (Grootaert and Kanbur 1995), and the impact of technology. Reflecting the former argument, case studies have illustrated that the wages of children are seen to be consistently below those of adults, even where both groups carry out the same jobs (Bequele and Boyden 1988; Jomo 1992). The outcome is therefore, that as a result of the wage differential, demand for child labor vis-à-vis adults will be higher. With reference to technology, in industries that are not capital intensive, children may be demanded more so than adults due to their ability to produce output more efficiently. This may be the case in areas such as carpet weaving or in the farming of crops such as cotton where children's nimble fingers allow them to work much quicker.

Over and above these economic motives and incentives, cultural or social factors such as the failure of the education system and the increased consumerist nature of modern society may also be important. One of the key non-economic explanatory variables has been the failure of the education system to deliver appropriate schooling. Basically, '[i]n an economic environment where survival depends on work in the informal sector, many parents conclude that taking children out of school and putting them to work is the most sensible solution for survival and the education method which offers the best prospects for the future' (Grootaert and Kanbur 1995: 193). With reference to this thesis, Bonnet (1993) suggests that reasons given for children seeking work reflect the fact that education is seen to provide no vocational qualifications, and does not prepare the child for the way of life they are likely to encounter once they finish school. Providing a specific case, Ahmed (1991: 262) argues that in 'Pakistan, 74% of the population is illiterate, and children who have no yearning for education constitute a considerable proportion of the labor force'.

It has been stated elsewhere (see Blackburn 1997) that as consumerism increases in society and producers and advertisers identify niche markets targeted at children, so to does the desire of children to earn money. To this extent the existence of an expanding consumerist orientation among residents of large cities is not lost on children. As has been noted elsewhere, the 'materialistic orientations and life-styles of the "new rich" class are beginning to enter into the psyche of their children with demonstrative and imitative effects for other youth' (Ariffin 1995: 348). For the urban poor in developing countries this may mean that if parents are unable to provide money to meet children's demands, then children will naturally want to earn money. Noting these changes with reference to Indonesia, White (1994: 868) suggested that

> Today's...children want to have money for their own use; this is the main reason behind the preference for wage employment outside the home...The desire for money among children and young people is not new, but in our view it is much more intimately felt by the present generation, in consequence of the form and strategy of development adopted in Indonesia.

Methodology

The study reported in this chapter covers 15 informal settlement areas in five city regions of Jakarta. Data was collected over three stages, with the sample being determined using information about the location of informal settlements that were supplied by the Jakarta Special Regency Regional Government. According to this information informal settlements accounted for approximately 2855 hectares in Jakarta in 1993/ 94. These were found in 38 sub districts (k*ecamatan*) and comprised approximately 1.6 million residents.

Information was collected in three stages using regional surveys, household surveys and working-children interviews. Sampling was carried out using a multistage sampling method. An initial sample of 15 locations was randomly selected, with 30 other locations chosen as back-ups. At this initial stage a regional survey was conducted in order to determine the eventual research location. In each chosen location, 30 households with children aged between 5 and 14 years were selected. Household surveys were then conducted to obtain social, economic and demographic data, including the presence or absence of working children. Of the 450 households surveyed, a final sample of 438 resulted. This comprised 2576 people and 883 children aged between 5 and 14 years of age. The final research stage comprised in-depth interviews with working children. Of the 883 children residing in the sample households, 21.5% (190) were classified as 'working children' and 160 of these children were questioned about their work, their demographic and social background and their aspirations for the future. The discussion presented in this chapter reflects this stage data collection.

Sample characteristics of working children

Working children in the sample were aged between 8 and 14 years, with the average being approximately 12.5 years. The majority (75 per cent) was male, and while many had been working in some form of paid employment since the age of 5 years, the average age at which they entered paid employment was 10.5 years.

Based on the birth order of the children, the majority of the working children were middle siblings (79.4 per cent), with 5 per cent first born and 15 per cent being the youngest. Most of these children came from large families (average size 4.6 persons) and the majority (78.8 per cent) still lived with their parents. In terms of education, 68.1 per cent was still attending formal education, with the majority (64.4 per cent) being at elementary school level or below. Of those children not attending formal education, a small proportion had never attended school (1.9 per cent), with the remainder leaving during elementary level.

Characteristics of child labor

Qualitative data from the surveys provided a rich source of background information about the working children in the sample. Working children were found in both the informal and formal sectors of the economy, and were typically employed in the service industry, although some were employed in manufacturing. Most often, the children in the sample worked as comic or newspaper sellers, umbrella bearers [1], '3-in-1' jockeys [2], food or toy vendors, scavengers, factory or construction workers, domestic workers or as shoe shiners. Other less common jobs included selling clean water, collecting alms, fishing or working as fishmongers, working in family enterprises, or working as bus assistants (k*enek*). In some cases the work performed such as fishing or scavenging was hazardous and could result in injuries to the children involved.

In discussions with working children and their parents, it was apparent that girls, especially those not attending school, tended to work in more settled or formal places of work. In these environments children were less likely to meet strangers and hence be more protected. This reflects the parental and community protective attitude towards young girls. Young girls were directed to work for certain persons (usually known to the family), at certain working times and at certain places. This was, according to one respondent '…so if anything happens to my daughter I know where to find someone to ask or make an inquiry.' In these cases, employment was therefore most likely to be found as factory hands, grocery store workers, cleaners and domestic servants or as helpers in restaurants – that is, in more formal settings.

In contrast, boys, especially those who had left school, tended to have more freedom and were less protected-unlike the girls in the sample there was less concern expressed by parents regarding the safety of sons. Young boys could choose to work on the street or in some other work place, and had more flexibility in their working hours. Reflecting this flexibility, they were often found in the informal sector of the economy. Boys worked as clean water sellers, scavengers, construction labor, helpers in restaurants, mechanic's assistants, neighborhood garbage collectors and bus assistants.

For the children who did gain employment in the informal sector, the uncertain and unstable nature of their jobs did not deliver high status or respect. As Nangia (1994: 285) asserts, the types of jobs which are characteristic of the urban informal sector 'are temporary and irregular because the child can leave them easily and because frequent staff changes allows employers to pay as little as possible. Children work in a situation where they can be hired or fired any time'. The low status associated with the types of jobs held by children was evident in conversations with both the children in the sample, as well as their parents. Most of the jobs held by the children were referred to as 'work for children' in that they were not seen as real work or were considered as activities only undertaken by children. This 'work for children' status can include scavenging or firewood collection and is often explained in terms of being shameful and low status work that is inappropriate for adults (Delap 2000). Further, as the jobs were not expected to result in long term employment or career options, they were not considered as 'proper work'. In many cases the children considered these jobs to be only short term and eventually they would do something else. Whilst these temporary jobs were the norm, there were some children who had obtained permanent employment or for them 'real work'.

For the majority of the children in the sample, job opportunities were to be found within their local environments. The majority worked close to their homes which meant that they could travel to their work on foot or by bicycle and for many their journey to work took less than 15 minutes. Children found work in residential or housing areas, on the streets, in factories or industrial areas, in or near shopping centers and markets, or at the bus terminal.

Influences of child worker's decisions

The main purpose of this chapter is to attempt to outline the determinants of the labor decision of children living in informal settlements in Jakarta. Responses gained during the survey provide a background to the choices made by children regarding the decisions to enter paid employment.

In terms of finding work, for many children it appeared that whilst they had not initially set out to obtain employment, when the opportunity to work presented itself, they took advantage of it. This seemed to be the case whether the child needed to work or not. It also appears that peer contacts played an important part in assisting working children to find work. Among the children sampled, approximately 40% obtained jobs via friends – through either being induced by friends in some way or through simply following along with friends who already worked. Similarly, a number of children obtained their work through direct offers from business owners, a neighbor, an older sibling or some other family member.

When working children talked about their work, a number of reasons were offered as to why they entered into paid employment. One reason mentioned by many children related to the enjoyment they gained from working, together with the existence of consumptive stimuli. Children in the sample mentioned that they received enjoyment from work, both in material and non-material senses, and that this sense of enjoyment influenced their working decisions. The material sources of enjoyment included having their own money and being able to spend it in the manner they choose. The non-material sources of enjoyment included being able to get together with friends, the opportunity to experience 'urban luxuries' such as visiting shopping malls and riding in luxury cars, something that was not usual for children living in informal settlements of the city. Another sense of fulfillment and enjoyment came from feeling as if they had done a good deed, especially in terms of contributing to the family. Closely associated with these arguments regarding the material gain from work, children in the sample also mentioned that paid employment offered them the chance to purchase consumer goods. Being from a poor background, many children or their families could not afford modern consumption goods that other middle class families take for granted. Undertaking some form of labor allowed some children to consume some modern lifestyle goods. In short, work decisions reflected a consumptive stimulus (Blackburn 1997; White 1994).

Apart from these reasons, which reflect a more individual orientation, many children directly mentioned that they sought paid employment in order to help their families. Reflecting popular arguments surrounding the reasons behind child labor, many children said that they worked so as to help boost the income of the household. There is also evidence that many children were working to provide a safety net in case other workers in the family became unemployed – the household response to risk mentioned by Grootaert and Kanbur (1995) above. Finally, reflecting the argument that failure of the education system may be a factor increasing the likelihood of child labor, many children said that they had sought paid employment because they had dropped out of school or that school no longer provided them with skills they would need in later life. In this case it was apparent that for many of the sample any more than a few years of education was considered as unimportant, because it may not result in better paid jobs in the future.

Probability of child labor

To further investigate the factors influencing child workers, regression analysis was undertaken using data from the household surveys. The household survey collected data on 883 children aged between 5 and 14 years of age. A selection of social, economic and demographic variables was analyzed using a regression method that looked at the impact of the selected independent variables on the dependent variable, to work or not work. The type of regression analysis used was logistic regression that required the dependent variable to be dichotomous. The analysis resulted in a series of coefficients (ß) that are interpreted in terms of the change in the log odds of working or not working, given the outcome on a particular independent variable. The alternative means of assessing the Betas (ß) is by considering the exponential of the coefficient (exp ß) which gives the likelihood of working given a particular outcome on the independent variable.

The survey provided several possibilities when it came to understanding the determinants of child labor. Eight variables were initially included in the model. These were:
- Sex of the child;
- Age of the child;
- School attendance;
- Household expenditure;
- Number of bread-winners;
- Education level;
- Human capital of parents; and
- Income of parents.

These variables were chosen as they represented important variables identified in previous work.

Initially, all variables were entered in the model and non-significant ones subsequently removed. The final model (table one) provides a good fit as measured by the model chi-square (320.34). Of the initial nine variables entered, five (plus a constant term) were significantly related to the likelihood of children undertaking paid employment. The regression model suggests that sex of the child, age of the child, school attendance, household expenditure and the number of household breadwinners, were all associated with the likelihood of a child in the sample working.

Considering the exponentials of the Betas, the model suggests that compared to girls, boys were four times more likely ($e^{1.3948}$ = 4.0343) to work. This finding is in line with previous studies (see for example Grootaert and Kanbur 1995), and may reflect cultural norms surrounding the position of boys work vis-à-vis schooling and the fact that in some cases boys may be a substitute for the labor of a female adult (Delap 2000). The second significant demographic

Table 12.1: Logistic regression results

Independent variable	β	Wald	Sig	Exp (β)
Sex	1.3948	32.1144	0.0000*	4.0343
Age (years)	0.5209	89.3255	0.0000*	1.6836
Schooling status	−1.4509	23.0527	0.0000*	0.2344
Household expenditure	−0.0012	8.7227	0.0031*	0.9988
Number of breadwinners	0.7674	45.5737	0.0000*	2.1542
Constant	−8.4872	111.0566	0.0000*	–

Model chi-squre= 320.336; df= 5; p=0.0008
* = significant at the 0.05 level

factor was age and not unexpectedly the Beta coefficient illustrates that an increase in age of one year increased the likelihood that a child would undertake work by 1.98 times ($e^{0.5206}$).

Akabayashi and Psacharopoulos (1999) reported findings to support the assertion that a trade off occurred between school and work for those involved in child labor. That is, work can for some children be considered as a perfect substitute for school with the choice being one or the other. Although a strong a strong case for such perfect substitutability is not reflected here, there is a small effect with children who are in school being less likely to be to be engaged in work – compared to children who were not attending school, attending children were 0.23 times as likely to work ($e^{-1.4509}$). The two variables specifically measuring the level of human capital were not significantly related to the likelihood of working.

Despite, evidence from the qualitative material to suggest that low income was an important factor in child labor, the results of the logistic regression suggest that with reference to the sample used here that parental income does not significantly influence the probability of child labor. This is in contrast to research by scholars including Delap (2000) who found a positive association between low-income households and child labor. The impact of income may have been accounted for by the variable measuring consumption of food, which suggests that increased spending of food reduces the likelihood of child labor. The regression analysis suggests that each additional 100 Rupiah of household expenditure on food consumption decreases the likelihood of children working by 0.99 times ($e^{-0.0012}$), suggesting that household who were better off and could spend more on food had a lower incidence of working children.

Finally, the regression analysis points to the impact that an extra bread winner has on the likelihood of child labor. As an extra bread winner is added to the household, the chances of a child working increases by 2.15 times ($e^{0.7674}$). While the reasons for his pattern are unclear, a possible explanation rests in the fact that a child's labor may be substituted for the labor of a mother in the home in families with more than one breadwinner.

Concluding comments

The problem of child labor is complex. The results of the study reported in this chapter illustrate that child labor is dependent on a number of separate, but interdependent factors. As elsewhere, the 'simple assumption that children worked because they were poor was quickly supplanted by a complex array of social factors' (Gunn and Ostos 1992: 638). Within our sample, children became workers due to opportunity, because of enjoyment or because they needed to in order to help their family's income. Furthermore, gender, the age of the child, school attendance, household expenditure and the number of breadwinners all impacted on the likelihood of child labor.

The question regarding the way ahead in addressing child labor is complex. As an important development issue, the position of child workers has been the cause for concern both within Indonesia and at a more global level with agencies such as the International Labor Organization. At the local Indonesian level, although polices may be implemented to address the problems of child workers, the policy environment can be a double edged sword- both assisting with the problems and causes of child labor, but also in some cases providing the means for child labor to occur. Government polices such as providing compulsory education or poverty reduction may go some way towards reducing the incidence of child labor (McDonald 1992). Alternatively, programs that improve the conditions and security of work for adults, may aid in a reduction of child labor by reducing the need for children to work as means of income insurance. Government rules and regulations, programs, and development strategies and goals can have non-intended outcomes in terms of increasing the likelihood of child workers. For example, a program, which aimed to reduce tricycles (*becak*) or sidewalk sellers in Jakarta, resulted in many people from informal settlement areas losing their jobs. As many of these workers relied on this income to support their families, this policy had the unintended consequence of placing many more families into more precarious financial positions. The result is that children are forced into employment as parents seek to improve their family's quality of life. Additionally, the decision by the state to introduce a restricted area whereby cars must have at least three passengers (3-in-1 area) opened up the possibility for children to become 3-in-1 jockeys. On a more macro scale, the success of development policies and the impact of a globalized market place have impacted on the level of consumerism and as was noted have had the unintended outcome of increasing the desire of children to work.

The policies and programs of international agencies are also important in terms of their impact on child labor. Agencies such as the International Labor Organization (ILO) and the United Nations have established successful projects in many developing countries, which have attempted to overcome many of the problems associated with child labor problem (Gunn and Ostos 1992; Lanskey 1997; UN Chronicle 1993). However, as Blackburn (1997: 104) observes in relation to Australian aid programs 'AusAID has the potential to help mitigate the worst aspects of child labor…At a minimum, however, the aim should be to ensure that the program does no harm in this respect'. She recognizes that in such situations there is a need for the programs put in place by international agencies to be 'monitored for their effects on child labor, analogous to the way in which development assistance is monitored for its effect on women and the environment'.

Associated with these concerns is the question of an outright ban on child labor. Simply banning child labor outright may not be the solution that some policy makers had hoped. Difficulties arise because of the different views held across the community and society regarding the seriousness of some forms of child labor (Roberts 1996). Additionally, placing a ban on the practice of child labor is of no use if such legislation is not backed up with thorough policing and enforcement. For instance, in India, although the government passed a child labor act essentially banning employment of children under 14 in certain industries, there was clear evidence of child labor practices continuing (McDonald 1992).

Important too, is the link between international trade and the question of reducing child labor. As Bouhdiba (1982: 3–14) notes,

> The international competitiveness of some of the goods produced by the third world countries is achieved largely at the price of the exploitation of the labor of their children...When a country is poor, in debt, and with budgetary difficulties, it is not always over-concerned about the price paid in terms of the toil of children to improve an export statistic or its coverage of the terms of the trade'.

An associated complication, is that internationally, whilst calls for boycotting of goods produced with child labor or labeling good as 'not being produced with child labor' may have an impact on export sector industries, they may not appreciable reduce child labor. The key point here is that 'if poverty and social customs require children to work, then they will do so where ever they can find jobs – export sector or elsewhere' (Hasnat 1995: 423). That is, because much child labor exists in the informal economy (Grootaert and Kanbur 1995), boycotts on goods which affect only the export sector may not have the desired impact. In some cases it is even suggested that such boycotts exacerbate the existing problem for many families living in poverty, and in fact may simply be protectionist measures taken by governments in developed countries (Hilowitz 1997; Lansky 1997).

A significant proportion of the debate around child labor has tended to focus on the way of reducing the propensity of children to enter into work. However, there are some who question the extent to which trying to stop child labor is in fact the best solution to the problem. It may be in fact preferable to ensure that the type of work children undertake, their level of remuneration and the conditions in which they work is controlled rather than simply trying to eradicate the use of child labor in enterprises. After all, countries, including those in the developing world have enacted legislation aimed at protecting adult workers from the kinds of conditions that child labor activists cite as being exploitive and hazardous for children (White 1994).

It seems that the final answer to the question of child labor is a complex one with many possible combinations and permutations. However, it is clear that one philosophy should guide program and policy development regardless of the solutions adopted. In short 'children should be given "opportunities and facilities, by law and by other means" to develop physically, mentally, morally, spiritually and socially "in a healthy and normal manner and in conditions of freedom and dignity'. (UN Chronicle 1989: 51).

Part IV
Conclusion

13 Social and Cultural Transformation in Asia: A Critical Assessment

Timothy J. Scrase
T.J.M. Holden
Scott Baum

In bringing this book to a close we wish to discuss the sociological prospects for Asia in the face of globalization. We will briefly identify some themes common to the eleven empirical contributions. After that, we will consider the lessons that might be drawn from each of the substantive sections that can serve as a research and policy guide for the future.

Asia is the world's most populous region. It boasts the world's two most populous nations, and six of the top ten.[1] In terms of regions, East Asia and Pacific and South Asia are far and away the world's two most populated regions. Economically, however, the story is reversed. While the Eastern region boasts what by many measures is the world's second largest economy (Japan),[2] and six of the world's 13 most competitive growth economies,[3] other indicators paint a less rosy portrait. According to a World Bank report, despite the fact that poverty rates have been lowered faster than anywhere else in the world, 'social indicators remain a matter of concern.'[4] The mortality rate for those less than five years of age remains high, at 45 per 1000 – with a rate of 96 per 1000 in South Asia. The latter region also features 'the lowest GNI per capita ($440) and some of the highest levels of child malnutrition in the world, with almost 50 percent of children below the standards for weight by age. It has the highest rate of youth illiteracy – 23 percent for males and 40 percent for females – and, at 37 percent, the lowest rate of access to sanitation facilities.'[5] While South Asia relies on agriculture more than any other region in the world, overall, the Asian regions require considerable support in improving infrastructure. The World Bank reports that 'at present only 75 percent of its population receives water from an improved source, 47 percent has access to improved sanitation facilities, and less than a quarter of its roads are paved.'[6]

The sociological contradictions of globalization

Thus, while we can speak – as many of the authors in this volume have – of an Asia that boasts bustling, dynamic urban environments, the most advanced means of communication, the most refined lifestyles and high rates of consumption, we also have to recognize that this is a region where the opposite of all of these conditions also prevails. For at least a decade now, the globalization paradigm has been about the dichotomy – if not dialectic – of heterogeneity versus homogeneity. But looking at Asia, and thinking about the chapters in this volume, it might in fact be more accurate to suggest a different sort of push/pull duality at work; indeed any number of paired oppositions.

For this reason – and for want of a better term – we might label this circumstance the 'sociological contradictions of globalization.' Sociological because these warring elements are not only expressed culturally – as in the conflicts between tradition and modernity that Bell (1976) spoke of in Western society and which Nilan uncovered in her study here of contemporary Indonesia (Chapter 8). They are also social contradictions, as Piper demonstrated in her study of female migrant laborers who leave their home countries due to discrimination but often end up victims of criminality and physical exploitation in the new countries they enter (Chapter 3). Political contradictions can also be observed, as Ganguly-Scrase showed in Chapter 4. Although market liberalization for lower middle class women in India has been touted as a gender equalizer by the State, the author's ethnographic data revealed that the inherent patriarchal ideologies of the neo-liberal state still determine female possibilities.

Chen, in her study of a Taiwanese sex scandal (Chapter 9) indicated that economic motive may have helped undo a political career, but media technology also helped liberate a woman from traditional patriarchal structuration. Thus, not only do globalization's sociological contradictions express themselves 'sectorally,' they also work within societies to pit sectors against one another. This was apparent in Goodman's contribution (Chapter 2) where political aspects such as a post-colonial political order, neo-liberal economic policies, and heightened consumption and materialism were shown to have worked to stimulate social divisions. In turn, these schisms have spawned a range of social movements challenging the established social, political and economic order. Hossain (Chapter 12) likewise demonstrated the contradictions engendered by economic development: in the case she analyzed, an increase in adverse mental health outcomes in Dhaka.

Finally, in Holden's discussion of various mediations of identity in Japan (Chapter 7) we encounter a society possessing particular, high levels of political and economic development. Consistent with the character of the context, information consumers employ media (such as television shows, fashion magazines, and body adornments) to proactively define and act on national, sub-group and individual identity. Though generally benign and non-problematic within the focal context, such identifications present potential for disjuncture (e.g. Appadurai 1990) – whether economic, cultural, political or moral – were they to be disembedded (Giddens 1990) and transplanted in other contexts in the Asian region.

The un/der-represented future

One of the undercurrents in this book has been how globalization touches groups whose voices often go un- or under-represented; above all, women and youth. Time and again in the preceding chapters we have seen the acts, interests, and possibilities of these publics influenced by global processes. From child labor to migrant workers, from young consumers to a new generation negotiating and embodying cultural, religious or political identifications, it is these groups – in articulation or confrontation with the dominant groups and/or pre-existing ideas and practices – who will determine the future of globalization in Asia. At the same time, obviously, it is the entrenched interests and structures – from economic organization to political elites to moral authority – whom influence the current course and consequences of globalization.

Recasting inequality and social change in Asia

Emerging from the arguments presented in this book is the need to re-assess the notion of social inequality and social change in Asia as a consequence of globalization. For instance, how significant is 'social class' as an analytical concept in light of mass consumption and the middle class explosion in various countries of Asia?

Moreover, should we reconsider class politics given the emergence of 'new' social movements? So, too, has there been an outpouring of interest in refugees and people trafficking (and migration issues generally), nationalist politics (for instance, East Timor), religious fundamentalism and extremism, population crises in various countries, questions of indigenous rights (including property and intellectual rights), ecological destruction, and forest and fisheries management, just to name a few. While these are largely global issues, they are nevertheless felt with force and significance throughout Asia. Piper, for instance, touched on several of these issues in her discussion of inter-regional, female labor migration. Moreover, the current reassertion of American and Western political and economic hegemony in the Middle East now reverberates throughout the Islamic countries and communities in the region, creating a sense of Islamic nationalism and solidarity as a countervailing force to the past decades of pro-Western, liberal capitalist path to modernization and development.

The recasting of inequality in terms of social class is evident when we explore two recent phenomena – the globalization of industrial production and the middle class explosion throughout the region. The shift to mass production in Asia, begun in the late 1950s with the so-called 'Asian Tigers', continues unabated. The globalization of technology and advances in transport, especially containerization, has meant that the rapid industrialization of many parts of Asia continues, particularly with respect to the automobile and associated industries, clothing, footwear and textiles manufacture, the electronics and computer industries (Sklair 1994), and selected (high added-value) primary industries like aquaculture (especially prawns). Moreover, while there have emerged new industries and a limited number of new jobs, older or traditional employment is fast diminishing. This was exemplified in Scrase's Chapter 5 whereby the survival of Asia's artisans was shown to be precarious, dependent on whimsical markets, the availability of scarce raw materials, and intense competition; and where artisans were drawn into minor, corrupt activities like bribery. The associated proletarianization of many of Asia's rural poor – swept-up into the various industrial towns and factories – coupled with the globalization of communications and culture, creates room for a degree of industrial strikes and political action. As Goodman described, various social movements in Asia have emerged in recent times, many of which are aligned with progressive Western-based, social movements which campaign for improvement of worker's rights, ecological sustainability and so forth. A good example of this 'global solidarity' is the 'Just Stop It' campaign aimed at highlighting the exploitation of Nike workers in Indonesia.

The rapid shifts in industrialization and manufacturing is felt at all levels of the economy, and nowhere is it more indicative of the 'rapidization' of production than in the fast-food industry; and, for that matter, no one company is more emblematic of this phenomenon than McDonalds. The 'McDonaldization of society' (Ritzer 1993) – where the core elements of the modern, fast food restaurant come to be the benchmark for wider industrial and professional work practices – represents not only an economic shift, but also a change in cultural values, tastes and expectations. Indeed, for many in Asia, eating at McDonald's has become the ultimate status symbol, whereby a McDonald's restaurant in Beijing or Seoul becomes an arena for conspicuous consumption (see Watson 1997).[7]

The detailed study of consumption in Asia thereby becomes an important prerequisite in developing an overall understanding of the cultural manifestations of class reconfiguration. Importantly, as the various contributors to Beng-Huat (2000a) show, there are various localized and regional patterns to contemporary capitalist consumption in Asia. What may be fashionable in one country may equally be distasteful in another. Moreover, as Beng-Huat (2000b: 18) argues when exploring Asia's new middle class: 'rather than diminishing in times of recession, the symbolic value of consumption becomes all the more important.' Moreover, 'The need to "maintain" a lifestyle is all the more necessary for one of the newly rich to communicate to all the world...' that they are largely unaffected by a declining economy. Such appearance must be upheld in hopes of preserving the confidence of colleagues and business associates alike.

While this is largely true for the upper middle class, the entrepreneurs, and the 'new rich', there are certainly differences when we look at the situation confronting the lower middle classes (see Ganguly-Scrase and Scrase 1999, 2001), due to their quest to maintain high status despite relatively lower and diminishing incomes. The intricacies of cultural expressions of class become more complex when one considers the dimension of gender. As Ganguly-Scrase (Chapter 4) pointed-out, a neo-liberal regime may have increased the desires of lower middle class Indians to consume, yet these would-be consumers deny that they have the increased economic wherewithal to buy the particular goods they want, when they want. Moreover, an important paradox has emerged between women's feelings of empowerment under globalizing conditions, and the reality of the overall negative impact of neo-liberal development policies on women. In other words, while some opportunities have arisen to challenge pre-existing gender ideologies which might enable women to assert their sense of self and personal agency, ultimately any challenges are constrained by patriarchal ideologies lodged within the neo-liberal state. Gender inequalities under the neo-liberal regime are thus left largely unchallenged.

Before addressing the question of media and identity, a final observation that can be made concerning the research in Chapters 2 to 5, is the effort to re-situate 'people' in the globalization of Asia debate. Both Ganguly-Scrase and Scrase, for example, demonstrate the need to 'recover the subject' as it were, and in so doing, contribute to the expanding literature of 'grounded globalization' – research that focuses on micro-level processes and impacts on peoples and communities[8]. Moreover, Goodman and Piper take great pains to show the interconnections of peoples and communities who, despite being victims of the economic globalization process, attempt – in many and varied ways – to forge new alliances to ameliorate the impact of emergent inequalities.

Asia's mediated future

Long before globalization was given a name, social philosophers and economic theorists apprehended the push and pull between homogeneity and heterogeneity and worried about the social effects. Marx and Engels, for instance, observed:

> ...in place of the old local and national self-sufficiency, we have intercourse in every direction, universal interdependence of nations... The intellectual creations of individual nations become common property. National one-sidedness and narrow mindedness become more and more impossible, and from the numerous national and local literatures, there arises a world literature. (1967: 84)

To these two, of course, media was but a metaphor or, at best, an indicator. The economy was the impetus, the under girding logic, the central homogenizer. But for a contemporary, John Stuart Mill, media was one among a battery of factors threatening the individual with 'assimilation.' These forces included: democratizing political processes, extensions in education, increasing commerce and manufacturing, the 'ascendancy of public opinion in the State,' as well as 'improvements in means of communication' (1956: 89).

The binaries of 'global' media

Of course, now we know – or at least think we know – about the contradictions inherent in globalization: the binary 'this and that,' 'but/and' nature of the beast. There is not only homogeneity, just as there isn't only heterogeneity; not only consensus and uniformity, just as there isn't exclusively dissent and diversity. As with globalization, so too, media – as the selections in this volume have made abundantly clear. There are many kinds of media, as Todd Holden emphasized, but they can often be employed for uniform ideational effect. Nationalism and sub-cultural identification are two unitary themes funneled through various media channels in Japan. At the same time, Roberta Julian demonstrated in Chapter 6, various media can work to assist the opening up of public space, enabling the inclusion of previously mute or ignored voices, and promoting the diversification of discourse. Interestingly, singular mediations can also produce multiplicity, as Ming-Chu Chen detailed in Chapter 9. There we saw one source – a pirated, mass-distributed VCD of an ostensibly private sexual act – spawned a multiplicity of interpretations: from legal, to moral, to gendered, to economic, to existential. In short, these chapters underscored that just as media is not any one thing, they do not necessarily produce any single effect. Like globalization, itself, 'media' is a multiplicity of instrumentalities, with variegated uses, strategies, possibilities, and outcomes – often simultaneously.

Another binary in which media are implicated – and which Mill and Marx and Engels also recognized – is tradition versus modernity. It is this competing discourse that Pam Nilan introduced us to in Chapter 8, showing how the messages from global (generally western) media can invade and threaten the integrity of local values and practices. This is the 'world literature' that the *Manifesto* identified, possessing the power to 'batter down all Chinese walls...to create...a world after its own image.' (Marx and

Engels 1967: 84). Since Appadurai (1990), local resistance to exogenous content has been a theme in writing on globalization.[9] In their chapters, both Nilan and Julian convincingly argued that the traditional views of identity are entrenched in communities and are influential. As the latter observes: 'The strategies (established elites) adopt at both the local and the global level reify "culture" and treat "tradition" as relatively fixed, uncontested, and uncontestable.' This is a local power with which western or exogenous globalization phenomena often have to contend.

So, too, though, must local voices on the margins deal with such local powers. As Chen demonstrated, the 'exogenous' content was actually indigenously produced. More, while its distribution may have been via global media and through a western/capitalist system of information production, its message worked to pit rival discourses rooted in the context against each another. Tradition – in the form of 'patriarchy' came to be opposed by modernity – in the guise of female 'liberation.' In this way, we again witness the binaries of global media. And befitting its paradoxical nature, disjuncture between modernity and tradition was spawned by, then resolved through, media. Beyond this, media served as both the undoing of a public figure, as well as the means for her public reincarnation.

Media and social transformation

It is not simply in individual cases that media can be transformative. Collectivities, as well, can undergo alteration due to media activity. As for the Asian region, in contemplating media's role in stimulating social change, we can locate three, somewhat interrelated conceptual concerns: 'disjuncture,' 'identity,' and 'power.'

Disjuncture

It is fashionable for academics contemplating globalization to invoke this term – pointing to the aftermath of a process in which hegemonic homogeneity wrought by the global flow of (primarily western) cultural ideas and practices (in this case, through media) rubs up against local diversity *in situ*. And, indeed, evidence of such contentious co-mingling can be found in all four chapters addressing Asian mediation. In the case of the story reported by Chen, it can be said that DVD is a media form whose content – a heterosexual liaison between two adults – can be found virtually worldwide. The disjuncture, Chen shows, lies in the reception of this content by two groups within the locality. Moreover, because of the traditional, historically circumscribed, values rooted in the particular locality, the outcomes differ from what might unfold elsewhere. Indicative of this, the fate of these protagonists differed: with the woman more severely judged, despite the fact that she was single while her male partner was married.

Another kind of disjuncture delineated in Nilan's work is the dissonance between what academics say about media (that it has a minimal or – at the very most – uncertain, complex, difficult-to trace, power) versus what respondents say (that media is extremely powerful). It is this *belief* in media power that, in part, inspired Nilan's respondents to express dislike for – even vent rage at – western values and practices. They viewed media – in potential, at least – as influential agents in identity formation and discourse.

Similarly, the population Julian studied – the Hmong – also expressed the view that media are proactive and efficacious. In the author's words, 'media comprise a powerful avenue for the creation of a diasporic public sphere.' One can imagine that as globalization and processes of advanced modernity create an environment in which further global movement of people and ideas transpires – as well as the awareness of exogenous 'others' will increase. In turn, so, too, should the prospect for configuring greater, more diverse and widely linked public spheres.

As for the matter of identity, along with Julian, we can agree that media will play a significant role in *how* identities – diasporic or otherwise – will be constructed and represented. We can also build on this view, averring that a large number of identities will be communicated, experienced and, one might imagine, even adopted, due to the extension of awareness of others. Media and the *diaspora of media content* will become increasingly significant in Asia's future – if only in prompting responses from indigenous peoples whose values and practices come into contact with these transcultural products.

Identity

While outright social transformation is far from guaranteed, we can expect the processes of global mediation to pose challenges to local, entrenched hegemonies. If so, one can anticipate that local identities will often offer reflex-like resistance to the incursion of global mediation. Such a response is at the core of Nilan's chapter, where Indonesian youth expressed their belief that Western lifestyles, 'free' sex, and 'freer lifestyle' are the result of Western media and technology. Even in more 'Westernized' Asian contexts, such as the Japan Holden observed, we can apprehend messages of foreign food and fashion practices working to stimulate stronger place- and group-based senses of (localized) identity.

Despite such unreflective challenges, it ought not to come as a surprise were media to end up *facilitating* social change. This is consistent with the contradictory logic of mediation under conditions of contemporary globalization. Often such change will not transpire within the context (*a la* Chen's reinvented sex-VCD victim); more likely it will transpire across contexts, or beyond any one context, where the roots of local resistance are planted most shallow. Media effect – in facilitating social transformation – would seem most likely in cases such as those described by Julian: where media assisted a de-placed people in successfully forging a collective identity, globally.

Power

For those in power media can be a threat, just as for those on the margins, media can be a promise – and vice-versa. This is another of media's simultaneous binaries: it is a force of control *and* liberation; a means of self-definition and self-expression, *as well as* a tool for externally imposed labeling and socialization. And, as Holden showed in his chapter, media carry a powerful invisible capacity to reign in members within the confines of nation and subgroup. At the same time, as discussed above, because media have the capacity to span boundaries, they threaten to render the old organization forms – of state, capital, patriarchy, and ethnic majority – less consequential. The greatest certitude in concluding about media in Asia's future is that they will be present – front and center – with increasing visibility and magnitude, as both tools of would-be domination and sought liberation.

Prospects and implications

So what, ultimately, are the prospects for Asia, in light of a globalized, media-assisted – even media-centered – future? That answer is as complex as the technologies yearly sprouting and the social processes they intersect. For one thing, Asia's mediated future depends as much on development as it does on technological innovation. Ito (1999) has offered an addendum to the Marx/Engels assessment: asserting that at the earliest stages of societal development media standardizes – they forge uniformities – but at the higher or more advanced stages of development, they embody and promote greater diversity. If so, we would anticipate seeing countries in Asia displaying more and more diversity in practices, world views, and the like – *because of media*; despite whatever differential rates of economic, political and social development may obtain as between any two or more societies.

It is this element of pan-regionality that is most implicated in the existence of media. It is the boundary spanning capability inherent in much media – measured in terms of physical, social and ideational 'geography' – that is most significant. Media possess the capability of nullifying or at least potentially rendering the boundaries of nations and interest groups less meaningful or determinative. In this way they have altered the political and moral and practical contours of the contemporary world. In a word, media carry the potential of affecting both tradition *and* modernity, at once.

Above all, what these chapters have demonstrated is that, in a variety of ways, media influence the lives of Asians today. And because media are so intimately connected with innovation, technological development, economy, and other processes associated with 'modernity', it is almost certain that as Asia continues to grapple with modernization (or, in the alternative, chooses to confront the world's globality), media will persist as a core agent in the everyday lives of Asians throughout the region.

Cities and urban areas

The latter third of this book touched on some of the issues that have confronted citizens living in the cities of the Asia region. While cities throughout the region stand at differing levels of urbanization and development, face different policy environments, and are driven by differing mixes of internal and external pressures, a common goal for all is to strive for livable urban systems, structures, and environments. The particular issues that are likely to confront those living in cities of the region will differ between cities in maturing economies and those in developing economies. Those in the former category (places such as Tokyo) face issues of high energy consumption and depletion of resources, aging population, deteriorating infrastructure, and contrasts between a highly educated and well paid mainstream and a disenfranchised minority. Some cities in Asia's most recently dynamic economies (for example Singapore, and cities in South Korea) will face similar issues as they continue to develop and deal with changing economic and social realities. As for cities in newly developed or developing economies (such as Dhaka or Jakarta), they face issues of a different order, including the prospect of rapid population growth, deficiencies in human capital, and shortfalls in the savings and investment needed to appreciably improve quality of life. Even given development projects, poverty in these cities will remain a pressing problem.

Of particular concern here are the Asian Mega Cities. Two were discussed in the chapters in this book – Dhaka and Jakarta – but others meriting attention include Tokyo, Mumbai, Metro Manila and Bangkok. No matter what their specific level of development, these mega-cities face the problems engendered by constant population pressure on infrastructure, natural resources and governmental inefficiencies. As these cities continue to expand (places such as Dhaka are estimated to grow at an annual rate of slightly less than 4 per cent) the logistical problems associated with supplying public goods, transporting both people and goods, and providing shelter will also multiply. The outcome is likely to be the ratcheting up of extreme pressure on quality of life, at least for those residents unable to pay to reduce urban nuisances.

Sound urban governance will become a key to the long term social and economic prosperity and development in all cities of the Asia region. The ability of governments to manage these places will be tested, with a key output being the development of policies and practices capable of creating sustainable cities. Sustainable urban development requires outcomes that 'ensure that it meets the needs of the present without compromising the ability of future generations' (World Commission on Environment and Development 1987: 8). Or, to put it another way, as the authors of *Urban Future 21* state: 'we must not rob the generations that come after us; rather, we should seek to leave them a larger and a better legacy than we have had ourselves' (Hall and Pfeiffer

2000: 17). Sustainable urban development is a multifaceted concept. It covers the environment (the facet of sustainability that is the most often quoted); but it also covers social, economic and cultural aspects. In addition, sustainability includes issues of employment, equity, safety and health. The aim of good urban policy must therefore be the production of cities that are economically prosperous, culturally vibrant, equitable, safe, green, enable citizens to live fruitful and fulfilling lives, and provide opportunities to participate in civil society. Cities should provide jobs for all citizens, affordable housing, sound health care, education for children, modern sanitation, affordable and efficient transport options, culture, and public safety. Citizens should also be given the opportunity to participate in the governance of their city and made to feel as though they are stakeholders in the cities of the future (Hall and Pfeiffer 2000).

However, the bringing together of these many facets of sustainable urban development is not without its problems, as developments in one area may conflict with goals in another. How can we reconcile the informal economic sectors discussed in Sanie and Baum's chapter with the views of city officials who see such sectors as a distraction from mainstream economic activities? Reducing informal activity may be part of a plan to improve economic development and seen as the epitome of a modern economy, but at what cost? Clearly, the goal of sustainable urban development in this case might require that these two sectors may have to co-exist for some time. Other problems may include how to push economic development and encourage the growth of the new knowledge sector economy without incurring side effects, some of which were noted in Baum's chapter on Singapore. There will be difficult tradeoffs, for sure, but some balance must be sought. Cities are going to continue to develop; *how* they proceed will depend on the way these considerations are balanced. Above all, the goal for urban governments, although difficult to achieve, should be for Pareto-optimal outcomes.

An ending (at the beginning)

It is hard to look at Asia today and – projecting into the short-term future – imagine securing Pareto-optimality; at least that is, absent conscious discourse and decision. To look only at the areas we have addressed in this text – labor, identity, cities, gender, social class, religiosity, technological and economic development – the phenomena associated with globality, freely operating, cannot avoid stimulating even greater disjuncture, even more inequality, disadvantaging even more groups.

Consider a recent advertisement in Japan for Sony mini-discs, running on network television during early evening 'golden hour.' In it, a large breasted woman with blond hair, garbed in a demi-T shirt and purple underpants, dances seductively in front of the camera. Suddenly, she grasps each of her breasts, then proceeds to knead and manipulate them provocatively as the camera zooms in on her torso. Her demeanor is unabashed, her expression challenging. This performance lasts for a good ten seconds before the company logo and product fade in, bringing the 'ad' to a close. In certain countries in the region – say the Philippines or Indonesia – such an ad would never be made, let alone shown. Malaysia's stringent advertising code would certainly forbid it, stating, as it does, that ads 'should not hurt the feelings (of various groups) or demean the sexes, politics or individuals.'[10] The government's 12-stage review process exists to ensure that no ad will come to air that might prove harmful to public morality or social order. Elsewhere, say in a country like North Korea, MDs are not an available technology; in Bangladesh or India MDs are not a ubiquitous part of daily life, as they are in Japan. The point is: Asia is a region *diverse* and *divided* – economically, politically, socially, culturally and morally. It is hard to imagine so many, often radical, fissures being patched over – such differences and inequalities brought into equilibrium; certainly not in the foreseeable future. For one thing, who could ever agree – between nations, even within any one nation – just what equilibrium is? For another, how could we ever determine by what means a society or collection of societies would get there? Even imagining such a dialogue transpiring – let alone formalized into consensual policy – strains credibility. Such an outcome certainly cannot be reconciled with what we know about human history, in this region or anywhere else in the world.

Asia's global career and the coming epoch of conflict

In this text we have introduced the concept of 'careers' of globalization, arguing that every nation has its own distinctive globalization signature. So, too, do regions. Looking at the current moment, we could say that this appears to be a distinct, and also critical, stage of Asia's globalization career. The widespread movement of people throughout the region, the increasing disparity in economic possibilities, the proliferation of media technologies – all contribute to the character of this career stage. These developments not only lend dynamism, though; they also stimulate concern. As we bring this book to conclusion, Asia appears on the cusp of a period of feverish political contestation. In the Philippines *Abu Sayyuf* rebels agitate for an Islamic state, prompting the Philippine government to enter into a cooperative agreement with United States, thereby allowing the latter to enter the fray. In Indonesia, it is said, *Al Qaeda* is regrouping, plotting the next terrorist campaign against Western-style governments and economic interests. A bomb in a Bali nightclub district in October 2002, fuels that belief. Nearly 200 revelers are killed and many more are maimed – with Australians, Indonesians, British, Canadians, Germans, and Swedes topping the list of victims. The Malaysian and Indonesian governments – equally mindful of their enormous Islamic populations, but also of their aspirations to conduct business with the world of nations – actively assist in investigating and even arresting suspected *Al Qaeda* members. North Korea has brought its nuclear reactors back on line – with the apparent intent of building weapons of mass destruction. Pyongyang claims that economic sanctions imposed by other nations – but in particular, America – amount to acts of war, which can only be met with by commensurate acts. China stands conspicuously quiet, while Japan and South Korea squirm in anticipation of potential nuclear holocaust. America responds by beefing up its military presence in the Pacific.

In some way, then, one could say that the more that globalization touches Asia, the more Asia remains the same. The flow of money, ideas, technology and goods are not the only tangible evidence of contemporary globalization in the region. So, too, are the delivery of military personnel from outside the region, the expansion of exogenous state power, and the reciprocal fomenting of local ideological resistance. These developments are sociological phenomena all; and interestingly, not very different from that of Asia's colonial past. One certainty about such phenomena: they are far from marking the final stage of Asia's globalization career.

Leading to one more certitude: in the future there will be a need to review the themes considered, the questions raised, and the findings presented in this volume. In that respect, globalizing Asia's future is wide open.

Notes

Chapter 1

1 Quoted from http://www.theoryhead.com/gender/extract.htm (Date last accessed: January 14, 2003).
2 Although McLuhan's writings have been derided as overly-deterministic, effects-oriented, microscopic, and unempirical, they have managed a measure of recovery. Certainly they have persisted in media theory, with second-generation writers such as Schwartz (1974), Boorstin (1978), and Ong (1982) highlighting the ways in which electronic media have altered patterns of thought and social organization. Even in general social theorization McLuhan's ideas have not been entirely dismissed (e.g. Meyerowitz 1986) and, in fact, endure in that they constitute the paradigm around which all contemporary globalization theory has been oriented (whether acknowledged or even apprehended).
3 See: http://www.vpro.nl/programma/dnw/download/Interview_Castells.shtml (Date last accessed: December 17, 2002).

Chapter 2

1 I would like to thank the Research Initiative on International Activism for supporting the research on which this Chapter is based. See www.international.activism.uts.edu.au
2 Post-crisis the IMF prescribed further devaluations, cuts to public expenditure, liberalization and privatization, thus deepening the recession and 'providing opportunities for Western transnational corporations to acquire new assets within East and Southeast Asia at bargain-basement prices' (Jones 2000: 251).
3 One profound example is the removal of communal property rights – *ejidos* – as part of NAFTA integration process, which

led to the reconstruction of indigenous demands for self-determination in the country, and a political ferment that still cannot be domesticated and contained within the existing formal political system (Morton 2000).

4 Castles distinguishes five major 'migration systems' in the Asia Pacific: out-migration from Asian countries, labor migration to the Gulf, migration between Asian countries, migration of professional and students, and movements of refugees and asylum seekers (Castles 1998). To this list may be added the migration flows from South to North America, with significant impacts on the politics of both Mexico and the US, and the existing and strengthening diasporas such as the Overseas Chinese diaspora, and the South Asian diaspora, which have key impacts on the politics of Malaysia and Taiwan for instance (Skeldon 2000). These dovetail with emerging professional diasporas, and the deepened inter-penetration of business and managerial classes across the region, expressed in Sklair's concept of the transnational capitalist class, a phenomenon that has had major impacts on political development (Sklair 2000).

5 The first clause states: 'The World Social Forum is an open meeting place for reflective thinking, democratic debate of ideas, formulation of proposals, free exchange of experiences and interlinking for effective action, by groups and movements of civil society that are opposed to neoliberalism and to domination of the world by capital and any form of imperialism, and are committed to building a planetary society directed towards fruitful relationships among Mankind and between it and the Earth.' (World Social Forum 2001: 1).

6 The Statement affirmed and extended the WEF slogan, 'We believe that not only is another world possible but that another world is necessary!'(Asian Social Forum 2003: 2). Reflecting its success, in January WSF announced it would hold the 2004 World Forum in Asia.

7 In 2001 for instance the Asia Pacific Research Network, a network of regional NGOs, brought together corporate campaigners from across the region to focus on the issue.

8 See Pesticides Action Network Asia Pacific (www.panap.net)

9 See Global Indymedia: www.indymedia.org

10 See Nike watch, Oxfam Australia: www.caa.org.au/campaigns/nike

11 Asia Monitor Resource Centre, www.amrc.org.hk

Chapter 3

1 With the exception of Sim (2001), Lisa Law (forthcoming) and Lim (2002).
2 Most studies derive from the empirical context of South or Latin America. For full literature review, see Piper & Uhlin, forthcoming.
3 ASEAN member states are: Indonesia, Malaysia, Philippines, Singapore, Thailand, Brunei Darussalam, Vietnam, Laos, Cambodia and Myanmar; the Plus 3-countries include China, Japan, and Korea.
4 I have argued elsewhere that the increase in marriages between Southeast Asian women and East Asian men is somewhat related to these restrictive and harsh visa policies. In other words, women opt for marriage as a method to migrate or to stay (Piper 1999).
5 Empowerment refers to the expansion of choice and action and is about individual and collective agency (Kilby 2002). 'Protection' as approached by policymakers has often the opposite result in limiting already constrained choices
6 It has been observed, however, that 'global' often meant 'western' in the early days of the ILO. According to Ghai, the ILO tended to treat problems of migrant workers in Europe differently from those in the developing countries. It now, however, seems to have adopted a global approach (1999).
7 Such as the legally binding Convention on the Elimination of Discrimination Against Women (CEDAW) from 1979 and the Declaration on the Elimination of Violence Against Women from 1993 (Lawasia, 1998:179).
8 In Singapore, for instance, foreign domestic workers are not allowed to marry local men and when getting pregnant while in Singapore, they risk being deported.
9 The campaign was launched on April 28, 1996 and was based on four demands: (1) complete amnesty for all illegal foreign workers; (2) the abolition of the industrial trainee system; (3) a repeal of the fine system; and (4) the establishment of a protection law for foreign workers. The full-text of signature campaign is available online at http://russia.shaps.hawaii.edu/social/foreign-workers/law3_1_eng.html
10 The 'trainee system' has been used in Japan and Korea to circumvent the issue of importing semi – or un-skilled migrant

workers. These are mostly men from mainly Southeast Asia who are supposed to receive job training by companies against a smaller than usual salary, but often are used as 'disguised unskilled labor' without receiving any proper training.

Chapter 4

1 This paper is an outcome of a broader collaborative research, with Dr Tim Scrase, University of Wollongong, on the social consequences of globalization and economic liberalization in India. It was funded by an Australian Research Council small grant and a visiting fellowship at the International Institute for Asian Studies, University of Amsterdam and University of Leiden. This research was further supported by a Strategic Development Research grant. Finally, I would like to express my sincere gratitude to our informants for their generous participation in this project.
2 For a detailed discussions see *Social Dimension of Structural Adjustment in India*, 1991, and Khatkhate, D. 1994. 'Intellectual Origins of Indian Economic Reform: A Review of Jagdish Bhagwati's India in Transition: Freeing the Economy (1993)' *World Development*, 22 (7), pp.1097–1102.
3 The approximate exchange rate at the time of fieldwork was Indian Rupees (Rs) 40.00 = US$1.00. Thus, their monthly household income ranged from US$50–200.
4 In neo-Weberian terms, following the sevenfold (seven scales) stratification model developed by British sociologists Goldthorpe and Hope (1974), this group forms part of Class II (lower professionals; technicians; lower administrators; small business managers; supervisors of non-manual workers) and Class III (clerks; sales personnel) – in their terms, the 'lower white collar classes'. In neo-Marxist terms, following the work of Erik Olin Wright and his colleagues, they may be seen to be in a contradictory class location, – semi-autonomous, professional employees laying somewhere between the proletariat and the petty bourgeoisie (Wright 1985; Wright et. al 1989).
5 It has been argued that in West Bengal '... class stratification is imbedded to a great extent within the hierarchy of castes' (Sinha and Bhattacharya 1969: 56). More significantly, a complex interlinkage of economic position, status and caste relations and

the dynamics of political power shape the formation of social classes in West Bengal. For accounts of class formation based on detailed household statistical data, participant observation and case studies, see Chatterjee (1979: 1–31) and Bardhan (1982: 73–94).

6 For a critique of the expansion of the Indian middle class and the conceptual problems associated with defining this category, see Lakha (1999, 263–5).

7 In developing countries the shifts towards non-interventionist approaches of governments in economic and social arenas, in particular the changes brought about by retreat from state intervention in trade, industrial social policies are constitutive of the process of liberalization and more broadly globalization. See Stewart Berry (1999: 150–186).

8 I was able to explore the complexity of social relationships through the process of an intense participation in the everyday life of the people being studied. The contradictions between what my informants claimed or believed rather than what they actually did became apparent. The strength of ethnographic research lies in the richness of the feedback, observations and responses of informants and interviewees together with our observations as researchers in the field.

9 The town of Siliguri in North Bengal presents an interesting contrast to the metropolis of Calcutta, particularly in terms of the uneven impact of globalization. It is a vibrant frontier town where there has been a considerable influx of migrant Bengalis amidst a largely diverse tribal population both in the pre and post partition periods. As migrant communities, Bengalis in North Bengal have had to grapple with questions of identity and this has made them more attuned to issues of Bengali-ness, particularly in this era of heightened cultural globalization. In addition, historically Siliguri has been a major center of both official and black-market trade in various foreign consumer goods from Thailand via Bangladesh and from Nepal. Finally, in comparison to Calcutta, Siliguri has had little in the way of industrial production (with the exception of the tea industry located around Siliguri) or infrastructural development. Despite the regional difference, cultural responses to globalization were not shaped by geographic location. While my co-researcher was largely responsible for researching the impact of global media, including conducting audience

research, I often commuted with women workers. The vast majority of our respondents working in Calcutta live in the surrounding suburbs and towns. They traveled long distances by train each day. The journeys allowed me to become involved in discussions with women and their friendship groups, providing me the opportunity to explore complex issues such as the significance of SAPs, the NEP and privatization.

10 The most poignant film made on this theme during that era was *Mahanagar* or the Great City by the widely acclaimed Indian director, Satyajit Ray. Based on the novel of the same title the film depicts the everyday life of a *bhadralok* family in hard times, in which the housewife goes to work as a sales girl, selling Singer sewing machines because her husband is unable to find work.

11 I use the term 'responsibility' rather than 'duty' or' task' since most middle class women would not be expected to engage in the actual sweeping, dusting or mopping.

12 Any specks or residues of food not wiped clean are not merely considered unhygienic. According to Hindu upper caste practice upheld in some *bhadralok* households they are designated as ritually polluting.

13 This is not a peculiarly Indian phenomenon. The notion of 'commodity feminism' shows that advertisers co-opt feminist rhetoric and repackage them in such a way that patriarchal ideologies can be maintained (Goldman, 1992). Global advertising campaigns such as 'Just Do It' by the Nike corporation are exemplars of commodity feminism's active involvement in generating and circulating images of the empowered 'new woman', whilst simultaneously masking unequal gender relations within and between nations. (Carty 1997; Cole and Hribar 1995; Goldman and Papson, 1998: 143–44).

Chapter 5

1 This chapter is based on papers presented at two recent conferences. The first paper was presented in an international workshop I co-convened with Prof Mario Rutten on 'Asian Artisans and Small Scale Producers in the Global Economy: Trends, Issues and Problems in the New Millennium' held at the International Institute for Asian Studies (IIAS), University of Amsterdam branch, 4 January 2002. The second version was

presented at the 5th Asia Pacific Sociological Association Conference – 'Asia Pacific Societies: Contrasts, Challenges and Crises', 4–7 July 2002, Queensland University of Technology, Brisbane, Australia. Research in India was conducted in New Delhi from October 2002 through to February 2003. In New Delhi, I would like to thank the research assistance of Ms Sayani Das and Ms Urvashi Chandra. I wish to also acknowledge the financial support of the University of Wollongong which provided funds under the URC Strategic Development Research Grants Scheme, Start-up Grant (jointly awarded with Dr Ruchira Ganguly-Scrase).

2 Interviews were conducted from late 2002 to February 2003 with artisans at two venues in New Delhi, India: *Dilli Haat* (Delhi Market) – a state run market offering stalls for artisans from all over India; and the Delhi Crafts Museum – a similar venue for artisans to display and sell their crafts.

3 As part of a pilot study, a small number of professional, upper middle class consumers were interviewed in depth in New Delhi during February 2003.

4 For instance, for detailed links, catalogues, details about retailers and producers, etc. see: http://www.fairtradefederation.com. 'Ten thousand villages' (http://www.villages.ca) is another important website for the promotion and marketing of third world handicrafts in North America.

5 AEN (Artisan Enterprise Network); Information about their curriculum and other details found at their website: http://www.artisanenterprisenetwork.org (accessed: 20/11/2002).

6 See: http://www.craftscenter.org (accessed: 29/11/2002). It appears that this center has linkages to the AEN.

Chapter 6

1 The Colombo Plan began as an initiative advanced by Commonwealth ministers at a meeting in 1950 in Colombo, Ceylon (now Sri Lanka). Its original aim was to assist economic development of Commonwealth countries in South and South East Asia, often via academic scholarships. During the Plan's thirty years, Asian students from non-Commonwealth countries such as Laos were awarded scholarships to study in nations such as Australia.

2 Note that the diasporic Hmong identity described here does not encompass the majority of the Hmong in China or South East

Asia. So, too, according to Maneeprasert (2001, personal communication), it fails to resonate with the identities of Hmong hill tribes in Northern Thailand, for whom the major arena for identity politics is the Thai political system.
3 'Miao' describes the ethnic minority in China which includes the Hmong.
4 'Hmong' is written 'Hmoob' in the Romanized Popular Alphabet (RPA) system.

Chapter 7

1 I gratefully acknowledge the assistance of *Ito Rie* and *Kawabata Miki* in collecting some of the data used in this analysis.
2 '*Gatsun*' being the word used to describe the sound made by a mallet striking a tree. It is applied to situations involving a forceful impact.
3 To this I would add the boom of *sports exports* over the past decade. This phenomenon is in equal parts economic, cultural and moral, and, abetted as it is by media, possesses concomitant societal impacts.
4 In fact, according to an October 2001, survey, 124 daily newspapers were in circulation in Japan, with a penetration rate of 1.1 newspapers per household. As compared to other countries, a 1996 UNESCO survey revealed that Japan not only had the highest circulation rate among nations in the world, but scaled to the population, nearly 6 of 10 people living in the country consumed daily newspapers, as compared with 4 out of 10 in South Korea, 3.5 out of 10 in England, 3 out of 10 in Germany, and 2 out of 10 in the United States and France. See: The Statistical Handbook of Japan, 2002, published by the Ministry of Public Management, Home Affairs, Posts and Telecommunications, http://www.stat.go.jp/english/data/handbook/c15cont.htm#cha15_4 (Date last accessed: January 12, 2003).
5 Source: http://www.stat.go.jp/english/data/handbook/c15cont.htm#cha15_4 (Date last accessed: January 12, 2003).
6 Although in 1998 more than 4 out of 10 books and magazines were returned to publishers unsold. See Mizoe Shogo and Giles Murray, 2002, *A Statistical Look at Japan*, Tokyo: Kodansha International Ltd., p.243.
7 A recent analysis suggested that the active user base is around 13 million; the population of active Internet-enabled mobile

telephone users is close to 20 million. See 'Japan's telecom revolution,' Japan Internet Report No. 54 – January 2001, (http://www.jir.net/jir1_01.html#users_overstated; site last accessed on December 10, 2002).

8 In fact, wired media is heavily gendered and generational: manifesting exceptionally high use rates until age 40, then declining dramatically. The highest female rates are found in the teens (89%), with steady drops thereafter: 86% in the 20s, 74% in the 30s, 57% in the 40s and 40% in the 50s. For men, the pattern is similar: 85% for teens, 94% in the 20s, 85% in the 30s, 85% in the 40s, and 70% in the 50s. The highest users by occupation are: students (at 90%), clerical and technical workers (at 86%), and management and professional (at 85%) [Kamimura and Ida 2002].

9 One of the major means of communicating this atomized identity is cell phones. Personalized content in the form of *machiuke gamen* – constantly changing downloadable screenshots – and *chakumelo* – call warning sounds in the form of famous voices, animal noises, and popular songs – enables users to employ phones as tools of fashion and self-expression (see Holden and Tsuruki 2003; Scuka 2000). So, too, are 'emoticons' (*kaomoji*) employed widely in email as a means of 'perform(ing) identities and emotions in well-defined cultural code' (Katsuno and Yano 2002).

10 For a full discussion of this subject see Befu (2001).

11 McVeigh has also explored this point in detail in the context of education and cell phone use among students. See his (2000) and (2003) works, respectively.

12 This is in addition to its other functions. Above all, food-talk is socializing. Often framed in the context of knowledge acquisition or competition, it also imparts values concerning planning, aesthetics, class, and consumption. Moreover, because it often arises in conjunction with television, film, sports, and recording stars, food discourse also works to reproduce popular culture. For more on this see Holden (2002, 1999a).

13 By comparison, news accounts for 15% of the broadcast day for all stations between 5 a.m. to Midnight.

14 With 'events' at number one. Food-related ads are roughly equivalent with ads for cars and sundries.

15 A good place to gain a sense of *Dochi?!* is on their home page. There one will find the competing meals for every show over

the past five years, the recipes for each prepared dish, interviews with the people associated with growing or preparing the featured ingredients in the localities around Japan, as well as maps to and pictures of key restaurants noted for the featured dish. Pictures from each telecast are also included. url: http://www.ytv.co.jp/docchi/dotch_set.html (Date last accessed: February, 20, 2003).

16 See, for example, Shufunotomo Publisher's website (http://www.shufunotomo.co.jp/company/prof2002B/In.html (Date last accessed: January 20, 2003); also *Japan's Periodicals in Print, 2002*. Tokyo: Media Research Center *kabushiki gasiha*

17 So-called 'office ladies.'

18 Data published by JMPA, the Japan Magazine Publishers Association (Date last accessed: January 20, 2003).

19 The others include: *Petitseven*, at 400,000, *Egg*, at 400,000, and *Fine*, at 367,000. Of these three, *Petitseven* is similar to Seventeen (and therefore a different target audience). *Egg* is targeted at the same '*gyaru*'-type group as *Cawaii!*. *Fine* targets 'active men and women in the 17 to 20 group.'

20 This according to Nomura (2000).

21 As quoted in Watrous (2000).

22 This is a complex signification. The word '*uchira*' although not a coarse word, is not generally used in public. '*Uchi*' means 'inside,' but is generally associated with the inside of a group or collectivity, such as a sports team, an organization or a household. '*Ra*' is a suffix referring to 'us.' In *Cawaii!* the term is written in *katakana*, the script associated with words that have been imported from outside Japan. Encountering them, the reader is struck by the sense of 'otherness'; of distinction for this particular group; of its existence in a world a world removed.

23 This is consistent with views of identity by non-media theorists, for instance, Hall (1991) and Jenkins (1996).

24 *Harajiku* is a trendy district in Tokyo.

25 Sources abound for this widely-trumpeted view. One of the most vocal is the novelist, Murakami Ryu. See his report in *Asiaweek*: 'Japan's New Attitude: While old-line politicians and businessmen struggle to catch up to the times, a new society is emerging — individual by individual', co-written with Jonathan Sprague.

27 An interesting point of note is that *ganguro* as a style has been marketed outside of Japan, in the guise of the Taiwan version

of the magazine *Cawaii*. Here, then, is a tangible exportation-related, media-based, 'globalization effect.'
28 'Jason,' quoted in *Tattoo Tribal*, Tokyo: Fujimi Publishing Company, Volume 5 (2003): 118.

Chapter 8

1 Four focus groups were convened in Bali; seven focus groups in Sulawesi.
2 In fact two separate questions were asked: (1) 'What is the influence of the mass media and electronic media on Indonesia?' and (2) 'What is the effect (of mass and electronic media) on young people?'
3 The New Order (Orde Baru) is the usual way to refer to the years under the authoritarian rule of President Suharto from 1966 to 1998. President Suharto was toppled from power by a 'people's revolution' and Indonesia now has a system of parliamentary democracy and free media.
4 This is even more likely if the young person in question had attended a Muslim religious school (five of the Muslim youths in this study) or was in part-time training for the priesthood (two of the Balinese youths and one of the Christian youths).
5 On the consumption of romance texts in Indonesia, see Nilan (2001); on television consumption in India, see Johnson (2001); on lifestyle consumption in Malaysian advertising, see Holden (2001).
6 This is not really surprising. As Nagata (1995) argues, wearing the veil in countries like Malaysia and Indonesia is an emphatically modern practice.
7 In presenting quotations I will employ the following convention regarding attribution: informant name, interview location, focus group number, gender, and religious affiliation. Names are fictitious to preserve confidentiality.
8 *Bandung – the Sea of Lust* is an Indonesian pornographic DVD.
9 This is often attempted through the constitution of a common enemy – although such a tack depends on constituting the 'other' as: 'those-who-are-as-different-from-us-as-they-can-possibly-be.' To be sure, Western counties do this too. For instance, in the 1950s communism was Australia's common enemy (the other); today it seems to be Muslim refugees.
10 In the case of the latter, see, for instance, Abou-El-Haj (1991).

11 A major reason 'Bollywood' has millions of non-Indian fans in the modest, Africa and Southeast Asia is because of the non-American quality of Indian movies. Particularly popular are the dreamily suggestive dance numbers, often placed in the midst of serious stories. As Power and Mazumdar (2000: 46) observe, 'given the choice between a Steve Martin divorce comedy and a musical about the virtues of God and family, Arabs, Africans and Southeast Asians often choose the latter.'

12 This latter reaction, in fact, may have been the result of some radical Muslim media which used the event to avidly fan the flames of anti-Westernism.

Chapter 9

1 Also known as VideoCD, this medium was developed in 1993 by Philips, JVC and Sony. It enables the storage of MPEG-1 video on a CD-ROM disk.

2 Chinese immigration to Taiwan began as early as the T'ang dynasty (618–907). In 1628, the Dutch took control of the island. In 1683, the Manchus of mainland China conquered the island and made Taiwan a province of China. The island was ceded to Japan following the Sino-Japanese War of 1895 and was under Japanese control until 1945. In 1949, the advancing communist forces of Mao Tse-tung forced President Chiang Kai-Shek's Nationalist government and nearly two million soldiers to flee from the mainland to Taiwan.

3 For instance, the principal and teachers of Hsin Wei Primary School in Pingtung county in southern Taiwan watched the pornographic video together in school in the teacher's room two months after its availability on the Internet. Lycos lists the topic as one of its top 50 search items of all-time. Chu topped the Lycos 50 for three weeks and spent 14 weeks on the list altogether. (See 'Lycos 50 Turns Three,' August 30–September 3, 2002; http://50.lycos.com/083002.asp [Date last accessed: January 22, 2003]).

4 A group formed in 1987 by women professionals in Taiwan. It aims at promoting concern about women's issues, vocalizing women's opinions, raising female consciousness and encouraging self-development.

Chapter 12

1 Umbrella bearers are workers who hold umbrellas for clients during rainstorms. These clients are usually well off.
2 Restrictions in certain areas of Jakarta which require at least 3 passengers in a car have resulted in some owners 'employing' young children to ride in their cars. To begin with people of all ages were employed, but later customers preferred children as they were likely to be less threatening as far as safety was concerned and also as they were willing to accept lower payment.

Chapter 13

1 According to the 1999 CIA World Fact book. Rankings list the following top ten: *China*, *India*, the United States, *Indonesia*, Brazil, Russia, *Pakistan*, *Bangladesh*, *Japan*, Nigeria. The *Philippines* was fourteenth, *Vietnam* fifteenth, *Iran* eighteenth, and *Thailand* nineteenth. Data can be found at the following URL: http://www.photius.com/wfb1999/rankings/population_0.html (Date last accessed: March 4, 2003).
2 See the following Economist report which offers a comparison to the U.S. Germany and China of 2001 indicators: url: http://www.economist.com/countries/Japan/profile.cfm?folder=Profile-Economic%20Structure (Date last accessed: March 4, 2003).
3 Source: The World Economic Forum's *Global Competitiveness Report 2001–2002*. The six countries include: Singapore (4th), Australia (5th), Taiwan (7th), New Zealand (10th), and Hong Kong (SAR) (13th). Other Asian Nations on the list include Japan (21st), South Korea (23rd), Malaysia (30th), Thailand (33rd), and China (39th). The full list can be found at: http://www.weforum.org/pdf/gcr/Overall_Competitiveness_Rankings.pdf (Date last accessed: March 4, 2003).
4 Source: http://www.worldbank.org/data/databytopic/reg_wdi.pdf (Date last accessed: March 4, 2003).
5 Ibid., 'Key indicators: regional data from the WDI database.'
6 Ibid.
7 Yet, as a representative of American imperialism, McDonald's has been bombed recently by Islamic fundamentalists in various Asian countries, including China (December 2001) and

Indonesia (December 2002), and a planned attack was thwarted in Pakistan (September 2002). In India, cow dung was smeared on a McDonald's mascot in protest of the corporation's use of beef in its hamburgers (May 2001). Finally, Malaysia began boycotting Coca-Cola (in December 2002) to protest perceived interference by the United States in Islamic countries.
8 See Burawoy *et.al.* (2000) for recent research and cases studies from a comparative, sociological perspective.
9 See also Santos (2002).
10 Malaysian Government, *Advertising Code for Television and Radio* (ACTR), Kuala Lumpur: Ministry of Information (1998), section 1.1.

References

Chapter 1

Anderson, Benedict (1983), *Imagined Communities: Reflections on the Origins and Spread of Nationalism,* London: Verso.

Appadurai, Arjun (1990), 'Disjuncture and difference in the global cultural economy,' in Mike Featherstone (ed), *Global Culture: Nationalism, Globalization and Modernity*, London and Newbury Park: Sage.

Ariffin, Jamilah and Adeline Louis (eds) (2001), *Social Challenges of Rapid Economic Transformation*, Proceedings of the Institute Sultan Iskandar and Swiss Academy of Development, Joint International Conference, Technology University of Malaysia, Johor: ISI Publications.

Boorstin, Daniel (1978), *The Republic of Technology: Reflections on Our Future Community*, New York: Harper and Row.

Burgess, Ernest W. (1967), 'The growth of the city', in Robert E. Park, Ernest W. Burgess, and R. D. McKenzie (eds), *The City*, Chicago: Chicago University Press.

Castells, Manuel (1977), *The Urban Question*, London: Edward Arnold.

Castells, Manuel (1996), *The Information Age: Economy, Society and Culture. Volume I: The Rise of the Network Society*. Cambridge MA. and Oxford UK: Blackwell.

Clammer, John (2001), *Japan and its Others: Globalization, Difference and the Critique of Modernity*, Melbourne: Trans Pacific Press.

Clammer, John (2002), *Diaspora and Identity: The Sociology of Culture in Southeast Asia*, Selangor Darul Ehsan, Malaysia: Pelanduk.

Clammer, John (2003), 'Globalisation, class, consumption and civil society in Southeast Asian cities, *Urban Studies*, 40 (2): 403–420.

Eades, Jerry F., Tom Gill and Harumi Befu (eds) (2000), *Globalization and Social Change in Contemporary Japan*, Melbourne: Trans Pacific Press.

Edwards, Louise and Mina Roces (eds) (2000), *Women in Asia: Tradition, Modernity and Globalisation*, Sydney: Allen and Unwin.

Evans, Grant (ed.) (1993), *Asia's Cultural Mosaic: An Anthropological Introduction*, New York: Prentice-Hall.

Frank, Andre Gunder (1998), *ReOrient: Global Economy in the Asian Age*, Berkeley: University of California Press.

Friedman, John. and Goetz Wolff (1982), 'World city formation: An agenda for research and action', *International Journal of Urban and Regional Research*, 6 (3), pp. 309–335.

Gauntlett, David (2002) *Media, Gender and Identity: An Introduction*, London: Routledge.

Giddens, Anthony (1990), *The Consequences of Modernity*, Stanford, CA: Stanford University Press.

Giddens, Anthony (1991), *Modernity and Self-Identity: Self and Society in the Late Modern Age*, Stanford, CA: Stanford University Press.

Gosovic, B. (2000), 'Global intellectual hegemony and the international development agenda', *International Social Science Journal,* 52 (4), pp. 447–456

Hall, Peter and Ulrich Pfeiffer (2000), *Urban Future 21: A Global Agenda for Twenty-First Cities*, London: E and F N Spon.

Ho, K. C. (1997), 'The global economy and urban society in Pacific Asia', *International Sociology*, 12 (3), pp.275–293.

Hung, R. (1996), 'The great U-turn in Taiwan: Economic restructuring and surge in inequality', *Journal of Contemporary Asia*, 26 (2), pp. 151–163.

Kinnvall, Catarina and Kristina Jonsson (eds) (2002), *Globalization and Democratization in Asia: The Construction of Identity*, London: Routledge.

Lull, James (1995), *Media, Communication, Culture: A Global Approach*, Cambridge: Polity Press.

Mills, C. Wright (1959), *The Sociological Imagination*, New York: Oxford University Press.

McLuhan, Marshall (1964), *Understanding Media: The Extensions of Man*, New York: The New American Library.

McLuhan, Marshall and Fiore Quentin (1967), *The Medium is the Massage: An Inventory of Effects*, New York: Bantam.

Meyerowitz, Joshua (1986), *No Sense of Place: The Impact of Electronic Media on Social Behavior*, New York and Oxford: Oxford University Press.

Morley, David and Kevin Robins (1995), *Spaces of Identity: Global Media, Electronic Landscapes and Cultural Boundaries*, London and New York: Routledge.

Olds, Kris, Peter Dicken and Philip F. Kelly (eds.), *Globalisation and the Asia Pacific: Contested Territories*, London: Routledge.

Ong, Walter (1982), *Orality and Literacy: The Technologizing of the Word*, Ithica, N.Y.: Cornell University Press.

Park, Robert E. (1967), 'The city: Suggestions for the investigation of human behavior in an urban environment', in Robert E. Park, Ernest W. Burgess, and R. D. McKenzie, (eds), *The City*, Chicago: Chicago University Press.

Pickvance, Chris (1976), *Urban Sociology: Critical Essays*, Melbourne: Tavistock.

Pinches, Michael (ed.) (1999), *Culture and Privilege in Capitalist Asia*, London and New York: Routledge.

Robertson, Roland (1992), *Globalization: Social Theory and Global Culture*, Thousand Oaks and New Dehli: Sage.

Robison, Richard and David Goodman (1996), *The New Rich in Asia: Mobile Phones, McDonald's and Middle-class Revolution*, London: Routledge.

Santos, Boaventura de Sousa (2002), '*Nuestra America*: reinventing a subaltern paradigm of recognition and redistribution,' in Scott Lash and Mike Featherstone (eds), *Recognition & Difference: Politics, Identity, Multiculture*, London and Thousand Oaks: Sage, pp. 185–217.

Sassen, Saskia (1991), *The Global City: New York, London, Tokyo*, Princeton NJ: Princeton University Press.

Savage, Mike and Alan Warde (1993), *Urban Sociology, Capitalism and Modernity*, London: Macmillan.

Schwartz, Tony (1974), *The Responsive Chord*, Garden City, N.J.: Anchor.

Slevin, James (2002), 'The Internet and forms of human association', in Denis McQuail (ed.), *McQuail's Reader in Mass Communication Theory*, London: Sage, pp. 147–56.

Tomlinson, John (1999), *Globalization and Culture*, Cambridge: Polity Press.

Yamashita, Shinji and Jerry F. Eades (eds) (2001), *Globalization* in *Southeast Asia: Local, National and Transnational Perspectives*, Oxford: Berghahn Books.

Tehranian, Majid (1999), *Global Communication and World Politics: Domination, Development, and Discourse*, Boulder, CO: Lynne Rienner.

Vervoorn, Aat (2002), *Re Orient: Change in Asian Societies*, (2nd edn.), South Melbourne: Oxford University Press.

Wallerstein, Immanuel (1976), *The Modern World-System I: Capitalist Agriculture and the Origins of the European World-Economy in the Sixteenth Century*, New York: Academic Press.

Wee, W-L.C.J. (ed.) (2002) *Local Cultures and the "New Asia": The State, Culture, and Capitalism in Southeast Asia*, Singapore: Institute of Southeast Asian Studies.

Werbner, Pnina (1998), 'Diasporic political imaginaries: A sphere of freedom or a sphere of illusions?', *Communal/Plural*, 6 (1), April, pp. 11–31.

The World Bank (2000), *Entering the 21st Century: World Development Report 1999/2000*, Oxford: Oxford University Press.

Yeung, Yue-Man (2000) *Globalization and Networked Societies: Urban-Regional Change in Pacific Asia,* Honolulu, HI: University of Hawai'i Press.

Chapter 2

Acharya, Amitav (1998), *Democratising Southeast Asia: Economic Crisis and Political Change,* Asia Research Centre, Working Paper 87, Perth, Australia: Murdoch University.

Acharya, Amitav and Richard Stubbs (1999), 'The Asia Pacific region in the post-Cold War era', in L. Fawcett and Y. Sayigh, (eds), *The Third World Beyond the Cold War: Continuity and Change*, Oxford: Oxford University Press, pp. 118–134.

Ahn, Byung-Joon (1997), 'The United States in Asia: defining a new role', in Chan Heng Chee (ed.), *The New Asia Pacific Order,* Singapore: Institute of SE Asian Studies.

Alagappa, Muthiah (1995), 'Contestation and crisis', in Muthiah Alagappa (ed.), *Political Legitimacy in Southeast Asia: The Quest for Moral Authority*, Stanford: Stanford University Press, pp.54–65.

Altman, Dennis (2000), 'The emergence of 'modern' gay identities and the question of human rights', in A. Hilson, et. al. (eds),

Human Rights and Gender Politics in the Asia Pacific, London: Routledge, pp. 211–228.

Antlov, Hans and Stein Tonnesson (1995), *Imperial Policy and Southeast Asian Nationalism, 1930–1957,* Nordic Instutute of Asian Studies, London: Curzon Press.

Asian Regional Exchange for New Alternatives (2000), *Re-imagining Asia: Re-defining 'human security' and 'alternative development' Movements and Alliances in the Twenty-First Century,* ARENA's three year program 2000–2003, Hong Kong: ARENA.

Asian Social Forum (2002), *Building Another World: Invitation to the ASF,* August 2002, Thailand: ASF.

Asian Social Forum (2003), *Statement Of The Asian Social Mass and Peoples' Movements and Organisations,* January 2003, India: ASF.

Asian Social Movements (2002), *Another World is Possible! Mobilise Against Neo-liberalism!,* Statement, August 2002, Thailand: ASM.

Bello, Walden (1998), 'East Asia: On the eve of the great transformation?', *Review of International Political Economy,* 5 (3), pp.424–445.

Bello, Walden (2003), *From Florence to Porto Alegre via Hyderbad: A Year in the Life of the World Social Forum,* Inter-Press Service, January 2003.

Berger, Mark (2001a), 'APEC and its enemies: The failure of the new regionalism in the Asia Pacific', *Third World Quarterly,* 20 (5) pp. 1013–30.

Berger, Mark (2001b), 'The rise and demise of national development and the origins of post-Cold War capitalism', *Millennium,* 30 (2), pp. 211–34.

Berger, Mark (2002), 'Battering down the Chinese walls: The antimonies of Anglo-American liberalism and the history of East Asian capitalism in the shadow of the Cold War', in C. Wee (ed.), *Local Cultures and the 'New Asia': The State, Culture and Capitalism in SE Asia,* Singapore: Institute of SE Asian Studies, pp. 77–106.

Burgmann, Verity (2003), *Power, Profit and Protest: Australian Social Movements and Globalization,* Sydney: Allen and Unwin.

Burke, A. (2001), 'Caught between national and human security: Knowledge and power in post-crisis Asia', *Pacifica Review,* 13 (3), pp. 215–239.

Camilleri, Joseph (2000), *States, Markets and Civil Society in Asia Pacific: Political Economy of the Asia Pacific Vol. 1,* London: Edward Elgar.

Castells, Manuel (1997), *The Power of Identity,* (vol. 2 of 'The Information Age: Economy, Society and Culture'), London: Blackwell.

Castles, Stephen (1998), 'New migrations in the Asia Pacific region: A force for social and political change', *International Social,Science Jouurnal,* 50 (156), pp. 215–228.

Chossudovsky, Michel (1998), *The Globalisation of Poverty: Impacts of IMF and WB Reforms,* Sydney: Pluto Press.

Clarke, Tony (1997), *Silent Coup: Confronting the Big Business Takeover of Canada,* Canadian Centre for Policy Alternative, Toronto: James Lorimer and Company.

Cox, Robert (1987), *Production, Power and World Order,* New York: Columbia University Press.

Crouch, Harold and James Morley (1999), 'The dynamics of political change', in James Morley, (ed.), *Driven by Growth: Political Change in the Asia Pacific Region,* New York: ME Sharpe, pp. 313–354.

Cruz, D. (2002), 'Undermined-values and foreign aid NGOs', *Review,* Magazine of the IPA, December, pp.26–29.

Curtis, Gerald (1998), 'A "recipe" for democratic development', in L. Diamond and M. Plattner, (eds), *Democracy in East Asia,* Baltimore: John Hopkins University Press, pp. 217–223.

Diller, J. (1999), 'A social conscience in the global marketplace? Labour dimensions of codes of conduct, social labelling and investor initiatives', *International Labour Review,* 138 (2), pp. 1–32.

Dokken, K. (2001), 'Environment security and regionalism in the Asia Pacific: Is environmental security a useful concept?', *The Pacific Review,* 14 (4), pp.509–530.

Doucet, Marc (2001), 'The possibility of deterritorialising democracy: Agonistic democratic politics and the APEC NGO forums', *Alternatives: Global Local Political,* 26 (3), pp. 283–314.

Ekins, Paul (1998), *A New World Order: Grassroots Movements for Global Change,* London: Routledge.

Ericson, Richard and Aaron Doyle (2000), 'Globalisation and the policing of protest', *British Journal of Sociology,* 50 (4), pp. 589–608.

Evans, Geoff, Nina Lansbury and James Goodman (2002), *Moving Mountains: Communities Confront Mining and Globalisation*, London: Mineral Policy Institute and Zed Press.

Fairbrother, Peter, S. Svensen and J. Teicher (1998), 'The ascendancy of neo-liberalism in Australia', *Capital and Class*, 63, pp. 1–12.

Falk, Richard (1999), *Predatory Globalisaton: A Critique*, Cambridge: Polity.

Faust, J. and U. Franke (2002), 'Attempts at diversification: Mexico and Pacific Asia', *The Pacific Review*, 15 (2), pp. 299–325.

Field, Heather and James Goodman (1999), 'Transforming Europe: New zones of dependency', *Democracy and Nature*, 5 (2) pp. 217–238.

Flynn, Norman (1999), *Miracle to Meltdown in Asia: Business, Government and Society*, Oxford: Oxford University Press.

Forrester, Geoff and R. May (eds), (1998), *The Fall of Soeharto*, London: Hurst.

Friedman, Thomas (1999), *The Lexus and the Olive Tree*, London: Harper Collins.

Friends of the Earth International (2002),*Clashes with Corporate Giants: 22 Campaigns for Biodiversity and Community*, Amsterdam: Friends of the Earth International.

Ghai, Yash (1996), 'From phoney debate to unholy alliance', in *ASEM Trading: New silk routes*, Thailand: Transnational Institute and Focus on the Global South.

Gill, Stephen (1998), 'New constitutionalism, democratisation and global political economy', *Pacifica Review*, 10 (1), pp. 23–38.

Goodman, James (2000a), 'Post-Cold War self-determination: Ireland and Timor', *Geopolitics*, 3 (3), pp. 53–82.

Goodman, James (2000b), 'Transnational contestation: Social movements beyond the state', in T. Cohn, S. McBride and J.Wiseman (eds), *Power in the Global Era: Grounding Globalization*, London: Macmillan, pp. 39–53.

Goodman. James (2001), 'The World Economic Forum: Capital's First International?', *Asia Pacific Journal*, 2.

Goodman, James (2002), 'Contesting corporate globalism: sources of power, channels for democratisation', in J. Anderson (ed.), *Possibilities of Transnational Democracy: Political Spaces and Border Crossings*, London: Routledge, pp. 215–236.

Goodman, James and Patricia Ranald (2000), *Stopping a*

Juggernaut: Public Interests Versus the Multilateral Agreement on Investment, Sydney: Pluto Press.

Goodman, James and Tony Tujan (2002),*Corporate Power or Peoples Power? Transnational Corporations and Globalization,* Paper presented at the Asia Pacific Research Network annual conference 2001, Manila: APRN.

Gopinath, Gayatri (1996), 'Funny boys and girls', in R. Leong (ed.), *Asian American Sexualities,* New York: Routledge, pp. 119–131.

Hardt, Micheal (2002), 'Porto Alegre: Today's Bandung?', *New Left Review,* 14, pp. 1–15.

Hernadez-Diaz, Jorge (1994), 'National identity and indigenous ethnicity in Mexico', *Canadian Review of Studies in Nationalism,* XX1 (1–2), pp. 71–83.

Hettne, Bjorn (1997), 'The double movement: global market versus regionalism', in R. Cox (ed.), *The New Realism: Perspectives on Multilateralism and World Order*, Tokyo: Macmillan and UN University Press, pp. 223–242.

Hewison, Kevin, Richard Robison and Garry Rodan (eds), (1993), *Southeast Asia in the 1990s: Authoritarianism, Democracy and Capitalism,* Sydney: Allen and Unwin.

Heywood, L. and Drake, J. (1997), *The Third Wave Agenda: Being Feminist, Doing Feminism*, Minneapolis: University of Minnesota Press.

Hsiung, James (1993), 'Asia Pacific in perspective: The impact of the end of the Cold War', in J. Hsiung (ed.), *Asia Pacific in the New World Politics,* Boulder, CO: Lynne Rienner, pp 213–233.

Huntington, Samuel (1991), *The Third Wave: Democratization in the Late Twentieth Century,* Norman, OK: University of Oklahoma Press.

Jarvis, Anthony and A. Paolini (1995), 'Locating the state', in Joseph Camilleri, Anthony Jarvis and A. Paolini (eds), *The State in Transition: Reimagining Political Space,* London: Lynne Reinner.

Johnson, C. (1987), 'Political institutions and economic performance', in Fred Dreyo (ed.) *The Political Economy of the New Asian Industrialism,* New York: Cornell University Press, pp. 136–165.

Jones, Barry (2000), *The World Turned Upside Down? Globalisation and the Future of the State,* Manchester: Manchester University Press.

Kelsey, Jane (1995), *Economic Fundamentalism: The New Zealand Experiment – A World Model for Structural Adjustment?*, Sydney: Pluto.

Khoo, Nicholas and Micheal Smith (2002), 'The future of American hegemony in the Asia Pacific: a concert of Asia or a clear pecking order?', *Australian Journal of International Affairs,* 56 (1), pp. 65–81.

Kothari, R. (1993), 'The yawning vacuum: A world without alternatives', *Alternatives: Global Local Political,* 18 (2), pp. 119–139.

Langton, Marcia (1997), 'Pauline as the thin end of the wedge', in Philip Adams (ed.), *The Retreat from Tolerance,* Sydney: ABC Books, pp. 86–108.

Laxer, Gordon (1992), 'Constitutional crises and continentalism: twin threats to Canada's continued existence', *Canadian Journal of Sociology,* 127 (2), pp. 199–222.

Luke, Timothy (1997), 'Localised spaces, globalised places: virtual community and geo-economics in the Asia Pacific', in Mark Berger and D. Borer (eds.), *The Rise of Asia: Critical Visions of the Pacific Century,* London: Routledge, pp. 241–259.

Ma, Shu-Yun (1998), 'Third World studies, development studies and post-communist studies: Definitions, distance and dynamism', *Third World Quarterly,* 19 (3), pp. 339–348.

Malhotra, Kamal (2002), 'Development enabler of disabler? The role of the state in Southeast Asia', in C. Wee (ed.), *Local Cultures and the 'New Asia': The State, Culture and Capitalism in Southeast Asia,* Singapore: Institute of Southeast Asian Studies, pp. 31–50.

Maiguashca, B. (1994), 'The transnational indigenous movement in a changing world order' in Y. Sakamoto (ed.), *Global Transformation: Challenges to the State System,* Tokyo: UN University Press, pp. 51–73.

Marchand, Marianne, Morten Boas and Timothy Shaw (1999), 'The political economy of new regionalisms', *Third World Quarterly,* 20 (5), pp. 897–910.

Martinez-Alier, J. (2000), 'Environmental justice as a force for sustainability', in J. Pierterse (ed.), *Global Futures: Shaping Globalization,* London: Zed, pp. 148–174.

Mertes, T. (2002), 'Grass-roots globalism: reply to Micheal Hardt', *New left Review,* 17, pp. 101–110.

Mittelman, James and Richard Falk (2000), 'Global hegemony and regionalism', in S. Calleya (ed.), *Regionalism in the Post-Cold War World,* Aldershot: Ashgate, pp. 3–22.

Morales, I. (1999), 'NAFTA: The institutionalisation of economic openness and the configuration of Mexican geo-economic spaces', *Third World Quarterly,* 20 (5), pp. 971–93.

Morton, A. (2000), 'Mexico, neo-liberal restructuring and the EZLN: A neo-Gramscian analysis', in B. Gills (ed.), *Globalisation and the Politics of Resistance,* Basingstoke: Palgrave, pp. 255–80.

Munck, Ronaldo (2002), 'Labour, globalisation and trans-national action', in James Goodman (ed.), *Protest and Globalization,* Sydney: Pluto Press, pp .50–71.

Niblo, Stephen (1995), 'The world economy and an economically active state: From economic radicalism to neoliberalism in Mexico', in Joseph Camilleri, Anthony Jarvis and A. Paolini (eds), *The State in Transition: Reimagining Political Space,* London: Lynne Reinner. pp.189–206.

Pang, Eul-Soo (2000), 'The financial crisis of 1997–1998 and the end of the Asian developmental state', *Contemporary Southeast Asia,* 22 (3), pp. 570–601.

Pettman, Jan (1996), *Worlding Women: A Feminist International Politics,* Sydney: Allen and Unwin.

Pinches, Michael (1997), 'Elite democracy, development and people power: Contending ideologies and changing practices in Philippine politics', *Asian Studies Review,* 21 (2–3), pp. 102–20.

Piper, Nicola and R. Ball (2001), 'Globalisation of Asian migrant labour: The Philippine-Japan connection', *Journal of Contemporary Asia,* 31 (4), pp. 1–15.

Polanyi, Karl (1944), *The Great Transformation,* New York: Octagon.

Prasad, S., J. Dakuvula and D. Snell (2001), *Economic Development, Democracy and Ethnic Conflict in the Fiji Islands,* London: Minority Rights Group International.

Preston, Peter (1998), *Pacific Asia in the Global System,* Oxford: Blackwell.

Ravenhill, John (2001), *APEC and the Construction of Pacific Rim Regionalism,* Cambridge: Cambridge University Press.

Reilly, B. (2002), 'Internal conflict and regional security in Asia and the Pacific', *Pacifica Review,* 14 (1), pp. 1–21.

Richardson, J. (1995), 'Problematic paradigm: Liberalism and the global order', in Joseph Camilleri, Anthony Jarvis and A. Paolini (eds), *The State in Transition: Reimagining Political Space,* London: Lynne Reinner, pp. 141–55.

Ruggie, James (1982), 'International regimes, transactions and change: Embedded liberalism in the postwar economic order', *International Organization,* 31 (4), pp. 379–415.

Sachsenroder, Wolfgang (1998), 'Party politics and democratic development in East and Southeast Asia: A comparative view', in W. Sachsenroder and U. Frings (eds), *Political Party Systems and Democratic Development in East and South East Asia,* Aldershot: Ashgate, pp. 1–35.

Scalapino, R. (1998), 'A tale of three systems', in L. Diamond and M. Plattner (eds), *Democracy in East Asia,* Baltimore, UK: John Hopkins University Press.

Schmidt, J. (2000),'Neoliberal globalization, social welfare and trade unions in Southeast Asia', in B. Gills (ed.), *Globalisation and the politics of resistance,* London: Palgrave, pp .220–241.

Serrano, Isagani (1994), 'Civil society in the Asia Pacific region', in M. Oliveira and R. Tandon (eds), *Citizens: Strengthening Global Civil Society,* Washington: Civicus, pp. 271–318.

Silliman, Sidney (1998), 'The transnational relations of Philippine NGOs', in G. Silliman and L. Noble (eds), *Organizing for Democracy: NGOs, Civil Society and the Philippine State,* Manila: Ateneo de Manila University Press.

Skeldon, Ronald (2000), 'Trends in international migration in Asian and Pacific region', *International Social Science Journal,* 52, pp. 369–382.

Sklair, Leslie (1996), 'The transnational capitalist class in Australia', *Australian and New Zealand Journal of Sociology,* 32 (2), pp. 85–115.

Sklair, Leslie (2000), *The transnational capitalist class,* Cambridge: Polity.

Soederberg, Susanne (2001) 'The new international financial architecture: Imposed leadership and emerging markets', in L. Panitch and Colin Leys (eds) *Socialist Register 2002: A World of Contradictions,* pp. 175–192.

Soros, George (1998), *The Crisis of Global Capitalism,* London: Little, Brown and Company.

Starr, Amory (2000), *Naming the Enemy: Anti-Corporate Movements Confront Globalization,* London: Zed.

Stiglitz, Joseph (2002), *Globalization and its Discontents*, New York: Norton and Co.
Stivens, Maila (2000), 'Introduction: Gender politics and the reimagining of human rights in the Asia Pacific', in A. Hilson, Martha Macintyre, Vera Mackie and Maila Stivens (eds), *Human Rights and Gender Politics: Asia Pacific Perspectives*, London: Routledge, pp. 1–36.
Stivens, Maila (ed.), (1991), *Why Gender Matters in Southeast Asian Politics*, Melbourne: Monash University.
Thompson, Mark (1996), 'Late industrialisers, late democratisers: Developmental states in the Asia Pacific', *Third World Quarterly*, 17 (4), pp. 625–47.
Tujan, Antonio and Rozario Guzman (1998),*Globalising Philippine Mining*, Manila: IBON Books.
Turner, Mark (1999), *Central-local Relations in Asia Pacific*, Basingstoke: Macmillan.
Uhlin, Anders (1999), *'Asian Values Democracy', Neither Asian nor Democratic: Discourses and Practices in Late New Order Indonesia*, Occasional Paper, Stockholm: Centre for Pacific Asia Studies.
Waterman, Peter (2002), *Globalization, Social Movements and the New Internationalism*, New York: Continuum.
Webber, Douglas (2001), 'Two funerals and a wedding? The ups and downs of regionalism in East Asia and the Asia Pacific after the Asian crisis', *The Pacific Review*, 14 (3), pp. 339–72.
Weiss, Linda (1998), *The Myth of the Powerless State*, Cambridge: Polity.
West, Lois (1997), *Feminist Nationalism*, New York: Routledge.
Willetts, Peter (1998),'Political globalization and the impact of NGOs upon transnational companies', in J. Mitchell (ed.), *Companies in a World of Conflict*, London: Royal Institute of International Affairs, pp. 195–225.
Wiseman, John (1996), *Global Nation? Australia and the Politics of Globalization*, Melbourne: Cambridge University Press.
Whitfield, D. (2001), *Public Services or Corporate Welfare*, London: Pluto.
World Bank (1997), *States in a Changing World: World Development Report 1997*, Washington: The World Bank.
World Social Forum (2001), *Charter of Principles*, (as approved by the WSF International Council, June 2001), Sao Paulo, Brazil: WSF.

Yamamoto, Tadashi (1995), *Emerging Civil Society in the Asia Pacific Community,* Osaka: Asia Pacific Philanthropy Consortium.

Yeung, H. (2000), 'Economic globalization, crisis and the emergence of Chinese business communities in Southeast Asia', *International Sociology,* 15 (2), pp. 266–88.

Yuval-Davis, Nira (1997), *Gender and Nation,* London: Sage.

Chapter 3

Aguilar, F.V. (1999), 'The triumph of instrumental citizenship? Migrations, identities and the nation-state in southeast Asia', *Asian Studies Review,* 23 (3), pp. 307–336.

Asian and Pacific Migration Journal (1996), 'Asian Women in Migration', Special Issue, 5 (1).

Athukorala, R.-C. and C. Manning (1999), *Structural Change and International Migration in East Asia,* Oxford: Oxford University Press.

Aviel, J. F. (2000), 'Placing human rights and environmental issues on ASEAN's agenda: The role of non-governmental organizations', *Asian Journal of Political Science,* 8 (2), pp. 17–34.

Buckley, S. (1994), 'A short history of the feminist movement in Japan', in J. Gelb and M.L. Palley (eds), *Women of Japan and Korea – Continuity and Change,* Philadelphia: Temple University Press, pp. 150–188.

Castles, Stephen and Mark Miller (1998) (2nd edn.), *The Age of Migration,* Basingstoke: Macmillan.

Chantavanich, Supang (1999), 'Thailand's responses to transnational migration during economic growth and economic downturn', *Sojourn – Journal of Social Issues in Southeast Asia,* 14 (1), pp. 159–77.

Chen Jie (2001), 'Burgeoning transnationalism of Taiwan's social movement NGOs', *Journal of Contemporary China,* 10 (29), pp. 613–644.

Cheng, Sealing (2002), Transnational Desires: 'Trafficked' Filipinas in US Military Camp Towns in South Korea, Unpublished PhD thesis, School of Anthropology, University of Oxford.

Chin, Christine B. N. (1998), *In Service and Servitude: Foreign Female Domestic Workers and the Malaysian 'Modernity' Project,* New York: Columbia University Press.

Cox, David (1997), 'The vulnerability of Asian women migrant workers to a lack of protection and to violence', *Asian and Pacific Migration Journal*, 6 (6), pp. 59–75.
Ghai, Y. (1999), 'Rights, social justice, and globalization in east Asia', in J. Bauer and D. Bell (eds), *The East Asian Challenge for Human Rights*, Cambridge: Cambridge University Press, pp. 241–263.
Gills, D. S. and Nicola Piper (eds) (2002), *Women and Work in Globalising Asia*, London: Routledge.
Gurowitz, Amy (1999), 'Mobilizing international norms: Domestic actors, immigrants, and the Japanese state', *World Politics*, 51 (3), pp. 413–445.
Harris, Nigel (1995), *The New Untouchables*, London: Penguin.
Hemming, Judith. (2002), 'Sex workers in Thailand – Victims or Agents?', Unpublished Paper, Canberra: ANU.
Hilsdon, A. M., Martha Macintyre, Vera Mackie and Maila Stivens (eds) (2000), *Human Rights and Gender Politics: Asia Pacific Perspectives*, London: Routledge.
Ho, L., C. Powell and L. Volpp (1996). '(Dis)Assembling rights of women workers along the global assembly line: Human rights and the garment industry', *Harvard Civil Rights-Civil Liberties Review*, 31, pp. 383–414.
Human Rights Law Group (2001), 'Initiative Against Trafficking in Persons', http://www.hrlawgroup.org/site/programs/traffic/No3.htm (07 Dec. 2001).
Human Rights Watch (2000), 'Owed justice – Thai women trafficked into debt bondage in Japan', http://www.hrw.org/reports/2000/japan/3-context.htm
Ito, Ruri (1996), 'Mouhitotsu-no Kokusai Roudouryoku Idou:Saiseisan roudou no chyo – Kokkyo teki iten to Nihon no zyosei izyuusya (Another international migration: transnational transfer of reproductive labour and migrant women in Japan)', in T. Iyotani and T. Sugihara (eds), *Nihon Syakai to Imin (Japanese Society and Migrants)*, Tokyo: Akashi Shoten, pp. 243–271.
Joachim, J. (1999), 'Shaping the human rights agenda: The case of violence against women', in M. K. Meyer and E. Pruegl (eds), *Gender Politics in Global Governance*, New York: Rowman and Littlefield, pp. 142–160.
Kempadoo, K. and J. Doezma (eds), *Global Sex Workers: Rights, Resistance and Redefinition*, London: Routledge.

Kilby, Patrick (2002), 'NGOs and civil society: The Indian case', Paper presented to the APSA Annual Conference, University of Queensland, Brisbane, July 2002.

Kofman, Eleonore (1999), 'Female "birds of passage" a decade later: Gender and immigration in the European Union', *International Migration Review*, 33 (2), pp. 269–299.

Law Association for Asia and the Pacific, Human Rights Committee (Lawasia) et. al. (1998), *Legal Protection for Asian Women Migrant Workers – Strategies for Action*. Makati, Philippines: Lawasia Human Rights Committee.

Law, Lisa (forthcoming), 'Sites of transnational activism – Filipino non-government organisations in Hong Kong', in Brenda Yeoh, Peggy Teo and Shirlena Huang (eds), *Gender Politics in the Asia Pacific Region*, London: Routledge.

Law, Lisa (2000), *Sex Work in Southeast Asia: The Place of Desire in a Time of AIDS*, London: Routledge.

Lim, Lin Lean and Nana Oishi (1996), 'International labor migration of Asian women: Distinctive characteristics and policy concerns', *Asia and Pacific Migration Journal*, 5 (1), pp. 85–116.

Lim, T.C. (2002), 'Racing from the bottom? The nexus between civil society and transnational migrants in South Korea', Paper presented at the American Anthropological Society conference, Washington, April 2002.

Mackie, Vera (1999), 'Dialogue, distance and difference: Feminism in contemporary Japan', *Women's Studies International Forum*, 21 (6), pp. 599–615.

Mills, K. (1998), *Human Rights in the Emerging Global Order: A New Sovereignty?*, Basingstoke: Macmillan.

OECD (SOPEMI) (1998), *Migration and Regional Economic Integration in Asia*, Paris: OECD.

Oxfam GB (2000), *Migration in Cambodia: Some Gender Issues*, Phnom Penh: Oxfam GB.

Philippines Overseas Employment Administration (POEA) (1999), (Unpublished Data), Department of Labour and Employment, Mandaluyong: Metro Manila.

Phongpaichit, Pasuk (1999), 'Trafficking in people in Thailand', in Phil Williams (ed.), *Illegal Immigration and Commercial Sex – The New Slave Trade*, London: Frank Cass.

Pietilae, H. and J. Vickers (1996) (3rd edn.), *Making Women Matter – The Role of the United Nations*, London: Zed Books.

Piper, Nicola (1999), 'Labour migration, trafficking and international marriage: Female cross-border movements into Japan', *Asian Journal of Women's Studies*, 5 (2), pp. 69–99.

Piper, Nicola (2001), 'Transnational women's activism in Japan and Korea: The unresolved issue of military sexual slavery', *Global Networks*, 1 (2), pp. 155–170.

Piper, Nicola (2002), 'Global labour markets and national responses – legal regimes governing female migrant workers in Japan', in: D. S. Gills, and Nicola Piper (eds.), *Women and Work in Globalizing Asia*. London: Routledge.

Piper, Nicola and R. Ball (2001), 'Globalisation of Asian migrant labour: The Philippine-Japan connection', *Journal of Contemporary Asia*, 31 (4), pp. 533–554.

Piper, Nicola and Mina Roces (forthcoming), *Wife or Worker? Asians' Marriage and Migration*, Boulder, Co.: Rowman and Littlefield.

Piper, Nicola and A. Uhlin (2002), 'Transnational advocacy networks and the issue of female labour migration and trafficking in east and southeast Asia: A gendered analysis of opportunities and obstacles', *Asian and Pacific Migration Journal*, 11 (2), pp. 171–196.

Piper, Nicola and A. Uhlin (eds) (forthcoming), *Transnational Activism, Power and Democracy: Contextualizing Networks in Asia*, London: Routledge.

Price, J. (1998), 'Shadowing APEC: Nongovernmental organizations build regional alliances', *Asian Perspective*, 22 (2), pp. 21–50.

Raghuram, Parvati (2000), 'Gendering skilled migratory streams: Implications for conceptualizations of migration', *Asian and Pacific Migration Journal*, 9 (4), pp. 429–457.

Raymond J.G. and D. M. Hughes (2001), *Sex Trafficking of Women in the United States – International and Domestic Trends*, New York: Coalition Against Trafficking in Women.

Roberts, G. (2000), 'NGO support for migrant labor in Japan', in M. Douglass and G. Roberts (eds), *Japan and Global Migration*, London: Routledge.

Sandy, L. (2002), 'It's all slavery anyway, isn't it?': An ethnographic study of female sex workers in Phnom Penh, Cambodia', Unpublished Paper, Canberra: ANU.

Shah, Nasra M. and Indu Menon (1997), 'Violence against women migrant workers: Issues, data and partial solutions', *Asian and Pacific Migration Journal*, 6 (1), pp. 5–30.

Shipper, A. (2000), 'Foreign workers, NGOs, and local governments in Japan', Paper presented at the Annual Meeting of the Association of Asian Studies, San Diego, March 11.

Sim, A. (2002), 'Organising discontent: NGOs for southeast Asian migrant workers in Hong Kong', SEARC (City University of Hong Kong), Working Papers Series No. 18.

Tirtorsudarmo, Riwanto (1999), 'The politics of regulating overseas migrant labor in Indonesia', Paper presented at the Workshop on 'Labor Migration and Socio-Economic Change in Southeast and East Asia', Lund University, 14–16 May 2001.

Truong, Thanh-Dam (1996), 'Gender, international migration and social reproduction: Implications for theory, policy, research and networking', *Asian and Pacific Migration Journal*, 5 (1), pp. 27–52.

Turner, Brian (ed.) (1993), *Citizenship and Social Theory*, London and New Delhi: Sage.

Tyner, James A. (1994), 'The social construction of gendered migration from the Philippines', *Asian and Pacific Migration Journal*, 3 (4), pp. 589–617.

Tyner, James A. (1999), 'The global context of gendered labor migration from the Philippines to the United States', *American Behavioral Scientist*, 42 (4), pp. 648–689.

Uçarer, Emek M. (1999), 'Trafficking in women: alternative migration or modern slave trade?', in M. K. Meyer and E. Prügl (eds), *Gender Politics in Global Governance*. Lanham, Maryland: Rowman and Littlefield, pp. 230–244.

Uhlin, A. (2001). 'The transnational dimension of civil society. Migration and independence movements in southeast Asia', in B. Beckman et. al. (eds), *Civil Society and Authoritarianism in the Third World*, Stockholm: PODSU/Stockholm University.

Weekley, Kathleen, (1999), 'Introduction', in Alastair Davidson and Kathleen Weekley (eds), *Globalization and citizenship in the Asia Pacific*, London: Macmillan, pp. 1–23.

Weiner, Myron (1995), *The Global Migration Crisis – Challenge to States and to Human Rights*, New York: Harper Collins College Publishers.

Yamanaka, Keiko (1999), 'Illegal immigration in Asia: Regional patterns and a case study of Nepalese workers in Japan,' in David W. Haines and Karen E. Rosenblum (eds), *Illegal Immigration in America*, Westport, Connecticut: Greenwood, pp. 11–34.

Yamanaka, Keiko (2002), 'Feminization of Japanese-Brazilian labor

migration to Japan,' in Jeffrey Lesser (ed.), *Searching for Home Abroad*, Durham, NC: Duke University Press.
Yeoh, Brenda S. A., Shirlena Huang and Joaquin Gonzalez II (1999), 'Migrant female domestic workers: Debating the economic, social and political impacts in Singapore', *International Migration Review*, 33 (1), pp. 114–136.

Chapter 4

Acharya, Swaran Kumari (1995), 'Spatial implications of the new economic policy – Reflections on some issues for north east India with special reference to women', *Man and Development*, 17 (1), pp. 6–64.
Afshar, Haleh and Stephanie Barrientos (eds) (1999), *Women, Globalization and Fragmentation in the Developing World*, London: Macmillan, pp. 1–17.
Agarwal, Bina (1992), 'Gender relations and food security: coping with seasonality, drought, and famine in South Asia', in Lourdes Beneria and Shelley Feldman (eds), *Unequal Burden: Economic Crises, Persistent Poverty, and Women's Work*, Boulder Co: Westview Press, pp. 161–218.
Appadurai, Arjun and Carol Breckenridge (1995), 'Public modernity in India', in Arjun Appadurai and Carol Breckenridge (eds), *Consuming Modernity: Public Culture in a South Asian World*, Minneapolis: University of Minnesota Press, pp. 1–20.
Arora, Dolly (1999), 'Structural adjustment programs and gender concerns in India', *Journal of Contemporary Asia*, 29 (1), pp.328–361.
Avashti, A. and Srivastava, A. K. (eds) (2001), *Modernity, Feminism and Women Empowerment*, Jaipur: Rawat Publishers.
Bagchi, Josodhara (1999), 'Women's empowerment: paradigms and paradoxes', in K. Sangari and U. Chakravarti (eds), *From Myths to Markets: Essays on Gender*, New Delhi: Manohar, pp. 368–379.
Bandyopadhyay, Dipendranath (1958), *Tritiya Bhuvan*, Calcutta: Mitralaya.
Bannerjee, Nirmala (1999), 'Can markets alter gender relations?' *Gender, Technology and Development*, 3 (1), pp.103–22.
Bardhan, Pranab (1982), 'Agrarian class formation in India', *Journal of Peasant Studies*, 10 (1), pp. 73–94.
Basu, Rumki (1996), 'New economic policies and social welfare programmes in India', *Social Action*, 46 (3), pp. 262–277.

References

Bhattacharya, D. (1999), 'Political economy of reforms', *Economic and Political Weekly*, XXXIV (23), pp.1408–10.
Carty, Victoria (1997), 'Ideologies and forms of domination in the organization of the global production and consumption of goods in the emerging post-modern era: A case study of Nike corporation and the implication for gender,' *Gender, Work and Organization*, 4 (4), pp.189–201.
Centre for Women's Development Studies [CWDS] (2000), *Shifting Sands: Women's Lives and Globalization*, Calcutta: Stree.
Chakravarti, Uma (2000), 'State, market and freedom of expression: Women and the electronic media', *Economic and Political Weekly*, (Special Issue: 'Review of Women's Studies'), XXXV (18), pp. ws12–ws17.
Chanana, Karuna (1996), 'Educational attainment, status production and women's autonomy: A study of two generations of Punjabi women', in Roger Jeffery and A. M. Basu (eds) *Girls' Schooling, Women's Autonomy and Fertility Change in South Asia*, Thousand Oaks, CA: Sage, pp. 107–132.
Chatterjee, Tapan (1979), 'Social stratification and dynamics of political power in the village of Kurumba', *Journal of the Indian Anthropological Society,* 14 (1), pp. 1–31.
Chaudhuri, Maitrayee (1996), Citizens, workers and emblems of culture: An analysis of the First Plan document on women' in Patricia Uberoi (ed.), *Social Reform, Sexuality and the State*, Thousand Oaks, CA: Sage.
Chaudhuri, Maitrayee (2001), 'Gender and advertisements: The rhetoric of globalisation', *Womens Studies International Forum*, 22 (3–4), pp. 373–385.
Cole, Cheryl L. and Amy Hribar (1995), 'Celebrity feminism: N*ike style*, post-fordism, transcendence, and consumer power,' *Sociology of Sport Journal*, 12, pp. 347–369.
Cowan, Ruth Schwartz (1983), *More Work For Mother: The Ironies of Household Technology from the Open Hearth to the Microwave,* New York: Basic Books.
Das, Vina (1994), 'Modernity and biography: Women's lives in contemporary India', *Thesis Eleven*, 39, pp. 52–62.
Dasgupta, Partha (1993), *An Inquiry into Well-Being and Destitution,* Oxford: Clarendon.
Desai, Neera (1996), 'Women's employment and their familial role in India', in A. M. Shah, B. S. Bhaviskar and E. A. Ramaswamy

(eds), *Social Structure and Change: Women in Indian Society*, Thousand Oaks, CA: Sage, pp. 98–112.

Deshpande, Satish (1998), 'After culture: Renewed agendas for the political economy of India', *Cultural Dynamics*, 10 (2), pp. 147–169.

Dewan, Ritu (1999), 'Gender implications of the "New" Economic Policy: A conceptual overview', *Women's Studies International Forum*, 22 (4), pp. 425–429.

Ehrenreich, Barbara and Deidre English (1979), *For Her Own Good: 150 Years Of The Experts' Advice To Women*, London: Pluto.

Einhorn, Barbara and Eileen Janes Yeo (eds) (1995), *Women and Market Societies: Crisis and Opportunity*, Aldershot: Edward Elgar.

Ganguly-Scrase, Ruchira (2000), 'Globalization and its discontents: An Indian response', *Journal Of Occupational Science: Australia*, 7 (3), pp. 138–147.

Ganguly-Scrase, Ruchira and Timothy J. Scrase (1999), 'A bitter pill or sweet nectar? Contradictory attitudes of salaried workers to economic liberalization in India', *Development and Society*, 28 (2), pp. 259–83.

Ganguly-Scrase, Ruchira and Timothy J. Scrase (2001), 'Who wins? who loses? and who even knows? – Responses to economic liberalisation and cultural globalisation', *South Asia*, (Special Issue 'Globalisation and Economic Liberalisation in South Asia'), 24 (1), pp. 141–158.

Goldman, Robert (1992), *Reading Ads Socially*, London: Routledge.

Goldman, Robert and Steven Papson (1998), *Nike Culture: The Sign of the Swoosh*, London: Sage.

Goldthorpe, John and Keith Hope (1974), *The Social Grading of Occupations*, Oxford: Clarendon.

ILO-ARTEP (1991), *Social dimension of Structural adjustment in India: Papers and Proceedings of a Tripartite Workshop in New Delhi*, (10–11 December), Geneva: ILO.

John, Mary (1998), 'Globalisation, sexuality and the visual field: Issues and non-issues for cultural critique' in M. E. John and J. Nair (eds), *A Question of Silence? The Sexual Economies of Modern India,* New Delhi: Kali for Women, pp. 368–396.

Kabeer, Naila (1999), 'Resources, agency achievement: Reflections on the measurement of women's empowerment', *Development and Change*, 30, pp. 435–464.

Kalpagam, U. (1994), *Labor and Gender: Survival in Urban India*. New Delhi: Sage.

Kar, Bimal (1956; 1958), *Deowal*, Calcutta: *Di Ema Laibreri*.

Khatkhate, Deena (1994), 'Intellectual origins of Indian economic reform: A review of Jagdish Bhagwati's "*India in Transition: Freeing the Economy*" (1993)', *World Development*, 22 (7), pp. 1097–1102.

Kulkarni, V. G. (1993), 'The middle class bulge', *Far Eastern Economic Review*, 156 (2), pp. 44–6.

Lakha, Salim (1999), 'The state, globalization, and the Indian middle-class identity', in Michael Pinches (ed.), *Culture and Privilege in Capitalist Asia*, London: Routledge, pp. 251–74.

Mankekar, Purnima (1999), *Screening Culture, Viewing Politics: An Ethnography of Television, Womanhood, and Nation in Postcolonial India*, Durham: Duke University Press.

Mitra, Gajendra Kumar (1957), *Kolkatar Kacchei*, Calcutta: Mitra and Ghosh Publishers Pvt. Ltd.

Mitra, Narendranath (1963), *Mahanagar*, Calcutta: Mukunda Publishers.

Moghadam, Valentine (1999), 'Gender and the global economy' in M. Ferree, *et al.* (eds), *Revisioning Gender*, Thousand Oaks, CA: Sage, pp.128–160.

Mohanty, Manoranjan (1995), 'On the concept of empowerment' *Indian Journal of Social Science*, 8 (4), pp. 333–38.

Mukherjee, Amitabha (1994), *Structural Adjustment Programme and Food Security, Hunger and Poverty in India*, Aldershot: Avebury.

Mukherjee, S. N. (1975), '*Bhadralok* in Bengali language and literature: An essay on the language of class and status', *Bengal Past and Present*, 95 (2), pp. 225–237.

Munshi, Shoma (1998), 'Wife/mother/daughter-in-law: Multiple avatars of homemaker in 1990's Indian advertising', *Media, Culture and Society*, 20 (4), pp. 573–591.

Murdock, Graham (2000), 'Reconstructing the ruined tower: Contemporary communications and questions of class', in James Curran and Michael Guervitch (eds), *Mass Media and Society*, London: Arnold, pp. 7–26.

Nagaraj, R. (1997), 'What has happened since 1991? An assessment of India's economic reforms', *Economic and Political Weekly*, XXXII (44–45), pp. 2869–79.

Oakley, Anne (1976), *Housewife*, Harmondsworth: Penguin.

Omvedt, Gail (1997), 'Rural women and the family in an era of liberalization : India in comparative Asian perspective', *Bulletin of Concerned Asian Scholars*, 29 (4), pp. 33–44.

Oshikawa, Fumiko (1999), *South Asia Under the Economic Reforms*, Osaka: National Museum of Ethnology.

Panini, M. (1995), 'The social logic of economic liberalization', *Sociological Bulletin*, 44 (1), pp. 33–62.

Pedersen, Jorgen Dige (2000), 'Explaining economic liberalization in India: State and society perspectives', *World Development*, 28 (2), pp. 265–282.

Puri, Joyti (1999), *Woman, Body, Desire in Post-Colonial India: Narratives of Gender and Sexuality*, New York: Routledge.

Scrase, Timothy J. (1993), *Image, Ideology and Inequality: Cultural Domination, Hegemony and Schooling in India*, New Delhi, London and Newbury Park: Sage.

Scrase, Timothy J. (2002), 'Television, the middle classes and the transformation of cultural identities in West Bengal, India', *Gazette: The International Journal for Communication Studies*, 64 (4), pp. 323–342.

Sen, Krishna and Maila Stivens (1998), *Gender and Power in Affluent Asia*, London: Routledge.

Sen, Samita (1997), 'Gendered exclusion: Domesticity and dependence in Bengal', *International Review of Social History*, 42, pp.65–86.

Sharma, Ursula (1986) *Women's Work, Class and The Urban Household*, London: Tavistock.

Sinha, Surajit and R. Bhattacharya (1969), '*Bhadralok* and *chotolok* in a rural area of West Bengal', *Sociological Bulletin*, 18, pp. 50–66.

Standing, Hilary (1991), *Dependence and Autonomy: Women's Employment and the Family in Calcutta*. London: Routledge.

Stewart, Frances and Albert Berry (1999), 'Globalization, liberalization and inequality: Expectations and experience' in Andrew Hurrel and Ngaire Woods (eds), *Inequality, Globalization and World Politics*, Oxford: Oxford University Press, pp. 150–186.

Sunder Rajan, Rajeshwari (1993), *Real and Imagined Women: Gender Culture and Post Colonialism*, London: Routledge.

Sunder Rajan, Rajeshwari (1999), *Signposts: Gender Issues in Post-Independence India*, New Delhi: Kali for Women.

Upadhyay, Ushma D. (2000), 'India's new Economic Policy of

1991 and its impact on poverty and AIDS', *Feminist Economics,* 6 (3), pp. 105–122.
Van Wessel, Margherita (1998), 'Wealth and its social worth: Consumers in the land of Gandhi', *Amsterdams Sociologisch Tijdschrif,* 25 (4), pp. 562–67.
Wright, Erik Olin (1985), *Classes.* London: Verso.
Wright, Erik Olin et al., (1989), *The Debate on Classes,* London: Verso.

Chapter 5

Anderson, Kym (ed.), (1992), *New Silk Roads: East Asia and World Textile Markets,* Cambridge: Cambridge University Press.
Appadurai, Arjun (1996), *Modernity At Large: The Cultural Dimensions of Globalization,* Minneapolis: University of Minnesota Press.
Balkwell, Carolyn and Kitty G. Dickerson, (1994), 'Apparel production in the Caribbean: A classic case of the new international division of labour', *Clothing and Textiles Research Journal,* 12 (3), pp. 6–15.
Basu, Kunal (1995), 'Marketing developing society crafts: A framework for analysis and change', in Janeen Arnold Costa and Gary J. Bamossy (eds), *Marketing in a Multicultural World: Ethnicity, Nationalism, and Cultural Identity,* Thousand Oaks, CA: Sage, pp. 257–98.
Bourdieu, Pierre (1984), *Distinction: A Social Critique of the Judgement of Taste,* London: Routledge.
Brohman, John (1996), 'New directions in tourism for third world development', *Annals of Tourism Research,* 23 (1), pp. 48–70.
Buchanan, Keith (1985), 'Center and periphery: Reflections on the irrelevance of a billion human beings', *Monthly Review,* 37 (3), pp. 86–97.
Chibnick, Michael (2000), 'The evolution of market niches in Oaxacan woodcarving', *Ethnology,* 39 (3), pp. 225–42.
Colloredo-Mansfield, Rudi (2002), 'An ethnography of neo-liberalism: Understanding competition in artisan economies', *Current Anthropology,* 43 (1), pp. 113–37.
Davis, Elizabeth A. (1999), 'Metamorphosis in the Culture Market of Niger', *American Anthropologist,* 101 (3), pp. 485–501.

Dickie, Virginia A. and Gelya Frank (1996), 'Artisan occupations in the global economy: A conceptual framework', *Journal of Occupational Science: Australia*, 3 (2), pp. 45–55.
Featherstone, Mike (1991), *Consumer Culture and Postmodernism*, London: Sage.
Fine, Ben and Ellen Leopold (1993), *The World of Consumption*, London: Routledge.
Ganguly-Scrase, Ruchira (2001), *Global Issues / Local Contexts: The Rabi Das of Bengal*, New Delhi: Orient Longman.
Grimes, Kimberly M. and B. Lynne Milgram (eds) (2000), *Artisans and Cooperatives: Developing Alternative Trade for the Global Economy*, Tuscon: The University of Arizona Press.
Guillermo, Alice G. (1995), 'Weaving: Women's art and power', in Lorna Kaino (ed.), *The Necessity of Craft*, Nedlands: University of Western Australia Press, pp. 35–56.
Helu-Thaman, Konai (1993), 'Beyond hula, hotels, and handicrafts: A Pacific islander's perspective of tourism development', *Contemporary Pacific*, 5 (1), pp. 104–11.
Hendrickson, Carol (1996), 'Selling Guatemala: Maya export products in US Mail-order catalogues', in David Howes (ed.), *Cross-cultural Consumption: Global Markets, Local Realities*, London and New York: Routledge, pp. 106–21.
Imhoff, Dan (1998), 'Artisans in the global bazaar', *Whole Earth*, Fall, pp. 76–81.
Jain, Jyotindra (1995), 'Art and artisans: Tribal and folk art in India', in Lorna Kaino (ed.), *The Necessity of Craft*, Nedlands: University of Western Australia Press, pp. 24–34.
Johnson, Josee (2002), 'Consuming global justice: fair trade shopping and alternative development', in James Goodman (ed.), *Protest and Globalization: Prospects for Transnational Solidarity*, Sydney: Pluto Press, pp. 38–56.
Kaino, Lorna (ed.) (1995), *The Necessity of Craft: Development and Women's Craft Practices in the Asian-Pacific Region*, Nedlands: University of Western Australia Press.
Kathuria, Sanjay (1988), 'Indian craft exports for the global market', in Sanjay Kathuria, Virginia Miralao and Rebecca Joseph, *Artisan Industries in Asia: Four Case Studies*, Ottawa: International Development Research Centre, pp. 1–29.
Kathuria, Sanjay, Virginia Miralao and Rebecca Joseph (1988), *Artisan Industries in Asia: Four Case Studies*, Ottawa: International Development Research Centre.

Knorringa, Peter (1999), 'Artisan labour in the Agra footwear industry: Continued informality and changing threats', *Contributions to Indian Sociology*, 33 (1–2), pp. 303–28.

Korovkin, Tanya (1998), 'Commodity production and ethnic culture: Otavalo, northern Ecuador', *Economic Development and Cultural Change*, 47 (1), pp. 125–54.

Kusakabe, Kyoko (2001), 'Cooperation and competition across border markets: Changes in the definition of women's weaving activity in Lao-Thai borderlands'. Paper presented at the 6th Conference of Women in Asia, Canberra, Australia.

MacHenry, Rachel (2000), 'Building on local strengths: Nepalese fair trade textiles', in Kimberly M. Grimes and B. Lynne Milgram (eds), *Artisans and Cooperatives: Developing Alternative Trade for the Global Economy*, Tuscon: The University of Arizona Press, pp. 25–44.

Milgram, B. Lynne (1999), 'Crafts, cultivation, and household economies: Women's work and positions in Ifugao, northern Philippines', *Research in Economic Anthropology*, 20, pp. 221–61.

Miller, Daniel (ed.) (1995), *Acknowledging Consumption*, London: Routledge.

Nakatani, Ayami (1999), ' "Eating threads": Brocades as cash crop for weaving mothers and daughters in Bali', in Raechelle Rubenstein and Linda H. Connor (eds), *Staying Local in the Global Village*, Honolulu: University of Hawai'i Press, pp. 203–29.

Nakatani, Ayami (2001), 'Exoticism and nostalgia: Consuming Southeast Asian handicrafts in Japan', Paper presented at the 3rd EUROSEAS Conference, London, 2001.

Nash, June (ed.) (1993a), *Crafts in the World Market*, Albany: SUNY Press.

Nash, June (1993b), 'Introduction: Traditional arts and changing markets in middle America', in June Nash (ed.), *Crafts in the World Market*, Albany: SUNY Press, pp. 1–22.

Riley, Mary and Katy Moran, (2001) 'Protecting indigenous intellectual property rights: Tools that work', *Cultural Survival Quarterly*, 24 (4), (http://www.culturalsurvival.org/newpage/publications/csq/back_issue_toc.cfm.cfm?id=24.4); accessed: 10/03/2003.

Rutten, Rosanne (2002), 'How craftworkers and small subcontractors may profit from the world market: A Philippine case'. Paper presented at a workshop on 'Asian Artisans and Small Scale Producers in the Global Economy: Trends, Issues and Problems in the New Millennium', International Institute for Asian Studies (IIAS), University of Amsterdam.

Seth, Shantum (1995), 'Towards a volunteer movement of artisan support', *Craft News*, 6 (1), pp. 1–4.

Steiner, Christopher B. (1994), *African Art in Transit*, Cambridge: Cambridge University Press.

Stephen, Lynn (1993), 'Weaving in the fast lane: Class, ethnicity and gender in Zapotec craft commercialization' in June Nash (ed.), *Crafts in the World Market*, Albany: SUNY Press, pp. 25–57.

Suratman, Suriani (1991), ' "Weaving" a development strategy: Cottage industries in the Philippines', *Sojourn*, 6 (2), pp. 263–89.

Tice, Karen (1995), *Kuna Crafts, Gender and the Global Economy*, Austin: University of Texas Press.

UNIFEM (United Nations Development Fund for Women) (1997), Report: 'Social security for artisans in the voluntary sector: Are human rights being denied?', New Delhi: UNIFEM.

Wilkinson-Weber, Claire M. (1997), 'Skill, dependency and differentiation: Artisans and agents in the Lucknow embroidery industry', *Ethnology*, 36 (1), pp. 49–65.

Wood, Warner W. (2000), 'Flexible production, households and fieldwork: Multisited Zapotec weavers in the era of late capitalism, *Ethnology*, 39 (2), pp. 133–48.

Chapter 6

Anderson, Benedict (1983), *Imagined Communities: Reflections on the Origins and Spread of Nationalism,* London: Verso.

Anderson, June (1996), *Mayko's Story: A Hmong Textile Artist in California*, San Francisco: California Academy of Sciences.

Ang, Ien (1993), 'The differential politics of Chineseness', in Ghassan Hage and Lesley Johnson (eds), *Community/Plural – Identity/Community/Change 1/1993,* Sydney: Research Centre in Intercommunal Studies, University of Western Sydney.

Bhabha, Homi (1994), *The Location of Culture,* London: Routledge.

Brah, Avtah (1996), *Cartographies of Diaspora: Contesting Identities,* London: Routledge.

Cha, Bee (2001), 'Being Hmong is not enough', *Paj Ntaub Voice,* 'Silence', 7 (2), pp. 8–11.

Chan, Sucheng (1994), *Hmong Means Free: Life in Laos and America*, Philadelphia: Temple University Press.

Cohen, Robin (1997), *Global Diasporas: An Introduction*, London: University College London Press.

Cooper, Robert, Nicholas Tapp, Gary Yia Lee, and Gretel Schworer-Kohl (1995), *The Hmong* (2nd edition), Bangkok: Artasia Press.

Dean, Elizabeth (1993), 'The Hmong in Hobart', *Post Migration*, No.91, April, Canberra: Department of Immigration and Ethnic Affairs (DIEA).

Donnelly, Nancy D. (1994), *The Changing Lives of Refugee Hmong Women*, Seattle: University of Washington Press.

Friend, Maria (2002), 'Bright garments with fading stitches: Recent transformations of Hmong costume in Australia', Paper presented at the *Australian Anthropological Society Annual Conference*, 3–5 October, Australian National University, Canberra.

Ganguly-Scrase, Ruchira and Roberta Julian (1999), 'Minority women and the experiences of migration', *Women's Studies International Forum*, 21 (6), pp. 633–48.

Gorman, Lyn and David McLean (2003), *Media and Society in the Twentieth Century*, Malden, MA: Blackwell.

Gramsci, Antonio (1971), *Selections from the Prison Notebooks*, London: Lawrence and Wishart.

Hall, Stuart (1976/2002), 'The television discourse: encoding and decoding', in Denis McQuail (ed), *McQuail's Reader in Mass Communication Theory*, London: Sage, pp. 302–8.

Hall, Stuart (1990), 'Cultural identity and diaspora', in Jonathan Rutherford (ed), *Identity: Community, Culture, Difference*, London: Lawrence and Wishart.

Hall, Stuart (1992), 'The question of cultural identity', in Stuart Hall, David Held, and Tony McGrew (eds), *Modernity and Its Futures*. Cambridge: Polity Press, in association with the Open University, pp.273–326.

Hein, Jeremy (1994), 'From migrant to minority: Hmong refugees and the social construction of identity in the United States', *Sociological Inquiry*, 64 (3), August, pp. 281–306.

Her, Mymee (1998), 'Hmong resiliency: Surviving a war and living a dream', Keynote address given at the *Fourth Annual Hmong National Conference* 'Living the Dream', 16–18 April, Denver, Colorado, USA.

Hmong Resource Center (2002), *Newsletter*, No. 10, St. Paul, MI: Hmong Resource Center.

Julian, Roberta (1998), '"I Love Driving!": Alternative constructions of Hmong femininity in the West', *Race, Gender and Class*, 5 (2), pp. 30–53.

Lee, Gary Yia (1996), 'Cultural identity in post-modern society: Reflections on what is a Hmong?', *Hmong Studies Journal*, 1 (1), Fall, http://members.aol.com/hmongstudiesjrnl/HSJv1n1_LeeFr.html (Date last accessed: January 27, 2003).

Lee, Pa Houa (2002), 'What's new with the Sounders', *Hmong American Journal*, 1, April, pp. 36–7.

Luke, Allan and Carmel Luke (2000), 'The differences language makes: The discourses on language of inter-ethnic Asian/Australian families', in Ien Ang, Sharon Chalmers, Lisa Law, and Mandy Thomas (eds), *Alter/Asians: Asian–Australian Identities in Art, Media and Popular Culture,* Sydney: Pluto Press.

Maneeprasert, Ralana (2001), Tribal Research Institute, Chiang Mai, Thailand. Personal communication.

Martin, Denis-Constant (1995), 'The choices of identity', *Social Identities*, 1 (1), pp. 5–20.

Moua, Mai Neng (2001), '"Silence" in the Hmoob community', *Paj Ntaub Voice*, 'Silence', 7 (2), p.4.

Pfaff, Tim (1995), *Hmong in America: Journey From a Secret War,* Eau Claire, WI: Chippewa Valley Museum Press.

Quincey, Keith (1995), *Hmong: History of a People* (2nd ed.), Washington: Eastern Washington University Press.

Rex, John (1995), 'Ethnic identity and the nation-state: The political sociology of multi-cultural societies', *Social Identities*, 1 (1), pp. 21–34.

Schein, Louisa (1999), 'Diaspora politics, homeland erotics, and the materializing of memory', *positions*, 7 (3), pp.697–729.

Schein, Louisa (2000), *Minority Rules: The Miao and the Feminine in China's Cultural Politics,* London: Duke University Press.

Sinclair, John and Stuart Cunningham (2000), 'Diaporas and the media', in Stuart Cunningham and John Sinclair (eds), *Floating Lives: The Media and Asian Diasporas*, St. Lucia: University of Queensland Press.

Slevin, James (2002), 'The Internet and forms of human association', in Denis McQuail (ed), *McQuail's Reader in Mass Communication Theory*, London: Sage, pp. 147–56.

Spivak, Gayatri Chakravorty (1990), *The Post-Colonial Critic: Interviews, Strategies, Dialogues*, Sarah Harasym (ed), London: Routledge.

Tapp, Nicholas (2000), 'Ritual relations and identity: Hmong and others', in Andrew Turton (ed), *Civility and Savagery: Social Identity in Tai States,* Richmond, Surrey: Curzon Press, pp. 84–103.
Theater Mu (2002), 'Theatre Mu Outreach Programs 2001–2002', Advertising Brochure.
Werbner, Pnina (1998), 'Diasporic political imaginaries: a sphere of freedom or a sphere of illusions?', *Communal/Plural*, 6 (1), April, pp. 11–31.
Xiong, Tou Ger (1998), *Hmong Means Free.* Video produced by Tou Ger Xiong.
Yang Dao (1993), *Hmong at the Turning Point*, Minneapolis: WorldBridge Associates.
Yang, Dara Carol (2002), 'Single…longer', *Hnub Tshiab*, 3 (1), pp. 1–2.
Yang, Naly (2001), 'I walk a fine line', *Paj Ntaub Voice*, 'Silence', 7 (2), p.46.

Chapter 7

Appadurai, Arjun (1990), 'Disjuncture and difference in the global cultural economy,' in Mike Featherstone (ed), *Global Culture: Nationalism, Globalization and Modernity*, London and Newbury Park: Sage.
Barber, Benjamin (1995), *Jihad vs. McWorld: How Globalism and Tribalism Are Reshaping the World*, New York: Ballantine.
Befu, Harumi (2000), 'Research proposal abstract: *Nikkei* in the context of globalizing Japan,' *The International Nikkei Research Project,* http://www.janm.org/inrp/english/sc_befu.htm (Date last accessed: December 13, 2002).
Befu, Harumi (2001), *Hegemony of Homogeneity: An Anthropological Analysis of Nihonjinron*, Melbourne: Trans Pacific Press.
Berger, Peter L. and Thomas Luckmann (1966), *The Social Construction of Reality: A Treatise on the Sociology of Knowledge,* Garden City, New York: Anchor Books.
Burton, Helena (2002), 'Oriental *irezumi* and Occidental tattooing in contemporary Japan,' *Alterasian.com*, http://www.asianesque.com/alterasian/arttattooirezumi.html (Date last accessed: January 15, 2003).
Castells, Manuel (1996), *The Information Age: Economy, Society*

and Culture. Volume I: The Rise of the Network Society. Cambridge MA. Oxford UK: Blackwell.

Clammer, John (2002), *Diaspora and Identity: The Sociology of Culture in Southeast Asia*, Selangor Darul Ehsan, Malaysia: Pelanduk.

Curran, James (2002), *Media and Power*, London and New York: Routledge.

Curran, James and Michael Gurevitch (eds) (1991), *Mass Media and Society*, London and New York: Edward Arnold.

Dale, Peter N. (1986), *The Myth of Japanese Uniqueness*, London: Croom Helm, Ltd.

Eades, Jerry, Tom Gill and Harumi Befu (eds) (2000), *Globalization and Social Change in Contemporary Japan,* Melbourne: Trans-Pacific Press.

Eriksen, Thomas Hylland (1999), 'Globalization and the politics of identity,' *UN Chronicle* (autumn), http://folk.uio.no/geirthe/UNChron.html, (Date last accessed: December 12, 2002).

Fiske, John (1989), *Understanding Popular Culture*, London and New York: Routledge.

Frith, Simon (1996), 'Music and identity' in Stuart Hall and Paul du Gay (eds), *Questions of Cultural Identity*, London and Thousand Oaks: SAGE Publications.

Gibney, Frank (1975/1987), *Japan: The Fragile Superpower*, Tokyo: Charles E. Tuttle Co., Publishers.

Giddens, Anthony (1990), *The Consequences of Modernity*, Stanford, CA: Stanford University Press.

Giddens, Anthony (1991), *Modernity and Self-Identity: Self and Society in the Late Modern Age*, Stanford, CA: Stanford University Press.

Hall, Stuart (1980), 'Encoding/decoding' in television discourse', in Simon During (ed), *The Cultural Studies Reader*, London and New York: Routledge, pp. 90–103.

Hall, Stuart (1991), 'The local and the global', in Anthony King (ed), *Culture, Globalization and the World System,* London & New York: Macmillan Press, pp. 19–40.

Hall, Stuart (1996), 'Introduction: who needs identity?' in Stuart Hall and Paul du Gay (eds), *Questions of Cultural Identity*, London and Thousand Oaks: Sage.

Halloran, Richard (1969/1985), *Japan: Images and Realities*, Tokyo: Charles E. Tuttle Co., Publishers.

Hannerz, Ulf (1992), *Cultural Complexity: Studies in the Social Organization of Meaning*, New York: Columbia University Press.

Holden, Todd Joseph Miles (1994), 'Surveillance: Japan's sustaining principle,' *Journal of Popular Culture*, 28 (1), pp. 193–208.

Holden, Todd Joseph Miles (1999a), ' "And now for the main (dis)course...," or: food as entree in contemporary Japanese television,' *M/C: A Journal of Media and Culture*, 2 (7), (October 20).

Holden, Todd Joseph Miles (1999b), 'The color of difference: critiquing cultural convergence via television advertising,' *Interdisciplinary Information Sciences*, 5 (1), (November), pp. 15–36.

Holden, Todd Joseph Miles (2000), '*Adentity*: Images of self in Japanese television advertising,' *The International Scope Review*, 2 (4) (Winter), http://www.internationalscope.com/journal/volume%202000/issue4/holden.htm (Date last accessed: January 11, 2002).

Holden, Todd Joseph Miles (2002), 'The Well Tempura'd Nation: Japan, television food shows and cultural nationalism,' presented at the 5th Conference of the *Asia Pacific Sociological Association*: "Asian Pacific Societies: Contrasts, Challenges and Crises," Queensland University of Technology, Brisbane, Australia, July.

Holden, Todd Joseph Miles (forthcoming), 'Hail Japan's Conquering Heroes: Sports reports and the discourse of national efficacy,' in Linda Fuller (ed), *Sexual Sports Rhetoric Globally: Teaming up gender with the language of sport*, The Haworth Press.

Holden, Todd Joseph Miles and Takako Tsuruki (2003), '*Deai Kei*: Japan's new culture of encounter', in Nanette Gottlieb and Mark McLelland (eds), *Japanese Cybercultures*, London: Routledge, pp. 34–49.

Irvine, Martin (1998), 'Cyberspace, identity, and the global informational city,' http://www.georgetown.edu/faculty/irvinem/articles/globalculture.html (Date last accessed: December 12, 2002).

Jenkins, Richard (1996), *Social Identity*, London, Routledge.

Kamimura, Shuichi and Mieko Ida (2002), 'Will the Internet take the place of television?' *NHK Broadcasting Culture and*

Research, 19 (New Year), http://www.nhk.or.jp/bunken/bcri-news/b5-e.html.

Kamimura, Shuichi, Chiho Ikoma and Sachiko Nakano (2000), 'The Japanese and Television, 2000 – The current state of TV viewing', *NHK Broadcasting Culture and Research*, 13 (Summer).

Katsuno, Hirofumi and Christine Yano (2002), 'Face to face: On-line subjectivity in contemporary Japan,' *Asian Studies Review*, 26 (2), pp. 205–232.

Kinnvall, Catarina and Kristina Jonsson (eds) (2002), *Globalization and Democratization in Asia: The Construction of Identity*, London: Routledge.

Lebra, Takie Sugiyama and William P. Lebra. (eds) (1986), *Japanese Culture and Behavior: Selected Readings*, Honolulu: University of Hawaii Press.

Lull, James (1995), *Media, Communication, Culture: A Global Approach*, Cambridge: Polity Press.

McLuhan, Marshall (1964), *Understanding Media: The Extensions of Man*, New York: The New American Library.

McLuhan, Marshall and Fiore, Quentin (1967), *The Medium is the Massage: An Inventory of Effects*, New York: Bantam.

McVeigh, Brian (2003), 'Individualization, individuality, interiority and the Internet: Japanese university students and e-mail', in Nanette Gottlieb and Mark McLelland (eds), *Japanese Cybercultures*, London: Routledge.

McVeigh, Brian (2000), *Wearing Ideology: State, Schooling, and Self-Presentation in Japan*, Oxford: Berg Publishers.

Meyerowitz, Joshua (1986), *No Sense of Place: The Impact of Electronic Media on Social Behavior*, New York and Oxford: Oxford University Press.

Ministry of Public Management, Home Affairs, Posts and Telecommunications, *Annual Survey* (2000), accessed from: *The Japanese Broadcasting Data*, http://www.nhk.or.jp/bunken/bcri-data/h16-d1.html (Date last accessed; December 17, 2002).

Mizoe, Shogo and Giles Murray (2002), *A Statistical Look at Japan*, Tokyo: Kodansha International Ltd.

Moeur, Ross and Yoshio Sugimoto (1986), *Images of Japanese Society*, London and New York: Kegan Paul International.

Nederveen Pieterse, Jan (2002), 'Hybridity, so what? The anti-hybridity backlash and the riddles of recognition,' in Scott Lash and Mike Featherstone (eds), *Recognition & Difference: Politics,*

Identity, Multiculture, London and Thousand Oaks: Sage, pp.219–245.
Nomura, Masaichi (2000), 'Driving my body,' (N. Onohara, translator), paper presented at the *JCAS Conference,* the Japanese Museum of Ethnology, August 24, http://brokenstones.tripod.co.jp/fashion/dmv.html (date last accessed: December 10, 2002).
Ozaki, Robert (1978), *The Japanese: A Cultural Portrait,* Tokyo: Charles E. Tuttle Company.
Reischauer, Edwin O. (1972), *Japan Past and Present,* Tokyo: Charles E. Tuttle Co., Publishers.
Robertson, Roland (1992), *Globalization: Social Theory and Global Culture,* Thousand Oaks and New Dehli: Sage.
Robertson, Rolan (1997), 'Comments on the "global triad" and "glocalization",' in Nobutaka Inoue (ed), *Globalization and Indigenous Culture,* Tokyo: Kokugakuin University, Institute for Japanese Culture and Classics, http://www.kokugakuin.ac.jp/ijcc/wp/global/index.html (Date last accessed: December 12, 2002).
Santos, Boaventura de Sousa (2002), '*Nuestra America*: Reinventing a subaltern paradigm of recognition and redistribution,' in Scott Lash and Mike Featherstone (eds), *Recognition & Difference: Politics, Identity, Multiculture,* London and Thousand Oaks: Sage, pp. 185–217.
Scuka, Daniel (2000), 'Unwired: Japan has the future in its pocket,' *J@pan.Inc: Business.Technology.People,* http://www.japaninc.com/mag/comp/2000/06/jun00_unwired2.html (Date last accessed: December 13, 2002).
Simmel, Georg (1950), *The Sociology of Georg Simmel* (Kurt H. Wolff, transl. and ed.), New York: The Free Press.
Sprague, Jonathan and Ryu Murakami (2000), 'Japan's new attitude: while old-line politicians and businessmen struggle to catch up to the times, a new society is emerging – individual by individual,' *Asiaweek.com,* Vol. 26, No. 41 (October 20), url: http://www.asiaweek.com/asiaweek/magazine/2000/1020/cover1.html (Date last accessed: February 20, 2003).
Talarowska-Kacprzak, Kinga (2001), 'Media and the construction of the *ganguro* trend in Japan,' *Journal of Mundane Behavior,* Volume 2, Number 1 (February), Url: http://www.mundanebehavior.org/issues/v2n1/kinga.htm. (Date last accessed: March 1, 2003).

Uður, Aydýn (1996), 'Media, identity and the search for a cultural synthesis,' *Privateview* (Winter), http://www.tusiad.org.tr/yayin/private/winter96/html/sec11.html

Watrous, Malena (2000), 'Hello Kitties,' *Salon.com* (http://dir.salon.com/people/feature/2000/03/08/kogaru/index.html?pn=3; Date last accessed: December 10, 2002).

Woodward, Kathryn (ed) (1997), *Identity and Difference (Culture, Media and Identities)*, London: Sage.

Wallerstein, Immanuel (1976), *The Modern World-System I. Capitalist Agriculture and the Origins of the European World-Economy in the Sixteenth Century*, New York: Academic Press. Record holder.

Chapter 8

Abou-El-Haj, Barbara (1991), 'Languages and models for cultural exchange', in Anthony King (ed), *Culture, Globalization and the World System,* London & New York: Macmillan Press in Association with the Department of Art and Art History, SUNY, Binghamton, pp. 139–44.

Abu-Lughod, Janet (1991), 'Going beyond global babble', in Anthony King (ed), *Culture, Globalization and the World System,* London & New York: Macmillan Press in Association with the Department of Art and Art History, SUNY, Binghamton, pp. 131–38.

Ainger, Kenneth (2001), 'Empires of the senseless', *New Internationalist,* 333, pp. 9–12.

Appadurai, Arjun (1990), 'Disjuncture and difference in the global political economy', *Public Culture,* 2 (2), pp. 1–24.

Barker, Chris (1999), *Television, Globalization and Cultural Identities,* Buckingham & Philadelphia: Open University Press.

Barthes, Roland (1977), *Image-Music-Text,* translated by Stephen Heath, London: Fontana.

Barton, Greg (2001), 'The prospects for Islam', in Grayson Lloyd and Shannon Smith (eds), *Indonesia Today: Challenges of History,* Singapore: Institute of Southeast Asian Studies, pp. 244–55.

Bayhaqi, Akhmad (2000), 'Social aspects of higher education: The case of Indonesia', *Ekonomi dan Keuangan Indonesia,* 68 (3), pp. 215–252.

Beck, Ulrich (1992), *Risk Society: Towards a New Modernity,* London: Sage.

Beck, Ulrich (1999), *World Risk Society,* Malden, MA: Polity Press.
Beck, Ulrich. (2000), *What is Globalization?* Translated by Patrick Camiller, Malden, Massachusetts: Polity Press.
Bhabha, Homi (1990), 'DissemiNation', in Homi Bhabha (ed), *Nation and Narration,* London & New York: Routledge, pp. 291–322.
Brayne, Katie (2002), 'Osama Bin Cool', *Inside Indonesia,* 69, January/March, p. 23.
Castells, Manuel (1997), *The Power of Identity, Volume 2, The Information Age: Economy, Society and Culture,* London: Blackwell.
Cieslik, Mark and Pollock, Gary (2002), 'Introduction: Studying young people in late modernity', in Mark Cieslik and Gary Pollock (eds), *Young People in Risk Society,* Aldershot: Ashgate, pp. 1–21.
CNN (2001), 'Sex scenes more frequent on television, study finds', 7 February, http://www.cnn.com/2001/SHOWBIZ/TV/02/06/sex.on.tv/index/html
Connor, Linda and Raechelle Rubinstein (1999), 'Introduction', in Linda Connor and Raechelle Rubinstein (eds), *Staying Local in the Global Village: Bali in the Twentieth Century,* Honolulu: University of Hawai'i Press.
Cribb, Robert (2001), 'Brief reflections on Indonesian social history', in Grayson Lloyd and Shannon Smith (eds), *Indonesia Today: Challenges of History,* Singapore: Institute of Southeast Asian Studies, pp. 231–233.
Facer, Kevin and Ruth Furlong (2001), 'Beyond the myth of the "cyberkid": Young people at the margins of the information revolution', *Journal of Youth Studies,* 4 (4), pp. 451–70.
Furlong, Andy and Fred Cartmel (1997), *Young People and Social Change: Individualization and Risk in Late Modernity,* Buckingham: Open University Press.
Gan, Steven (2001), 'Malaysia's virtual democracy', in Uwe Johannen and James Gomez (eds), *Democratic Transitions in Asia,* Singapore: Select Publishing in association with Friedrich Naumann Foundation, pp. 137–42.
Gerke, Solvey (2000), 'Global lifestyles under local conditions: The new Indonesian middle class', in Beng-Huat Chua (ed), *Consumption in Asia,* London & New York: Routledge, pp. 116–28.

Giddens, Anthony (1991a), *Modernity and Self-Identity: Self and Society in the Late Modern Age*, Cambridge: Polity Press.

Giddens, Anthony (1991b), *The Consequences of Modernity*, Stanford, CA: Stanford University Press.

Golding, Peter and Graham Murdock (1996), 'Culture, communications and political economy', in James Curran and Michael Gurevitch (eds), *Mass Media and Society* (Second Edition), London & New York: Arnold, pp. 11–30.

Hall, Stuart (1991), 'The local and the global', in Anthony King (ed), *Culture, Globalization and the World System,* London and New York: Macmillan Press in Association with the Department of Art and Art History, SUNY, Binghamton, pp. 19–40.

Hassan, Riaz (2002), *Faithlines: Muslim Conceptions of Islam and Society,* Oxford & New York: Oxford University Press.

Holden, Todd Joseph Miles (2001), 'The Malaysian dilemma: Advertising's catalytic and cataclysmic role in social development', *Media, Culture and Society,* 23, pp. 275–297.

Hourani, Albert (1946), *Syria and Lebanon: A Political Essay,* London: Oxford University Press.

Johnson, Kirk (2001), 'Media and social change: The modernizing influences of television in rural India', *Media, Culture and Society,* 23, pp. 147–169.

Klein, Naomi (2000), *No Logo,* Hammersmith: Flamingo/HarperCollins.

Leigh, Barbara (2002), 'Education? Indonesia needs more of it under decentralization', paper delivered at the *Autonomy in Education in the Indonesian Context Conference*, Canberra: Australian National University, 29 September.

Lent, John (1995), 'Introduction', in John Lent (ed), *Asian Popular Culture*, Boulder, San Francisco and Oxford: Westview Press, pp. 1–10.

Liechty, Mark (1995), 'Media, markets and modernization: Youth identities and the experience of modernity in Kathmandu, Nepal', in Vered Amit-Talai and Helena Wulff (eds), *Youth Cultures: A Cross-Cultural Perspective,* London: Routledge, pp. 166–201.

Livingstone, Sonia (2002), *Young People and New Media: Childhood and the Changing Media Environment*, London: Sage.

Mitchell, David (2001), 'Internet content regulation in Southeast

Asia: Directions', *Media International Australia*, 101, November, pp. 43–55.

Morley, David and Kevin Robins (1995), *Spaces of Identity: Global Media, Electronic Landscapes and Cultural Boundaries*, London and New York: Routledge.

Nagata, Judith (1995), 'Modern Malay women and the message of the veil', in Wazir Karim (ed), *'Male' and 'Female' in Developing Southeast Asia*, Oxford and Verndon: Berg Publishers, pp. 101–20.

Nilan, Pam (2001), 'Young Indonesian women and the discourse of romance', paper presented at the *Women in Asia Conference*, Canberra: Australian National University, September 24–26.

Parker, Lynette (2000), 'The introduction of Western-style education to Bali: Domination by consent?' in Adrian Vickers, I. Nyoman Darma Putra and Michele Ford, (eds), *To Change Bali: Essays in Honour of I Gusti Ngurah Bagus*, Denpasar: Bali Post in conjunction with Institute of Social Change and Critical Inquiry, University of Wollongong: Australia, pp. 47–70.

Power, Carla and Sudip Mazumdar (2000), 'Bollywood goes global', *Newsweek*, Feb. 28, pp. 42–48.

Pradadimara, Dias and Burhaman Junedding (2002), 'Who is calling for Islamic law?' *Indonesia*, 72, October–December, p. 25.

Robinson, Kathryn (2002), 'Inter-ethnic violence: The *Bugis* and the problem of explanation', in Minako Sakai (ed), *Beyond Jakarta*, Adelaide: Crawford House Publishing, pp. 145–172.

Romano, Angela (1999), *Journalistic Identity and Practices in Late New Order Indonesia*, Ph.D thesis, Queensland University of Technology, Australia.

Said, Edward (1978), *Orientalism*, Harmondsworth: Penguin.

Scrase, Tim (2002), 'Television, the middle classes and the transformation of cultural identities in West Bengal, India', *Gazette: The International Journal for Communication Studies*, 64 (4), pp. 323–342.

Sen, Krishna and David Hill (2000), *Media, Culture and Politics in Indonesia*, South Melbourne: Oxford University Press.

Thompson, John (1995), *The Media and Modernity*, Cambridge: Polity Press.

Tomlinson, John (1997), 'Internationalisation, globalisation and cultural imperialism', in Kenneth Thompson (ed), *Media and*

Cultural Regulation, London and Thousand Oaks CA: Sage, pp. 98–101.
Van den Bulck, Hilde (2001), 'Public service television and national identity as a project of modernity: The example of Flemish television', *Media, Culture and Society,* 23, pp. 53–69.
Vatikiotis, Michael (2001), 'Freedom and truth: Cultivating the free press in emerging democracies', in Uwe Johannen and James Gomez (eds), *Democratic Transitions in Asia,* Singapore: Select Publishing in association with Friedrich Naumann Foundation, pp.143–50.
Vickers, Adrian (2002), *'Bali Merdeka?* Internal migration, tourism and Hindu revivalism', in Minako Sakai (ed), *Beyond Jakarta: Local Autonomy and Local Society in Indonesia,* Adelaide: Crawford House Publishing, pp. 80–101.
Wilson, Rob and Wimal Dissanyake (1996), 'Introduction: Tracking the global/local', in Rob Wilson and Wimal Dissanyake (eds), *Global/Local: Cultural Production and the Transnational Imaginary,* Durham & London: Duke University Press, pp. 1–20.

Chapter 9

Althusser, Louis (1971), *Lenin and Philosophy and Other Essay,* NY and London: Monthly Review Press.
Battersby, Christine (1998), *The Phenomenal Women: Feminist Metaphysics and the Patterns of Identity,* Cambridge and Oxford: Polity Press.
Baudrillard, Jean (1988), *Selected Writings*, Stanford: Stanford University Press.
Benjamin, Walter (1968), *Illuminations: Walter Benjamin Essays and Reflections* (Trans. by Harry Zohn), NY: Schocken Books.
Berger, John (1972), *Ways of Seeing,* London: British Broadcasting Corporation and Penguin Books.
Butler, Judith (1990), *Gender Trouble: Feminism and the Subversion of Identity*, NY and London: Routledge.
China Times.
Foucault, Michel (1979), *Discipline and Punish: The Birth of the Prison* (Trans. by Alan Sheridan), NY: Vintage Books.
Gatens, Moira (1996), *Imaginary Bodies: Ethics, Power and Corporeality,* NY: Routledge.
Grosz, Elizabeth (1994), *Volatile Bodies: Toward a Corporeal*

Feminism, Bloomington and Indianapolis: Indiana University Press.
Hall, Stuart (1996), 'Introduction: Who needs identity?', in Stuart Hall and Paul du Gay (eds), *Questions of Cultural Identity*, London: Sage, pp. 1–17.
Haraway, Donna (1988), 'Situated knowledge: The science question in feminism and the privilege of partial perspective', *Feminist Studies,* 14 (3), pp. 575–599.
Lingis, Alphonso (1984), *Excesses: Eros and Culture,* Albany: State University of New York Press.
Mulvey, Laura (1989), *Visual and Other Pleasures,* Bloomington: Indiana University Press.
Nelson, Jenny L. (1989), 'Phenomenology as feminist methodology: Explicating interviews', in Kathryn Carter and Carole Spitzack (eds), *Doing Research on Women's Communication: Perspectives on Theory and Method,* Norwood: Ablex, pp. 221–241.
The Taipei Times Online (http://www.taipeitimes.com/news/)
Woodward, Kathryn (1997), 'Introduction', in Kathryn Woodward (ed), *Identity and Difference*, London, Thousand Oaks and New Delhi: Sage, pp. 1–6.

Chapter 10

Baum, Scott (1997), 'Sydney, Australia: A global city? Testing the social polarisation thesis', *Urban Studies*, 34 (11), pp.1881–1901.
Beaverstock, Jonathan V. (1996), 'Revisiting high waged labour markets demand in the global cities: British professional and managerial workers in New York City', *International Journal of Urban and Regional Research*, 20, pp. 422–445.
Beng, Cheah-Hock (1993), 'Responding to global challenges: the changing international economy', in G. Rodan (ed) *Singapore Changes Guard: Social, Political and Economic Direction in the 1990s*, New York: Longman Cheshire, pp. 101–115.
Chia, S. Y. (1997), 'Singapore: advanced production base and smart hub of the electronics industry', in W. Dobson and S.Y. Chia (eds.) *Multinationals and East Asian Integration*, Canada: IDRC, pp. 31–61.
Cho, Myung-Rae (1997), 'Flexibilisation through metropolis: The case of post-fordist Seoul, Korea', *International Journal of Urban and Regional Research*, 21(2), pp. 180–201.

Deyo, Frederic (1991), 'Singapore developmental paternalism', in Steven Goldstein (ed) *Mini-Dragons: Fragile Economic Miracles in the Pacific,* Boulder: Westview Press.
Dicken, Peter (1987), 'A tale of two NICs: Hong Kong and Singapore at the crosswords', *Geoforum*, 18, pp. 151–164.
Friedmann, John and Goetz Wolff (1982), 'World city formation: an agenda for research and action', *International Journal of Urban and Regional Research*, 6(3), pp. 309–344.
Fujita, Kuniko (1991), 'A world city and flexible specialisation: Restructuring of the Tokyo metropolis', *International Journal of Urban and Regional Research*, 15 (2), pp. 269–289.
Hamnett, Chris (1994), 'Social polarisation in global cities: theory and evidence', *Urban Studies*, 31 (3), pp. 401–424.
Hamnett, Chris (1996), 'Social polarisation, economic restructuring and welfare state regimes', *Urban Studies*, 33 (8), pp. 1407–1430.
Hamnett, Chris and D. Cross (1996), *Income equality trends in London, 1979–1994*, (unpublished manuscript).
Harrison, Bennett and Barry Bluestone (1988), *The Great U-Turn*, New York: Basic Books.
Ho, K. C. (1997), 'The global economy and urban society in Pacific Asia', *International Sociology*, 12 (3), pp.275–293.
Hung, Rudy (1996), The great U-turn in Taiwan: Economic restructuring and surge in inequality, *Journal of Contemporary Asia*, 26 (2), pp. 151–163.
Hymer, Stephen (1972) The multinational corporation and the law of uneven development, in Jagdish W. Bhagwati (ed.), *Economics and the World Order from the 1970s to the 1990s*, New York: MacMillan, pp. 113–140.
International Monetary Fund (1997), *Globalisation: Opportunities and Challenges, World Economic Outlook*, International Monetary Fund, May.
Kanter, Rosabeth (1997), *World Class: Thriving Locally in the Global Economy*, New York: Touchstone.
King, Anthony D. (1990), *Global Cities, Post Imperialism and the Internationalisation of London*, London: Routledge.
Kuttner, P. (1983), 'The declining middle', *Atlantic Monthly*, July, pp. 60–72.
Lawrence, R. (1984), 'Sectoral shifts and the size of the middle class', *The Brookings Review*, Fall, pp. 3–11.

Lepani, B. (1994), 'The economic role of cities: Australia in the global economy' *Urban Futures*, September, pp. 14–22.

Levy, P. (1987), 'The middle class: is it really vanishing?' *The Brookings Review*, Summer, pp. 77–122.

Lim, Lydia (2002), 'S'poreans in 7 cities play a bigger role', *The Straits Times Interactive*, October 3, 2002, http://straitstimes.asia1.com.sg/primenews/story/0,1870,146661,00.html, accessed October 3, 2002.

Macleod, Scott and Terry McGee (1996), 'The Singapore-Johore-Riau growth triangle: An emerging extended metropolitan region', in Fu-Chen Lo and Yue-Man Yeung (eds.) *Emerging World Cities in Pacific Asia*, Tokyo: United Nations University Press, pp. 417–464 .

Marcuse, Peter (1989), 'Dual city: A muddy metaphor for a quartered city' *International Journal of Urban and Regional Research*, 13, pp. 697–708.

Markusen, Ann and Vicky Gwiasda (1994), 'Multipolarity and the layering of functions in world cities: New York City's struggle to stay on top', *International Journal of Urban and Regional Research*, 18 (2), pp. 167–193.

Martin, Hans-Peter and Harald Schumann (1997), *The Global Trap: Globalisation and the Assault on Democracy and Prosperity*, translated from German by P. Camiller, London: Zed Books.

Ministry of Information and the Arts (1999), *Singapore 1999*, Singapore: Ministry of Information, Communications and the Arts.

Ministry of Information, Communications and the Arts (2002a), *Singapore 2002*, Singapore: Ministry of Information, Communications and the Arts.

Ministry of Information, Communications and the Arts (2002b), *Singapore Government Press Release, Speech by George Yeo, Minister for Trade and Industry, Singapore*, at the Asia Europe Forum in Copenhagen, 20th September 2002.

Ministry of Information, Communications and the Arts (2002c), *Speech by Goh Chok Tong, Prime Minister, Singapore National Day Speech*, Singapore, August 2002.

Ministry of Manpower (2000), *Speech by Dr. Lee Boon Yang, Minister for Manpower at the Ministry of Manpower National Day Observance Ceremony 2000*, Singapore, 8th August 2000.

Ministry of Manpower (2002), *Report on the Labor Force in*

Singapore 2001, Singapore: Manpower Research and Statistics Department, Ministry of Manpower.

Ministry of Transport (2001), *An Effective Land Transport Network in Singapore*, http://www.mot.gov.sg/policies_nav/main0.htm [Date accessed November 17th 2002].

Ooi, Giok-Ling and Gillian Koh (1998), 'State-society synergies: New stakes, new partnership', in Arun Mahizhnan and Lee-Tsao Yuan (eds.) *Singapore: Re-Engineering Success*, Singapore: Oxford University Press, pp. 98–111.

Perry, Martin, Lily Kong and Brenda Yeoh (1997), *Singapore: A Developmental City State*, New York: John Wiley and Sons.

Pryke, M. (1991), 'An international city going global: Spatial change in the city of London' *Environment and Planning D, Society and Space,* 9 (2), pp. 197–222.

Sassen, Saskia (1991), *The Global City: New York, London, Tokyo*, Princeton: Princeton University Press.

Sassen, Saskia (1994), 'The urban complex in a world economy', *International Social Science Journal*, 139, pp. 43–62.

Sassen-Koob, Saskia (1984) 'The new labour demand in global cities', in M. Smith (ed.) *Cities in Transition,* Beverley Hills: Sage, pp.139–171.

Savage, Victor and C. P. Pow (2001) 'Model Singapore: Crossing urban boundaries', in Williams, Jack and Stimson, Robert (eds.) *International Planning Settings: Lessons of Success*, Amsterdam: JAI, pp. 87–121.

Singapore Department of Statistics (2000), *Singapore Census of Population, 2000, advance data release no. 4, Economic characteristics of Singapore resident population*, Singapore: Department of Statistics.

Singapore Department of Statistics (2002a), *Yearbook of Statistics, 2002*, Singapore: Department of Statistics.

Singapore Department of Statistics (2002b), *Changing Education Profile of Singapore Population*, Paper presented at the Conference on Chinese Population and Socioeconomic Studies, Hong Kong University of Science and Technology, 19–21 June.

Smith, David and Michael Timberlake (1995), 'Conceptualising and mapping the structure of the world systems' city system', *Urban Studies, Special issue: Cities, Enterprises and Society as the Eve of the 21st Century*, 32 (2), pp. 287–303.

Stark, T. (1992), *Income and wealth in the 1980s, 3rd edition*, Working Group Papers, London: Fabian Society.

Straits Times Interactive (1997), 'PM Gohs vision of a new era for Singapore', http://web3.asia1.com.sg/archive/st/4/pages/q06071.html, [date accessed: 9th May 1997].
Taylor, Peter J. and D. R. Walker (2001), 'World cities: A first multivariate analysis of their computer service complexes', *Urban Studies*, 38 (1), pp. 23–47.
The Straits Times, various issues, Singapore Press Holdings, Singapore.
Thrift, Nigel (1994), 'On the social and cultural determinants of international financial centres: The case of the city of London', in Stuart Corbridge, Nigel Thrift and Ron Martin (eds.) *Money, Power and Space*, Oxford: Blackwell, pp. 327–355.
Wirth, Louis (1969), 'Urbanisation as a way of life' in R. Sennett (ed) *Classic Essays on the Culture of Cities*, New York: Appleton-Century-Crofts, pp. 143–164.
Yamazawa, Ippei, Akira Hirata and Kazuhko Yokota (1991), 'Evolving patterns of comparative advantage in the pacific economies', in Mohamed Ariff, (ed) *The Pacific Economy: Growth and External Stability*, Sydney: Allen and Unwin, pp. 213–232.
Yeoh, Brenda and T. Chang (2001), 'Globalising Singapore: Debating transnational flows in the city', *Urban Studies*, 38 (7), pp. 1025–1044.
Yuan, L. and M. Choo (1995), 'Singapore as a global city: Strategies and key issues', *Urban Futures*, 19, pp. 90–96.
Zukin, Susan (1992), 'The city as a landscape of power: London and New York as global financial capitals', in Leslie Budd and Sam Whimster (eds.) *Global Finance and Urban Living: A Study of Metropolitan Change,* London: Routledge, pp. 195–223.

Chapter 11

Ahmed, N. and M. Baqee (1996), 'Urban crimes in Bangladesh' in N. Islam and R. Majid Ahsan (eds.) *Urban Bangladesh,* Dhaka: Urban Studies Programme.
Arts, W. Hermkens, P. and P. Van Wijck (1995), 'Anomie, distributive justice and dissatisfaction with material well-being in Eastern Europe: A Comparative Study', *International Journal of Comparative Sociology*, 36 (1): pp. 5–16.
Asian Development Bank (2002a), *Bangladesh: Progress in*

Poverty Reduction, Background Paper, Bangladesh Development Forum, Paris, March 13–15.
Asian Development Bank (2002b), *Bangladesh: Public Expenditure Review Summary*, Background Paper, Bangladesh Development Forum, Paris, March, 13–15.
Asian Development Bank (2002c), *Key Indicators of Developing Asian and Pacific Countries*, Philippines: Asian Development Bank.
Atteslander, Peter (1995), 'Social destabilisation and the development of early warning systems', *International Journal of Sociology and Social Policy,* 15 (8–10), pp. 9–24.
Atteslander, Peter (1999) 'Social change, development and anomie', in Peter Atteslander, Bettina Gransow and John Western (eds.) *Comparative Anomie Research: Hidden Barriers – Hidden Potential for Social Development*, Aldershot: Ashgate, pp. 3–22.
Atteslander, Peter, Bettina Gransow and John Western (1999), *Comparative Anomie Research: Hidden Barriers – Hidden Potential for Social Development*, Aldershot: Ashgate.
Bhuiyanm, S. (1999), *Dhaka City, Bangladesh*, paper presented at the Asian City Development Strategy Conference, Tokyo.
Deflem, Mathieu (1999), 'The Future of Anomie Theory, Book Review' *Social Forces*, 78 (1), pp. 364–368.
Durkheim, Emile (1893), *The Division of Labor in Society*, New York: Free Press.
Eichengreen, B. (2002), 'Capitalizing on Globalization', *Asian Development Review*, 19(1), pp. 14–66.
Enayetullah, I. and M. Maqsood Sinha (2000), *Community Based Decentralized Composting in Dhaka: An Ecological and Sustainable Approach to Solid Waste,* Retrieved May,8, 2002 from http://mc2000.arch.hku.hk/Abstracts/Environment Technology/Sinha/Sinha.html.
Fujita, Kuniko (1991), 'A world city and flexible specialisation: Restructuring of the Tokyo metropolis', *International Journal of Urban and Regional Research*, 15 (2), pp. 269–289.
GOV-ADB, (1996), *A Study of Urban Poverty, Final Report, Vol. 1&2,* Dhaka: Asian Development Bank.
Gunewardena, Dileni (1999), *Urban Poverty in South Asia: What do we Know? What do we Need to Know?*, Paper presented at Poverty Reduction and Social Progress: New Trends and Emerging Issues, Regional dialogue and consultation on WDR2001 for South Asia, April 4–6, Rajendrapur, Bangladesh.

Hardoy, Jorge, Susan Cairncross and David Satterthwaite (1990), *The Poor Die Young: Housing and Health in Third World Cities*, London: Earthscan Publications.

Hardoy, Jorge, Diana Mitlin and David Satterthwaite (1992), *Environmental Problems in Third World Cities*, London: Earthscan Publications.

Hall, Peter and Ulrich Pfeiffer (2000), *Urban Future 21: A Global Agenda for Twenty-First Cities*, London: E & F N Spon.

Hossain, H. (1987), *Urban Travel Behaviour in Bangladesh: A Case Study of Dhaka*. Calcutta: Centre for Human Settlement.

Li, Han-Lin, Peter Atteslander, Judith Tanur and Qi Wang (1999), 'Anomie Scales: Measuring Social Instability', in Peter Atteslander, Bettina Gransow and John Western (eds), *Comparative Anomie Research: Hidden Barriers – Hidden Potential for Social Development*, Aldershot: Ashgate, pp. 23–46.

Lo Fu-Chen and Yue-Man Yeung (1996) (eds.) *Emerging World Cities in Pacific Asia*, Tokyo: United Nations University Press.

Louis Berger International, (1991), *Secondary Towns Infrastructure and Services Development Project, Bangladesh Final Report*, Dhaka: Louis Berger International Inc.

Merton, Robert (1968) *Social Theory and Social Structure*, New York: Free Press.

Passas, Nikos and Robert Agnew (1997), (eds) *The Future of Anomie Theory*, Chicago: Northeastern University Press.

Shahjahan, M. (1998), 'Improvement of Dhaka City's law and order situation: Some proposals' in *Seminar Volume on the problems of Dhaka Metropolis and an Integrated Approach towards their Solution*, Dhaka: The Institute of Engineers.

Siddiqui, K. (2000), *Overcoming The Governance Crisis in Dhaka City*, Dhaka: University Press Limited.

Temple, Frederick (2002), *Dhaka Urban Transport Project Launching Workshop*, Introductory Remarks by the World Bank Country Director, Washington: The World Bank.

Travis, R. (1993), 'The MOS Alienation Scale: An alternative to Srole's Anomia Scale', *Social Indicators Research*, 28, pp. 71–91.

Western, John and Andrea Lanyon (1999), 'Anomie in the Asia Pacific Region: The Australian study', in Peter Atteslander, Bettina Gransow and John Western (eds.) *Comparative Anomie Research: Hidden Barriers – Hidden Potential for Social Development*, Aldershot: Ashgate, pp. 73–98.

World Bank (1997), *World Bank Development Report, 1997*, Washington: World Bank.
World Bank (2000), *World Bank Development Report, 2000*, Washington: World Bank.
World Bank (2002), *Globalization, Growth and Poverty*, Washington: World Bank.

Chapter 12

Ahmed, Mian A. (1991), 'Child labor in Pakistan: A study of the Lahore area', *Child Welfare*, March–April, pp. 261–267.
Akabayashi, Hideo and George Psacharopoulos (1999), 'The trade off between child labor and human capital formation: a Tanzanian case study', *Journal of Development Studies*, 35(5), pp. 120–129.
Angel, Shlome, Raymon Archer, Sidhijai Tanphiphat and Emiel Wegelin (1983), (eds.), *Land for Housing the Poor*, Singapore: Select Books.
Ariffin, Jamilah (1995), 'At the crossroads of rapid development: Malaysian society and anomie', in Peter Atteslander (ed) *Anomie: Social Destabilisation and the Development of Early Warning Systems, International Journal of Sociology and Social Policy*, 15 (8/9/10), pp. 343–371.
Ariffin, Jamilah and Adeline Louis (2001), (eds.), *Social Challenges of Rapid Economic Transformation*, Proceedings of the Institute Sultan Iskandar and Swiss Academy of Development, Joint International Conference, Technology University of Malaysia, Johor: ISI Publications.
Atteslander, Peter Bettina Gransow and John Western (1999), *Comparative Anomie Research: Hidden Barriers-Hidden Potential for Social Development*, Aldershot: Ashgate.
Bequele A. and J. Boyden (1988), (eds), *Combating Child Labor*, Geneva: International Labor Organization.
Blackburn, Susan (1997), 'Indonesia' in Malcolm Falkus, Susan Blackburn, Howard Brasted, Amarjit Kaur and Denis Wright (eds.), *Child Labor in Asia: Some Perspectives on Selected Countries*, International Development Issues, No. 49, Canberra: Australian Agency for International Development, pp. 91–111.
Bonnett Michel (1993), 'Child labour in Africa', *International Labour Review*, 132(3), pp. 371–389.

Bouhdiba, A. (1982), *Exploitation of Child Labor*. New York: United Nations.
Brookfield, Harold and Yvonne Byron (1993), (eds.), *South East Asia's Environmental Future: The Search for Sustainability*, Singapore: Oxford University Press.
Delap, Emily (2001), 'Economic and cultural forces in the child labor debate: Evidence from urban Bangladesh', *Journal of Development Studies*, 37(4), pp.1–22.
Falkus, Malcolm, Susan Blackburn, Howard Brasted, Amarjit Kaur and Denis Wright (1997), 'Introduction', in Malcolm Falkus, Susan Blackburn, Howard Brasted, Amarjit Kaur and Denis Wright (eds.), *Child Labor in Asia: Some Perspectives on Selected Countries*, International Development Issues, no. 49, Canberra: Australian Agency for International Development, pp. 1–12.
Forbes, Dean (1996), *Asian Metropolis: Urbanisation and the South East Asian City*, Oxford: Oxford University Press.
Gilbert, Richard, Don Stevenson, Herbert Girardet and Richard Stren (1996), *Making Cities Work: The Role of Local Authorities in the Urban Environment*, London: Earthscan Publications.
Grootaert, Christiaan and Ravi Kanbur (1995), 'Child labor: An economic perspective', *International Labor Review*, 134(2), pp. 187–204.
Gunn, Susan and Zenaida Ostos (1992), 'Dilemmas in tackling child labour: The case of scavenger children in the Philippines', *International Labour Review*, 131(6), pp. 629–646.
Hall, Peter and Ulrich Pfeiffer (2000), *Urban Future 21: A Global Agenda for Twenty-First Century Cities*, London: E & FN Spon.
Hardoy, Jorge and David Satterthwaite (1989), *Squatter Citizen: Life in the Urban Third World*, London: Earthscan Publications.
Hardoy, Jorge, Susan Cairncross and David Satterthwaite (1990), *The Poor Die Young: Housing and Health in Third World Cities*, London: Earthscan Publications.
Hasnat, Baban (1995), 'International trade and child labor', *Journal of Economic Issues*, 29 (2), pp. 419–426.
Hilowitz, Janet (1997), 'Social labeling to combat child labor: some considerations', *International Labor Review*, 136 (2), pp. 215–232.
ILO (1992), *World Labor Report 1992*, Geneva: International Labor Organization, Geneva.

Jacoby, H. and E. Skoufias (1994), *Risk, financial markets and human capital in a developing country*, Mimeo World Bank Policy Research Department, Washington, DC: The World Bank.

Jomo K. S. (ed), (1992), *Child Labor in Malaysia*, Kuala Lumpur: Varlin Press.

Kaur, Amarjit (1997), 'Philippines', in Malcolm Falkus, Susan Blackburn, Howard Brasted, Amarjit Kaur and Denis Wright (eds.), *Child Labor in Asia: Some Perspectives on Selected Countries*, International Development Issues, No. 49, Canberra: Australian Agency for International Development, pp. 113–144.

Lansky, Mark (1997), 'Child labor: How the challenge is being met', *International Labor Review*, 136 (2), pp. 233–257.

Levy, Victor (1985), 'Cropping pattern, mechanization, child labor and fertility behavior in a farming economy: rural Egypt', *Economic Development and Cultural Change*, 33 (4), pp. 777–791.

McDonald, H. (1992), 'Boys of bondage', *Far Eastern Economic Review*, 9 July, 155, pp. 18–20.

Mahizhnan, Arun and Lee-Tsao Yuan (1998), (eds), *Singapore: Re-engineering Success*, Singapore: Oxford University Press.

Marcuse, Peter (1997), 'The enclave, the citadel, and the ghetto: What has changed in the post-Fordist U.S. city', *Urban Affairs Review*, 33(2), pp. 228–264.

Nangia, P. (1994), 'Children in the urban informal sector: A tragedy of the developing countries in Asia', in A. Dutt, F. Costa, S. Aggarwal and A. Noble (eds), *The Asian City: Processes of Development, Characteristics and Planning*. The GeoJournal Library, Dordrecht: Kluwer Academic Publishers, pp. 274–294.

Psacharopoulos, George (1997), 'Child labor versus educational attainment: Some evidence form Latin America', *Journal of Population Economics*, 10(4), pp. 377–386.

Roberts, L. (1996), 'Child labor: A form of slavery', in *World Federation of the Sporting Goods Industry (Committee on Ethics and Fair Trade), The Way Forward*. Proceedings of the Conference on Human rights held in Verbier, Switzerland, 3–4 November, London: Brassey's.

Rodgers, G. and G. Standing (1981), (eds), *Child work, poverty and underdevelopment*. Geneva: International Labor Organization.

Sharma, B. and V. Mitter (1990), *Child Labor and Informal Sector*, New Delhi: Deep and Deep Publications.

UN Chronicle (1993), 'Global plan on child labor adopted: third racism decade asked', *UN Chronicle*, 30, pp.54–57.
UN Chronicle (1996), 'Child labor: developing country estimates double', *UN Chronicle*, 4, pp. 19–20.
UN Chronicle, (1989), 'So they may have a happy childhood… (1959 Declaration on the Rights of the Child) (The Best Mankind Has To Give)', *UN Chronicle,* Sept 26, 3, p. 51.
UNICEF (1986), *Exploitation of working children and street children*, UNICEF, Executive Board, 1986 Session, Report E/ICEF/1986/CRP.3. New York.
UNICEF (1991), *The state of the world's children 1991*, Oxford: Oxford University Press.
White, Ben (1994), 'Children, work and "Child Labor": Changing Responses to the Employment of Children', *Development and Change*, 25, pp. 849–878.
Williams, Jack and Robert Stimson (2001), (eds), *International Planning Settings: Lessons of Success*, Amsterdam: JAI.

Chapter 13

Appadurai, Arjun (1990), 'Disjuncture and difference in the global cultural economy,' in Mike Featherstone (ed.), *Global Culture: Nationalism, Globalization and Modernity*, London and Newbury Park: Sage, pp. 295–310.
Bell, Daniel (1976), *The Cultural Contradictions of Capitalism*, New York: Basic Books.
Beng-Huat, Chua (ed.) (2000a), *Consumption in Asia: Lifestyles and Identities*, London: Routledge.
Beng-Huat, Chua (2000b), 'Consuming Asians: Ideas and issues' in Beng-Huat, Chua (ed.) *Consumption in Asia: Lifestyles and Identities*, London: Routledge, pp. 1–34.
Burawoy, Michael et.al. (2000), *Global Ethnography: Forces, Connections, and Imaginations in a Postmodern World*, Berkeley: University of California Press.
Ganguly-Scrase, Ruchira and Timothy J. Scrase (1999), 'A bitter pill or sweet nectar? Contradictory attitudes of salaried workers to economic liberalisation in India', *Development and Society*, 28 (2), pp. 259–83.
Ganguly-Scrase, Ruchira and Timothy J. Scrase (2001), 'Who wins? who loses? and who even knows? – Responses to

economic liberalization and cultural globalization in India', *South Asia*, 24 (1), pp. 141–58.
Giddens, Anthony (1990), *The Consequences of Modernity*, Stanford: Stanford University Press.
Hall, Peter and U. Pfeiffer (2000), *Urban Future 21: A Global Agenda for Twenty-First Cities*, London: E and F N Spon.
Ito, Youichi (1999), 'Theories on the mass media and ethnicity: How do the mass media affect ethnicity and related problems?', in Anura Goonasekera and Youichi Ito (eds), *Mass Media and Cultural Identity: Ethnic Reporting in Asia*, London and Sterling, VA: Pluto Press.
Marx, Karl and Friedrich Engels (1888/1967), *The Communist Manifesto*, (Translated by Samuel Moore), Harmondsworth, Middlesex: Penguin.
Mill, John Stuart (1859/1956), *On Liberty*, Indianapolis and New York: Bobbs-Merrill.
Ritzer, George (1993), *The McDonaldization of Society: An Investigation into the Changing Character of Contemporary Social Life*, Thousand Oaks, CA: Pine Forge Press.
Santos, Boaventura de Sousa (2002), '*Nuestra America*: Reinventing a subaltern paradigm of recognition and redistribution,' in Scott Lash and Mike Featherstone (eds), *Recognition & Difference: Politics, Identity, Multiculture*, London and Thousand Oaks: Sage, pp. 185–217.
Sklair, Leslie (ed.) (1994), *Capitalism and Development*, London: Routledge.
Watson, James L. (ed.) (1997), *Golden Arches East: McDonald's in East Asia*, Stanford: Stanford University Press.
World Commission of Environment and Development (1987), *Our Common Future* (The Brundtland Report), Oxford: Oxford University Press.

Name Index

Abou-El-Haj, B. 295 n.10
Abu-Lughod, J. 187
Acharya, A. 33, 34
Acharya, S.K. 71
Afshar, H. 71
Agarwal, B. 71
Agnew, R. 235
Aguilar, F.V. 54
Ahmad, N. 240
Ahmed, M. 250, 253, 254
Ahn, B. 27
Ainger, K. 173
Akabayashi, H. 261
Alagappa, M. 30, 31, 47
Althusser, L. 197
Altman, D. 38
Anderson, B. 11, 121
Anderson, J. 127
Anderson, K. 97
Ang, I. 129
Angel, S. 250
Antlov, H. 31, 36
Appadurai, A. 5, 7, 15, 73, 108, 146, 173, 174, 185, 188, 271, 276
Ariffin, J. 16, 249, 255
Arora, D. 69
Arts, W. 235
Asian and Pacific Migration Journal 50
Asian Regional Exchange for New Alternatives (ARENA) 24
Asian Social Forum 41, 286 n.6

Asian Social Movements 40
Athukorala, R.-C. 50
Atteslander, P. 234, 235, 236, 249
Avashti, A. 69
Aviel, J.F. 49

Bagchi, J. 76
Balkwell, C. 97
Ball, R. 38, 50
Bandyopadhyay, D. 79
Bannerjee, N. 69
Baqee, M. 240
Barber, B. 144
Bardhan, P. 289 n.5
Barker, C. 176, 183
Barrientos, S. 71
Barthes, R. 172
Barton, G. 188
Basu, K. 104
Basu, R. 69
Battersby, C. 210
Baudrillard, J. 197
Baum, S. iii, v, vi, xi, 1, 6, 16, 17, 215, 216, 234, 249, 269, 281
Bayhaqi, A. 186
Beaverstock, J. 225
Beck, U. 174, 177, 178, 186
Befu, H. 148, 150, 293 n.10
Bell, D. 270
Bello, W. 28, 41
Beng-Huat, C. 218, 222, 273
Benjamin, W. 201, 202
Bequele, A. 254

Berger, J. 197
Berger, M. 28, 32, 34
Berger, P.L. 156
Berry, A. 71, 289 n.7
Bhabha, H. 121, 123, 174
Bhattacharya, D. 74
Bhattacharya, R. 288 n.5
Bhuiyanm, S. 239
Blackburn, S. 253, 255, 259
Bluestone, B. 216
Bonnet, M. 254
Boorstin, D. 285 n.2
Bouhdiba, A. 251, 264
Bourdieu, P. 102
Boyden, J. 254
Brah, A. 120, 121, 122
Brayne, K. 188
Breckenridge, C. 73
Brohman, J. 101
Buchanan, K. 98
Buckley, S. 66
Burawoy, M. 298
Burgess, E.W. 15
Burgmann, V. 45
Burke, A. 35
Burton, H. 160
Butler, J. 211

Cairncross, S. 241, 250
Camilleri, J. 28, 29, 31, 34, 35
Cartmel, F. 186
Carty, V. 290 n.13
Castells, M. 13, 15, 41, 149, 177, 285 n.3
Castles, S. 48, 51, 286 n.4
Cha, B. 136
Chakravarti, U. 91, 92
Chan, S. 124
Chanana, K. 82
Chang, T. 225
Chantavanich, S. 51

Chatterjee, T. 289 n.5
Chaudhuri, M. 76, 91
Chen J. 49, 58, 60, 62, 65
Chen, M.C. v, xi, 5, 7, 14, 191, 270, 275, 276, 277, 278
Cheng, S. 63, 64
Chia, S. 221
Chibnick, M. 97
Chin, C.B.N. 51
Cho, M.R. 216
Choo, M. 218
Chossudovsky, M. 28
Cieslik, M. 177
Clammer, J. 2, 6, 16, 144, 165
Clarke, T. 28
Cohen, R. 120, 121
Cole, C.L. 290 n.13
Colloredo-Mansfield, R. 98
Connor, L.H. 184
Cooper, R. 124
Cowan, R.S. 88
Cox, D. 52
Cox, R. 29
Cribb, R. 187
Cross, D. 216
Crouch, H. 31, 32, 34
Cruz, D. 44
Cunningham, S. 121, 139, 140
Curran, J. 164
Curtis, G. 33
CWDS (Centre for Women's Development Studies) 69

Dale, P.N. 150
Das, V. 69, 93
Dasgupta, P. 71
Davis, E. A. 105
Dean, E. 124
Deflem, M. 234
Delap, E. 250, 253, 258, 260, 261

Name Index

Desai, N. 82
Deshpande, S. 73, 74
Dewan, R. 69
Deyo, F. 226
Dicken, P. 226
Dickerson, K.G. 97
Dickie, V.A. 96
Diller, J. 43
Dissanyake, W. 187
Doezma, J. 56
Dokken, K. 34
Donnelly, N.D. 124
Doucet, M. 45, 46
Doyle, A. 45
Drake, J. 38
Durkheim, E. 234, 235

Eades, J.F. 2, 146
Edwards, L. 2
Ehrenreich, B. 88
Eichengreen, B. 248
Einhorn, B. 68
Ekins, P. 43
Enayetullah, I. 241
Engels, F. 274, 275, 279
English, D. 88
Ericson, R. 45
Eriksen, T.H. 144
Evans, Geoff, 44
Evans, Grant, 1

Facer, K. 180
Fairbrother, P. 28
Falk, R. 25, 35, 46
Falkus, M. 252
Faust, J. 30
Featherstone, M. 115
Field, H. 29
Fine, B. 115
Fiore, Q. 145
Fiske, J. 165

Flynn, N. 29
Forbes, D. 249
Forrester, G. 36
Foucault, M. 210
Frank, A.G. 2
Frank, G. 96
Franke, U. 30
Friedman, J.
Friedman, T. 25
Friedmann, J. 16, 215
Friend, M. 130
Friends of the Earth
 International 44
Frith, S. 163
Fujita, K. 217, 234
Furlong, A. 186
Furlong, R. 180

Gan, S. 181
Ganguly-Scrase, R. v, xi, 9,
 10, 68, 73, 97, 102, 130,
 270, 273, 274, 291
Gatens, M. 208
Gauntlett, D. 12
Gerke, S. 187
Ghai, Y. 38, 53, 287 n.6
Gibney, F. 148
Giddens, A. 5, 10, 12, 145,
 146, 147, 178, 183, 186,
 189, 271
Gill, S. 25
Goh, C. T. 225, 232
Golding, P. 172
Goldman, R. 290 n.13
Goldthorpe, J. 288 n.4
Gonzalez II, J. 51
Goodman, D. 2, 16
Goodman, J. v, xii, 8, 21, 29,
 36, 37, 39, 43, 45, 270,
 272, 274
Gopinath, G. 38

Gorman, L. 125
Gosovic, B. 9
Gramsci, A. 141
Grasnow, B. 235
Grimes, K.M. 97, 103, 113
Grootaert, C. 252, 253, 254, 259, 264
Grosz, E. 209
Guillermo, A.G. 99
Gunewardena, D. 239
Gunn, S. 250, 251, 262, 263
Gurevitch, M. 164
Gurowitz, A. 49, 56, 57, 60, 61
Guzman, R. 33
Gwiasda, V. 217

Hall, P. 15, 239, 240, 249, 250, 280, 281
Hall, S. 120, 121, 122, 123, 134, 135, 139, 142, 146, 151, 156, 165, 184, 211, 294 n.23
Halloran, R. 148
Hamnett, C. 215, 216, 224, 232
Hannerz, U. 165
Haraway, D. 195
Hardoy, J. 241, 250
Hardt, M. 40
Harris, N. 57
Harrison, B. 216
Hasnat, B. 251, 264
Hassan, R. 187, 188
Hein, J. 125
Helu-Thaman, K. 101
Hemming, J. 63
Hendrickson, C. 106, 114
Her, M. 128, 129
Hernadez-Diaz, J. 32
Hettne, B. 25
Hewison, K. 28
Heywood, L. 38

Hill, D. 169, 181, 189
Hilowitz, J. 264
Hilsdon, A.M. 61
Ho, K.C. 16, 28, 228
Ho, L. 65
Holden, T.J.M. iii, v, vi, xii, 1, 5, 7, 12, 144, 149, 151, 155, 176, 269, 271, 275, 278, 293 n.9, 293 n.12, 295 n.5
Hope, K. 288 n.4
Hossain, H. 241
Hossain, Z. vi, xiv, 6, 16, 17, 271
Hourani, A. 186
Hribar, A. 290 n.13
Hsiung, J. 36
Huang, A.S. 51
Hughes, D.M. 53
Human Rights Law Group 55
Human Rights Watch 50, 51
Hung, R. 16, 216
Huntington, S. 33
Hymer, S. 217

Ida, M. 150, 293 n.8
Ikoma, C. 149
ILO (International Labor Organization) 250
Imhoff, D. 100, 101
Irvine, M. 144
Ito, R. 50
Ito, Y. 279

Jacoby, H. 254
Jain, J. 108
Jarvis, A. 47
Jenkins, R. 294 n.23
Joachim, J. 54
John, M. 69
Johnson, C. 26

Johnson, J. 106
Johnson, K. 176, 295 n.5
Jomo, K. S. 254
Jones, B. 285 n.2
Jonsson, K. 3, 144
Julian, R. v, xii, xiii, 7, 11, 12, 14, 119, 130, 135, 275, 276, 277, 278
Junedding, B. 170

Kabeer, N. 84
Kaino, L. 99
Kalpagam, U. 69
Kamimura, S. 149, 150, 293 n.8
Kanbur, R. 252, 253, 254, 259, 264
Kanter, R. 225, 227
Kar, B. 79
Kathuria, S. 97, 100
Katsuno, H. 293 n.9
Kaur, A. 250
Kelsey, J. 28
Kempadoo, K. 56
Khatkhate, D. 288 n.2
Khoo, N. 24, 27, 28
Kilby, P. 287 n.5
King, A. 217
Kinnvall, C. 3, 144
Klein, N. 173
Knorringa, P. 97, 102
Kofman, E. 51
Koh, G. 233
Korovkin, T. 98
Kothari, R. 47
Kulkarni, V. G. 73
Kusakabe, K. 101
Kuttner, P. 216

Lakha, S. 73, 74, 289 n.6
Langton, M. 36
Lansky, M. 263, 264
Lanyon, A. 236, 246, 248
Law, L. 59, 62, 66, 287 n.1
Lawasia (Law Association for Asia and the Pacific) 50, 54, 57, 287 n.7
Lawrence, R. 216
Laxer, G. 32
Lebra, T.S. 150
Lebra, W.P. 150
Lee, G.Y. 130, 131
Lee, P.H. 137
Leigh, B. 181
Lent, J. 176, 189
Leopold, E. 115
Lepani, B. 216
Levy, P. 216
Li, H. L. 236
Liechty, M. 171, 188
Lim, L. 221
Lim, L.L. 48, 52
Lim, T.C. 58, 287 n.1
Lingis, A. 208
Livingstone, S. 180
Lo, F. C. 234
Loong, L. H. 230
Louis, A. 16, 249
Luckmann, T. 156
Luke, A. 123
Luke, C. 123
Luke, T. 46
Lull, J. 7, 148

Ma, S-Y. 29
MacHenry, R. 99, 100, 103, 113
Macintyre, M. 61
Mackie, V. 58, 66
MacLeod, S. 221
Mahizhnan, A. 249
Maiguashca, B. 38

Malhotra, K. 29, 33
Maneeprasert, R. 292 n.2
Mankekar, P. 69
Manning, C. 50
Marchand, M. 46
Marcuse, P. 216, 228, 249
Markusen, A. 217
Martin, D.C. 120, 121
Martin, H. P. 231
Martinez-Alier, J. 38
Marx, K. 274, 275, 279
May, R. 36
Mazumdar, S. 296 n.11
McDonald, H. 262, 263
McGee, T. 221
McLean, D. 125
McLuhan, M. 10, 12, 14, 145, 285 n.2
McVeigh, B. 151, 293 n.11
Menon, I. 52
Mertes, T. 40
Merton, R. 234, 235
Meyerowitz, J. 14, 147, 285 n.2
Milgram, B.L. 97, 100, 103, 113
Mill, J.S. 275
Miller, D. 115
Miller, M. 48, 51
Mills, C.W. 18
Mills, K. 57
Mitchell, D. 181
Mitlin, D. 241
Mitra, G.K. 79
Mitra, N. 79
Mittelman, J. 25, 35
Mitter, V. 253
Mizoe, S. 292 n.6
Moeur, R. 150
Moghadam, V. 71
Mohanty, M. 76

Morales, I. 30
Moran, K. 112
Morley, D. 11, 171, 174
Morley, J. 31, 32, 34
Morton, A. 286 n.3
Moua, M.N. 134
Mukherjee, A. 71
Mukherjee, S.N. 72
Mulvey, L. 196
Munck, R. 39
Munshi, S. 69, 83
Murakami, R. 294 n.25
Murdock, G. 73, 172
Murray, G. 292 n.6

Nagaraj, R. 74
Nagata, J. 295 n.6
Nakano, S. 149
Nakatani, A. 99, 102, 114
Nangia, P. 250, 251, 253, 257
Nash, J. 96, 97, 101, 103
Nederveen-Pieterse, J. 165
Nelson, J.L. 208
Niblo, S. 28
Nilan, P. v, xiii, 5, 7, 13, 168, 174, 187, 270, 274, 275, 276, 277, 278, 295 n.5
Nomura, M. 158, 294 n.20

Oakley, A. 88
OECD (SOPEMI) 50
Oishi, N. 48, 52
Omvedt, G. 71
Ong, W. 285 n.2
Ooi, G. L. 233
Oshikawa, F. 74
Ostos, Z. 250, 251, 262, 263
Oxfam GB 67
Ozaki, R. 166

Pang, E-S. 27, 28, 29

Name Index

Panini, M. 68
Paolini, A. 47
Papson, S. 290 n.13
Park, R.E. 15
Parker, L. 169
Parsons, T. 234
Passas, N. 235
Pedersen, J.D. 74
Perry, M. 231
Pettman, J. 37
Pfaff, T. 127
Pfeiffer, U. 15, 239, 240, 249, 250, 280, 281
Philippines Overseas Employment Administration (POEA) 50
Phongpaichit, P. 51
Pickvance, C. 15
Pietila, H. 65
Pinches, M. 2, 6, 33
Piper, N. v, xiii, 5, 8, 9, 38, 48, 49, 50, 51, 52, 55, 57, 58, 62, 270, 272, 274, 287 n.2, 287 n.4
Polanyi, K. 23, 26, 47
Pollock, G. 177
Pow, C. P. 219, 220, 226, 230, 232, 233
Power, C. 296 n.11
Pradadimara, D. 170
Prasad, S. 36
Preston, P. 27
Price, J. 49
Pryke, M. 217
Psacharopoulos, G. 251, 261
Puri, J. 69

Quincey, K. 124

Raghuram, P. 51
Ranald, P. 45

Ravenhill, J. 45
Raymond J.G. 53
Reilly, B. 30
Reischauer, E.O. 148
Rex, J. 120, 121
Richardson, J. 47
Riley, M. 112
Ritzer, G. 273
Roberts, G. 57, 58
Roberts, L. 263
Robertson, R. 11, 146, 166
Robins, K. 11, 171, 174
Robinson, K. 174, 187
Robison, R. 2, 16, 28
Roces, M. 2, 51
Rodan, G. 28
Rodgers, G. 252
Romano, A. 170, 178
Rubinstein, R. 184
Ruggie, J. 46
Rutten, R. 101

Sachsenroder, W. 34
Said, E. 181
Sandy, L. 63
Sanie, S.Y.R. vi, xiii, 6, 17, 249, 281
Santos, B.S. 7, 146, 165, 298 n.9
Sassen, S. 16, 215, 217, 223, 224, 225, 228, 232
Sassen-Koob, S. 223
Satterthwaite, D. 241, 250
Savage, M. 16
Savage, V. 219, 220, 226, 230, 232, 233
Scalapino, R. 35
Schein, L. 120, 130
Schmidt, J. 33, 44
Schumann, H. 231
Schwartz, T. 285 n.2

Scrase, T.J. iii, v, vi, xi, xiii, 1, 5, 9, 10, 72, 73, 91, 95, 182, 184, 269, 272, 273, 274, 288 n.1
Scuka, D. 293 n.9
Sen, K. 74, 169, 181, 189
Sen, S. 83
Serrano, I. 34
Seth, S. 96
Shah, N.M. 52
Shahjahan, M. 240
Sharma, B. 253
Sharma, U. 82
Shipper, A. 58
Siddiqui, K. 240
Silliman, S. 39
Sim, A. 49, 59, 60, 287 n.1
Simmel, G. 159
Sinclair, J. 121, 139, 140
Sinha, M.M. 241
Sinha, S. 288 n.5
Skeldon, R. 286 n.4
Sklair, L. 21, 28, 272, 286 n.4
Skoufias, E. 254
Slevin, J. 11, 131, 139, 142
Smith, D. 216
Smith, M. 24, 27, 28
Soederberg, S. 25
Soros, G. 26
Spivak, G.C. 129
Sprague, J. 294 n.25
Srivasthava, A.K. 69
Standing, G. 252
Standing, H. 82
Stark, T. 216
Starr, A. 41
Steiner, C. B. 97
Stephen, L. 107
Stewart, F. 71
Stiglitz, J. 26
Stimson, R. 249

Stivens, M. 22, 39, 74
Stubbs, R. 33
Sugimoto, Y. xv, 150
Sunder Rajan, R. 69
Suratman, S. 108

Taipei Times, The 199, 202, 205, 207
Talarowska-Kacprzak, K. 157
Tanur, J. 236
Tapp, N. 130
Taylor, P. 217
Tehranian, M. 3
Temple, F. 240
Thompson, M. 33
Thrift, N. 217
Tice, K. 97
Timberlake, M. 216
Tirtorsudarmo, R. 50
Tomlinson, J. 15, 184
Tonnesson, S. 31, 36
Travis, R. 236, 237
Truong, T-D. 54, 64
Tsuruki, T. 293 n.9
Tujan, A (Tony). 33, 43
Turner, B. 53
Turner, M. 30
Tyner, J.A. 52

Uçarer, E. 53, 56
Uður, A. 159
Uhlin, A. 27, 49, 60, 62, 287 n.2
UNIFEM (United Nations Development Fund for Women) 110, 111

Van den Bulck, H. 180
Van Wessel, M. 74
Vatikiotis, M. 181
Vervoorn, A. 1, 6

Vickers, A. 185, 187
Vickers, J. 65

Walker, D.R. 217
Wallerstein, I. 5, 146
Wang, Q. 236
Warde, A. 16
Waterman, P. 41
Watrous, M. 294 n.21
Watson, J.L. 273
Webber, D. 28
Wee, W-L.C.J. 2
Weekley, K. 54
Weiner, M. 54
Weiss, L. 26
Werbner, P. 11, 120, 121, 122, 125, 131, 140
West, L. 36
Western, J. 235, 236, 246, 248
White, B. 253, 255, 259, 264
Whitfield, D. 46
Wilkinson-Weber, C.M. 99
Willetts, P. 43
Williams, J. 249
Wilson, R. 187
Wirth, L. 228
Wiseman, J. 28
Wolff, G. 16, 215
Wood, W.W. 97
Woodward, K. 146, 209
World Bank (The) 15, 29
World Social Forum 40, 286 n.5
Wright, E.O. 288 n.4

Xiong, T.G. 126, 133

Yamamoto, T. 34
Yamanaka, K. 52
Yamashita, S. 2

Yamazaawa, I. 222
Yang, D. 124, 126
Yang, D.C. 142
Yang, L.B. 227
Yang, N. 137
Yano, C. 293
Yeo, E.J. 68
Yeo, G. 230
Yeoh, B. 51, 225
Yeung, H. 27
Yeung, Y.M. 2, 27, 234
Yuan, L-T. 218, 249
Yuval-Davis, N. 39

Zukin, S. 217

Subject Index

advocacy, 9, 37, 48, 49, 62, 65, 67
anomie, 4, 7, 17, 234–248
artisan exploitation,
  gender concerns, 98–100
  health concerns, 98–100
artisan labor, 95–116
artisan/s, 5, 10, 95–116
ASEAN, 45, 50, 287 n.3
Asia Pacific, 8, 21, 22, 23, 24, 26, 29, 30, 34, 36, 38, 40, 43, 45, 46, 47, 58, 61, 65, 68, 216, 286 n.4, n.7, 291 n.1
Asian Development Bank, 45, 239
Asian values, 1, 27, 176, 181
Australia, 11, 23, 27, 28, 29, 31, 35, 36, 37, 66, 119, 124, 125, 130, 132, 143, 145, 148, 202, 217, 219, 236, 248, 263, 283, 291 n.1, 295 n.9, 297 n.3

Bali, 168, 170, 175, 176, 178, 179, 182, 183, 185, 188, 283, 295 n.1
Bangkok, 40, 65, 66, 130, 217, 280
bhadralok, 71–72, 78, 79, 83, 84, 85, 86, 290 n.10, n,12
Broadcasting and Television Law, 191, 199
Brunei, 287 n.3
Burma, 31, 51, 65, 189

Cambodia, 51, 52, 54, 61, 63, 64, 287 n.3
Canada, 27, 28, 32, 35, 37, 124, 130, 132, 161, 202
Ceylon, 291 n.1
child labor, 17, 249–265, 271
  & formal education, 250
  & gender, 262
  characteristics of, 256–258
  impact of education system on, 254–255, 259
  impact of family members on, 258
  international policy, 17
  negative impacts of, 250–251
  probability of, 259–262
child laborers, 5
China, 15, 28, 29, 31, 36, 37, 115, 124, 130, 136, 145, 161, 193, 202, 221, 226, 283, 287 n.3, 291 n.2, 292 n.3, 296 n.2, 297 n.1, n.3
Chinese, 32, 36, 60, 124, 160, 275
Chinese Anomie Project, 236
Chinese communism, 24
Chinese culture,
  & women, 205
Chinese Hmong, 130
Chinese immigration, 296 n.2
Chinese morality, 200
Chinese toys, 44
cities, 15, 16, 216, 217, 227, 234, 239, 249, 255, 280

& sustainable urban
    development, 280–281
  Asian, 16
  economic functions of, 223
  global network of, 232
  modern, 3
  mosaics of social worlds, 228
  North American, 216
  sociology of, 215
  treatment in social sciences,
    231
cities and urban areas, 279–281
civil society, 4, 16, 29, , 39, 43,
    49, 57, 60, 61, 215, 233,
    248, 249, 281, 286 n.5
  & family, 34
  & religion, 34
  political space of, 34
class, 2, 73, 76, 86, 142, 293
    n.12
  & gender, 273
  Bengali society, 72, 93
  differences, 124
  identity, 59, 94
  industrial entrepreneurial, 221
  lower, 9
  lower middle, 9, 69, 71, 72,
    73–74, 75, 83, 93, 270, 273
  middle, 9, 63, 64, 69, 73,
    74, 77, 89, 96, 103, 104,
    107, 114, 170, 187, 188,
    189, 190, 232, 259, 271,
    272, 289 n.6, 290 n.11
  new middle, 273
  new rich, 255
  social, 4, 271, 272, 281, 289
    n.5
  transnational business, 21
  transnational capitalist, 21,
    28, 286 n.4
  transnational technocrats, 28

transnationalized middle, 27
upper, 75, 76, 103, 104
upper middle, 83, 87, 105,
    291 n.3
working, 63
class differentials, 71
class discrimination,
  & female migrants, 52
class divisions, 223
class formation, 289 n.5
class fraction/s, 71, 72, 83
class inequalities, 100
class politics, 272
class reconfiguration,
  & consumption, 273
class stratification, 288 n.4
classes, 6
  business, 32
  executive, 28
  lower, 112
  lower middle, 68, 73, 74, 94
  middle, 9, 27, 94, 115
  upper, 105
  upper middle, 112
consumption, 8, 10, 44, 87–
    91, 164, 185, 188, 270,
    293 n.12
  & feminization, 69
  & the new middle class, 73
  alcohol, Indonesia, 184
  conspicuous, 5, 72, 187, 273
  energy, 280
  family, 100
  food, 261
  local, 103
  mass, 102, 271
  status of women, 101
consumption community,
  creating a, 158–160
consumption goods,
  & child labor, 259

craft consumption, 101–108, 114
craft styles, 101–108
crime, 55, 160, 194, 217, 239, 240, 242
culinary culture,
 Japan, 152
culture, 15, 16, 26, 122, 165, 201, 211, 237, 276
 & cities, 281
 Arab, 186
 Bengali, 71, 72; see also *bhadralok*
 Chinese, 193, 194, 204, 205, 206, 209
 consumer, 16
 Eastern, 193
 foreign, 185
 gendered, 208, 211
 globalization of, 272
 Hmong, 119, 137, 142
 Indian, 107
 indigenous, 32
 Indonesian, 170, 178, 181
 international, 181
 Islamic, 186
 Japanese, 156
 local, 4, 18
 man-made, 197
 national, 121, 182
 of capitalism, 33
 of the nation, 33
 political, 23, 37
 popular, 2–3, 92, 132, 133, 140, 166, 176, 293 n.12
 Quichua, 98
 school, 157
 social structure & anomie, 235
 Taiwanese, 193
 traditional, 15, 126, 192, 209
 Western, 174, 193
cultures, 122, 204
 political, 47

Dhaka, 6, 16, 17, 234, 236, 238, 239, 240, 241, 242, 246, 248, 271, 280
diaspora, 4, 7, 11, 22, 37, 38, 119, 140, 165, 286 n.4
 Asian, 119
 Chinese, 27, 286 n. 4
 corporate, 21
 dimensions of, 121
 Hmong, v, xii, 7, 119–124, 126, 131, 132, 139, 141
 Japanese, 148, 149
 of media content, 277
 South Asian, 286 n. 4
diasporas,
 social, 37
 cultural, 37
diasporic public sphere, 11, 120, 122, 123, 125 131, 132, 135, 139–142, 277
division of labor, 99
decoding, 193

economic development, 2, 6, 50, 216, 221, 248, 271, 281, 282, 291 n.1
economic restructuring, 6, 215, 216, 217, 223, 231
 & gender, 270
education, 94, 237, 251, 252, 275, 293 n.11
 & artisan laborers, 112
 & *bhadralok* children, 72
 & cities, 281
 & economic policy, 220
 & gender discrimination, 84
 & gender relations, 69
 & Hmong femininity, 135

& Japanese culture, 156
& migrants, 57
& the status of women, 2, 75, 193
  child workers, Jakarta, 156
  civil, 169
  compulsory, 262
  formal, 100, 236
  high school, 236
  higher, 85, 94, 126
  HIV/AIDS, 66
  Hmong, 126, 127
  mass, 33
  moral, 169
  secondary, 236
  tertiary, 168, 186
  women's, 78, 79–80, 132, 141
education levels, 51
educational status,
  & anomie, 245, 247, 248
educational stratification, 232
educational upgrading, 226–228
employment, 177, 224, 257, 263, 281
  & artisan laborers, 114
  & economic liberalization, 75, 94
  & empowerment, 76, 77–79
  & gender relations, 69
  & the status of women, 2
  female, 80
  paid, 82, 250, 259, 253, 254, 256, 258, 260
  participation policies, 108
  traditional, 272
  wage, 255
  women's, 79, 80, 83–86, 98
employment conditions, 111
employment growth, 238
employment opportunities,
  polarization of, 223
employment passes,
  in Singapore, 225
employment rights, 111
employment status, 237, 243, 246, 247
empowerment, 87–91
  language of, 77
encoding, 135, 139, 182
environmental conditions, 147
environmental costs, 26
environmental degradation, 249
environmental goals,
  & urban infrastructure, 219
environmental impacts, 106
environmental problems, 100, 239, 240, 241
environmental security, 33–34, 35
environmental wastelands, 3
equality,
  women's, 9
equity,
  gender, 35
ethnicity, 2, 52, 185
Europe, 216

family, 78, 86, 89, 90, 94, 110, 114, 136, 163, 184, 205, 296 n11
  & gender relations, 71
  & Hmong community, 137
  & women's empowerment, 92
  & women's status, 52
  & youth education, 179
  bhadralok, 290 n.10
family honor, 79
family economy, 87
family enterprises, 257
family income, 82, 262

family quality of life, 263
family survival, 79
  impact of child labor on, 259
film (movies), 7, 12, 108, 173, 183, 187, 191, 194, 196, 197, 198, 199, 201, 203, 204, 219, 290 n.10, 293 n.12, 296 n.11
foreign investment, 44, 221

gender, 4, 12, 14, 35, 37, 54, 69, 78, 96, 100, 123, 130, 131, 140, 141, 150, 156, 192, 193, 194, 196–197, 200, 201, 204, 207, 208, 209, 210, 211, 212, 262, 270, 273, 274, 275, 281, 290 n.13, 293 n.8, 295 n.4
  social construction of, 11
gender & traditional Taiwanese culture, 205–206
gender disadvantage, 87
gender discrimination, 84, 93, 97, 99
gender discourse, 198
gender division of labor, 99
gender equality, 68–94, 201
gender hierarchies, 83
gender identity, 192, 193, 196–197, 198, 204, 206, 208, 209, 211, 212
gender ideology, 71, 92, 94
gender/ed inequality/ies, 9, 69, 79, 87, 100, 130, 203–204, 205, 206, 208, 211, 274
  & class, 87
  mediated, 204–205
gender relations, 87, 71, 91, 92, 93, 290 n.13
gender roles, 14, 69, 196
gender segregation, 97

gender socialization, 87
gender/ed identity, 196–197, 198, 204, 210
global cities, 16, 30, 215, 216, 223, 224, 225, 231, 232
global city, 16, 217–220
global economy, 2, 5, 33, 71, 95, 96, 177, 217, 226, 227, 228, 231, 232, 238, 290 n.1
global media corporations, 69
globalization, 1–18, 48, 68–94, 95–98, 115, 120–123, 144–146, 157, 164–167, 174, 180, 183, 189, 215, 219, 220, 228, 230, 234–248, 269, 270, 271, 274, 276, 278
  & change, 4
  & growth, 27
  & Japan, 148–149
  & the Internet, 193
  & trade liberalization, 70
  contradictions of, 270–271, 275
  cultural, 289 n.9
  discourse, 49
  financial, 29
  impacts of, 57, 271, 289, 295 n.27
  neo-liberal, 35
  status of women, 80
  theory, 5–8, 10–11, 120–121, 165
globalization career, 3–4, 148–149, 282–284

health, 44, 66, 100, 177, 240, 241, 249, 251, 271, 281
  & the status of women, 2
  migrant women, 52

Subject Index

health care, 220
Hmong, 5, 7, 8, 11, 14, 119–143, 277, 291 n.2, 292 n.3, n.4
Hmong diaspora, 7, 11, 119–143
  & class, 131
  & gender, 131
  & religion, 131
Hmong identity, 7, 11, 119–143, 291 n.2
  & gender, 8, 140
  & women, 141
  & youth, 141
Hong Kong (SAR), 15, 59, 60, 155, 173, 187, 217, 297 n.3
household income, 71, 72, 228, 229, 253, 254, 259, 288 n.3
human capital, 222, 227, 260, 261, 280
human rights, 38, 41, 53, 54, 55, 56, 60, 62, 65, 66, 194, 195, 199
  advocates, 38
  language of, 64
  U.N. charter of, 53
hybrid- ity/ization, 7, 10, 165, 166
  & craft, 115
  & fashion, 104
  & food, 155
  & identity, 32, 115, 132, 139, 140
  & political systems, 31
  & Taiwanese culture, 193

identit- y/ies, 2–3, 4, 73, 120–123, 168–190, 192, 200, 281, 294 n.23
  & advertising (*adentity*), 144, 148
  & gender, 12, 200
  & globalization, 144
  local culture, 38
  atomized, 293 n.9
  Bengali, 289 n.9; see also *bhadralok*
  Chinese cultural, 210
  class, 77
  collective, 278
  construction of, 12, 123
  cultural, 35, 38, 44, 157, 163, 195
  cultural politics of, 38
  defining, 174
  diasporic, 127, 130
  discourse, 7, 11, 12, 13, 145–148, 150, 151, 152, 161–163, 168–169, 179, 185
  ethnic, 107, 139
  ethno-local, 182, 187
  female, 198, 210
  global, 125, 154
  group, 73
  gyaru, 158
  hybrid, 115
  Indian, 104
  indigenous, 155
  individual, 163, 271
  Japanese, 144–167
  lesbian and gay 38
  local, 13, 147, 154, 172, 174, 185, 278
  mediated, 144–167
  national, 32, 36, 152, 153, 154
  performing 293
  regional, 33
  resistance/oppositional 27, 140
  self, 157, 163, 211
  social, 197

space of, 157
spaces, 160
Taiwanese, 199
identity formation, 5, 14
identity representations, 187
identity subgroups,
  in Japan, 160
IMF, 9, 25, 28, 36, 45, 70,
  170, 285 n.2
immigrant labor, 224–225
immigration,
  policies, 55
income, 10, 111, 187, 215,
  230, 232, 239, 253, 254,
  261, 262
  distribution, 16, 223
  high , 231
  low, 215, 231, 261
  middle, 216, 229
  parental, 260, 261
  subsistence, 111
income disparities, 228–231,
  253
income inequality, 230, 232,
  239
income polarization, 229
income structure, 228, 229
India, 5, 9, 15, 40, 68–116,
  145, 226, 254, 263, 270,
  282, 288 n.1, 291 n.1,
  295 n.5, 297 n.1, 298 n.7
indigenization, 7
individual income, 229
Indonesia, 5, 13, 15, 31, 32,
  35, 36, 37, 38, 44, 52,
  61, 100, 168–190, 221,
  226, 252, 255, 262, 270,
  273, 282, 283, 298
Indonesian identity and
  globalization, 172–173
inequalities, 8

inequality, 2, 4, 6, 10, 15,
  16, 71, 98, 122, 125,
  192, 232, 249, 271, 272,
  282
  & female migrant labor, 8, 52
  structural, 106
  women, 9
informal economy, 96, 264
informal sector, 6, 74, 252,
  254, 256, 257
informal settlements, 17, 240,
  249, 250, 255, 258, 259
  families in, 250
  sustainable employment in,
    249–250
infrastructure, 46, 148, 218,
  219, 220, 239, 240, 241,
  269, 280
International Labor
  Organization, 53, 113,
  250, 262, 263
international women's
  movement, 54
Internet, 11, 12, 13, 14, 95,
  106, 119, 125, 130–131,
  132, 140, 142, 166, 179–
  180, 187, 192, 195, 196,
  200, 202–203, 204, 208,
  211, 218, 292 n.7, 293
  n.7, 296 n.3
  & privacy, 193–194
  control of, 181, 182, 184
  global reach of, 13, 183
  in Japan, 149, 150
  on-line shopping, 95, 106
intellectual property rights,
  111

Jakarta, 6, 17, 174, 186, 217,
  231, 249, 250, 255, 258,
  263, 280, 297

Subject Index

Japan, 2, 5, 12, 15, 28, 31, 37, 38, 53, 57, 58, 63, 66, 144–167, 193, 217, 219, 220, 269, 271, 275, 278, 282, 283, 287 n.3, n.10, 292 n.4, n.6 , 293, 294, 296 n.2, 297 n1, n.3

Kuala Lumpur, 217

labor, 4, 6, 10, 33, 48, 88, 281
 domestic, 226
 female, 48
 flows, 37
 international division of, 5, 32
 laws, 9
 low-skilled, 226
 menial, 3
 sexual division of, 89
 transnational flow, 225
 unskilled, 288
 women's, 71
labor autonomy, 96
labor force, 69, 74, 223, 224, 255
labor force participation, 75
labor force policy,
 in global cities, 217
labor force structure,
 in global cities, 217
labor market/s, 53, 226, 230
labor migration, 3, 48–67
 & women, 50
labor movement/s, 38, 76, 80
labor saving devices, 88
language, 7, 131, 153, 162, 166, 184, 237
 & Hmong identity, 132
 Hmong, 141
Laos, 11, 51, 101, 119, 124, 126, 127, 128, 129, 130, 132, 133, 135, 136, 141, 287 n.3
law, 2, 59, 195, 198, 199, 200, 201, 206, 211, 265
 & the status of women, 2
 adultery, 207
 international, 49, 54, 64
 Islamic, 170
 labor, 51
law enforcement agencies, 65, 240
law of origin, 122
London, 255

Malaysia, 31, 32, 37, 43, 60, 61, 145, 176, 202, 210, 217, 221, 282, 283, 286 n.4, 287 n.3, 295 n.6, 297 n.3, 298 n.7
magazines, 12, 86, 87, 88, 114, 145, 147, 149, 150, 156, 157, 158, 160, 161, 163, 164, 173, 271, 292 n.6, 294 n.27
Manila, 30, 45, 60, 217, 251, 280
media, 2, 4, 12–15, 91, 93, 119–212, 271, 274, 275, 276, 278, 279, 292 n.4
 & empowerment, 91–93
 & gender relations, 92, 192, 201
 & identity, 4, 15, 169, 170–171, 177, 274, 276–278
 & social transformation, 276–277
 commercial, 157, 166, 177, 188
 contemporary, 167
 digital, 3

electronic, 14, 87, 132, 175, 285 n.2, 295 n.2
ethics, 194, 195
free, 295
global, 7, 14, 92, 171, 172, 173, 275–276, 289 n.9
Hmong, 140
impact on culture, 11
in Indonesia, 168–190
influences, in India, 83, 88, 91–93
Japanese, 7, 12, 156, 164
mainstream, 140
mass, 79, 130, 149, 168, 169, 170, 171, 172, 173, 174, 175, 177, 178, 179, 181, 184, 185, 190, 295 n.2
mono-aural, 125
Muslim, 296 n.12
new, 132, 142, 143
non-traditional, 119
popular, 75–77
print, 87
public, 169
traditional, 194–195
Western, 1, 7, 182, 186, 189, 278
wired, 293 n.8
written, 172
media advertising, 173
media anxiety, Indonesia, 182
media audience, 193
media communications, 131
media conglomerations, 44
media consumers, 193
media consumers, 209
media consumption, 139, 149, 173, 193
media discourses, 173, 192
media equality, 92
media imperialism, 189

media organizations, 13, 201
media practice, 198
media representation, 198, 201
media systems, 44
media technologies, 192, 204, 283
media technology, 270
media texts, 134
media theory, 10, 14, 134–139, 285 n.2
mediated identity, 146, 166, 171, 184
& Japan, 151–167
Melbourne, 45, 217
mega city, 234, 236, 239, 280
migrant,
female labor, 5, 8, 9, 48–67, 270
politics, 61
migrant labor, 49, 50
migrant status, 133
migrant women, 51
migrant workers, 37–38, 56, 271, 287 n.10
protection of, 53, 54
Thailand, 51
migrants, 50, 51, 53, 54, 108, 125, 289 n.9
undocumented, 54
women, 48, 55, 56
migration, 37, 48, 50, 52, 55, 234, 239, 286 n.4
chain, 119
female, 48, 272
feminization of, 48–67
forced, 128
gendered, 49–53
international, 51
involuntary, 65
labor, 3, 55, 60, 61, 67
legal, 51

mass, 235
professional, 37
repeat, 51
voluntary, 65
migration patterns,
  in global cities, 217
modernity, 7, 27, 68–94,
    123, 168, 171, 174, 176,
    183, 187, 189, 270, 275,
    276, 279
  & religion, 170
  & tradition, 276, 279
  advanced, 156, 277
  contradictions of, 173–174
  late, 139, 142
  mediated, 169
  postcolonial, 106
  Western, 13
Myanmar, 226, 287

New Economic Policy, 69, 70
new economy, 215, 217, 222, 223, 225, 226, 227, 231
new knowledge economy, 16, 281
new urban sociology, 15
New Zealand, 23, 27, 28, 37, 154, 297 n.3
NGOs, 9, 34, 35, 39, 45, 49, 56, 57, 58, 59, 60, 61, 62, 63, 64, 65, 66, 67, 102, 108, 110, 113, 230, 286 n.7
North Korea, 282, 283
New York, 225

Osaka, 217

Pakistan, 253, 254, 297 n.1, 298 n.7

Philippines, 28, 29, 32, 33, 35, 36, 37, 38, 39, 50, 52, 58, 65, 66, 99, 100, 101, 148, 193, 226, 282, 283, 287 n.3, 297 n.1
policy, 4, 62, 69, 70, 108, 217, 225, 232, 239, 254, 262, 263, 264, 269, 279, 281, 282, 287 n.4
  APEC, 45
  domestic, 45
  economic, 9, 73, 218
  economic liberalization, 68
  immigration, 62
  industry, 26
  labor migration, 60
  neo-liberal, 9, 274
  neo-liberal, 73
  political-economic, 149
  social, 73, 218
  transport, 219
  U.S. Cold War foreign, 24
  urban, 281
policy makers, 54, 65, 231
politics, 22, 23, 25, 36, 46, 76, 80, 123, 142, 211, 282, 286 n.4
  & the status of women, 2
  Asia Pacific, 22, 47
  cultural, 32, 37, 38
  grassroots, 49
  national, 29, 40, 47
  nationalist, 272
  of diaspora, 38
  of division, 38
  of environmental justice, 38
  of identity, 122, 129, 135, 141, 292
  of moral and cultural community, 35
  of position, 122

of sexual rights, 38
of shared humanity, 39
of solidarity and recognition, 39
of transition and transformation, 47
social movement, 21, 39
transnational, 47
transversal mode of, 39
poverty, 4, 10, 68, 69, 96, 113, 115, 177, 238, 239, 240, 253, 262, 264, 269, 280

reading (text)
  & the gaze, 196
  of Taiwan's sex VCD, 198–201
  pluralistic/multiple, 139, 188, 204
  practices, 192, 193, 197, 211
  resistant/oppositional, 139, 165
refugees, 36, 37, 79, 119, 123, 124, 128, 130, 132, 133, 142, 272, 286 n.4, 295 n.9
religion, 2, 31, 34, 131, 142, 169, 171, 173, 185, 186, 237
resistance, 3, 6, 7, 40, 41, 44, 47, 123, 131, 139, 140, 141, 142, 162, 165–166, 183, 185, 188, 212, 276, 278, 283
  & Hmong, 134–138
  & popular culture, 133–134
rights, 23, 54, 54, 59, 66, 67
  child, 66
  citizen's, 204
  citizenship, 54

democratic, 35
indigenous, 38, 272
institutionalization of, 53
intellectual, 272
labor, 58, 67
language of, 62
legal, 57
migrant's, 49, 52, 53, 54, 58, 60, 62, 67
of foreign workers, 9, 57
of states, 54
property, 272, 285
sex worker's, 56, 63, 66
universal, 38
women's, 9, 54, 66, 71, 193, 194, 207
women's labor, 55
worker's, 273

Seoul, 217
Shanghai, 217
Singapore, 5, 6, 15, 16, 29, 31, 37, 60, 181, 182, 202, 210, 215–233, 280, 281, 287 n.3, 297 n.8
slums, 6, 220, 240
social change, 1, 2, 4, 10, 11, 14, 16, 17, 49, 77, 234, 236, 238, 246, 248, 271, 276, 278
social class, see 'class'
social movement/s, 4, 8, 21–47, 49, 57, 60, 271, 272, 273
social polarization, in global cities, 216
social stratification, 8
social structure, 12, 15, 16, 215
South Korea, 36, 53, 42, 59, 63, 64, 65, 145, 148, 280,

283, 287 n.3, 292 n.4, 297 n.3
sports exports, 149, 166
squatter settlements, 220, 240
Sri Lanka, 226, 291
Sydney, 217

Taipei, 191, 199, 200, 202, 203, 204, 205, 206, 207, 217
Taiwan, 5, 6, 7, 14, 31, 32, 36, 53, 58, 60, 65, 164, 191–212, 270, 286 n.4, 294 n.27, 296 n.2, n.3, n.4, 297 n.3
television, 12, 86, 87, 89, 92, 93, 134, 144, 145, 147, 149, 151, 152, 154, 166, 171, 172, 173, 175, 176, 178, 182, 184, 186, 187, 188, 191, 194, 199, 205, 210, 271, 282, 293 n.12, 295 n.5, 298 n.10
Thailand, 31, 51, 52, 61, 64, 65, 101, 119, 124, 127, 128, 129, 132, 136, 145, 202, 226, 287 n.3, 289 n.9, 292 n.2, 297 n.1, n.3
Tokyo, 58, 153, 217, 225, 280, 294 n.24
transculturation, 7, 164–165

unemployment, 10, 115, 177, 238
UNICEF, 65, 250, 251
United Kingdom, 216
United States of America, 8, 119, 120, 124, 125, 126, 128, 129, 130, 131, 132, 133, 135, 141, 189, 220, 283, 292 n.4, 297 n.1, 298 n.7
urban, 15, 16, 108, 152
 & sustainable development, 4, 280, 281
urban artisans, 100
urban center/s, 2, 15, 16, 103, 186, 231
urban character, 239
urban environments, 16, 270
urban fringe, 6
urban governance, 280
urban infrastructure, 218–220
urban infrastructure, 218
urban livability, 240
urban luxuries, 259
urban planning, 220
urban poor 33, 240, 255
urban population, 239
urban scholarship, 15
urban social structures, 16
urban social life, 16, 232
urban social problems, 240, 241
urban society, 228
urban societies, 149
urban spaces, 18
urban sprawl, 242
urban *yamamba*, 157
urbanization, 6, 234, 235, 238, 239, 246, 249, 250
urbanization and development, 279

Vietnam, 29, 31, 36, 51, 52, 54, 61, 63, 64, 124, 126, 127, 182, 287 n.3, 297 n.1

wage labor/ers, 76, 82, 96

women, 5, 99, 101, 182, 271, 287
& anomie, 243
& crime, 240
& development assistance, 263
as domestic workers, 37
discrimination, 8
& economic liberalization, India, 68–71, 77–87
emancipation, 10
employment participation, 75, 206
empowerment, 68, 274
Harajiku, 159
Hmong, 8, 129, 130, 131, 132, 137, 141, 142
impact of market reform on, 68–95
in patriarchal society, 14, 191
inequality, 99
& modernity, India, 68–94
Muslim, 174
professionals, 296 n.4
status of, 2, 204
women in Bangladesh society, 246
women in Chinese culture, 209
women in Indian society, 68–94
women in Taiwanese society, 207–208
women's exploitation, 8
& class, 99
& gender, 99
women's issues, 296
women's magazines, 114
working children, 6, 17, 249–265
World Bank, 15, 29, 30, 113, 238, 241, 246, 269

World Health Organization, 220, 250

youth, 11, 78, 163, 255, 271
Balinese, 295 n.4
Christian, 295 n.4
Hmong, 8, 141
Indonesian, 7, 13–14, 168–190, 278
Japanese, 160
Muslim, 295 n.4
youth culture, 173, 189
youth illiteracy, 269